Football in Asia

This book is the first comprehensive study on history, culture, and business of football in Asia. Football has been a symbol of the modern invention, a catalyst of local, national and regional identities, all time favourite among kids and youths, and even a harbinger for cultural globalization and consumerism in Asia. The economic growth and the current proliferation of football culture in Asia make it imperative to examine the complex relationship between the globalization of football and the local appropriation. The essays in the book deal with various topics on football in Asia from history of football in Asia, football and local, national and regional identities, to commercialization of football cultures, global mobility and athletes' migration, and then new Asianism and football. This book argues that football in Asia contributes to reconfiguring both national and regional identities among football fans in the active interconnection with the global flows of football and cultural globalization without homogenizing Asian identities into a cosmopolitan one.

This is the textbook to presents football's implication and influence on Asian populace and social changes while using football as a lens assessing the modern development and current diversification of Asia.

This book was originally published as a special issue of *Soccer & Society*.

Younghan Cho is Associate Professor of Korean Studies at Hankuk University of Foreign Studies (Seoul, South Korea). He is co-editor of many special issues including *Glocalization of Sports in Asia*, *Modern Sports in Asia: Cultural Perspectives*, *Colonial Modernity and Beyond*, and *American Pop Culture*.

Football in Asia

History, Culture and Business

Edited by
Younghan Cho

LONDON AND NEW YORK

First published 2015
by Routledge
2 Park Square, Milton Park, Abingdon, Oxon, OX14 4RN, UK

and by Routledge
711 Third Avenue, New York, NY 10017, USA

Routledge is an imprint of the Taylor & Francis Group, an informa business

© 2015 Taylor & Francis

All rights reserved. No part of this book may be reprinted or reproduced or utilised in any form or by any electronic, mechanical, or other means, now known or hereafter invented, including photocopying and recording, or in any information storage or retrieval system, without permission in writing from the publishers.

Trademark notice: Product or corporate names may be trademarks or registered trademarks, and are used only for identification and explanation without intent to infringe.

British Library Cataloguing in Publication Data
A catalogue record for this book is available from the British Library

ISBN 13: 978-1-138-81602-2

Typeset in Times New Roman
by RefineCatch Limited, Bungay, Suffolk

Publisher's Note
The publisher accepts responsibility for any inconsistencies that may have arisen during the conversion of this book from journal articles to book chapters, namely the possible inclusion of journal terminology.

Disclaimer
Every effort has been made to contact copyright holders for their permission to reprint material in this book. The publishers would be grateful to hear from any copyright holder who is not here acknowledged and will undertake to rectify any errors or omissions in future editions of this book.

Sport in the Global Society – Contemporary Perspectives
Series Editor: Boria Majumdar

The social, cultural (including media) and political study of sport is an expanding area of scholarship and related research. While this area has been well served by the *Sport in the Global Society* series, the surge in quality scholarship over the last few years has necessitated the creation of *Sport in the Global Society: Contemporary Perspectives*. The series will publish the work of leading scholars in fields as diverse as sociology, cultural studies, media studies, gender studies, cultural geography and history, political science and political economy.† If the social and cultural study of sport is to receive the scholarly attention and readership it warrants, a cross-disciplinary series dedicated to taking sport beyond the narrow confines of physical education and sport science academic domains is necessary. *Sport in the Global Society: Contemporary Perspectives* will answer this need.

Titles in the Series

Australian Sport
Antipodean Waves of Change
Edited by Kristine Toohey and Tracy Taylor

Australia's Asian Sporting Context
1920s and 1930s
Edited by Sean Brawley and Nick Guoth

Bearing Light: Flame Relays and the Struggle for the Olympic Movement
Edited by John J. MacAloon

'Critical Support' for Sport
Bruce Kidd

Disability in the Global Sport Arena
A Sporting Chance
Edited by Jill M. Clair

Diversity, Equity and Inclusion in Sport and Leisure
Edited by Katherine Dashper and Thomas Fletcher

Documenting the Beijing Olympics
Edited by D. P. Martinez and Kevin Latham

Ethnicity and Race in Association Football
Case Study analyses in Europe, Africa and the USA
Edited by David Hassan

Exploring the cultural, ideological and economic legacies of Euro 2012
Edited by Peter Kennedy and Christos Kassimeris

Fan Culture in European Football and the Influence of Left Wing Ideology
Edited by Peter Kennedy and David Kennedy

Football in Asia
History, Culture and Business
Edited by Younghan Cho

Football in Southeastern Europe
From Ethnic Homogenization to Reconciliation
Edited by John Hughson and Fiona Skillen

Football Supporters and the Commercialisation of Football
Comparative Responses across Europe
Edited by Peter Kennedy and David Kennedy

Forty Years of Sport and Social Change, 1968-2008
"To Remember is to Resist"
Edited by Russell Field and Bruce Kidd

Global Perspectives on Football in Africa
Visualising the Game
Edited by Susann Baller, Giorgio Miescher and Ciraj Rassool

Global Sport Business
Community Impacts of Commercial Sport
Edited by Hans Westerbeek

Governance, Citizenship and the New European Football Championships
The European Spectacle
Edited by Wolfram Manzenreiter and Georg Spitaler

Indigenous People, Race Relations and Australian Sport
Edited by Christopher J. Hallinan and Barry Judd

Modern Sports in Asia
Cultural Perspectives
Edited by Younghan Cho and Charles Leary

Olympic Reform Ten Years Later
Edited by Heather Dichter and Bruce Kidd

Reflections on Process Sociology and Sport
'Walking the Line'
Joseph Maguire

Security and Sport Mega Events
A Complex Relation
Edited by Diamantis Mastrogiannakis

Soccer in Brazil
Edited by Martin Curi

Soccer in the Middle East
Edited by Alon Raab and Issam Khalidi

South Africa and the Global Game
Football, Apartheid and Beyond
Edited by Peter Alegi and Chris Bolsmann

Sport – Race, Ethnicity and Identity
Building Global Understanding
Edited by Daryl Adair

Sport and Communities
Edited by David Hassan and Sean Brown

Sport, Culture and Identity in the State of Israel
Edited by Yair Galily and Amir Ben-Porat

Sport in Australian National Identity
Kicking Goals
Tony Ward

Sport in the City
Cultural Connections
Edited by Michael Sam and John E. Hughson

Sport, Memory and Nationhood in Japan
Remembering the Glory Days
Edited by Andreas Niehaus and Christian Tagsold

Sport, Music, Identities
Edited by Anthony Bateman

Sport, Race and Ethnicity
The Scope of Belonging?
Edited by Katie Liston and Paddy Dolan

The Changing Face of Cricket
From Imperial to Global Game
Edited by Dominic Malcolm, Jon Gemmell and Nalin Mehta

The Consumption and Representation of Lifestyle Sports
Edited by Belinda Wheaton

The Containment of Soccer in Australia
Fencing Off the World Game
Edited by Christopher J. Hallinan and John E. Hughson

The History of Motor Sport
A Case Study Analysis
Edited by David Hassan

The Making of Sporting Cultures
John E. Hughson

The Olympic Movement and the Sport of Peacemaking
Edited by Ramón Spaaij and Cindy Burleson

The Olympic Games: Meeting New Challenges
Edited by David Hassan and Shakya Mitra

The Other Sport Mega-Event: Rugby World Cup 2011
Edited by Steven J. Jackson

The Politics of Sport
Community, Mobility, Identity
Edited by Paul Gilchrist and Russell Holden

The Politics of Sport in South Asia
Edited by Subhas Ranjan Chakraborty, Shantanu Chakrabarti and Kingshuk Chatterjee

The Social Impact of Sport
Edited by Ramón Spaaij

Towards a Social Science of Drugs in Sport
Edited by Jason Mazanov

Twenty20 and the Future of Cricket
Edited by Chris Rumford

Who Owns Football?
The Governance and Management of the Club Game Worldwide
Edited by David Hassan and Sean Hamil

Why Minorities Play or Don't Play Soccer
A Global Exploration
Edited by Kausik Bandyopadhyay

Women's Football in the UK
Continuing with Gender Analyses
Edited by Jayne Caudwell

Women's Sport in Africa
Edited by Michelle Sikes and John Bale

Contents

Citation Information	xi
1. Introduction: football in Asia *Younghan Cho*	1
2. The slow contagion of Scottish example: association football in nineteenth-century colonial Singapore *Nick Aplin*	10
3. From shamateurism to pioneer of Asia's professional football: the introduction of professional football in Hong Kong *Chun Wing Lee*	25
4. The politics of Indonesian and Turkish soccer: a comparative analysis *James M. Dorsey and Leonard C. Sebastian*	37
5. 'Hamlet without the Prince': understanding Singapore–Malaysian relations through football *Charles Little*	57
6. The otherness of self: football, fandom and fragmented (sub) nationalism in Bengal *Madhuja Mukherjee*	74
7. 'Hope for the win and hope for the defeat': constructions of South Korean identity and the 2010 FIFA World Cup *Miyoung Oh*	92
8. South Asia and South-East Asia: new paths of African footballer migration *Gerard A. Akindes*	106
9. Twenty years of development of the J-League: analysing the business parameters of professional football in Japan *Harald Dolles and Sten Söderman*	124
10. Latin America, football and the Japanese diaspora *Jorge E. Cuéllar*	144
11. 'A' is for Australia: New Football's billionaires, consumers and the 'Asian Century'. How the A-League defines the new Australia *Zoran Pajic*	156

CONTENTS

12. Australia, Asia and the new football opportunity 173
    Chris Hallinan and Tom Heenan

    Index 191

Citation Information

The chapters in this book were originally published in *Soccer & Society*, volume 14, issue 5 (September 2013). When citing this material, please use the original page numbering for each article, as follows:

Chapter 1
Introduction: football in Asia
Younghan Cho
Soccer & Society, volume 14, issue 5 (September 2013) pp. 579–587

Chapter 2
The slow contagion of Scottish example: association football in nineteenth-century colonial Singapore
Nick Aplin
Soccer & Society, volume 14, issue 5 (September 2013) pp. 588–602

Chapter 3
From shamateurism to pioneer of Asia's professional football: the introduction of professional football in Hong Kong
Chun Wing Lee
Soccer & Society, volume 14, issue 5 (September 2013) pp. 603–614

Chapter 4
The politics of Indonesian and Turkish soccer: a comparative analysis
James M. Dorsey and Leonard C. Sebastian
Soccer & Society, volume 14, issue 5 (September 2013) pp. 615–634

Chapter 5
'Hamlet without the Prince': understanding Singapore–Malaysian relations through football
Charles Little
Soccer & Society, volume 14, issue 5 (September 2013) pp. 635–651

Chapter 6
The otherness of self: football, fandom and fragmented (sub) nationalism in Bengal
Madhuja Mukherjee
Soccer & Society, volume 14, issue 5 (September 2013) pp. 652–669

CITATION INFORMATION

Chapter 7
'Hope for the win and hope for the defeat': constructions of South Korean identity and the 2010 FIFA World Cup
Miyoung Oh
Soccer & Society, volume 14, issue 5 (September 2013) pp. 670–683

Chapter 8
South Asia and South-East Asia: new paths of African footballer migration
Gerard A. Akindes
Soccer & Society, volume 14, issue 5 (September 2013) pp. 684–701

Chapter 9
Twenty years of development of the J-League: analysing the business parameters of professional football in Japan
Harald Dolles and Sten Söderman
Soccer & Society, volume 14, issue 5 (September 2013) pp. 702–721

Chapter 10
Latin America, football and the Japanese diaspora
Jorge E. Cuéllar
Soccer & Society, volume 14, issue 5 (September 2013) pp. 722–733

Chapter 11
'A' is for Australia: New Football's billionaires, consumers and the 'Asian Century'. How the A-League defines the new Australia
Zoran Pajic
Soccer & Society, volume 14, issue 5 (September 2013) pp. 734–750

Chapter 12
Australia, Asia and the new football opportunity
Chris Hallinan and Tom Heenan
Soccer & Society, volume 14, issue 5 (September 2013) pp. 751–767

Please direct any queries you may have about the citations to
clsuk.permissions@cengage.com

Introduction: football in Asia

Younghan Cho

Graduate School of International and Area Studies, Hankuk University of Foreign Studies, South Korea

Introduction: football in Asia

Football is by far the most globalized sport in the world and since its introduction in Asia, football has engendered inspiration and excitement among people in various locations throughout Asia. Football is particularly important in Asia, given the complexities of the landscape of Asian sports. While there is a lack of real pan-Asian sporting culture, 'perhaps only soccer [football] can lay claim to being Pan-Asian sporting phenomenon'.[1] Despite the vast differences and traditions in Asian sports culture, it is only football that connects Asia more or less. However, it is too naïve to assume that there would be one Asian football culture: rather, football and its associated cultures have been vastly diversified in Asia depending on its associated conditions and different periods.

Since its introduction to Asia about one and a half centuries ago, football has been undergoing different and complex implications in relation to Asian societies. Football has been a symbol of modern inventions, a tool for imperial forces, a catalyst of local, national and regional identities, a convenient and all time favorite leisure activity and even a harbinger for cultural globalization and emerging consumerism in Asia. Asia has been increasingly important in football, while vast numbers of Asians enjoy football as practitioners, audiences and fans; hence the Asian markets for broadcasting football events and football-related goods have been recently expanded. Furthermore, a couple of regional football leagues, such as the Asian Cup and Asian Champions League, have also been rejuvenated. Within the past couple of decades, several club leagues in Asian countries have received vast investments and subsequently are emerging on global stages by recruiting international football players and coaches.

Despite the 'emergence of 'sport studies' as a thriving, differentiated zone of multi-disciplinary scholarship' since the mid-1990s,[2] sports issues in Asia have either been ignored or poorly addressed. In particular, Asian football has been, by and large, overlooked and is still in the margin in terms of professional, institutional and academic attention. In this sense, it is both opportune and imperative to estimate the trajectories, traditions and recent developments of football in Asia which would provide another venue of examining diverse and dynamic roles of football in Asian societies and their populace. This special issue aims to assess the history and development of football in Asia as well as to inquire about football's implications and influences on Asian histories and social changes. That is, we intend to use football as a lens assessing the modern development and current diversification of Asia. Due to the economic growth and the current proliferation of football in Asia, the imperative to examine the complex relationship between the globalization of football and the local reception or appropriation grows stronger.

Football as western coloniality and national aspiration

As the largest and most diverse continent, Asia has a vast history and tradition of sports. On contrary to such traditional sports, football began to take its root in Asia as a modern invention along with other modern sports in the mid-late nineteenth century.[3] It was primarily European soldiers and merchants who introduced football to many Asian locations and their people.[4] By stating that 'the language of the modern sports is English', Guttman illustrates, 'not until after the World War II did Americans finally supplant the British as the primary agents in the diffusion of modern sports'.[5]

Similar to other modern sports, football initially symbolized both Western modernity and imperial forces.[6] As a part of the extensive imperial baggage, modern sports were used for the use of the imperialist and as a means of attempted control over the colonies and the colonized.[7] Therefore, in its beginning, football was played exclusively by imperial subjects in Asia, and like other modern sports, football was used for teaching the rules and systems to the colonial subjects, i.e. disciplining colonial bodies. However, it does not mean that football was forcefully enforced to the Asian populace. Rather, football was actively adopted and first played by the royal families and local elites. To play football symbolized exercising modern skills and furthermore, participating in modern ways of life.[8] Meanwhile, Asian nationalists intended to utilize sports, as ways of strengthening their own nationals and of increasing national competitiveness, ultimately for maintaining or re-acquiring national independence against the imperial forces. By beating opponents in the fields, playing football against imperial subjects provided rare moments of fighting against and even subverting the colonial rules and hierarchies. In Asia, therefore, football is not solely a physical activity during leisure time, but a Western encroachment, modern development, national inspiration and even subversive desire. Particularly under Japanese occupation, instruments of Western imperial sports were used against Western imperialist and Eastern (Japanese) imperial desires.[9] In this sense, Guttman suggests the term hegemony, rather than imperialism, as the most accurate concept for describing the British and American dominance in the process of diffusion of modern sports and highlights 'the emancipatory potential as well the undeniable role of modern sports as a means of social control and imperial rule'.[10]

During the post-World War II period, sports have been crucial for uniting national people and promoting national identities within newly independent countries in Asia. Football events, such as the Asian Cup, King's Cup and Merdeka Tournaments, 'invokes[invoked] the nation as an enduring space of identity and provokes[provoked] nationalism in its fans'.[11] The Asian Football Confederation (AFC), based in Kuala Lumpur, was formed in 1954, and has organized the Asian Cup since 1956. Besides the Asian Cup, the King's Cup, which is an international football competition held in Thailand since 1968, and the Merdeka Tournament, which is a football tournament held in Malaysia annually from 1957 to 1988, and then held seven times from 1989 to 2007, were popular within Asian countries during the 1960s and 1970s. Currently in Asian leagues, East Asian countries, such as South Korea and Japan, and the Middle-East ones, such as Iraq and Saudi Arabia, are becoming the most successful teams.[12]

At the same time, there has to be the reminder that Asia has not accomplished international victories in football, nor has it been the centre for international events (there are some exceptions, of which the most remarkable exception would be the 2002 Korea–Japan Football World Cup). Nonetheless, football was crucial in developing national identities and unities as well as with igniting newly forged regional rivalries in Asia. As illustrated in Little[12], for instance, football was the major focus in which Singapore and Malaysia have competed, negotiated and played with. During the 1960s and 1970s, two Koreas (North and South) had been the most-heated rivalries in regional matches; South Korea still places national emphasis on its matches against Japan, i.e. its former colonizer. According to Cha, 'not only is sport political, but it is arguably more political in Asia than elsewhere in the world'.[13]

In this sense, football in Asia served not only for the purposes of imperial control, but also for the desire for modernity and national aspiration. According to Mangan, 'for Asians and others, it [sport] provides powerfully evidence of an elitism that breeds confidence, redefines superiority, pays off old imperial scores and establishes post-imperial ways of looking at the world'.[14]

Football as a global commodity and professionalization

As one of the pop cultures, global sports came to replace the role of Hollywood in the process of cultural globalization.[15] Given the central roles of the USA or American power in global sports, it is only football that is exceptionally unpopular with the USA.[16] Contrarily, several European countries and Latin-American ones emerge as the powerhouses in football, and the Fédération Internationale de Football Association (FIFA), which controls the FIFA World Cup, plays central roles in its organizational and institutional managements. As a result, a 'soccerscape' in the globe portrays very different dimensions and dynamics, which have multiple centres and peripheries, and diversified trajectories.[17]

As aforementioned, Asia has not accomplished many international successes or emerged as a powerhouse in international club competitions. Nonetheless, the importance of Asia in football should not be ignored due to its massive population (and possible audiences and fans for any football leagues and clubs), its rapid economic developments and increasing consumer powers. Such potential as well as the increasing market power already exerts influences in the international sporting broadcasting rights (both for international football events, such as the FIFA World Cup, and for several club leagues in England, Spain, Germany, France and so on). Several elite football clubs are making annual trips to Asia in order to have invitational matches against national teams or local clubs of the inviting nations. After the collapse of the football bubble economy in 2001, 'the economically vibrant East Asian region has been a preferential destination for marketing manager and promotion tour'.[18] Several Asian players who have been recruited by such European clubs have become national and even regional celebrities; further, they are the central figures for attracting local sports (or football) fans to the international clubs.

Despite the global dominance of European football leagues and clubs, it is noteworthy that several Asian club leagues are making successful establishments, and Asian regional football events are recently obtaining local and regional attention. It is still true that Asian football fans are orienting much of their attention to European or Latin American leagues; however, many Asian countries have their own professional football leagues and clubs. Particularly in East Asia, South Korea launched the K-league in 1983, Japan established the J-League in 1993 and China did the same with the Chinese Football Association Super League in 2004. The J-League made rapid establishment and economic success with shrewd marketing tactics thereby gaining popularity among female students and people aged 15 – 25.[19] As Dolles and Söderman show in this volume, J-League demonstrates a successful and economic viable model in launching a professional league as a relative newcomer. With the successful holding of the 2002 Korea – Japan Football World Cup, both leagues successfully drew domestic audiences and made contracts with high-profile international players (particularly by the J-League). China is still a sleeping giant in the field of football, while its clubs are slowly attracting global attention: a couple of clubs in China are investing huge amounts of money by contracting such football celebrities.

The regional economic development and financial affluence in Asia also make different trajectories possible in global sports. Within a global sports complex, we can easily observe a New International Division of Cultural Labour.[20] In the soccerscape, however, there are some exchanges with the non-West. That is, players from Latin America and Africa often migrate to East Asia and South-East Asia in order to play in their professional clubs. As Akindes and Cuellar illustrate in this issue, it is no longer unusual to witness Latin American and American players in Asian football leagues and Asian Champions League. Moreover, several players from Asia, particularly youth players, choose to play in Latin America in order to learn the developed skills. It is still arguable as to whether Japan and South Korea belong to the First-World or not: however, it is noteworthy that in football, there are increasingly different or even alternative routes, which directly connect Asia to Latin America and Africa without being mediated through the West.

Football as a new Asian regionalism

In recent decades, Asia's 'growing political economic power has also seen it become increasingly central to the political economy of global sport'.[21] For instance, several major international sporting events, such as the 2008 Beijing Summer Olympics, the 2002 Korea – Japan FIFA World Cup and several Formula-1 races have been held in various countries in Asia. The 2008 Beijing Olympics 'provided a rich opportunity to consider not only the forays of China and Asia onto the international stage, but also the construction of Asianness and regional connections as they function in Asia'.[22] Also, such international sporting events contribute to reconfiguring the relationships among Asian countries: for instance, the 2008 Olympics elicited a mixed response from Japan, from admiration to anxiety, and also signalled replacing the USA – Japan relationship by the ambivalent Sino – Japanese relationships.[23]

One remarkable change in football in Asia is that Australia has become a member of the AFC since 2006. Such a change might be simply a tactical decision for making it easy for the Australian national team to advance to the final World Cup tournament; yet, it would be one of the outcomes from Australia's efforts for being part of Asia. In Australia, the significance of Asia has been keenly felt during the past decades, and according to Ang, 'the idea that Australia has an Asian future was promoted in the early 1990s'.[24] Despite the recent efforts, it is 'clear that the distance between 'Australia' and 'Asia' is still very wide'.[25] Another example would be the lack of the pan-Asian popular flows in Australia.[26] In this sense, the inclusion of Australia in the AFC might provide another opportunity as well as a challenge for the future relationship between Australia and Asia as well as for the new regional definition of Asia. It is still uncertain whether football would increase the actual encounters, develop emotional and passionate relationships and make regular connections between Australia and Asia.[27] In this issue, Hallinan and Heenan, and Pajic explore the developments and changes of the Australian football league.

Furthermore, the growing power in global sports and the expansion of the AFC might provide larger implications and impacts on new Asian identities and regionalism. Along with its economic development, Asia developed a new relationship to globalization, and meanwhile, regionalism has strengthened.[28] Furthermore, the Asian liquid crisis made Asian countries feel the new regional co-operation imperative,[29] and enabled sports to rebuild national building in a symbolic way. Cha succinctly points out that 'the 2002 World Cup might have had less significance if it did not mark South Korea's recovery after the 1998 Asian financial crisis'.[30] The changing identities and regional relationships are also observed in the increasing Asian audiences and fans of European football leagues and clubs. Along with this trend, some might be conserved about the economic deficit and the demolition of national identity. However, many critics already highlight that this trend can be better explained not by cultural imperialism, but by glocalization.[31] Guiliannoti and Robertson aptly highlight that 'Asian sports provide a distinctive field for exploring the duality of glocality, or the interplay between processes of homogenization and heterogenization'.[32] By examining Israeli's football fandom, Ben-Porat and Ben-Porat describe that Israeli players abroad are admired and fans follow their games via satellite TV and the internet; however, they also conclude that 'while Israeli soccer fans are globalized, local identities are far from erased'.[33] In this sense, football in Asia contributes to reconfiguring both national and regional identities among football fans in the active interconnection with the global flows of football and cultural globalization without homogenizing Asian identities into a cosmopolitan one.

Essays in the issue

The essays in the issue deal with various topics on football in Asia from history of football in Asia, and Football and local, national and regional identities to commercialization of football cultures, global mobility and athletes' migration, and then new Asiannism and football. Nonetheless, it needs to be noted that this special issue cannot represent all the diverse ramifications of football in Asia and the developing research on them.

The issue opens with the study on the historical trajectory of football in Asia and its roles in developing national and regional identities. Aplin explores the historic process of the establishment of the Singapore Football Association in 1892, which would be the first institution on football in Asia. By tracing the process of diffusion of sport, Aplin illustrates that football was transformed from a colonial distraction to a tool of cultural imperialism, being promoted as a civilizing agent. Lee also examines the introduction of football in Hong Kong in the early post-war period with focus on the issues on 'shamateurism' in football clubs and players there. For that purpose, Lee reviews the developments that led to the professionalization of football, which was made happen by and large as the response to shamteurism.

Football in Asia also leads to the development of the national identities and regional rivalries in Asia. Dorsey and Sebastian take on the political role of football in Turkey and Indonesia. Despite the distance between the two countries, authors highlight, the similarities in the politics of soccer which they suggest originates from the struggle for independence in which pro- and anti-colonial soccer clubs played an important role. Little delves into the Singapore – Malaysian relations through football in the post-war periods. While two neighbouring countries had a tumultuous relationship in relation to economics, personality and race, Little demonstrates that footballing tensions predated the ill-relations between two nations, and that, despite the mutual antipathy, the two states are locked together in an inescapable inter-dependence.

From a similar perspective, Oh examines the reconstruction of national identity in South Korea in relation to its two major others, i.e. North Korea and Japan. By examining the ways in which South Koreans produce shared memories and differentiate themselves from North Koreans and the Japanese, Oh explores the intricate workings of ethnic and postcolonial identities in the construction of South Korean identity. Mukherjee explores the football cultures and the development of national identity in Bengal in relation to the global media and their influence on daily lives. In order to understand the connections between (sub) nationalist fervour and global sport event, Mukerjee relocates the question of club football in Bengal within the framework of World football.

In the past decades, football in Asia has been also commercialized: as noted, several professional football leagues and their clubs have made economic success and strongly emerged. Such successes also promote the regional and even global mobility of international players into Asian clubs, which in turn project a new transnational trajectory of soccerscope and add a new dimension to Asian societies. Dolles and Söderman consider the implementation and the immediate success of the Japanese professional soccer league during its first two decades. By identifying three dimensions within the business parameters of professional football, they reveal different practices, product marketing and merchandising and the distribution of media revenues in the management of football in Japan compared with Europe. Akindes traces a new dimension of the migrations in global football in which African footballers are present in many Asian competitions, particularly towards South and South-East Asia. By analysing the condition of the recruitment of African players and their experiences in Asian club, Akindes illustrates the emergence of semi-peripheral economies and migration pattern in African football. Cuéllar explores the presence of Asian players in Latin American football, which tells the unique history of Asian people and growing importance for the sustainment of football clubs. By focusing on the relation of the Japanese diaspora to sports culture, Cuéllar highlights the intersecting issues around the questions of Asian identity, politics, capitalism and its relationship to conceptions of the nation in Latin America.

Finally, this issue pays attention to the new relationship between Asia and Australia with focus on the development of Australian football league. Pajic explores the creation of new football in Australia as a new elite, a new culture, a new commodity for a new economy and a new industry. In this sense, Pajic suggests that the A-League not only represents a change from old soccer to new football, but rather the transition from old Australia to new Australia. Hallinan and Heenan examine how Australia's joining of the AFC coincided with corporatization of the game exemplified in the establishment of the A-League. They further explore how the changes in Australian football are connected both to its multi-culturalism model and its place in Asia.

Acknowledgement

I would like to thank Boria Majumdar for inspring and supporting this project, and Eunha Koh for sharing the thoughts for the project. This work was supported by Hankuk University of Foreign Studies Research Fund.

Notes

1. Little, 'Sports History', 176.
2. Giulianotti and Robertson, 'Introduction', 108.
3. For more detailed discussion on the implications of modern sports in Asia, please refer to the special issue on 'Modern Sports in Asia' in Sport in Society, and its introduction by Cho and Leary (2012).
4. Guiliannotti (1999) explains that football underwent rationalization and seculization in Britain and began to expand during the late nineteenth century via trade connections and imperial links.
5. Guttmann, *Games and Empires*, 1–2.
6. Appadurai, *Modernity at Large*; Mangan, 'Prologue' and Cho and Leary, 'Introduction'.
7. Mangan, 'Prologue', 2002.
8. Appadurai (1996) illustrates a similar pattern in exploring the sport of cricket in India: In India, cricket worked as an instrument of elite formation.
9. Lin and Lee, 'Sport as a Medium'.
10. Guttman, 'Games and Empires'.
11. Cho and Charley, 'Introduction', 1325–6.
12. Little, 'Sports History', 186.
13. Cha, *Beyond the Final Score*, 23. While suggesting that 'sport acts as an outlet for pent-up historical resentment', Cha adds that 'Japan's imperial past in Asia causes most former colonies to view every contest with Japan as a historical grudge match' (Ibid., 25).
14. Mangan, 'Prologue', 6.
15. Cho, 'Broadcasting'; Hong, 'Epilogue'; Miller et al., *Globalization and Sport*. Hong similarly suggests that 'the desire of international organizations to conquer new markets has brought a new version of the internationalization of sport to the Asian world' (2002, 403).
16. Markovits and Hellerman, *Offside*.
17. Guiliannotti uses the term 'soccerscape' to 'refer to the geo-cultural circulation of football's constituent parts: players and coaches, fans and officials, goods and services, or information and artifacts' (1999, 24).
18. Horne and Manzenreiter, 'Football, Culture, Globalization', 11.
19. Guttmann and Thompson, *Japanese Sports*.
20. Miller et al., *Globalization and Sport*. By tracking the relationship of sports to globalization, they discern five processes: Globalization, Governmentalization, Americanization, Televisualization, and Commodification (GGATaC). They further suggest that GGATaC are governed by the NICL. Ultimately, they argue that the global sports complex via GGATaC and the NICL is 'against the singular phenomenon of globalization' (2001, 8).
21. Little, 'Sports History', 173.
22. Cho et al., 'Introduction', 421.
23. Kelly, 'Asia Pride'.
24. Ang, 'Australia, China', 129.

25. Ang, The Cultural Intimacy, 305.
26. Ang, 'Australia, China' and Cho, 'Desperately Seeking'.
27. Ang, 'Australia, China'. Similarly, Ang suggests that whether or not Australia is part of Asia 'would grow out of the complex web of actual interconnections between Australia and different parts of Asia through the myriad human interactions which make societies work' (2010, 135).
28. Duara, 'Asia Redux'.
29. Duara, 'Asia Redux'. Duara suggests that the Asian financial crisis seems to have awakened the states with the reality of regional networks and the attention on regional cooperation.
30. Cha, *Beyond the Final Score*, 27.
31. For a detailed discussion, refer to a special issue on 'glocalization of sports in Asia' in the Sociology of Sport Journal, co-edited by Cho et al. (2012). For the development of the term glocalization in Asian sports, refer to Guiliannotti and Robertson's article in the same issue.
32. Guiliannoti and Robertson, 'Glocalization and Sport in Asia', 443.
33. Ben-Porat and Ben-Porat, '(Un)Bounded Soccer', 434. Also, see Kobayashi's research on corporate nationalism and glocalization of Nike advertising in Asia (2012), and Satoshi's research on 'Beckham fever' among Japanese identity since the 2002 World Cup (2004).

References

Ang, Ien. 'The Cultural Intimacy of TV Drama'. In *Feeling Asian Modernities: Transnational Consumption of Japanese TV Dramas*, ed. Koichi Iwabuchi, 303–9. Hong Kong: Hong Kong University Press, 2004.

Ang, Ien. 'Australia, China and Asian Regionalism: Navigating Distant Proximity'. *Amerasia Journal* 36, no. 2 (2010): 127–40.

Appadurai, Arjun. *Modernity at Large: Cultural Dimensions of Globalization*. Minneapolis, MN: University of Minnesota Press, 1996.

Ben-Porat, Guy, and Amir Ben-Porat. '(Un)Bounded Soccer: Globalization and Localization of the Game in Israel'. *International Review for the Sociology of Sport* 39, no. 4 (2004): 421–36.

Cha, Victor D. *Beyond the Final Score: The Politics of Sport in Asia*. New York, NY: Columbia University Press, 2009.

Cho, Younghan. 'Broadcasting Major League Baseball as a Governmental Instrument in South Korea'. *Journal of Sport and Social Issues* 32, no. 3 (2008): 240–54.

Cho, Younghan. 'Desperately Seeking East Asia amidst the Popularity of South Korean Pop Culture in Asia'. *Cultural Studies* 25, no. 3 (2011): 383–404.

Cho, Younghan and Leary Charles. ed. *Modern Sports in Asia: Cultural Perspectives*. Special Issue in *Sport in Society* 15, no. 10 (2012).

Cho, Younghan, and Leary Charles. 'Introduction: Modern Sports in Asia: Cultural Perspectives'. *Sport in Society* 15, no. 10 (2012): 421–32.

Cho, Younghan, Leary Charles, and Steve Jackson, ed. *Glocalization of Sports in Asia*. Special Issue in *Sociology of Sport Journal* 29, no. 4 (2012): 421–558.

Cho, Younghan, Leary Charles, and Steve Jackson. 'Introduction: Glocalization of Sports in Asia'. *Sociology of Sport Journal* 29, no. 4 (2012): 421–558.

Duara, Prasenjit. 'Asia Redux: Conceptualizing a Region for Our Times'. *The Journal of Asian Studies* 69, no. 4 (2010): 963–83.

Giulianotti, Richard. *Football: A Sociology of the Global Game*. Cambridge: Polity Press, 1999.

Giulianottti, Richard, and Roland Robertson. 'Introduction: Sport and Globalization: Transnational Dimensions'. *Global Networks* 7, no. 2 (2007): 107–12.

Guilanotti, Richard, and Roland Robertson. 'Glocalization and Sport in Asia: Diverse Perspectives and Future Possibilities'. *Sociology of Sport Journal* 29, no. 4 (2012): 433–54.

Guttman, Allen. *Games and Empires: Modern Sports and Cultural Imperialism*. New York, NY: Columbia University Press, 1994.

Guttman, Allen, and Lee Thompson. *Japanese Sports: A History*. Honolulu, HI: University of Hawaii Press, 2001.

Hong, Fan. 'Epilogue Into the Future: Asian Sport and Globalization'. In *Sport in Asian Society: Past and Present*, ed. J. A. Mangan and Fan Hong, 401–7. London: Frank Cass, 2002.

Horne, John and Wolfram Manzenreiter. 'Football, Culture, Globalization: Why Professional Football has been Going East'. In *Football Goes East: Business, Culture and the People's Game in China, Japan and South Korea*, ed. John Horne and Wolfram Manzenreiter, 1–17. New York: Routledge, 2004.

Kelly, William W. 'Asia Pride, China Fear, Tokyo Anxiety: Japan Looks Back at Beijing 2008 and Forward to London 2012 and Tokyo 2016". *The International Journal of the History of Sport* 27, no. 14–15 (2010): 2428–39.

Kobayashi, Koji. 'Corporate Nationalism and Glocalization of Nike Advertising in "Asia": Production and Representation Practices of Cultural Intermediaries'. *Sociology of Sport Journal* 29 (2012): 42–61.

Lin, Chien-Yu, and Ping-Chao Lee. 'Sport as a Medium of National Resistance: Politics and Baseball in Taiwan during Japanese Colonialism, 1895–1945'. *The International Journal of the History of Sport* 24, no. 3 (2007): 319–37.

Little, Charles. 'Sports History, Culture, and Practice in Asia'. In *Sports around the World: History, Culture, and Practice*, ed. J. Nauright and C. Parrish, 173–184. Santa Barbara, CA: ABC-CLIO, 2012.

Mangan, J. A. 'Prologue. Asian Sport: From the Recent Past'. In *Sport in Asian Society: Past and Present*, ed. J. A. Mangan and Fan Hong, 1–10. London: Frank Cass, 2002.

Markovits, Andrei S., and Steven L. Hellerman. *Offside: Soccer and American Exceptionalism*. Princeton, NJ: Princeton University Press, 2001.

Miller, Toby, Geoffrey Lawrence, Jim McKay, and David Rowe. *Globalization and Sport: Playing the World*. Thousand Oaks, CA: Sage, 2001.

Satoshi, Shimizu. 'Football, Nationalism and Celebrity Culture: Reflection on the Impact of Difference Discourses on Japanese Identity since the 2002 World Cup'. In *Football Goes East: Business, Culture and the People's Game in China, Japan and South Korea*, ed. John Horne and Wolfram Manzenreiter, 180–193. New York: Routledge, 2004.

The slow contagion of Scottish example: association football in nineteenth-century colonial Singapore

Nick Aplin

Physical Education and Sports Science Academic Group, National Institute of Education, Nanyang Technological University, Singapore, Singapore

> The Singapore Football Association was established in 1892, the first institution of its kind in Asia. Only football really captured the imagination of the predominantly migrant population and subsequently it became the national game. Football was introduced by marine engineers, many of whom were Scots, and their friends from the Singapore Cricket Club (SCC). This paper establishes that the process of diffusion of sport was hesitant and often exclusive. Interest in the game spread quickly to the Asian communities, notably the Malay population and the Straits Chinese population, but then stalled as it lacked complete support from the British. Based on news reports at the time, it emerges that the game was transformed from a colonial distraction to a tool of cultural imperialism, being promoted as a civilizing agent. Yet the reluctance of the SCC to play against the Chinese prevented more rapid growth.

Introduction

The first recognized football association to appear in Asia was established in 1892 on the small island of Singapore.[1] Parochial in scale, the Singapore Football Association (SFA) was a small working committee formed by Scotsmen and Englishmen, who were motivated to initiate and organize a challenge cup competition involving all racial communities. In a setting normally characterized by isolation, disease, physical hardship, racial segregation and colonial hegemony, the altruism implied by the desire of the SFA stimulated sporadic, yet often intense interest amongst the more stable sections of a predominantly migrant population.[2] However, the process of accommodating so-called 'native teams' into a competitive environment remained problematic well into the twentieth century, because of resistance from unidentifiable yet influential members of the Singapore Cricket Club (SCC). Despite the efforts of younger members and frequent statements of encouragement in the press, the process of inclusion stalled periodically.

Football arrived at a time when trade was booming. Singapore was viewed as a land of opportunity for young merchants' assistants, bank clerks, telegraphists and engineers. Industrial growth was rapid and a flood of itinerant workers was being drawn from China and India.[3] The game in Singapore was then transformed, almost by chance, from a private distraction to a tool of imperialism. Within five years of its introduction, the game was being promoted as a civilizing agent. How the

British viewed themselves and their role as empire builders would be reflected in all aspects of life and, therefore, in the growth of the game.

> A predominant power which looks for means outside coercion or despotism for the maintenance of its prestige, and which seeks not to suppress, but to encourage, the moral and physical development of those races which on the threshold of their introduction to civilization are for the time necessarily in a subservient state, cannot be otherwise than keenly alive as to all those conditions indispensable to the permanent establishment of a well-conducted administration.[4]

This exploratory paper seeks to document the pioneering efforts to establish football in a small multicultural colony and to identify landmark events in the introduction of the game to the Asian population. While the few reports available on the development of the game are usually a reflection of the imperial perspective, it is clear that the process of diffusion provoked discomfort amongst the colonial supporters of the game themselves. Newspaper reports and correspondence, which represent the main sources of data, portray divisions within the colonial establishment and resistance to the inclusion of the Chinese. Little is reported about the Chinese and the Malay response to the hegemony of the Europeans. What emerges is a picture of quick exposure, yet slow immersion.

The leather makes its entry

Kicking a ball was rarely deemed worthy of documentation in Singapore in the early years. During the first three decades of its existence as a settlement under British East India Company control, only one reference highlighted the inclusion of such a game, one which was included in the New Year sports festivities in 1849.[5] One unsubstantiated suggestion is that the 'British Army team, which from the time the game was first inaugurated in 1849, conducted regular association football matches with the Chinese and Malays on land near Tank Road'.[6] Even then there was no indication as to which style of play was adopted.[7] It took another 40 years before the game – governed by Association rules – would be established. The game had been slower to reach Singapore than rugby football. Yet in the context of Asia, Singapore was amongst the first to enjoy organized competitions in what would become known as the beautiful game. Notwithstanding the relatively late arrival of football, once it was instituted, it rapidly became the people's game based on its appeal to a wider range of devotees.[8]

Colonial settlers viewed recreation and exercise as fundamental to their existence, and initially reserved the game for their own benefit and amusement. For the younger Europeans, playing the game was an appealing distraction as more and more activities were added to the list of physical amusements.[9] For the small European population, the 'manly' sport became an adjunct to 'healthful living' in what was an environment plagued by heat, high humidity and disease – typhoid, dysentery and cholera were among the common threats to life.[10] However, playing the game was no guarantee of immunity, as at least two locally well-known devotees of the game – John Lawson and Lt. Clement Sarel – would fall victim to 'malignant fever' during the 1890s.[11]

The equatorial climate was not an obliging setting, as a typical game could only be endured with short 20- or 25-min halves, assuming that frequent tropical thunderstorms did not make the ground unplayable. Some observers questioned the sense in even playing at all.

> I take leave to doubt whether football is a good game for the average European in the tropics. It is an excellent game in the country of its origin in winter. But they don't play football in England in summer – they are more sensible. Why then should it be played in the heat of a tropical afternoon?[12]

But play they did. To accommodate the game, open tracts of land were utilized by Asian players with increasing frequency. The best playing fields were the preserve of the private clubs, or found in the British military camps. To satisfy the increasing local demand, pitches would be located temporarily on reclaimed land near the sea.

The pioneers: the Scottish influence

Any discussion of the evolution of the modern game of football must acknowledge the significant contributions of both Englishmen and Scotsmen. It is not surprising that this cooperative effort was reflected in the introduction of the game in Singapore. In the case of this small Straits Settlement, the contribution of Scotsmen had taken on particular significance.

> To Scotland we have learned to look for a large part of our leaders in Singapore; the porridge-trap still works, and bankers, merchants, and governors still come to remind us that in Scotland is bred a race without which our British Empire would not have been and would not be now.[13]

The acknowledged pioneers of the game in 1889 were the marine engineers, many of whom were Scotsmen. One of them, the same John Lawson, was credited as being the 'introducer of football in Singapore'.[14] Together with friends and acquaintances from the SCC and the Garrison, the Engineers set the scene. The first games took place on the Police cricket ground at Tank Road, where Robert Scoular and his friend James McKenzie, also a Scot, apparently linked up with the marine engineers in 1889.[15] Scoular, a young merchant's assistant, was instrumental in attracting much more prolonged interest in the game than Francis Villiers Hornby the other candidate for recognition.[16]

There were other men in Singapore with experience of football. Military personnel were enthusiastic advocates and provided competition for the civilians. A team of infantrymen from the 2nd Battalion, the 58th (the Northamptonshire) Regiment of Foot materialized very rapidly. The 'Steelbacks' accepted an early challenge from the SCC. There was clearly considerable interest in playing the game even though the actual standard of play was difficult to predict.

> The 58th make the Association Rules their game and they have been trained to it, and with forwards and half backs ... the team from the 58th is not to be beaten by imperfect players. Probably the members of the SCC have been good at the game, but taking into consideration the long time that has elapsed since the last game, and that they had no previous practice to the match, is it to be wondered that their performance on Friday was not as it might have been.[17]

Significantly, the military were far more willing than the SCC members to engage in matches against Chinese and Malay teams. The reluctance on the part of the

SCC to embrace the Chinese community, in particular, was a reflection of a general tendency to minimize contact with other racial groups in social settings. The military were much less exclusive in their pastimes.

The local newspapers played an important role in establishing the game. The Straits Times announced games and the proposed starting times. Team lists were appended and the players were reminded to wear the correct coloured shirt. The Engineers could be relied upon to wear red, but the SCC members might turn out in their old school colours. The matches were reported in minimal detail but gradually players were assessed on their variable quality of skill. Referees were criticized for inconsistency in decision-making and for poor interpretation of the rules. A full understanding of the rules by all the players could not be expected. Some volunteers – coerced to make up the numbers – had been brought up on rugby and sometimes they found it difficult to resist the temptation to handle the ball.

There were other constraints to the growth of the game. As interest widened there was increasing demand for pitches. The SCC teams had to share the Esplanade with other games, notably lawn tennis and rugby. The Singapore Recreation Club occupied the opposite end of the *padang*.[18] The Police utilized their own cricket ground. The Engineers relied on invitations to play at those grounds because they had no field of their own. Only military teams had easy access to fields in their barracks and this, in part, explains their successes. Football provided immediate interest for spectators, but only at the Esplanade which was the ground most accessible to the public after business hours.[19]

The SCC

The SCC represented the fulcrum of sporting endeavour as football was being introduced. One in four members of the male European population was affiliated to the Club. However, it was difficult to build up a critical mass of members who could sustain interest in the growing number of games. Although as many as 100 new members might join the club during the course of a year, a significant number would also return home or be posted elsewhere. There was a constant need for new blood. When the SFA began, there were 400 members of the SCC.[20] Only a quarter of that number were truly active and 50 of them were tennis players. Football and cricket teams drew their players from the other 50.[21] Tennis was the game of choice amongst the older and better established members. As the most recent arrival, football assumed a subordinate position in the hierarchy of interests. Conflicts invariably arose between the different social circles that were represented at the SCC. The younger and more active members, who favoured a higher intensity of exertion, faced resistance and even disdain from some of the tennis players.[22] It was clearly difficult to sustain the growth of the game based purely on young European members of the community and the military.

> Owing to the departure from the Colony of several active supporters and the withdrawal of others, less football than usual was played towards the end of last year and the beginning of this.[23]

For the game to survive, the local population and later the migrant population had to take an interest in football.

Early beginnings for the local communities

Many Europeans perceived that they were the only ones really interested in sport, though the tiny Eurasian community, with closer cultural ties and in possession of their own club facilities were seen to be exceptions.[24] However, when the game arrived, it soon became an attraction to established non-European communities, notably the Straits-born Chinese[25] and the indigenous Malays. The wealthier Straits Chinese had begun to adopt British leisure customs when the Straits Chinese Recreation Club (SCRC) was formed in 1884.[26]

The recognition of this interest amongst the Straits Chinese eventually led to the realization that 'chasing the leather' could become an important component of the imperial drive towards dominance and economic expansion. Initially, there had been no intent to actively encourage the game as a form of recreation for the Chinese and Malay communities, but it became a useful medium for promoting value systems built on power, conformity and an acceptance of authority. The younger Straits-born Chinese adopted the game in order to emulate their colonial associates. The minority indigenous Malay section took rapidly to the game as it could be played informally in the *kampongs*.[27] Kicking a rattan ball in *sepak raga* was a familiar pastime, albeit one that was based on cooperation rather than competition. The progress of the Malay population in football was slow but ultimately enjoyed the benefit of a closer interest in their affairs by the British.

The Chinese experience

In 1891, the population of Singapore was 66% Chinese. They may have represented the dominant racial group in Singapore, yet there were significant differences between the clans represented in terms of dialect and cultural background. The pre-existing clan system of the Chinese meant that they found little need for the game of football to enhance social bonding and the majority were quite comfortable following the system of segregated lives imposed by the hegemonic Europeans.[28] However, those who interacted more directly with the Europeans found the additional links provided by the game to be profitable. The majority migrant China-born population was slower to include football among their limited range of pastimes. The China-born Chinese came to Singapore as coolies prepared to undertake manual labour. They were tightly packed into meagre accommodation in Chinatown, with little space for pastimes other than gambling and smoking opium. Clans and secret societies, which were designed to provide mutual aid and assistance, created an environment where a game like football had little chance to thrive.

As a spectacle, the game of football initially provided amusement laced with bewilderment for the Chinese. Kicking a ball, in a competitive sense, was an alien activity to the majority of Asians. An 'educated' Chinese view of sport suggested that a game like football would not have universal support.

> Physical strength is often held in slight estimation by those who cultivate the intellect, and they who take delight in sports and those exercises which call it forth, are rather looked down upon as men of low tastes.[29]

Earlier exposure to rugby football had generated scepticism amongst local observers. Body contact was not viewed favourably, and the confrontational style of playing – particularly as advocated by regimental teams – ran counter to a collective

Asian lifestyle. Europeans sometimes interpreted this unwillingness to be physically active as laziness or apathy.

> To anyone who studies the Chinese and Malay character, it becomes very soon obvious that any pastime which calls for active exercise is at a discount. The average Chinese youth will play at tops and marbles with some zest, but he fails to appreciate the running after a ball in the cricket field or the engaging in a scrimmage at football ...[30]

Throughout the decade, there was a cultural constraint that limited Chinese involvement in football. The *towchang* (or queue) was an awkward 'tonsorial appendage'. Also known as a 'pigtail', the *towchang* had to be tied up as it impeded movement and represented a danger to opponents, if left to swing free. Once the *towchang* was discarded by more and more Chinese at the turn of the century, it no longer represented an obstacle to playing.[31] The potential threat of more serious types of injury in a physically punishing game may have persuaded many Chinese not to participate, but it became clear that the younger advocates were prepared to take the risk.

> It is gratifying to note the progress of football among the Singapore Chinese. Within the last day or so one doctor had had cases of a broken rib and of a broken arm for Chinese football players; and there is reason to believe that other medical men may have been employed on football accidents. Considering that the game is only beginning to take hold, the record is creditable. Even in northern English towns the average of surgical cases from football is seldom above two or so a week, and it is often less.[32]

The Europeans were proved misguided in their assumptions about football and about how the Chinese might respond to the challenge. The game would be received and adopted with relish. At a club level, the Chinese became involved in mid-1891 when members of the SCRC created a team that could play at their own club ground at Hong Lim Green.[33] Later the Straits National Football Association (SNFA) and the Chinese Football Club joined in too.[34] The SNFA was inaugurated in 1891 and grew to a membership of about 50 within three years. Within that period, the team defeated the Singapore Recreation Club team, the European Police team and the civilian Engineers team.[35]

More Chinese teams were soon vying for opportunities to play. This was a surprise to members of the European community, some of whom doubted that cultural advances of this type were possible amongst the Chinese and expressed their feelings in condescending and sanctimonious tones.

> The football craze is apparently at its height. Hardly a single day passes without football. Even the Chinese Babas have taken to it and who knows who will follow next.[36]

> ... football seems to find popular favour here among Europeans, Eurasians and natives, and hardly a single week passes by without seeing this game played somewhere, and the young man who is not versed in the intricacies of the game is regarded as one behind the age ... the contagion of example seems to have spread to the Celestial element. Who will dispute, after this that this is the age of enlightenment.[37]

Initially games tended to be played between teams of the same race, with referees coming from the same clubs. So the first inter-race game involving the British and the Chinese represented a real landmark in the development of the game. After a match between the SCRC and the Chinese Football Club, it was announced that the next opponents for the SCRC would be a team from the Royal Artillery (RA).[38] The proposed contest prompted positive correspondence from a Chinese observer.

> It must be highly satisfactory indeed to my countrymen to see the advancement made by their friends in this game; and whatever may be the result, it cannot otherwise than be to their credit, as they are only novices in the game, besides being men of little or no physique compared with the men of the other team; and it is creditable also to see that the RA do not disdain to try their mettle with the long-tailed Chinee (sic).[39]

Although the SCRC lost the game, the Chinese 'played a plucky and determined game'.[40] Emboldened by their experience with the RA, the Chinese now envisaged a greater challenge, but they would be frustrated by the tactless refusal of the SCC to entertain the idea of a game. The Chinese teams had to be satisfied with matches against community rivals, or against military and navy teams.[41] In the New Year, the Police and the boys of Raffles School and Anglo-Chinese School were added to the list of potential adversaries. An inter-settlement game was even played between the Chinese scholars of Penang (400 miles to the north) and Chinese scholars form Singapore.[42]

The European scene

By 1892 the European community had created seven recognizable teams.[43] An informal structure meant that any player might be eligible to play for more than one team. Different combinations of players could be drawn from those teams to provide additional variety. From time to time, informal selections of players challenged each other. And even one of the most influential newspapers – The Singapore Free Press – began to provide coverage of the new sporting trend.[44] Amongst the younger settlers and the transient clerks, assistants and military men, football was fast becoming the fashionable game. Navy teams, after long spells at sea, featured on the playing fields too.[45] The military played all-comers, and although the SCC would play against the Eurasian Singapore Recreation Club, they stubbornly refused to 'try conclusions' against the Chinese.

A pivotal moment

In early 1892, Robert Scoular and his associates conceived the idea of the SFA Challenge Cup. Their intention was to run the competition on a league basis. However, with minimal resources and uncertainly about the number of teams involved, a knock-out system was adopted. In view of the perceived eagerness of the Chinese to adopt the game, it was intended to open the competition to any team in the colony. Many Europeans supported the move. However, there was sufficient resistance from unnamed senior members of the SCC to preclude the inclusion of the Chinese. The Cup ties were to be played between March and September, so as not to interfere with rugby, cricket and tennis tournaments. There would be prizes too. A $50 trophy would be sent from 'Home' and each winning player would receive a small gold medal. The Honourable W.E. Maxwell, who was to become the next Governor of the Straits Settlements, was invited to become the first President of the SFA. When the competition actually began, there were only European and military teams.

It had been too early for some advocates to invite Asian teams to join in. It took another two years for the next opportunity to arise, when the military, not the SCC, recognized that the expansion of the competitive game should accommodate all communities. The Warren Challenge Shield was introduced in 1894 for competitions in four sports.[46] The first competition featured six teams including the SCC.[47] The first winners of the Shield were players from the Singapore Volunteer Artillery (SVA) team, which included Scoular, McKenzie and Lawson.[48] Just four months later, a second competition was organized with a team from the SCRC as a new entry. The SCC chose to withdraw for unspecified reasons and an air of uncertainty prevailed.

> … the Committee of the Garrison Sports Club should take steps to ascertain the standing of any native teams that may enter for the Warren Football Challenge Shield. It may be noted that in India no football matches are allowed between native and European military teams, for sufficiently understood reasons … We should think at all events that the Committee have it in their discretion to enquire into the status and pretensions of any Asiatic team offering to enter. The Straits Chinese Recreation Club … is as far as is known, the only Club of any standing.[49]

When the second competition began on the SRC ground at the Esplanade, a Chinese correspondent wrote that there was a great deal of betting on the result of the game between the SVA and the SCRC. The odds were 10–1 or 12–1 in favour of the SVA.[50] A crushing 9–0 defeat for the Chinese was witnessed and this effectively ruled the SCRC out of consideration in the near future. The rules were altered in December 1895 to reflect the sentiment that the competition should be open only to European or Eurasian teams. The Chinese and potentially the Malays were excluded. Whatever games were being played by the Chinese, they ceased to be of interest to the newspapers until the following year. In late 1896, the revitalized SCRC team visited Johore on the Malaya Peninsula to play in the Johore Challenge Cup.[51] During the following weeks, the SCRC repeated their successes and won through to the final against the Johore Football Club. There is no record of whether they returned to Singapore with the Cup.

Aspects of expansion: after 1894

As the game became a popular public spectacle and rivalries became more intense, observers were becoming more critical in their appreciation of the game of 'socker'.[52] There was a 'dark side' to the game, when it was recognized that the result was not always a reflection of an all-out endeavour to win. In the SFA Cup, the two Lincolnshire Regiment teams played five matches in the final and were accused, by some, of fixing their games with repeated draws.[53] Opportunities to bet on the result and extra time away from military duties were the incentives.

It was reckoned that the majority of the spectators at the Esplanade were Malays, who devoted time and energy making their way from the outskirts of the town to see the white men play.[54] As time passed and the numbers of spectators increased, there were more complaints about unruly behaviour. The Europeans preferred to enjoy the seclusion of an enclosure near the SCC clubhouse. But as interest gathered pace, such segregation was not feasible and extreme patronizing tones of the colonial community were periodically expressed.

> What a howling mass of native riff-raff there was when the football cup was presented. Surely members of SCC could keep their enclosure free from such; a stick or a dog is all that is necessary.[55]

Football reinforced existing divided cultural identities. The Chinese community had been left to create its own opportunities for play. However, the Malay community received more assistance from the colonial British. It was said that the British favoured the more docile Malay population in day-to-day life. Some European Civil Servants found the Malay language easier to learn and this facilitated communication. The Malays themselves were often given significant responsibilities in the running of civil society – notably as an integral part of the police force.[56]

One of the consequences of increased interest in football was the call for more playing fields and a centralized location for different sports, not just football.

> A decent football ground would be always in demand for matches: at present if the RA, the RE, the Police, the marine engineers want to play a match there is endless difficulty in getting a suitable ground. We commend the formation of a 'Singapore Gymkhana Ground' to the attention of all interested in athletics and manly games.[57]

This was a reflection of the desire to spread the game more widely. The first example of a team venturing beyond the island to play occurred when the SCC were invited to play at the Selangor Club in Kuala Lumpur. Primarily an opportunity to play cricket, the Selangor Contests included football as a bonus for those who displayed greater stamina and competitive urges.[58] This ongoing rivalry between the leading European Clubs represented a forerunner of the Malaya Cup which would be established in 1921.

The expansion of football continued with the first visit of an SCC team to neighbouring Johore in late 1894. The Tunku Makota (or Crown Prince) invited the SCC to play against a team of Malay players that had been assembled by Norman Gawler.[59] As expected, the SCC team included Scoular, McKenzie and Lawson, who were clearly making a point to the senior members of the SCC that the game was not just a European affair. It was judged that the standard of play by the Malays had reached a level at which they 'could be pitted against the best Chinese team in Singapore with every confidence of success'.[60] A return match was initially scheduled for the New Year.[61] The game was postponed because of the approach of the Mohammedan fasting month, but eventually took place in June 1895, and represented the first time a Malay football team had appeared in public on the Esplanade.[62]

Civilization by soccer and the Malay experience

Although the introduction of football represented an opportunity for different racial groups to engage in recreational and then competitive games, it was also identified by the imperial masters as an avenue for pursuing an important agenda. Underlying the motivation for promoting football games was the imperial directive to help 'civilize through soccer'.

> All these native races have taken readily to various forms of athletic sport, and the sight of every race, colour and creed assembled together on the cricket or football field affords striking evidence of the good results attending British protection, whilst the mere assembly for a common purpose by teaching men of different races to know and respect one another exercises a by no means unimportant influence on their general civilization.[63]

The irony was that the civilizing process initially focused on providing role models, rather than actual opponents. Civilization was not synonymous with integration. The Warren Challenge Shield provided an opportunity for all the racial communities to observe and learn about the game. In one match, spectators were lined four deep all-round the field and many of the Asian contingent took a deep interest in the play. As a necessary prelude to guiding the Malay community, a translation of the rules of football into Malay was issued for the Darul Adab Association by the American Mission Press.[64] There is no record of a similar effort being made on behalf of the diverse Chinese community.

School teams were included as opponents in matches organized by the leading Malay Clubs. Boys from Raffles Institution were strong enough to play a combined team from the Darul-Adab club and the Darul-Bahar club. The latter club included Malay professionals, who were considered to be the strongest players from the community.[65] There were also signs of greater racial integration in the Darul Adab Football Cup – the first of the Malay-organized competitions – which included a team representing the Straits Chinese National team.[66] It was not uncommon for some teams to include individual players of other races.[67] The Malay Royal Engineers would often be assisted by European sappers.[68]

The formation of recreation clubs where Malays could play football was seen as a gratifying sign that young local men were growing in their enthusiasm for healthy physical recreation and therefore following the colonial model.[69] If the local teams demonstrated that they could adopt the European code of play – as reflected in the promotion of team spirit, fair play, graciousness, acceptance of the decisions made by the referee, discipline, for example – there would be encouragement to develop their participation further. A regular feature of life in Singapore was the arrival of British naval vessels. There was always time to arrange friendly games against the various teams that were emerging in Singapore. The Malay Policemen benefited from their connections and were quick learners when it came to taking on the Jack Tars from HMS Pique and later HMS Plover. With help from their European officers, they were able to gain sweet revenge for an earlier painful loss in which they had been 'frightened by the impetuosity of the Tars'.[70] Such was their progress that the Malay policemen even considered issuing a challenge to the SCC.[71] There was a notable reward for the Malay Police team later in 1897 when they were invited to travel to London to play during the festivities associated with the celebration of Queen Victoria's Golden Jubilee.[72]

Conclusions

As the last decade of the century was drawing to a close there were clear indications of change. First, soccer had supplanted rugby because of its general appeal.

> It is not often we witness a game of Rugby nowadays. Since the days of the old England and Scotland battle, of 6 or 8 years ago, it may almost be said that Rugger is a dead letter. 'Socker' to all appearances has permanently taken its place.[73]

The Europeans were still dominating the competitive scene, and there were signs that Malay football, in particular, was establishing a firm footing.[74] The Chinese game, however, did not receive much publicity. Second, the early style of play, which centred on an individualistic approach to the game was being replaced. The rush and the long dribble by a speedy winger were common occurrences. A more scientific approach was gradually being encouraged as football news arrived more regularly from Britain. The strategy of 'combination' was the great goal scorer and the soul of the game according the more enlightened writers.[75] Third, the game was now in the limelight because of its association with cultural imperialism. The game was praised as a suitable vehicle for spreading moral benefits.

> This is no small thing. It is not least than a Mission of the worthiest character, and it means a promise of native manhood of a greatly superior type. There are to be learnt, in the game, lessons of pluck, cooperation, endurance, fair-play, good temper, honesty, truthfulness and obedience to law ...[76]

Yet, five years later there were concerns that some of the European exponents, notably the military, were providing the wrong example. It was not just the physicality of their game, which was becoming increasingly belligerent. Indeed, the physical dangers associated with football were becoming newsworthy.[77] Nor was it their willingness to mutually control the outcome of a game, but mainly their raucous approach to supporting teammates from the touchline and abusing the referees.[78] For some observers this was a danger sign. The constant reminder was that the Europeans had to retain their dignity and grace if they were to be respected as leaders and administrators. The aim to encourage soccer as a civilizing agent was being undermined.

> It is ... unpleasant to hears howls of 'Yah Bah Boo Tyke 'im orf' from white skinned men wearing a uniform that implies discipline and respect to authority, before crowds of Asiatics who are quite quick enough to form their own ideas as to the propriety of such conduct. Bad enough as it is, it doesn't matter what goes on amongst the mobs that form the ordinary gallery at football matches in England: for the often dignified non-European races of the Queen's Empire are happily far themselves out of earshot. But that sort of thing should be left on the other side of the Suez Canal. To conduct himself with obvious fairness as a bystander at games is part of the 'White man's burden' when the White man is under the observation of large numbers of what he perhaps looks upon as inferior races.[79]

At the Annual General Meeting of SFA in 1898, which, as usual, took place at the SCC, Robert Scoular was re-elected as President. His committee consisted of a Treasurer Mr Thomas C.B. Miller, once the treasurer of Glasgow Rangers apparently, who refereed many of the games, and two representatives each from the RA, Royal Engineers, the West Yorkshire Regiment and the SCC itself.[80] There were only six entries for the SFA Cup competition and, as yet, no Asian teams.[81] Even though Robert Scoular and James McKenzie were still representing Scotland against England and Robert Scoular was to continue as President of the SFA until 1907, they were unable to fulfil a collective vision of complete integration in soccer.

Notes

1. *The Straits Times Weekly Issue*, January 27, 1892, 42.
2. The census of 1891 indicated that the total population of Singapore was 181,602. Europeans numbered 2302 (1434 males and 868 females). As a garrison town, Singapore also housed 1160 military men. The indigenous Malay community accounted for 35,992; the Chinese community represented 66% of the population at 121908. The Indian community numbered 16,035 and the Eurasian community 3589.
3. Industry focused on mining and the manufacture and export of such products as gambier, an astringent used in tanning and dyeing.
4. *The Singapore Free Press*, December 13, 1893, 3.
5. *The Singapore Free Press*, January 4, 1849, 3.
6. Edwards, *The Singapore House and Residential Life*, 107.
7. Handling style, hacking style or even sepak raga; a traditional Asian game involving a rattan ball and a collective effort to keep the ball in the air for as long as possible.
8. The indigenous Malay population and the migrant population – predominantly Chinese and Indians – and a proportion of the European colonialists favoured the game.
9. Football was not without its rivals for attention amongst the European population. Tennis had been the dominant recreational activity for men and women since the late 1870s. In 1891, the Singapore Golf Club was created, attaining a membership of 30 in five months. Sailing had been a staple throughout the Colony's history and cycling was coming into vogue as an option for the individual. Rowing was seen as a means to a healthy existence in a social setting.
10. *The Straits Times Weekly*, December 31, 1889, 8. Rabies was also highlighted in the press.
11. *The Straits Times*, September 7, 1896, 3 and *The Singapore Free Press*, July 22, 1895, 2. Lawson, a Scottish engineer, and Sarel, a young lieutenant with the 2nd Battalion Northumberland Fusiliers, both died after short, but severe illnesses.
12. *The Straits Times*, July 10, 1897, 3.
13. Roland St J. Braddell, in Makepeace et al., *100 years of Singapore*, 466. In all aspects of colonial life in Singapore during the nineteenth century Scotsmen figured prominently. In business and administration, the names of Scotsmen appeared regularly. William Farquhar and John Crawfurd were the first colonial administrators or Residents, once Sir Stamford Raffles the founder of Singapore had departed. Alexander Laurie Johnston was one of the first traders to make his mark. In sport, the first advocate of competitive games had been Raffles' own surgeon Dr William Montgomerie, who created an awareness of the benefits of physical activity by promoting the game of fives in 1835. Scotsmen were at the heart of life in the small settlement.
14. *The Singapore Free Press*, November 24, 1894, 2.
15. Makepeace, *100 Years of Singapore*, 333. This recollection may not be accurate as Scoular only arrived in Singapore on the steamer from Marseille in late November of that year.
16. *The Straits Times*, October 12, 1894, 2. It was suggested in 1894 that credit for actually introducing the game of football in Singapore should go to Englishman Francis Villiers Hornby, a senior member of the SCC. Indeed he featured actively in a number of early games, and, as the Captain of the SCC, he was in a position to create a platform for a new team game. However, Hornby (like Raffles before him) quickly departed from Singapore, in Hornby's case in January 1891, before the Football Association was created. Robert Scoular (1865–1930) came to Singapore as a clerk and assistant at John Little and Co. a well-established merchant's enterprise. He did not play in many of the first reported games, but became one of the first administrators as Vice President of the SFA in 1892. The name of Robert Scoular, as a player, as a referee and as an administrator, appears prominently throughout the first decade of the game and he was at the forefront of efforts to establish the game on a permanent basis. Had he recovered from the fever in 1896, John Lawson would have been a prime candidate for similar recognition.
17. *The Straits Times Weekly Issue*, June 7, 1889, 4.
18. 'Padang' is the local name for the open space occupied by the SCC.
19. *The Straits Times Weekly Issue*, 22 October 1890, 44. The idea of playing football during the evening hours was one innovation designed to obviate the problem of the

equatorial climate and the dearth of pitches. As yet there was no electric light, but an experiment was tried on the Tank Road ground with a series of oil lights lining a small pitch. The 'Well's' lights provided insufficient illumination to be considered worthy of regular use.

20. *The Straits Times Weekly Issue*, September 1, 1891, 6. In 1890, the year after football was introduced, there were 351 SCC members, a number which grew to 378 the following year and to 392 in 1892 – the year in which SFA was formed.
21. *The Singapore Free Press*, July 9, 1892, 2.
22. *The Straits Times*, September 8, 1896, 3. In one incident, a number of senior government officials and some military officers insisted on playing tennis at the same time as the funeral of John Lawson was taking place. An earlier club notification that play at the courts would be suspended as a sign respect for the Scotsman was disregarded.
23. *The Straits Times*, August 17, 1893, 3.
24. *The Straits Times Weekly Issue*, February 16, 1892, 6. On Friday, 12 February 1892 it was reported that 'an association football match will be played this afternoon between the Singapore Cricket Club and the past and present pupils of the Raffles Institution'. Raffles Institution was a school for children of local leaders. See Wijeysingha, *The Eagle Breeds a Gryphon,* 1–11.
25. Also known as Peranakans or 'Babas', the Straits-born Chinese had been living in the region for generations and had adopted many of the local cultural practices. Many also emulated the European settlers, speaking English and adopting their customs and habits. The China-born Chinese were more recent immigrants with little awareness or concern for European social life.
26. Tennis and billiards were the most popular games when the club opened and team games such as cricket followed.
27. Kampongs were small village communities outside the town.
28. Edwards, *The Singapore House and Residential Life*, 105.
29. *Straits Chinese Magazine*, Vol. 1, 9.
30. *The Straits Times Weekly Issue*, September 30 1889, 7.
31. *The Straits Times*, January 27, 1898, 3. There was resistance to the idea, but Dr. Lim Boon Keng was one of the first prominent Straits Chinese to remove his *towchang* in 1899.
32. *The Straits Times*, June 15, 1891, 2 and *Straits Chinese Herald*, March 27, 1894, 2. On a more serious note, there was even an unfortunate case of 'death from playing football'. An 18-year-old clerk who worked at the Straits Times expired during a game at the Old Jail ground.
33. *Daily Advertiser*, June 19, 1891, 3.
34. *The Straits Times Weekly Issue*, September 1, 1891, 6. The Societies Ordinance was invoked in 1889 to prevent problems associated with Chinese secret societies. New associations were required to maintain standards of rules and regulations relating to the activities of their members. Among the first to be exempted from the Ordinance were the SCC, the Engineers Association, the Masonic Club, the Rowing Club, the Cycling Club, the Ladies Lawn Tennis Club and the SCRC.
35. *The Straits Times*, February 8, 1894, 3.
36. *Daily Advertiser*, May 6, 1891, 3.
37. *Daily Advertiser*, August 3, 1891, 2.
38. *The Straits Times Weekly Issue*, September 1, 1891, 7.
39. *Daily Advertiser*, September 5, 1891, 2.
40. *The Straits Times Weekly Issue*, September 9, 1891, 8.
41. The Royal Engineers and the crew of the HMS *Egeria* provided opposition. In the following years, men from HMS *Severn*, HMS *Archer* and HMS *Peacock* also played against the SCRC.
42. *The Straits Times Weekly Issue*, May 17, 1893, 2.
43. Marine (or Maritime) Engineers; Singapore Cricket Club; 58th Regiment; Police; Royal Artillery; Royal Engineers and Singapore Volunteer Artillery.
44. The first reference to football in the Singapore Free Press came on the 1 September 1891.
45. *The Straits Times Weekly Issue*, July 21, 1891, 6. SCC vs HMS *Hyacinth* and HMS *Rattler*.

46. The General Officer Commanding the Straits Settlements, Sir Charles Warren, presented trophies for four 'sports': tug-of-war, rifle shooting, golf and football. The first two were restricted to the army, navy and volunteers. Golf was open to members of clubs. The football competition was open to all teams in the Malay Peninsula.
47. The other teams were the Singapore Volunteer Artillery, the Royal Artillery, the Royal Engineers and two teams from the Lincolnshire Regiment.
48. *The Singapore Free Press*, July 13, 1894, 3.
49. *The Singapore Free Press*, November 16, 1894, 3.
50. *The Straits Times*, November 23, 1894, 2.
51. *The Straits Times*, August 24, 1896, 2. The first match resulted in their favour of the Chinese by ten goals to nil.
52. *The Singapore Free Press*, November 19, 1894, 2. In news reports, the word 'socker' was changed to 'soccer' in 1900.
53. *The Straits Times*, October 12, 1894, 2.
54. *The Straits Times*, January 18, 1896, 3.
55. *The Singapore Free Press*, September 1, 1898, 3.
56. Olympiu G. Urcan. *Surviving Changi: E.E.Colman,* 46.
57. *The Singapore Free Press*, December 26, 1893, 2.
58. *The Singapore Free Press*, February 8, 1894, 3. These matches were played during the Chinese New Year holiday period or at Easter and Christmas and continued on a reciprocal basis well into the twentieth century. The first of the Selangor Contests took place early in 1894, when a team accompanied cricketers and tennis players. The cricket match was the main event. Two of the cricketers also played in the 25-min-each-way football game that concluded the proceedings.
59. Norman Gawler (1866–1938) was an Englishman. He had come to Johore initially as a teacher in 1892, but later became associated with the rubber industry.
60. *The Straits Times*, November 19, 1894, 3.
61. The invitation to the team was seen as a sign of respect for the Malay Crown Prince, the Tunku Mahkota.
62. *The Singapore Free Press*, June 5, 1895, 3.
63. *The Singapore Free Press*, July 15, 1895, 3.
64. *The Singapore Free Press*, January 10, 1896, 2.
65. *The Singapore Free Press*, October 18, 1897, 2. This year represented the first in which professional players were acknowledged in Singapore.
66. *The Straits Times*, December 7, 1897, 3.
67. *The Straits Times*, August 16, 1898, 2. In the 5th round of the Darul Adab Association Cup the team representing the Darul Afiah Club included two Chinese. Their opponents were aided by a number of players from Johore.
68. *The Straits Times*, October 11, 1898, 3.
69. *The Singapore Free Press*, January 25, 1897, 2.
70. *The Straits Times*, February 8, 1897, 3.
71. *The Straits Times*, March 8, 1897, 3.
72. *The Straits Times*, August 14, 1897, 3.
73. *The Singapore Free Press*, July 15, 1895, 3.
74. *The Straits Times*, May 10, 1899, 3.
75. *The Straits Times*, July 6, 1898, 3, and *The Straits Times*, October 6, 1899, 3. The thoughts of one of the early football stars, Ernest Needham, of Sheffield United, were published in Singapore in an attempt encourage a more elaborate passing game.
76. *The Singapore Free Press*, November 19, 1894, 2.
77. *The Straits Times*, July 11, 1899, 2.
78. *The Straits Times*, August 6, 1898, 3.
79. *The Singapore Free Press*, June 5, 1899, 2.
80. *The Straits Times*, June 17, 1898, 2.
81. *The Singapore Free Press*, June 27, 1898, 3. The only newcomers were the European dock employees from Tanjong Pagar FC.

References

Edwards, N. *The Singapore House and Residential Life: 1819–1939*. Oxford: Oxford University Press, 1991.

Makepeace, W., G.E. Blake, and R. St. J. Braddell. *One Hundred Years of Singapore*, Vol. II. London: John Murray, 1921.

Needham, E. *Association Football*. Cleethorpes: Soccer Books Limited, 2003.

Straits Chinese Magazine: A Quarterly Journal, Volume 1. Edited by Lim Boon Keng and Ong Song Siang. Singapore: Koh Yew Heng Press, 1897.

Urcan, Olympiu G. *Surviving Changi. E.E. Colman: A Chess Biography*. Singapore: Singapore Heritage Society, 2007.

Wijeysingha, E. *The Eagle Breeds a Gryphon*. Singapore: Raffles Institution, 2004.

From shamateurism to pioneer of Asia's professional football: the introduction of professional football in Hong Kong

Chun Wing Lee*

Hong Kong Community College, The Hong Kong Polytechnic University, Hong Kong, China

> Football in early post-war Hong Kong was rife with shamateurism. Since getting rid of under-the-table payments was all but impossible, in the mid-1950s there began to appear suggestions to introduce professional football into Hong Kong. But at the time, the unique situation of Hong Kong football meant that neither the clubs nor the top players supported legalizing professional football. The status quo was finally shaken by a bitter feud between the Amateur Sports Federation and Olympic Committee of Hong Kong (ASF&OC) and the Hong Kong Football Association (HKFA), triggered when the ASF&OC refused to endorse Hong Kong's participation in the 1968 pre-Olympic football competition in response to allegations of professionalism. The strong stance taken by the ASF&OC eventually prompted the HKFA to sanction professional football in the 1968–1969 season, making Hong Kong the first location in Asia to legalize professional football.

Introduction

As in many former British colonies, football in Hong Kong was originally dominated by the expatriate community, who dominated the top competitions in Hong Kong football, namely, the Challenge Shield and the League, which were formed in the 1890s and the 1900s, respectively. Not until the 1920s did South China become the first ethnic Chinese club to take away trophies from the expatriates. After the Second World War, Chinese clubs began to dominate both competitions. Beginning with the 1946–1947 season, no expatriate club ever won either competition again. The playing strength of the Hong Kong Chinese was also confirmed in international competitions. Even before the Second World War, the Republic of China (ROC) was able to dominate football competition in the Far East Games, thanks largely to the contribution of players who played club football in Hong Kong.

The practice of Hong Kong Chinese players representing the ROC continued after the Second World War. The bulk of the Chinese team that participated in the 1948 Olympic Games came from Hong Kong. Even after the ROC regime retreated to Taiwan following the Communist victory in the Chinese Civil War, Hong Kong players continued to represent the ROC in international competitions; they also helped the ROC win gold medals in the 1954 and 1958 Asian Games and secured qualification to participate in the 1960 Rome Olympics. With such an excellent record on the international stage and a league that witnessed sold-out crowds for many big matches, Hong Kong became known as the Football Kingdom of the Far East.

The popularity of football in Hong Kong also led inevitably to the emergence of 'shamateurism'. It was an open secret that top players were well paid for their contribution on the pitch. In the 1950s, the Chinese-language press often reported how clubs competed to sign the top players. Yiu Cheuk-yin, the ROC national team captain and widely recognized as the best player in the 1950s, even earned the nickname 'forty thousand feet' because it was widely believed that he once received a signing fee of HK$40,000.[1]

Although the Hong Kong Football Association (HKFA) had begun investigating shamateurism as early as 1951, without concrete evidence it was powerless to stamp it out.[2] Yet, ultimately the battle against shamateurism would lead to legalizing professional football in the 1968–1969 season, making Hong Kong the first place in Asia to introduce professional football, 15 years before South Korea and more than 20 years before professional football was introduced in Japan and China. While the origins of these leagues have been discussed elsewhere,[3] so far there have been no studies on the emergence of the first league set up for professional footballers in Asia. In the rest of this paper, therefore, I review the developments that led to the professionalization of football in Hong Kong. As will be shown, these changes were largely a response to shamateurism, and so I begin by reviewing how the HKFA attempted to deal with the problem in the 1950s.

Combatting shamateurism

It is impossible not to mention Leslie C Channing when discussing the fight against shamateurism in Hong Kong football. Channing was an Australian Chinese who worked in Hong Kong as a journalist for Hong Kong English-language newspapers in the early post-war years. In the 1950s, he had different stints representing both First Division clubs (including Sing Tao and Eastern) and the lower division clubs in the HKFA Council. In the Chinese press, Channing was given the nickname 'Cannon' for his often critical views raised in HKFA Council meetings. It appears that Channing saw the combating of shamateurism in Hong Kong football as his mission.

In an HKFA Council meeting in October 1955, Channing suggested that restrictions should be imposed on player transfers during the season to deal with the problem of requests by players for such transfers under financial inducements offered by the clubs.[4] This suggestion prompted another Council member, Major Elrick (the Army representative), to propose that the allegation of professionalism be investigated by a sub-committee; Channing also argued that a commission of inquiry should be formed. Two months later, the HKFA Council decided that the investigation would be conducted by the Appeals Board, which consisted of the HKFA president and three vice-presidents.[5] In February 1956, Elrick recommended that the investigation be abandoned and a professional league established.[6] Although Elrick's idea was not followed up, his suggestion, which was probably the first ever proposal for professionalization in an official meeting of the HKFA, showed that the HKFA's attempts to investigate the violation of amateur rules were probably not based on any commitment to amateurism.

Since the investigation by the Appeals Board never came to any conclusion on the issue, Channing urged in the Council meeting held in October 1956 that the investigation be restarted. In the same meeting, Channing also proposed a motion that all registered players sign within one month a declaration that they had received no financial benefits from the football clubs they were playing for.[7] But, although the motion narrowly passed (seven to six), no declaration forms were ever sent out to the clubs or players, showing that the issue of shamateurism was indeed an extremely thorny one.[8]

After his proposal on signing declarations, Channing left for Australia, never to return to Hong Kong. But, this did not mean the end of his fight against shamateurism in Hong Kong. In Australia, Channing wrote to international sporting organizations like the International Olympic Committee (IOC) and the Fédération Internationale de Football Association (FIFA). The IOC, after receiving his complaints, referred the case to the Amateur Sports Federation and Olympic Committee of Hong Kong (ASF&OC), which then requested the HKFA to investigate the issue.[9] The HKFA, however, never gave a satisfactory response to the charges of violating amateurism. As will be explained later, the HKFA's failure to deal with the ASF&OC's request would eventually lead to football in Hong Kong becoming professionalised.

Other ills of Hong Kong football

While professionalizing football could be used to deal with shamateurism, in the late 1950s and early 1960s it was also seen as a way to solve other problems within Hong Kong football. In 1960, one year after the HKFA failed to follow up on a proposal by Council member John Charles Weston to introduce professional football, Maximo Antoney Cheng became the first Chinese HKFA Council member to raise the idea of starting a professional league.[10] Cheng made it clear that he was advocating professional football to revive Hong Kong football, which by that time was suffering from allegations of match-fixing, declining standards and falling attendance.[11] Whereas, the relationship of professionalization to raising playing standards and attracting more spectators looks rather straightforward, its connection to match-fixing needs some elaboration. Since the mid-1950s, there had been many allegations of match-fixing in Hong Kong football. Reports in newspapers sometimes hinted that matches were rigged. For example, after the 1959 Senior Shield Final between South China and Tung Wah (won by South China 4–2), journalist Haobo commented in the *Hong Kong Times* that 'judging from the performance of Tung Wah, it was clear that many of their players were willing (or even liked) to lose by three goals'.[12] But, before 1960, the HKFA had done nothing serious to tackle the problem. As explained by I. M. MacTavish, a sports journalist employed by local English newspapers and a fierce critic of shamateurism, professional football could be used 'as a means of wiping out the complex evils of gambling' because it would force the HKFA to deal with gambling seriously.[13]

Even though Cheng was the representative of the Division One club Kitchee in the HKFA Council, this did not induce the club to back his suggestion. Indeed, when the HKFA then invited all clubs to share their stance on professionalization, none of the meeting participants favoured professionalizing football in Hong Kong.[14] Yet, although the clubs' stance meant that Cheng's proposal could not proceed further, some members of the HKFA Council were open to the idea of introducing professional football. One of these was Raleigh Leung, who would later play an important role in professionalizing Hong Kong football.

President's move

After his failure to clean up the Hong Kong game in the late 1950s, Channing began new attack on shamateurism in 1962 from Australia. In a statutory declaration that he signed, Channing claimed that 'registered soccer players of the Hongkong Football Association from First Division Chinese Clubs in Hongkong, who had lost their amateur status, took part in the Third Asian Games in Tokyo in 1958 and the 1960 Olympic Games in Rome'.[15] He then sent letters to the HKFA and the Hong Kong newspapers. In response to these allegations, the HKFA set up a special committee and HKFA President Albert Rodrigues, through the Policy and Planning Committee, pushed forward a proposal to study the feasibility of introducing professional football. It was decided to seek opinions from FIFA and the English Football Association on forming a league in which both professional and amateur players could compete.[16] In December 1962, the HKFA special committee issued a memorandum to the football community concerning the introduction of an 'open league' that would include both professional and amateur players in Hong Kong. The authors of the document clearly favoured introducing such a league, since they not only claimed that fans were largely positive about the idea, but they also outlined the advantages (though not the disadvantages) that professionalization would bring to the HKFA, the clubs and the players.[17]

As for the HKFA, one chief advantage was that it would no longer have to deal with allegations about professionalism in the future. Also, important to the HKFA was reviving Hong Kong's status as the Football Kingdom of the Far East by improving playing standards. According to the memorandum, this could happen in three ways. First, it could put a hold on off-season overseas tours by Chinese clubs, since only those clubs that performed well could travel overseas.[18] Second, clubs would protect players by not allowing them to play too often and third, players would get sufficient rest before the start of a new season. Taking into account that many of the overseas tours by Chinese clubs had very hectic schedules, both the second and third considerations could also be understood as targeting the overseas tours taken by Chinese clubs.

As for the clubs, some advantages they would enjoy after professionalization were as follows: clubs would be able to control players through contractual obligations; they would be able to discipline players (implicitly referring to the various allegations against match-fixing in the late 1950s and early 1960s); players could not leave clubs freely; and clubs could invite overseas players to participate in the future professional league. The players, on the other hand, would receive the following benefits: contracts would offer them security, they could command higher salaries if they performed well, professional training would improve their standards and they would gain recognition and respect from the public as professional players.

In other words, what the memorandum pictured was wholesale changes to Hong Kong football with professionalization. It was, therefore, no surprise that neither the Chinese clubs nor the players supported the idea. Most Chinese clubs in the First Division were supported financially by a small group of Chinese elites (usually businesspeople), who backed their clubs mainly for publicity. They had no long-term plans for developing their teams, and they were free to withdraw support after just one season. Asking them to increase their investment and to commit financially to a long-term project was clearly not something they were interested in.

The Chinese clubs, therefore, made their opinion clear when they unanimously voiced their opposition to professional football in March 1963.[19]

For the players, their views were less clear, but the top players certainly were not enthusiastic about the idea. When the Hong Kong Chinese Footballer's Fraternity organized a meeting to discuss the proposed changes, few players bothered to show up.[20] Its chairman, Au Chi-yin, later stated publicly that he was against professionalism by appealing to the ideal of amateurism. He argued that turning professional would cost players the opportunity to participate in the Olympic Games, which could bring them honour that money could not buy, and that sacrificing one's freedom for the sake of playing professionally would mean the loss of one's autonomy and meaning in life.[21] Although Au himself had a proper job as a policeman, it was unlikely that he really was a custodian of the Corinthian spirit since many his fellow Fraternity members were obviously shamateurs. The icon of Hong Kong football at that time, Yiu Cheuk-yin, also opposed the plan and, fearing that payments to players by the clubs would be subject to taxation after professionalization, questioned whether it would improve player income.[22] Also worth remembering is that for the top players, the freedom to join whichever club offered them the best terms every season gave them a lot of bargaining power in the shamateur system. Even though bosses may have paid them only during the football season, in the summer they could earn additional income by participating in the off-season tours.

Additionally, the political context may also help explain why most Chinese involved in Hong Kong football were not keen on going professional. Without the support of the Chinese clubs in Hong Kong, it was highly unlikely that the ROC could select Hong Kong players to represent the ROC in international competitions. It is safe to argue that most Chinese clubs were at least sympathetic to the ROC regime in the 1950s and 1960s. If Hong Kong introduced professional football, the Hong Kong Chinese players would no longer be eligible to play for the ROC in the Asian Games or Olympic Games. For the top players, this would mean a loss of a stream of income and also the opportunity to gain sporting prestige. Moreover, considering the propaganda value of a successful ROC team made up of Hong Kong players in the overseas Chinese community,[23] the ROC would be a potential loser if professional football were instituted in Hong Kong. This may explain why the day after the HKFA published its memo on professional football, the *Hong Kong Times*, a pro-ROC newspaper, invited former ROC player and coach Lee Wai-tong, widely recognized as the greatest Hong Kong player ever who had always been loyal to the ROC regime, to explain why he opposed the idea of introducing professional football in Hong Kong.[24]

Towards professional football

Despite this lack of support, the HKFA special committee released in the summer of 1963 a white paper that outlined the regulations governing non-amateur players.[25] But unsurprisingly, the proposal failed to gain traction without the support from clubs, players and the majority of Council members. The issue of professionalization was no longer mentioned publicly until 1966, although it is highly likely that some behind-the-scenes action was being taken to move Hong Kong football towards going professional, as shown by the publication of a set of draft rules on professional football in August 1966. These draft rules had been drawn up by the HKFA's Rules Revisions Committee during the 1965–1966 season, but upon receiving them HKFA chairman Mok Hing decided to shelve the issue.[26] They were, however, made public just a fortnight after the HKFA's annual meeting in July 1966 for two reasons. First, in the annual meeting, retiring President Rodrigues voiced his preference for professional football in his speech, stating: 'I still hold the view that players of great ability deserve and should be allowed to make soccer their career. We could well pioneer this move in Asia'.[27] Another important development was that the election for chairman in that meeting resulted in a defeat for Mok Hing, who had never shown any enthusiasm for professional football. The winner was Raleigh Leung, who (as shown earlier) was open to introducing professional football in Hong Kong. While Leung's victory in the chairman election did not necessarily mean that the clubs were now ready to embrace professional football, a chairman sympathetic to professional football would undoubtedly make the path towards professionalism less difficult. Led by Leung, who would win a second term in office the following summer (but Leung never finished it because he passed away in April 1968),[28] the HKFA began streamlining its rules to facilitate the future introduction of professional football in the second half of 1967.

Although the HKFA was busy fine-tuning the regulations in preparation for professionalizing the game in 1967, professional football could not be legalized without the support of the clubs, which had never welcomed the idea. But in November 1967, journalist MacTavish reported in his column in the *South China Morning Post* that several clubs had agreed in a private meeting to form professional teams in the 1968–1969 season.[29] Although it is impossible to verify the validity of the report, it is worth quoting how an unidentified club official made sense of going professional, according to MacTavish's column: 'Administration is lax and slipping and the standard of the game is inevitably getting lower each year. Professionalism will not act like a magic wand but it will provide the necessary solid foundation on which something worthwhile can be built and furnish the clearly defined framework within which clubs will be able to plan on a long term basis'. In other words, if there were clubs that were eager to embrace professional football, it was because the bosses of these clubs saw professionalism as a way to improve standards and serve as a foundation for making long-term plans, which up to that point had not been a concern of those bosses who supported the Chinese clubs. But, even if MacTavish's information was true, just 4 years earlier, both the Chinese clubs and the players had made clear that they had no interest in professional football, and so its advocates still had a long way to go to persuade the vested interests in the status quo to accept professionalism.

ASF&OC vs. HKFA

Eventually, a feud between the ASF&OC and the HKFA, triggered by Hong Kong's participation in the Olympic football qualifying competition in January 1968, served as a catalyst for bringing professional football to Hong Kong in the 1968–1969 seasons. This feud should be understood by taking the global Olympic movement into account. Although the growing pressures of commercialism and the rise of athletes sponsored by states in the socialist bloc were challenging the hegemony of amateurism in global sports in the 1950s and the 1960s, Avery Brundage, the IOC President between 1952 and 1972, was determined to defend the spirit of amateurism.[30] The ASF&OC was, therefore, obliged to uphold the amateurism ideal in the Hong Kong sporting community as well. Since the ASF&OC had urged the HKFA to clean up shamateurism to no avail before, a showdown between the two organizations was inevitable. It finally occurred only in late 1967 because, ever since the 1958 Asian Games, Hong Kong had not entered either the Olympic or the Asian Games football competitions. With international competitions restricted to those organized by the Asian Football Confederation (AFC), such as the Asian Cup or the Asian Youth Cup, the ASF&OC had had no opportunity to intervene in local football.

But, now the participation of the Hong Kong team in the pre-Olympic competition to be held in Thailand in January 1968 was subject to the ASF&OC's endorsement. The ROC had already fielded a team made up solely of Hong Kong players in another group of qualifiers in the summer of 1967, but when the HKFA submitted the 18 players of the Hong Kong team to the ASF&OC in December 1967, its chairman A. de O. Sales refused to countersign the player list, stating that 'the Hong Kong FA failed to satisfy us as to the amateur status of the players concerned'.[31] An HKFA Council meeting was quickly held where it was proposed that the club presidents of the players in the Hong Kong squad be invited to sign statements to prove that the players were amateurs.[32] But, such a proposal failed to convince Sales, who insisted that the players should *swear* in front of a Justice of the Peace to prove that they did indeed have amateur status.[33] Despite the setback, the HKFA did not give up and subsequently organized the players to *declare* in front of a JP that

> We, the undersigned, being players registered as amateurs with the Hongkong Football Association, do hereby solemnly declare that we have all the time been playing amateur football in Hongkong and at no time have we played professional football here or elsewhere, nor have we received any inducement to become professional footballers or to play professional football.[34]

Yet, the players' declarations failed to satisfy Sales, who again declined to endorse the player list since, according to him, what was needed was an oath (rather than a declaration) in front of a JP.[35] The next response of the HKFA was to ask the players to sign the official Olympic statement on amateurism, again in the presence of a JP.[36] But without an oath, Sales insisted that he would not countersign the player list. Writing to the HKFA Council, Sales stated that the ASF&OC would now approve the player list only if all members of the Council could give the ASF&OC 'a written official guarantee as to their veracity, that is to say, that there is no doubt whatsoever in the minds of all your Councillors that such players have never contravened the Olympic Eligibility Code'.[37] Sales also referred to the long-standing allegations about professionalism in Hong Kong football: 'We must once more ask your Association to take account of press and other allegations of professionalism in local football which your Association is accused of condoning. We insist that your Council take adequate and effective measures, in advance of the next football season, to distinguish clearly between amateur and professional players'.[38] This latest request from the ASF&OC could be seen as an insult to the integrity of the HKFA Council members, and with the pre-Olympic competition scheduled to start on 14 January, the HKFA finally gave up on the team's first ever participation in the Olympic Games qualifiers.[39]

This was not, however, the end of the saga. In late January 1968, the ASF&OC offered the HKFA a three-month time limit to set up a separate Amateur Football Association; otherwise, the HKFA might be expelled from the ASF&OC.[40]

The HKFA, unsurprisingly, had no intention of conceding to the ASF&OC's demand. The HKFA's stance was backed up by the English FA Secretary Dennis Follows, who suggested that there was no need for a separate Amateur Football Association,[41] and by FIFA, which told the HKFA that it should be able to decide how to administer amateur and professional football without outside intervention.[42] The ASF&OC thereupon suspended the membership of the HKFA from June onwards.[43]

Although the HKFA was not prepared to set up a separate amateur FA, the feud with the ASF&OC meant that it was now impossible for the HKFA not to deal with shamateurism. With rules and regulations already streamlined to prepare for the earlier anticipated introduction of professional football, the clubs no longer openly opposed the idea of professionalization when the HKFA Council asked FIFA whether it could control both professional football and amateur football simultaneously.[44] Clubs like Sing Tao, Rangers and Yuen Long even made quick preparations for professional football.[45] With no opposition from within the Hong Kong football community, the process of professionalizing the game now moved swiftly. In the April HKFA Council meeting, a special committee was set up to contact foreign football governing bodies so that it could instruct member clubs on the introduction of professional football in the 1968–1969 seasons.[46] Rules governing professional footballers were drafted and agreed to by the clubs in June.[47]

In the new season, five of the 12 First Division clubs – Rangers, Sing Tao, Kowloon Motor Bus (KMB), Jardine and Yuen Long – had players with professional status on their squads. None of these five clubs were typical Chinese athletics clubs like the powerhouse South China. Both Rangers and the newly promoted Jardine, a club backed by Jardine Matheson (one of the biggest businesses in Hong Kong), were controlled by members of the expatriate community. Colonial official David Akers-Jones was an influential figure in Yuen Long. Both Sing Tao and KMB were backed by businesses – the Sing Tao Group and the Kowloon Motor Bus Company, respectively – meaning that neither club needed to seek new backers every season.[48] In other words, most Chinese athletics clubs still preferred to operate without constraints bounded by contracts. The introduction of professional football, therefore, did not mean that the Hong Kong football community had fully embraced professionalism.

Conclusion

In advanced footballing nations in Western Europe and South America, the legalization of professional football was often a response to the pressures of commercialism or the power and influence of the best clubs that had been paying players in the amateur era.[49] But in Hong Kong, which had the best developed Far East football league from the 1950s to the 1970s, professional football was introduced not to deal with threats that clubs that had been breaking amateur rules would break away or to keep players from joining overseas leagues. In fact, the best-paid players and the clubs that could offer under-the-table payments were not interested in professional football because both parties enjoyed the flexibility of shamateurism. Adding to the fact that the ROC could field Hong Kong players in the Asian Games and the Olympic Games because Hong Kong players were amateurs in name, neither the clubs nor the top players had any reason to support professional football.

Therefore, the impetus to professionalize the game came mainly from officials of the HKFA.[50] Early attempts to defeat shamateurism were launched not to safeguard amateurism but to combat hypocrisy. And, since it was all but impossible to stop clubs from paying players, coupled with the perceived decline in Hong Kong football in the late 1950s and early 1960s, focus was turned towards professionalizing the game. But in 1963, the proposal to introduce professional football was defeated because both the Chinese clubs and the top players preferred clinging to the status quo they were enjoying. Eventually, an external force was needed to smooth the path towards professional football. That external factor was the ASF&OC's refusal to endorse Hong Kong's participation in the pre-Olympic competition in 1968 and its subsequent threat to expel the HKFA from its membership.

As suggested earlier, the firm stance taken by Sales should be understood by taking the global Olympic movement into account. First, the IOC had earlier asked the ASF&OC to investigate the professionalization of football in Hong Kong because of the allegations made by Channing, who probably knew that the Hong Kong football community would never deal with shamateurism unless there were sufficient external pressures. Also, the IOC at that time was led by Brundage, who was well known for his critical attitude towards professionalism.[51] What Sales and the ASF&OC did during the saga with the HKFA should, therefore, be considered part of the IOC's attempt to combat professionalism and safeguard the hegemony of amateurism in global sports. In the end, the interplay of such global forces and the attempts by those within the Hong Kong football community to introduce professional football resulted in professional football finally emerging in the 1968–1969 season.

Yet, despite being the first league in Asia to legalize professional football and being able to attract the likes of Dick Nanninga, Theo de Jong and Tommy Hutchison to play professionally in the early 1980s, Hong Kong has never qualified for the Asian Cup Finals since turning professional in 1968.[52] There are two possible reasons why the results of Hong Kong declined on the international stage after the introduction of professional football. Firstly, Hong Kong began to face tougher competition in the 1970s after the inclusion of North Korea and the People's Republic of China in AFC competitions. Also, the differences in professionalization between Hong Kong and other countries in East Asia are worth highlighting. In countries like China, Japan, Singapore and South Korea, professional leagues came into existence to improve the standards of football in those places.[53] But in Hong Kong, professional football was introduced in 1968 largely in response to the firm stance taken by the ASF&OC on the issue of amateurism. Professional football, therefore, did not mean introducing professional attitudes or commercializing the game in this context. The term only implied making under-the-table payments public and transforming the relationship between clubs and players into an employer–employee relationship. Although figures like Lee Wai-tong and newspapers like the *Hong Kong Times* opposed professionalism because they were defending the interests of the ROC, some of the concerns they raised about introducing professional football in the 1960s were legitimate. Ironically, some of the problems they identified have yet to be resolved in the twenty-first century. For example, most clubs still do not own training facilities, and few backers of Division One teams are ready to offer long-term commitment to clubs. Therefore, while professionalization improved the standards of football in many Asian countries in recent decades, the introduction of professional football probably did little to improve the quality of Hong Kong football players. The name 'Football Kingdom of the Far East' is now a distant memory. At the time of this writing, the HKFA is planning to introduce a fully professional league in the near future. But, if the problems noted above are not addressed, it is difficult to see how replacing the current First Division, which is open to both professional and non-professional teams, could revive the fortunes of the game in Hong Kong.

Notes

1. In the mid-1950s, the average daily wage of a skilled worker in Hong Kong was around HK$7.0 to HK$12.0. See England and Rear, *Chinese Labour under British Rule*, 30.
2. Ailin, 'FA Writes to Rebuke MacTavish Again Yesterday' [in Chinese], *Hong Kong Times*, September 17, 1959, 8.
3. Hirose, 'The Making of a Professional Football League'. Horne and Bleakley, 'The Development of Football in Japan'. Jones, 'Football in the People's Republic of China'; 'The Emergence of Professional Sport'. Lee, 'The Development of Football in Korea'. Manzenreiter and Horne, 'Playing the Post-Fordist Game'.
4. 'Chinese Members Fail to Answer Soccer Pro Charge', *Hong Kong Standard*, October 12, 1955, 8.
5. 'HKFA Council Meeting: Appeals Board to Investigate Allegations of Professionalism; Four Clubs Fined', *South China Morning Post*, 13 December 1955, 8.
6. Sima Niu, 'Can Hong Kong Organise a Professional League?' [in Chinese], *Hong Kong Times*, March 1, 1956, 8.
7. 'Channing Drops a Bomb Yesterday by Suggesting a Motion Requiring Players from Clubs to Declare They are Completely Amateur. Motion Passes 7–6' [in Chinese], *Hong Kong Times*, October 3, 1966, 8.
8. 'No Follow-up on Players' Declaration' [in Chinese], *Sing Tao Daily*, October 17, 1956, 4.
9. Chuanshanja, 'The Amateur Status of Hong Kong Football: FA Given Late June Deadline to Respond' [in Chinese], *Hong Kong Times*, May 27, 1959, 8.
10. 'Special Committees Set Up to Study Exterminating Gambling by Players, Organising a Professional League, Investigating Professionalization' [in Chinese], *Hong Kong Times*, September 28, 1960, 8.
11. In hindsight, there are few objective indicators showing that the standard of football was declining in the late 1950s. Although South Korea won the Asian Cup in 1956, the ROC football team, formed solely by Hong Kong players, was able to defend their gold medal in the 1958 Asian Games and qualify for the 1960 Olympic Games in Rome. Nevertheless, judging from sports pages in that period, there appears to have been a consensus regarding the decline in standards. Concerning falling attendance, there are no official statistics that could show that fewer spectators were going to the stadia, although some fixtures that were sold out in the mid-1950s could no longer attract a capacity crowd in the late 1950s.
12. Haobo, 'I was Wrong' [in Chinese], *Hong Kong Times*, May 18, 1959, 8.
13. Ian M. MacTavish, 'The Football Flutter Causes Quite a Splutter', *The China Mail*, October 22, 1960, 15.
14. Boguang, 'Representatives of Clubs Do Not Support Professional Football' [in Chinese], *Hong Kong Times*, October 21, 1960, 8.
15. 'Shock Pro. Claim', *Hong Kong Standard*, November 9, 1962, 18.
16. Weiduoli, 'Channing Attacks Hong Kong Football. FA Adopts Two Measures and Seeks Opinions from FIFA and the English FA' [in Chinese], *Hong Kong Times*, November 15, 1962, 8.
17. Haobao, 'FA to Introduce Professional Football, Writes to Relevant Parties for Opinions' [in Chinese], *Hong Kong Times*, December 12, 1962, 8.
18. In the 1950s and 1960s, the Chinese clubs often organized off-season overseas tours. The destinations of these tours were usually Southeast Asia, but could be as far away as Australia, New Zealand and East Africa. Very often, these tour teams included players who were playing for other clubs during the football season.
19. 'Chinese Clubs Unanimously Opposed to Football Reforms Yesterday', [in Chinese], *Hong Kong Times*, March 15, 1963, 8.

20. Boguang, 'Footballer's Fraternity Decides Yesterday to Ask the FA to Publish Proposals First' [in Chinese], *Hong Kong Times*, January 5, 1963, 8.
21. 'Au Chi Yin Offers Five Reasons to Oppose Professional Football' [in Chinese], *Hong Kong Times*, January 15, 1963, 8.
22. Weiduoli, 'Opinions within the Football Community on the Introduction of Professional Football' [in Chinese], *Hong Kong Times*, December 13, 1962, 8.
23. Lee, 'Politics, Identity and Football during the Cold War'.
24. Chuanshanja, 'Lee Wai-tong and Wong Shek-to Firmly Oppose Introducing Professional Football in Hong Kong' [in Chinese], *Hong Kong Times*, December 12, 1962, 8. Some of the reasons Lee suggested were as follows: Hong Kong lacked quality players; there was insufficient financial commitment from bosses; football standards would probably decline because Hong Kong players could no longer participate in amateur international competitions; professionalism could make match-fixing worse; top players would not support professionalism because they were already enjoying lives better than many professionals overseas; and most clubs in Hong Kong lacked stadia.
25. Weiduoli, 'Lee Man Kit: Non-amateur Football Will be Implemented, but Professional Competitions Will Not Happen' [in Chinese], *Hong Kong Times*, July 3, 1963, 8.
26. 'Rules Drafted for Professional Soccer', *South China Morning Post*, August 11, 1966, 3.
27. 'Raleigh Leung is New HKFA Chairman', *The China Mail*, July 27, 1966, 8.
28. Weiduoli, 'FA Chairman Raleigh Leung Passes Away from Illness Yesterday', [in Chinese] *Hong Kong Times*, April 16, 1968, 8.
29. I.M. MacTavish, 'Professionals in H.K. Next Season', *South China Morning Post*, November 17, 1967, 2.
30. Allison, *Amateurism in Sport*. At least one letter received by the ASF&OC after Channing's complaint to the IOC about shamateurism in Hong Kong football was signed by Brundage. 'The IOC Writes to the ASF&OC Again to Follow Up on the Professionalization of Hong Kong Football' [in Chinese], *Hong Kong Times*, October 16, 1959, 8.
31. 'Amateur Status of H.K. Players Questioned', *South China Morning Post*, December 27, 1967, 2.
32. 'Counter Proposal by the HKFA', *South China Morning Post*, December 29, 1967, 2.
33. 'Hongkong Withdraws', *South China Morning Post*, December 30, 1967, 3.
34. 'Sales May Still Say 'No'', *The China Mail*, January 4, 1968, 12.
35. 'Sales Rejects Statement', *South China Morning Post*, January 5, 1968, 2.
36. 'Colony Players Sign Statement', *South China Morning Post*, January 6, 1968, 2. The statement that Olympic participants had to sign in 1967 was to the effect that 'I, the undersigned, declare my honour that I am an amateur and that I have read and comply with the Eligibility Code of the Olympic Games as specified on this form'. Cited in Glader, *Amateurism and Athletics*, 157.
37. 'Mr Sales' Reply', *South China Morning Post*, January 9, 1968, 2.
38. Ibid.
39. 'H.K. Pull Out of Pre-Olympics', *South China Morning Post*, January 9, 1968, 2.
40. 'Get into Line, Or Get Out', *South China Morning Post*, January 25, 1968, 2.
41. 'Top UK Official Supports F.A.', *South China Morning Post*, February 16, 1968, 2.
42. 'FIFA Intervenes in Soccer Row', *South China Morning Post*, February 24, 1968, 2.
43. Boguang, 'ASF&OC Suspends FA Membership Effective Beginning of Next Month' [in Chinese], *Hong Kong Times*, May 23, 1968, 8.
44. Boguang, 'The FA Sets Up a Delegation to Discuss Amateur FA with the ASF&OC' [in Chinese], *Hong Kong Times*, February 7, 1968, 8.
45. Weiduoli, 'Professional Football Will Come, Clubs Start to Plan for Next Season, Facilitating Management and Improving Standards' [in Chinese], *Hong Kong Times*, February 10, 1968, 8.
46. 'Colony Wants Postponement', *South China Morning Post,* April 9, 1968, 2.
47. Boguang, 'Clubs Agree on Rules for Football Reform' [in Chinese], *Hong Kong Times*, June 29, 1968, 8.
48. It is likely that some of these five clubs had already agreed to form professional teams in late 1967, as reported in MacTavish's column.
49. For a general overview of the professionalization of football in Europe and South America, see Goldblatt, *The Ball is Round*, 171–226. See Russell, *Football and the*

English, 22–27 for the legalisation of professional football in England. The case in France was described in Hare, *Football in France*, 20–26. For the experience in Germany, see Hesse-Lichtenberger, *Tor! The Story of German Football*. The professionalization of football in Argentina, Brazil and Uruguay was documented in Mason, *Passion of the People*, 45–54.

50. Although all HKFA Council members were either sent to represent a First Division club or were elected by the clubs, it appears that many of them had a certain degree of autonomy when making decisions. It should be emphasized, however, that most of those who were eager to deal with shamateurism or to introduce professional football were from the expatriate community.
51. Allison, *Amateurism in Sport*. Glader, *Amateurism and Athletics*, 151.
52. Hong Kong participated in the inaugural competition as host in 1956, which reflected the status of Hong Kong football in those years. Hong Kong football players also participated in the three subsequent tournaments. The ROC qualified at the expense of Hong Kong in 1960. Hong Kong did qualify for the 1964 finals, and in 1968, both the ROC and Hong Kong played in the finals competition held in Iran.
53. See note 3.

References

Allison, Lincoln. *Amateurism in Sport: An Analysis and a Defence*. Abingdon: Routledge, 2001.

England, Joe, and John Rear. *Chinese Labour under British Rule*. Hong Kong: Oxford University Press, 1975.

Glader, Eugene A. *Amateurism and Athletics*. West Point: Leisure Press, 1978.

Goldblatt, David. *The Ball is Round: A Global History of Football*. London: Viking, 2006.

Hare, Geoff. *Football in France: A Cultural History*. Oxford: Berg, 2003.

Hesse-Lichtenberger, Ulrich. *Tor! The Story of German Football*. London: WSC Books, 2003.

Hirose, Ichiro. 'The Making of a Professional Football League: The Design of the J. League System'. In *Football Goes East: Business, Culture and the People's Game in China, Japan and South Korea*, ed. Wolfram Manzenreiter and John Horne, 38–53. New York, NY: Routledge, 2004.

Horne, John and Derek Bleakley. 'The Development of Football in Japan'. In *Japan, Korea and the 2002 World Cup*, ed. John Horne and Wolfram Manzenreiter, 89–105. London: Routledge, 2002.

Jones, Robin. 'Football in the People's Republic of China'. In *Football Goes East: Business, Culture and the People's Game in China, Japan and South Korea*, ed. Wolfram Manzenreiter and John Horne, 54–66. New York, NY: Routledge, 2004.

Jones, Robin. 'The Emergence of Professional Sport: The Case of Soccer'. In *Sport and Physical Education in China*, ed. James Riordan and Robin Jones, 185–201. London: Spon Press, 1999.

Lee, Chun Wing. 'Politics, Identity and Football during the Cold War: When Hong Kong Played the Republic of China in 1959'. *The International Journal of Sport & Society* 1, no. 1 (2010): 59–70.

Lee, Johng-young. 'The Development of Football in Korea'. In *Japan, Korea and the 2002 World Cup*, ed. John Horne and Wolfram Manzenreiter, 73–88. London: Routledge, 2002.

Manzenreiter, Wolfram, and John Horne. 'Playing the Post-Fordist Game in/to the Far East: The Footballisation of China, Japan and South Korea'. *Soccer and Society* 8, no. 4 (2007): 561–77.

Mason, Tony. *Passion of the People? Football in South America*. London: Verson, 1995. 45–54.

Russell, Dave. *Football and the English*. Preston: Carnegie Publishing, 1997.

The politics of Indonesian and Turkish soccer: a comparative analysis

James M. Dorsey and Leonard C. Sebastian*

S. Rajaratnam School of International Studies, Nanyang Technological University, Singapore, Singapore

> With soccer playing an increasingly important political role in both Turkey and Indonesia, this essay seeks to highlight similarities in the politics of soccer in two parts of the world that share cultural and political traits but are geographically distant from one another.

Introduction

Comparative analysis of the politics and economics as well as the social role of soccer in Indonesia and Turkey produces striking similarities. These similarities are rooted in the politicization of soccer in both countries and the fact that the game traces its origins to the struggles for independence in which pro- and anti-colonial soccer clubs played an important role.

That politicization is evident until today with rival political and commercial forces in both countries capitalizing on the sport's immense popularity in an environment of widespread corruption. In doing so, they often exploit historical differences between clubs that often are little more than a perception from the past rather than a reality and at times threaten the integrity of the sport.

In Turkey, political rivalries and corruption underlie a massive match fixing scandal and a battle for control of Turkey's biggest and best supported club, with millions of supporters and substantial assets. Similarly, contention in Indonesia has produced rival leagues that have undermined performance.

Moreover, in both countries, soccer lends itself as a tool of mass mobilization that political and economic forces as well as rulers exploit to garner support, improve their image and syphon off financial resources. Soccer's effectiveness is enhanced by the games immense news value in Indonesia as well as in Turkey, benefits that allow political and economic forces as well as rulers to score public relations points, distract public attention and at times manipulate public emotions.

Similarly, fan opposition to political interference and corruption in the sport plays a major role in both nations as do cultural clashes and socio-economic vulnerability and disadvantage.

Finally, identity politics spills into soccer in Indonesia as well as in Turkey. In predominantly Kurdish south-eastern Turkey, several municipalities governed by the pro-Kurdish Peace and Democracy Party launched in 2012 a regional football league to emphasize the area's distinct ethnic identity against the background of renewed insurgent violence that has cost more than 40,000 lives since 1986.

In Indonesia, the divide is primarily between Java and Papua with Papuans interpreting the game as a struggle against Javanese hegemony and animosity between clubs like Persebaya (Surabaya) Arema (Malang) rooted in the shift of cultural power from Malang to Surabaya.

Politics of football in Indonesia[1]

Competitive football in Indonesia is in dire straits. Both the national team and football clubs, have not won any international competition since winning the Gold Medal in SEA Games 1991.Currently, Indonesia's position in FIFA Global Ranking is 168th among 206 members. Despite having suffered its largest loss in over three decades, when losing to Bahrain 10–0 on 29 February 2012 in a World Cup qualifier, at the grassroots level however, football as a sport is booming. According to former Minister of Youth and Sports Andi Mallarangeng,

> Football continues to make money even when matches are broadcast free to air on TV. The game also brings development to industries and our local economy. Football is booming in Indonesia. There are now "soccer moms" and parents who are willing to pay thousands for their kids to play. There are 400 soccer schools for kids in Jakarta alone.[2]

Indonesia has a history of performing well at the international level. They were the first Asian side to qualify for a World Cup in 1938 competing, while still under occupation, as the Dutch East Indies. It performed credibly in the Tiger Cup ASEAN football championship in 2002 finishing runners up. Indonesian league football remains credible and the standard of competition between the clubs is high despite many scandals it faces off the pitch. Footballers who decide to play in the domestic leagues have an opportunity to earn lucrative salaries and foreigners do come to Indonesia to play. But a downward spiral is increasingly evident in international competition and there have been a spate of disappointing results. At the 2010 U-16 ASEAN tournament Indonesia, as host, lost to a novice Timor-Leste side and were dumped out of the competition early. Indonesia got off to the worse possible start in 2012 Suzuki Cup by managing a draw in their opening game with Laos averting defeat with an equalising goal in the final minute of the game, however, yet again crashed out at the group stage of the competition.

A legacy of polarisation

Pundits have regularly identified the politicization of football as the main source of the problems in Indonesian football.[3] While it is difficult to point to a direct connection or correlation between Indonesia's football humiliation at the hands of Bahrain in a recent World Cup qualifier as the consequence of corruption and political interference in football administration in the country, in reality, Indonesia's football team is far weaker as compared to Bahrain. Based on FIFA's world rankings, Bahrain's position is better than Indonesia. Yet, on-field technical issues, be it, bad strategy, lack of discipline and the poor mentality of the players, are the actual reasons behind the defeat. However, these on-field issues cannot be isolated from the off-field shenanigans that plague Indonesian football and have its origins in the politicization of football that has afflicted the sport since Indonesia's independence and can be now observed through the climate of perpetual conflict within the *Persatuan Sepakbola Seluruh Indonesia* (PSSI). When seen in that light, we can observe a logical connection between football and politics.

In July 2011 Nurdin Halid's[4] controversial tenure as Chairman of the Football Association of Indonesia (PSSI) finally came to an end. No stranger to the national political party scene, he ran the FA from his prison cell while serving a sentence having been convicted of the illegal importation of goods. Upon his release, he spearheaded the bid for the 2022 World Cup ultimately rejected by FIFA on 19 March 2010 due to lack of support from the Indonesian government. He is living proof of how entrenched football and politics has become in the country. Club football remains heavily dependent on government funding. Majority of clubs rely on local government funds, some as much as up to 95%, to run their programmes, and many are owned by local governments while those who operate as private companies are staffed by civil servants. As the most popular sport in Indonesia, football has attracted many suitors, including politicians and political parties.

Scholarly writings on the relationship between football and politics in Indonesia are limited.[5] Additionally, much of the available research is written in *Bahasa Indonesia*, not in English.[6] The politicization of football in Indonesia had its origins in the Dutch colonial era. In the Netherlands Indies, football spread from the elite to the workers. Initially, football used to be an exclusive game primarily for the Dutch. Later on, Chinese and *pribumi* (indigenous people) became interested in football and they established their own football clubs. Football actively contributed to societal changes.[7] Freek Colombijn (2000) argues that the football–politics–society nexus in Indonesia is closely related and by analyzing the relationship between them, links are evident especially when analyzed in tandem with the development of Indonesia's national integration, nationalism and modernization.

Football played an important role during the nation's struggle to gain and defend its independence. Football associations have both paid the price and become an instrument in power struggles. The contest between PSSI and the Netherlands Indies Football Association (*Nederlandsch Indische Voetbal Bond*), the Netherlands Indies Football Union (*Nederlandsch Indische Voetbal Unie*) and the Football Union for the United States of Indonesia (*Voetbal Unie in de Verenigde Staten van Indonesie*, or *Ikatan Sepakraga Negara Indonesia Serikat*) from the 1930s to the 1950s also represented different dimensions of the nationalist vs. the colonial political system. Furthermore, in terms of the nation building process, the inter-insular league had been crucial in the process of defining the Archipelago or *Nusantara* as a single nation.

During the Suharto regime, football continued to be politicized[8] when PSSI appointed Bardasono as the Chairman of the Association.[9] He introduced the concept of 'Pancasila[10] Football (*Sepakbola Pancasila*)' and a 'Joint Champions (*Juara Bersama*)' initiative in order to avoid a greater horizontal conflict within society.

The State also treated football as a tool to showcase national prestige. Observing the decline of Indonesian football in the international competition, Suharto warned PSSI to perform better. By doing so, Suharto had intended improve his public image as a leader who cared for Indonesia's favourite sport. Later on, it became common for political figures to follow Suharto's strategy by creating a connection between them and football.[11] Based on rational calculations, there is no obvious benefit for politicians to get involved in football-related matters because such an association may compromise their image. With Indonesia's football image deteriorating due to problems within the PSSI, persistent hooliganism, and the zero achievement of its national team at international level, what motivates politicians to take an interest in football?

Statistics attest to the popularity of football – 17.2% of Indonesians from the age of 10–65 chose football as their primary sports activity.[12] Additionally, in terms of age, the numbers of young Indonesians who actively play football as their sports activity are as follows:

- 15–19 years old: 23.9% or the equivalent of 4,990,495 people
- 20–24 years old: 32.6% or the equivalent of 6,484,672 people
- 25–29 years old: 24.6% or the equivalent of 5,242,369 people

The total population in this range is 62.1 million people or 26.12% of Indonesia's overall population. Such large numbers, specifically those in the age groups of 15–29 years old are potential voters and could possibly have a multiplier effect being able to influence their family members, relatives, friends and colleagues to vote for particular political candidates. These numbers would be larger if those who enjoy watching football as passive recreational activity are included.

Indonesian football's political fault-lines

There are two national leagues in Indonesia, the Indonesian Super League (*Liga Super Indonesia*, LSI) and the Indonesian Premier League (*Liga Prima Indonesia*, LPI). The latter was established and sponsored by Arifin Panigoro, owner of the Medco Group, to counter balance the LSI, then controlled by the PSSI under Nurdin Halid's chairmanship. Nurdin Halid being a Functional Group Party (*Golongan Karya*, Golkar) cadre and backed by the luminaries of the Bakrie family, Nirwan Bakrie and Aburizal Bakrie, the current Chairman of Golkar and the party's likely nominee for the Indonesian presidency in the 2014 presidential election. Their direct competitor, Arifin Panigoro used to be a leading member and financier of the Indonesian Democratic Party of Struggle (*Partai Demokrasi Indonesia Perjuangan*) and later established his own personal political vehicle, the New Democratic Party (*Partai Demokrasi Pembaruan*).

Nurdin Halid was unable to face down enormous pressure to resign as PSSI Chairman after the national team failed to win the 2010 AFF Cup. Although allegedly backed by the Golkar party, he accused his opponents of being supported by the government and President Yudhoyono's Democratic Party (*Partai Demokrat*, PD). Yet in reality, government intervention through the Ministry of Youth and Sports was limited primarily because FIFA does not tolerate such forms of intervention. Nevertheless, the opposition to Nurdin Halid was able to install Djohar Arifin Husein, an expert staff of the Minister of Youth and Sports, as the chairman of the PSSI and the PD's Deputy Secretary General Ramadhan Pohan as the manager of the national team. Djohar Arifin Husein's leadership has faced opposition from number of LSI clubs who remain loyal to Nurdin Halid. To further consolidate opposition to the current PSSI leadership, Nurdin Halid's camp then established the Committee to save the Indonesian Football (*Komite Penyelamatan Sepak Bola Indonesia*, KPSI) led by La Nyalla Mattalitti (former president of Persebaya).[13] Nurdin

Table 1. At the regional level.[a]

Club	Name of politician	Position in the club	Party/political organisation	Position in the party	Remark
Sriwijaya FC	Dodi Reza Alex Noerdin	CEO	Golkar	MP	
Persela Lamongan	Fadeli Hasan	Chairman	Golkar	Cadre	Regent of Lamongan
PSPS Pekanbaru	Herman Abdullah	Chairman	Golkar	Head of Kosgoro	
Mitra Kukar	Endri Erawa	CEO	Golkar	Former treasurer	
Persipura Jayapura	Benhur Tommy Mano	Chairman	Golkar	Cadre	Mayor of Jayapura
Persidafon	Habel Melkias Suwae	Chairman	Golkar	Cadre	
Pelita Jaya	Owned by Bakrie family				Owned by Bakrie's
PS Deltras	Mafiron	Chairman			Former Nurdin Halid's ExCo
Persebaya Surabaya	La Nyalla	Chairman	MPW Permuda Pancasila East Java Chapter		Golkar supporter
Persiba Balikpapan	Syahril HM Taher	Chairman	MPW Permuda Pancasila Balikpapan		
Persija Jakarta	Fery Paulus	Chairman			Former Nurdin Halid's ExCo
PSMS Medan	Rahudman Harahap	Chairman	Golkar	Cadre	Mayor of Medan
Gresik United	HM Sambari	Chairman	Golkar	Cadre	

[a]Information is compiled from Koran Baru. (19 April 2012). 'Bakrie Biang Keladi Kehancuran Sepakbola Indonesia?'. [Is Bakrie the Culprit of Indonesian Football Disaster?]. *Koranbaru.com*, http://koranbaru.com/bakrie-biang-keladi-kehancuran-sepakbola-indonesia/ (accessed November 29, 2012).

Halid used his knowledge of football politics to lobby the Asian Football Confederation (AFC) and FIFA for support placing him at a distinct advantage. Unsurprisingly, the AFC and FIFA have given their support to KPSI and the organisation is now considered by them as an important stakeholder for Indonesian football. Currently, AFC is working together with the new PSSI and the KPSI to find a durable solution.[14] However, this current format for cooperation has added greater complications to an uncertain situation. Currently there are two national competitions (LSI and LPI) and two national football administrations (PSSI and KPSI).[15]

The implications of this competition dualism are threefold. First, some of the clubs under the PSSI and LSI have decided to join LPI.[16] Further organisational chaos is evident at the club level with some clubs being torn asunder with internal competition within their organizations due to the national level administrative dualism. A case in point is the split between Persebaya Surabaya and Persebaya 1927, which originated from Persebaya, and who have now joined separate competitions. Persebaya joined the LSI, while Persebaya 1927 is with the LPI. Second, players belonging to LPI clubs are not permitted to play for the national team. Third, The AFC and FIFA have threatened the PSSI to overcome the dualism, or else face a ban on Indonesia's participation in all international and regional tournaments.

The difficulty for the PSSI is that the organisational dualism at the national level is deeply mired in a multi-dimensional political conflict involving a multiplicity of interest groups. It involves competition between the political parties – the Golkar–PD rivalry; organisational rivalry for the management and control of the game – KPSI vs. PSSI; competition between the leaders of the two principal football organizations – La Nyalla Mattalitti (seemingly identified as be part of Nurdin Halid's camp) vs. Djohar Arifin Husein (perceived to have the support of the government); and further complicated by the personal interests of political figures (see also Table 1) – Aburizal Bakrie, Nirwan Bakrie's personal rivalry Arifin Panigoro,[17] plus the Yudhoyono camp which includes Ramadhan Pohan[18] and Yudhoyono confidant George Toisutta (the former Army Chief of Staff and former PSSI Chairman).

Rationale why politics and football are closely intertwined in Indonesia

In Indonesia, football remains a channel for mass mobilization and a source of support.[19] Politicians see supporters of the national team and football clubs as potential voters in an election.[20] Football continues to be used by politicians to create 'metaphors' to generate a positive image, for both the individual politician and their political party, thereby justifying their activities and enabling them to establish a varied array of relationships between them and their target audience (Semino and Masci 1996).[21] The uses of slogans like 'Selamatkan Sepakbola Indonesia' (Save Indonesian Football) and public relations exercises like inviting the national team to a lunch sessions are examples how politicians try to create a positive public image and gain support from potential voters.

Politicians are also able to tap into lucrative football-related funding sources. Funding for football activities, both at the national and local level, is generally derived from the state budget (*Anggaran Pendapatan Belanja Negara*) and regional budget (*Anggaran Pendapatan Belanja Daerah*) as well as corporate sponsorship. The utilization of state or regional budget is prone to corruption. Funds are allegedly siphoned from football related revenues to bankroll the campaigns of politicians or political parties.

In Indonesia, football has immense news value whether at the national or local level.[22] By making contact and maintaining a relationship with a club or the national team, politicians would expect to receive greater news coverage related to their political ambitions. Such strategies are aimed at improving their image and raising their profile. For instance, Dodi Reza Alex Nurdin used his capacity as the CEO of Sriwijaya FC to sustain media coverage during his candidacy to become the regent of Musi Banyuasin.[23] In turn it is customary for local clubs to seek 'protection' by including the regent or governor to become the Chairman or a member of Board of Patrons of football clubs.

As in many countries, football has become a lucrative business in Indonesia. There also exist co-relations between football and business and the business-politics dimensions, resulting in intertwined relationships between football, business and politics (see Figure 1). Compared to the regional level, the relationship between football and business is more apparent at the national level. Though hard to prove, lucrative financial under-table agreements and access to football gambling revenues makes a takeover of PSSI a lucrative proposition and therefore many parties are attracted to competing over who controls it.[24] Income from broadcast rights can be as much as 130 billion rupiah per year (USD 13 billion) and from major sponsors like PT. Djarum (a tobacco company) can reach to 40–41 billion rupiah (USD 4 billion) per year. These figures do not include other sources of revenue, for example, player transfer fees, government aid and ticketing fees. The PSSI and PT. Liga Indonesia are also responsible for the management and distribution of these incomes to all LSI clubs. However, only half the revenue is ever received by a football clubs with much of it lost through corruption.[24] Suspicions also abound that funds are also allocated to finance a particular political party or regional leaders' election campaign.

Society is trapped in the middle of three (football-politics-business) elements (see Figure 1). Ideally, these three elements should work together to contribute to the society. However, the actual situation in Indonesia suggests that the society has not only become a victim but remains trapped within a conflict of interests between

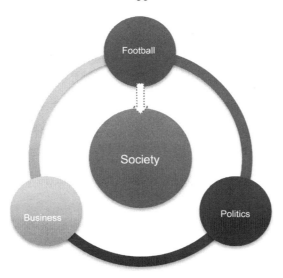

Figure 1. The nexus between football–politics–business and society.

predatory and rapacious actors in the tumultuous world of Indonesian football. Indonesian society has to sacrifice their hard earned tax dollars (particularly to the State and Regional budget); their dignity (lack of achievement by their clubs and the national team); and on occasions, even their lives (through incidences of hooliganism).

When it comes to violence and hooliganism, and its impact on Indonesian football, Freek Colombijn (2000) cautions that characteristics of the actors and the context for conflict in Indonesia is different compared to football hooliganism in the West. Utilising a Javanese cultural perspective, Colombijn observed that playing or supporting football is problematic for most Javanese players and supporters because football is played in situations where direct conflict is unavoidable. In Javanese culture, explicit conflict or open conflict should be avoided at all costs. The culturally prescribed reaction of conflict avoidance is practically impossible in a football match.

The resulting situation leads to an accumulation of tension for Javanese players and supporters alike which is unmanageable with the potential for numerous flashpoints during a football match. According to Lanang, a reporter from the Indonesian edition of *FourFourTwo* magazine, supporters resort to hooliganism because of peer pressure, socio-economic factors, or irrational motivations. To some extent, his view supports the argument of Limbergen, Colaers and Walgrave who emphasized that the main source of hooliganism is the social vulnerability of young people. According to Lanang, for the average Indonesian football fan, football clubs are an extension of their social identity providing them a rationale for a meaningful role in the society.[25] Non-football issues could also trigger conflict. For example, a supporter of a Jakarta football team Persija clashed with a supporter from a Bandung football club Persib during a television quiz programme in 2001 and ever since that incident, the supporters of the two clubs have always clashed during a Persija–Persib football match.

Conflict commonly occurs at the end of every football match, especially in Java and Papua. Supporters seem eager to initiate conflict irrespective of whether their team may have won or lost. Yet much of the conflict can be traced to structural issues. For example, if Persipura (Papua) lost to Persija (Jakarta), the defeat would be portrayed to symbolize Papua's defeat by Jakarta representing the Central Government or perceived Javanese hegemony over Papua. Persebaya (Surabaya) rivalry with Arema (Malang) is viewed in cultural/socio-political terms with Malang formerly the centre of culture during Indonesia's independence, while today Surabaya is more the regional focal point as the region's administrative centre.

The politics of soccer in Turkey

Like elsewhere in the Middle East and North Africa, soccer in Turkey traces its roots to the era of British colonialism when British residents of the Ottoman empire introduced the game in the late nineteenth century. With Ottomans of Turkish descent banned from embracing the sport, soccer was initially the game of the empire's European, Jewish, Greek and Armenian minorities.

It took however little more than two decades for Turks to challenge the ban with their feet with the emergence in 1899 of the Black Stockings (Siyah Çoraplılar), the first club formed by Turkish players and headed by a Naval Academy student. Its English name was intended to persuade security forces that it was a British club and spare it the invasion of pitches and arrest of players. Such measures constituted a doomed effort to halt the soccer wildfire that erupted with the emergence of various Istanbul-based clubs, including Kadikoy FRC, Moda FC, Elpis and Imogene FC as well as similar teams in the port city of Izmir.

'In Turkey, football has long been a metaphor for life', notes Al Jazeera Turk reporter Eylam Kaftan. In a documentary, she plays excerpts of a decades old Turkish black and white film. 'Brothers and sisters, be my referee. This is like a match. Play on the pitch of life. We are the players. The ball is our conscience. Tell me, is this not a goal?' says an emotional, moustachioed soccer fan. Turning to a judge, he adds: 'I take refuge in your justice. Your honour, is this not a goal?' The judge bangs his hand on the table. 'It's a goal', he says as the court room applauds and the film switches to a soccer match.[26]

The turn-of-the-century ban by Sultan Abdulhamit II, who viewed public gatherings of more than three people as a threat, reflected the then Ottoman elite's animosity towards Western modernity which it viewed as a menace to indigenous and Islamic culture as well as a potential political challenge by highly educated urban Turks who were enamoured by the game. In a foretaste of modern day opposition to soccer by segments of the militant Islamist community, Ottoman clerics denounced the game as a distraction from the study of Koran, promoting inappropriate dress and the display of naked flesh and symbolizing blasphemy because it resembled the kicking round in 680 CE of the severed head of the Prophet Mohammed's grandson Hussein by his killers.

The tide began to change however towards the end of the first decade of the twentieth century as the sultan's power increasingly made way for the rise of the reformist Committee for Union and Progress or Young Turks. Turkish clubs joined the league established in 1904 while educational institutions attended by Muslims and non-Muslims gave birth to some of modern Turkey's foremost clubs: gymnastics club Besiktas JK, elite French school Galatasaray's Galatasaray Spor Kulubu and St. Joseph's Fenerbahce Spor Kulubu.

The publication in that period of Istanbul's first sports magazine bore witness to the explosion of the city's repressed passion for soccer. In the words of Cem Emrence, the newly established Turkish clubs served 'to support the nationalist project under the auspices of the intelligentsia'[27] as the empire neared its demise. They were tools in the effort of the Young Turks to 'bolster popular Turkish nationalist sentiment and challenge non-Muslim cultural supremacy'[28] as well European prerogatives. Not unlike present day Arab autocrats who view soccer as a threat as well as an opportunity, the Young Turks saw soccer not only as a policy tool but also as a potential political rallying point. As a result, they focused on the sport as physical education rather than a way to align nationalist sentiment and reduce the risk of political and social mobilization.

This first defining period of Turkish soccer was followed by the post-World War Two emergence of soccer as a tool of expression of competing economic, ethnic and religious regional identities that often challenged the supremacy of Istanbul's three dominant clubs – Besiktas, Fenerbahce and Galatasaray. Anatolian clubs frequently did so from the position of the underdog given the Istanbul clubs' greater access to resources.

Despite making it to World Cup finals for the first time in 1954, Turkey's initial march to glory began only in the late 1950s with a first wave of professionalism. That did not prevent the political, geo-political and commercial rivalries and associated violence, corruption and match fixing that underlid Turkish soccer from exploding in the deaths of 42 people and wounding of 300 others in 1967 in the central Anatolian city of Kayseri in one of the worst incidents in Turkish sporting history. The incident occurred against the backdrop of local often more pious Anatolian political and economic bosses organized around communal and religious networks manipulating soccer for their own purpose and as a way of challenging the country's dominant political elite (Akin).[29]

The emergence of provincial teams highlighted competing efforts by Anatolian cities to wield political and economic influence as regional centres, established a civic and local identity of their own and integrated the mass influx of rural migrants. Competition between Kayseri and Sivas, dating back to the early days of the modern Turkish republic carved out of the ruins of the Ottoman empires was particularly fierce with Kayseri being viewed as the wealthier, more developed and economically dominant of the two. Fighting erupted in the stands during a match in 1967 between Kayseri's Kayserispor and Sivas' Sivasspor following a controversial decision by the referee to cancel a red card he had shown to a Kayseri striker. Hundreds of primarily Sivas fans were crushed unable to exit tunnels because the gates were locked.[30]

The wedge between Istanbul and much of the rest of the country was initially deepened as soccer further professionalized and commercialized in the last quarter of the twentieth century. Clubs located in Turkey's more globalized commercial hubs with Istanbul in the forefront pulled ahead by attracting a wealthy benefactor, often a businessman who made his fortune in construction or the media, forcing those that didn't to compete by becoming more and more dependent on funding from local government (Emrence 2010).[31] The new wealthy owners ran their clubs much like their family-owned business as their personal fiefdoms. They used the clubs to increase their own public recognition as well as that of politicians, leverage ownership to create new business opportunities. The club often served to launch the political career of the new owner who counted on fans grateful for his coming to the rescue of their club voting for him.

Controversial media and communications industry mogul Cem Uzan, scion of a family, viewed either as robber barons or the Turkish equivalent of the early, rough playing Rockefellers, established for example his own political party partly with the support of fans of two long neglected historic clubs, Istanbulspor and Adanaspor acquired by his family. The soccer holdings helped him boost his media properties with the repeated winning of the broadcast rights of the Turkish Super League and the European Championship League. Ultimately however, the two clubs suffered the fate of their owners. They went into bankruptcy in 2005 after the Uzans became embroiled in multi-billion dollar law suits with their communications industry partners, Mototorla and Nokia, and had many of their companies confiscated. Uzan's father and brother evaded arrest by fleeing the country. Cem Uzan's right-wing, nationalist Genc (Youth) Party emerged as a strong contender from the 2002 elections having won the third largest number of votes. Those were however insufficient for the party to cross the 10% threshold needed for a seat in the Turkish parliament.

Parallels can be drawn between the political role of the first militant Turkish fans in the 1960s and 1970s and those of contemporary Indonesia. Like in Indonesia where soccer until today is divided by vested political and commercial interests, Turkey's first militants forged close ties to the heads of clubs who used them as leverage to strengthen their positions. In contrast to North African ultras who prided themselves from their founding on their financial independence, the early Turkish militants were rewarded with funding for their paraphernalia such as flags and banners.

Militant fans of the major Istanbul clubs since then have come to view their loyalty to their club as universal much like their counterparts in North Africa who played key roles in recent popular uprisings that radically changed the region's political landscape. This universal approach contrasted starkly with the more locally focused identity of soccer fans in Indonesia. The Turkish definition of support transcended local, political, ethnic and religious identities. 'By rejecting the deep schisms that divide the country, the fans' group can be viewed as a new model of a national community', wrote French scholar Adrien Battini in an analysis of UltrAslan, militant Galatasaray supporters,[32] who traditionally greeted supporters of visiting clubs with the words: 'Welcome to Hell'.

Turkish researcher Itir Erhat, who in a break with tradition was introduced to soccer by her father and other male relatives at a young age recalls suddenly realizing in her mid-twenties the macho nature of the songs she was chanting.

> I caught myself singing the chant 'Suck my cock Fener' to the tune of 'Those Were the Days'4 during a derby match and making the appropriate hand gesture. That was a moment of epiphany for me: for years, I had been passionately singing about actions I cannot perform as a woman and had completely adopted the hegemonic male discourse to fit in with the men in the family, to fit in with the football stadium environment.

she wrote.[33]

Erhat's realization highlighted one source of soccer violence in Muslim societies like Turkey and Indonesia irrespective of whether they define themselves as secular or not.

> In Turkey, the stadia are masculine, hetero-normative spaces. They are seen as fortresses of masculinity (Tanir 2007). What Simić (1969) calls the machismo syndrome can be exemplified in various ways. Terrorizing the passersby before or after the games, vandalizing the stadia, tearing the seats, smashing bathroom mirrors are common practices in Turkey. These actions arise from the desire to prove strength and dominance. After the games the visiting team is given a half-hour head start to clear the area to avoid possible clashes. Fans take pride in calling themselves delikanlı, a Turkish expression which means 'crazy-blooded'.

she wrote.[34]

The use of sexual innuendo in the chants and slogans of Turkish fans sets them apart from their counterparts in Indonesia and most other Muslim countries. It reflects the imposition of western cultural concepts at the birth of modern Turkey as well as its control of women by stripping them of their sexuality rather than confining them to their homes (Ibid. Erhart).[35]

> Turkish fans distance themselves from homosexuality and insult the enemy (the rival team, the fans, the referees, sometimes their own players) by attributing to them sexual weakness and, hence, feminizing them. The most common insults are 'sons of whores' and 'fag' (Tanir 2007, 16). These insults aim at undermining male respectability ... Players and referees are also abused by references to their wives, mothers, sisters or girlfriends

Erhat wrote. Turks further refer to scoring a goal as entering, inserting or penetrating. They often chant about anal rape when a team scores a goal.[36]

The influence of business fed on the fact that Turkish soccer clubs remained from their inception elitist organizations whose management was populated by close-knit often impenetrable groups. It also benefitted from the fact that support of a soccer team is in Turkey as in the Middle East and North Africa as important as religious and ethnic identity. In the same vein of wealthy businessmen taking over major clubs, second and third tier clubs became more dependent on municipal funding. This turned them into tools of support bases for politicians who controlled the municipality. Mayors often became part of a club's management.

As a result, soccer was subjected to commercial interests and vulnerable to political corruption. Turkey's economic and soccer integration with the European Union accelerated the trend. Liberalization led to clubs becoming economic actors in their own right.[37] Galatasaray with an estimated fan base of 20 million becoming the first Turkish club to list on the Istanbul stock exchange and attract foreign investment.[38] Besiktas was quick to follow. The move transformed Turkish soccer from a national pastime into an industry with revenues in the hundreds of millions of dollars.

As a result, the management of soccer clubs changed fundamentally. Political bosses, their cronies and businessmen were joined by financial, business development, legal, marketing, merchandising, branding, sponsorship and communications experts in the running of the club. These new executives were tasked with maximalizing income, generating new revenue streams, improving cash flow, reducing debt and funding expanded infrastructure, including stadiums. Following the example of Europe's top leagues, Turkey's exploding privately owned media meant that broadcast rights significantly helped to produce cash needed to create a super league and acquire increasingly costly international players to be able to compete at a European and global level.

To integrate soccer economically and socially into Europe and revive the country's moribund economy, Turkish President Turgut Ozal, who assumed office immediately after a period of military rule in the early 1980s and put Turkey firmly on the road towards economic liberalization, loosened the tight grip on the game imposed by the generals. He granted the the Turkish Football Federation (TFF) greater political autonomy in a bid to encourage greater competitiveness and created financial muscle so that the national team and club would perform in Europe. As a result, soccer increasingly became a barometer of Turkish ambitions to join the European Union. When in 1991, for example, a match between Fenerbahce and Atletico Madrid was cancelled because of a power failure, Turkish newspapers reported the incident in terms of a national disgrace.[39]

Similarly, Galatasaray's 1993 and Fenerbahce's 1996 success against Manchester United, the Turkish national team's first appearance in a Euro competition in 1996 and Galatasaray's winning of the UEFA Cup and European Super Cup in 2000 were seen as evidence of Turkish progress, vitality and growing strength (Goldblatt)[40] Galatasaray's firsts made them the first team from a Muslim nation to excel in European competitions. Turkish justice minister Hikmet Sami Turkey hailed Galatasaray's winning of the 2000 Union of European Football Associations' UEFA Cup in Copenhagen as Turkey's fulfilling of the European Union's Copenhagen criteria.[41] 'A winning Turkish sport team ... helps the Turkish authorities ease the erratic process of integration into the European Union and therefore to affirm that

Turkey is indeed part of Europe and belongs to part of its organizations', wrote political scientist Adrien Battini.[42] The game also served to highlight Turkey's place as a bridge between east and west. 'Fenerbahce is the first place in Asia when you arrive from the European side. Your first step into Asia brings you to Fenerbahce', said one of the club's cheer leaders.[43]

Increasingly, the economics and politics of twenty-first century Turkish soccer mirrored the country's debt-driven economic model. They also reflected social shifts from Istanbul to the Anatolian hinterland that stemmed from a decade of rule by a democratically elected Islamist government as well as political struggles that were being waged across the Middle East and North Africa as Turkey emerged as a military and economic powerhouse in a region populated by former Ottoman colonies in the throes of political change.

As a result, a 2012 research note issued by Moscow-based investment house Renaissance Capital[44] concluded that Turkish soccer, estimated to be the world's sixth largest football market, and the country's economy faced the same risks. These risks stemmed from increasing deficits – current account for the state, debt for clubs – and rising inflation.

'Turkey's declining success in football can be mapped to economics', the Renaissance capital note said.[45] The investment house noted that Turkish soccer like the Turkish economy 'imports almost all their best players from abroad, and exports one or two good players every year'.[46] In doing so clubs incurred high levels of debt to attract star players with top clubs like Fenerbahce, Besiktas and Galatasaray operating as commercial companies that eschewed competitiveness for profit. The acquired stars were often expensive, old has been such as former Real Madrid stars Roberto Carlos and midfielder José María Gutiérrez Hernández (Guti). Their celebrity boosted merchandising, but contributed little if any added value to the team. The focus on sales rather than performance on the pitch produced the same ills many Turkish companies faced: complacency and reduced competitiveness. 'Without an increase in competitiveness Turkey is trapped with manic depressive success', Renaissance Capital said.[47]

Soccer results proved the point. Turkey's top clubs have dominated the country's soccer for decades but failed twice in a row in 2011 and 2012 to win the Turkish league or qualify for the UEFA Champions League. The poor performance of the three major Istanbul clubs mirrored a trend in Turkish economic development as growth shifted and political power expanded from the country's economic capital to booming urban centres in the Anatolian inland. Two of Turkey's more recent most successful teams, Bursapor and TrabzonSpor, hail from the former Ottoman capital of Bursa and Trabzon on the Black Sea, two cities that at the same time boasted trade surpluses while Istanbul accounted for 60% of Turkey's trade deficit.[48]

Economic change and innovation did little to take politics and the corruption associated with it out of the game. At the beginning of the second decade of the twenty-first century, scandal-ridden Turkish soccer was playing two simultaneous existential matches: one to eradicate widespread corruption and match-fixing embedded in Turkish soccer since its birth in clandestinity, the other pitting two Islamist teams competing for the hearts and minds of Turkish soccer fans. The political battle in many ways resembled that being waged in Indonesian soccer, but has proven less divisive and less disruptive of performance despite its high stakes.

Turkish Prime Minister Recep Tayyip Erdogan, a former soccer player, member of Fenerbahce – Turkey's biggest and best supported club, and leader of the ruling

Justice and Development Party (AKP), emerged the apparent victor, albeit to the detriment of the sport itself. The prime minister determined to preserve Fenerbahce, Turkish soccer's most valuable political asset, as his unrivalled domain against attempted encroachments by self-exiled, Pennsylvania-based cleric Fethullah Gulen and his supporters within AKP, compromised on dealing harshly with those guilty of match fixing, first and foremost Fenerbahce chairman Aziz Yildirim.[49] By contrast, Gulen, in a bid to reduce Erdogan's grip on the club, favored harsh punishment, including relegation, of those involved in the scandal. Gulen was believed to have wanted to see Yildirim removed to pave the way for someone closer to his movement to take control of the club. Erdogan however was catering to soccer bosses and their corporate backers as well as the fans themselves in advance of elections in 2014. The elections as well as the push for constitutional change in the run-up to the poll are crucial for Erdogan who after three terms as prime minister was widely believed to be eying the presidency, a largely ceremonial post that he would like to see endowed with enhanced power.[50]

In months of battles in 2012 in parliament and in the TFF, Erdogan pushed for leniency as Yildirim and 92 others were charged and convicted of match fixing. Three months after the TFF rejected a proposal backed by the prime minister that would have shielded clubs guilty of match fixing from being relegated, Erdogan succeeded in getting the federation to clear Fenerbahce as a club and 15 others of charges of involvement in match fixing. Erdogan's successful interference prompted the TFF's three top officials, including its vice chairman, Goksel Gumusdag, a brother-in-law of Erdogan, to resign.[51] Erdogan defended the controversial TFF decision on the grounds that punishing institutions rather than individuals would amount to penalizing 'millions of fans who set their hearts on these institutions'.[52] The decision followed Erdogan's earlier success in driving through parliament against the will of President Abdullah Gul, believed to be a Gulen ally, a bill that limited punishment of match fixing.

The battle for Fenerbahce was politically sensitive given Gulen's support for the AKP and its significant influence based on its vast network of schools, businesses, media assets, including major Turkish media, and NGOs across the globe, and its significant sway over Turkey's police force. The movement played an important role in the rise of Turkey's appeal across the Middle East, North Africa and sub-Saharan Africa with its network often paving the way for Turkish diplomacy and business.

Erdogan increasingly, however, has come to see Gulen as a liability rather than an asset. The cleric's inroads into the judiciary and the police have meant that critics of his movement have more often than not found themselves behind bars on charges of involvement in the murky and controversial Ergenekon affair, involving Turkey's Kemalist, ultra-nationalist deep state. The affair has led to massive military arrests and made Turkey one of the world's foremost jailers of journalists. The arrests have sparked international criticism and portrayed Erdogan as increasingly arrogant and authoritarian. Gulen left Turkey in 1998 ostensibly for health reasons but more likely to avoid standing trial for a recording in which he allegedly advocated an Islamic regime.

In supporting opposition to the reduction of penalties for match fixing, the Gulen movement has signalled that it would continue to support the AKP, but could well side with elements in the party eager to curb the prime minister's unchallenged grip. Erdogan has earned domestic and international praise for his presiding over years of tremendous economic growth and positioning Turkey as a regional and international power house. Privately, however, critics within his party complain about his increasingly autocratic streak, his measures against the media that have made Turkey one of the world's largest incarcerator of journalists and his emotionalism that has prompted him at times to narrow Turkey's options.

Conclusion

Indonesian and Turkish soccer have similar roots in struggles for independence and suffer both from exploitation by political and commercial interests. Turkey's historical focus on Europe and its quest for European Union membership however has spared it some of the worst tribulations suffered by Indonesian soccer. As a result Turkey despite a major match fixing scandal and political battles for control has unlike Indonesia made its mark on the international soccer stage. In doing so, Turkey constitutes a model for badly needed reform of Indonesian soccer that would shield the game from the worst paralyzing effects of political and commercial manipulation even if it fails to liberate it from the manipulative influence of external forces.

Notes

1. Leonard C. Sebastian would like to credit Yoes C. Kenawas for research assistance during the writing of this article.
2. Interview with Andi Mallarangeng, Minister of Youth and Sports, 26 June 2012. On 7 December 2012, Andi Mallarangeng was indicted for corruption and subsequently resigned as Indonesia's Youth and Sports Minister. He is alleged to have abused his powers and illegally delegated signing authority to a subordinate in the graft-ridden construction of West Java's Hambalang sports complex, which cost the state US$24 million in losses. A presidential favourite he was President Susilo Bambang Yudhoyono's spokesman on domestic affairs for five years before being rewarded with a cabinet postion in 2009.
3. 'Clubs cannot survive without support from the government whether it is national or local. Hence politicians have become the Chairpersons football clubs not purely as benefactors but because football is important to Indonesian society and could become a platform for their political aspirations'. Interview with Andi Mallarangeng, Minister of Youth and Sports, 26 June 2012.
4. A supporter of Sepp Blatter, Nurdin also derived his position due to a close friendship with embattled former AFC President Mohammed Bin Hammam. Interview with Lanang, Editor, Indonesian edition of *FourFourTwo* magazine and Rio Josia, Reporter, *Tabloid Bola*, 26 June 2012.
5. Freek Colombijn, 'The Politics of Indonesian Football', *Archipel* 59 (2000): 171–200.
6. Arief Natakusumah, *Drama Itu Bernama Sepak Bola: Gambaran Silang Sengkarut Olah Raga, Politik, dan Budaya* (Jakarta: PT Elex Media Komputindo, 2008).
7. Colombijn, 'The Politics of Indonesian Football', 171–200.
8. See, Inilah.com. (2011, September 15). *Guncangan Politik Dalam Sepakbola Indonesia*, from Inilah.com: http://bola.inilah.com/read/detail/1774387/guncangan-politik-dalam-sepakbola-indonesia (accessed November 29, 2012).
9. During the Suharto era, PSSI Chairman was an aide to former president Soekarno. Soeharto put him in prison without any clear reasons.
10. The Pancasila is the formal organizing ideology of the Indonesian state since 1945. Its purpose was to create a consensus for the establishment of a state that would resonate with all Indonesians regardless of their religious, ethnic and regional identities. While the Pancasila acknowledges that Indonesia is fundamentally a religious country, the state respects the religious diversity of its citizens and does not endorse any particular religion. For a useful discussion, see, Douglas E. Ramage, *Politics in Indonesia: Democracy, Islam and the Ideology of Tolerance* (London: Routledge, 1995).

11. 'SBY: PSSI Jangan Sibuk Berantem!' Tempo.co, http://www.tempo.co/read/news/2012/03/05/099388061/SBY-PSSI-Jangan-Sibuk-Berantem (accessed August 20, 2012).
12. *Statistik Sosial Budaya 2009*. (Jakarta: Badan Pusat Statistik).
13. Okezone. (2012, March 21). 'Menpora: Rekonsiliasi, Solusi Terbaik Kisruh PSSI' ['Youth and Sports Minister: Reconciliation, the Best Solution for PSSI Conflict'], from bola.okezone.com: http://bola.okezone.com/read/2012/03/21/51/597744/menpora-rekonsiliasi-solusi-terbaik-kisruh-pssi (accessed November 29, 2012).
14. A Normalization Committee was established to address PSSI's difficulties and took a long time to overcome the problem due to political issues that compromised attempts at reaching a settlement. Taufik Jursal Effendi, the Head of Indonesian Football School Association implored all parties concerned to prioritize national interest before personal interest in order to find a solution to PSSI's problems. Yahoo (2011, June 12). 'Persoalan Kongres PSSI Dinilai Sudah Masuk Ranah Politik' ['The PSSI Congress has entered the political arena'], from id.berita.yahoo.com: http://id.berita.yahoo.com/persoalan-kongres-pssi-dinilai-sudah-masuk-ranah-politik-073609113.html (accessed November 29, 2012).
15. 'Timnas Versi La Nyalla Incar Riedl atau Bendol', Tempo.co, http://www.tempo.co/read/news/2012/08/10/099422529/Timnas-Versi-La-Nyalla-Incar-Riedl-atau-Bendol (accessed August 18, 2012); 'La Nyalla Tantang Timnas PSSI Lawan Timnasnya', http://www.tempo.co/read/news/2012/08/10/099422526/La-Nyalla-Tantang-Timnas-PSSI-Lawan-Timnasnya (accessed August 18, 2012); and 'No end to the chaos', *World Soccer*, December 2011: 38.
16. Tempo (2011, January 24). 'Kompetisi dengan Spesialis Blunder dan Kado Penalti' ['A Competition with Confusion and Penalty Gift'], from tempointeraktif.com: http://majalah.tempointeraktif.com/id/arsip/2011/01/24/LU/mbm.20110124.LU135733.id.html (accessed November 29, 2012).
17. Arema (Malang football club) is contested by Bakrie and Panigoro. This contestation represents the race between the two men for oil exploration in Malang region. Prince Ali Bin Al Hussein, Vice President of FIFA, is a friend of Arifin Panigoro and business partner of Bakrie, thereby complicating FIFA's ability to resolve the PSSI-KPSI conflict. Interview with Lanang, Editor, Indonesian edition of *FourFourTwo* magazine and Rio Josia, Reporter, *Tabloid Bola*, 26 June 2012. See also, Berita Satu. (2011, January 5). 'Politik sepakbola Arifin dan Bakrie' ['The Politics of Football Between Arifin and Bakrie'], from Beritasatu.com: http://www.beritasatu.com/ekonomi/8817-politik-sepakbola-arifin-dan-bakrie.html (accessed November 29, 2012).
18. The debate on Ramadhan Pohan's new position as the manager of the national team revolved around his suitability owing to his background as a PD legislator. It was alleged that politics was the deciding factor in his appointment particularly to smoothen the lobby with the Ministry of Youth and Sports. Ramadhan Pohan was viewed as useful to the PSSI to gain financial aid from the ministry and the parliament. Mr. Pohan, however, rejected this accusation saying that his main duties were to look after the needs of the national team and protecting the players the negative influence of external parties. Suara Merdeka. (2012, April 30). 'Pro-Kontra Ramadhan Pohan Jabat Manajer Timnas'. ['Pros and Cons on Ramadhan Pohan's Position as the Manager of the National Team'], from suaramerdeka.com: http://www.suaramerdeka.com/v1/index.php/read/sport/2012/04/30/16234/Pro-Kontra-Ramadhan-Pohan-Jabat-Manajer-Timnas (accessed November 29, 2012).
19. In a *Bola* magazine article, PSSI is compared to the Helen of Troy whose beauty attracts many people, with many striving to get her attention and ready to die for her. Several governors and district leaders (mayor or regents) are using local football clubs to attract public support. Fauzi Bowo (former Governor of Jakarta) supported Persija Jakarta as a means attracting the support of the club followers, who are well known in the city as the Jakmania. Alex Nurdin (Governor of South Sumatera) was similarly using Sriwijaya FC for the same purposes as was Peni Suparto (Mayor of Malang) with Arema FC (Aremania) in order to support his wife's candidacy in the local election. The most recent and observable connection between politics and football was seen during the leadership of Nurdin Halid (a Golkar Party cadre) when arranged for the national team to have lunch with the Golkar Party Chairman, Aburizal Bakrie, during the AFF Cup in 2010. Ramadhan Pohan's appointment as the Manager cum Operational Director of the

national team was the consequence of an ultimatum given by then Youth and Sports Minister, Andi Mallarangeng (then Secretary of PD's Supervisory Council), who threatened that the ministry would not provide the annual budget for PSSI. Pohan's appointment was seen as an answer to the Minister's ultimatum. See, 'Helen of Troy, PSSI, dan Politik' [Helen of Troy, PSSI, and Politics] in Bola.net. (2012, April 25), from Bola.net: http://www.bola.net/editorial/helen-of-troy-pssi-dan-politik.html and Tribun News. (2010, December 21). 'Staf Khusus Presiden Sindir Kunjungan Timnas ke Rumah Ical'. ['Presidential Expert Staff Criticizes the National Team's Visit to Ical's House'] (accessed November 29, 2012), from tribunnews.com: http://www.tribunnews.com/2010/12/21/staf-khusus-presiden-sindir-kunjungan-timnas-ke-rumah-ical (accessed November 29, 2012).

20. Many people want Indonesian football to be free from political interference. One of the proponents is Ari Junaidi of the University of Indonesia who noted that several numbers of politicians were holding important positions in the PSSI's structure. Achsanul Kosasih of PD is the treasurer of the PSSI. Adjie Massaid of PD was the manager of U-23 national team. TM Nurlif and Ahmadi Supit of Golkar as well as Syarifuddin Sudding of Hanura were also part of the PSSI. The highest position in the PSSI was held by Nurdin Halid (Coordinator for Sulawesi Region of Golkar Party). Indonesian Democratic Party of Struggle (PDIP) legislator Dedy Gumelar wanted politics kept out of football through a constitutional mechanism. (Kompas. (2011, January 14). 'Jauhkan Sepak Bola dari Politik!' [Keep the Football Out of Politics], from Kompas.com: http://bola.kompas.com/read/2011/01/14/18134356/Jauhkan.Sepak.Bola.dari.Politik (accessed November 29, 2012).

21. E. Semino, and M. Masci, 'Politics is Football: Metaphor in the Discourse of Silvio Berlusconi in Italy', *Discourse and Society* 7, no. 2 (April 1996): 243–69.

22. The National Team's success in AFF 2011 had been claimed by several political parties. Politicians came to the stadium, gave comments on the media, and hosted a special lunch. Indra Jaya Piliang of Golkar said, 'if it is the case, then PD had beaten Golkar by 3-1'. PD through Susilo Bambang Yudhoyono (SBY) was far more aggressive than Golkar. The first defeat was the media coverage when President Yudhoyono watched the national team's match (*nonton bareng*). The second and third defeats were when the President came to the Stadium to support the national team. Skala News. (2010, December 21). 'Timnas Jadi Lumbung Pencitraan Parpol?' ['National Team has become the tool for Political Parties to Create Good Image?'], from Skalanews.com: http://skalanews.com/baca/news/8/0/89733/politik/timnas_jadi_lumbung_pencitraan_parpol__.html (accessed November 29, 2012).

23. Sutiyoso, former governor of Jakarta and founder of *Jak Mania* (a group of Persija supporters) successfully maintained his position as a governor for two terms utilising such a support base. These *Jak Mania* members also joined a demonstration to back Sutiyoso when he faced criminal proceedings. Heru Joko, a leading football supporter of the local football team in Bandung was elected as member of the Regional People's Consultative Assembly (*Dewan Perwakilan Rakyat Daerah*, DPRD) Bandung. Interview with Lanang, Editor, Indonesian edition of *FourFourTwo* magazine and Rio Josia, Reporter, *Tabloid Bola*, 26 June 2012.

24. Interview with Lanang, Editor, Indonesian edition of *FourFourTwo* magazine and Rio Josia, Reporter, *Tabloid Bola*, 26 June 2012.

25. Interview with Lanang, Reporter, Indonesian edition of *FourFourTwo* magazine, 26 June 2012; and K. van Limbergen, C. Colaers, and L. Walgrave, 'The societal and psycho-sociological background of football hooliganism', *Current Psychology* 8, no. 1 (Spring 1989): 4–14.

26. Eylem Kaftan, Al Jazeera English, The Passion and the Penalty, November 8, 2012, http://www.aljazeera.com/programmes/aljazeeraworld/2012/11/201211572928581576.html.

27. Cem Emrence, 'From Elite Circles to Power Networks: Turkish Soccer Clubs in a Global Age, 1903–2005', *Soccer and Society* 11, no. 3 (2010): 242–52.

28. Emrence ibid.

29. Akin, 'Not Just a Game: The Kayseri vs. Sivas, Football Disaster', *Soccer and Society* 5, no. 2 (Summer 2004): 219–32.

30. Ibid.

31. Emrence, ibid.
32. Adrien Battini, 'Reshaping the National Bounds through Fandom: The UltrAslan of Galatasaray', *Soccer and Society* (2012), doi:10.1080/14660970.2012.730771.
33. Itir Erhart (2011), Ladies of Besiktas: A dismantling of male hegemony at Inönü Stadium, International Review for the Sociology of Sport.
34. Ibid.
35. Ibid.
36. James M. Dorsey, 'Istanbul Club Spurs Change in Turkey's Soccer World – Galatasaray Hopes to Float Shares', *Forms Plan for Stadium Complex*, November 4, 1996.
37. James M. Dorsey, 'Galatasaray Plans to Seek Listing For Some Assets', *The Wall Street Journal*, November 14, 2000.
38. David Goldblatt, *The Ball is Round, A Global History of Soccer* (New York: Riverhead Books, 2006, p. 759) and C. Kozangolu, 'Beyond Edirne: Football and the National Identity Crisis in Turkey', in *Football Culture and Identities*, ed. G. Armstrong and R. Giulianotti (London: MacMillan, 1999).
39. Ibid. Goldblatt, 758–9.
40. Kerim Balci, 'Galatasaray Enters the EU in Copenhagen, Hurriyet', *Daily News*, May 19, 2000, http://www.hurriyetdailynews.com/default.aspx?pageid=438&n=galatasaray-enters-the-eu-in-copenhagen-2000-05-19
41. Ibid. Battini.
42. Ibid. Kaftan.
43. quoted in James M. Dorsey, 'Debt Fuels Turkish Soccer but Threatens Country's Economic Growth', *The Turbulent World of Middle East Soccer*, January 1, 2012, http://mideastsoccer.blogspot.com/2012/01/turkish-soccer-crisis-dents-erdogans.html
44. Ibid. Turkey's current account deficit soared from 6 to 10% in the first half of 2012.
45. Ibid.
46. Trabnzonspor secured government approval for a 28 MW plant in the hills above Trabzon, the city it helped make famous and that is known for its fanatical football fans and hot-blooded residents who pick a fight first and think later. The plant is expected to cost up to $50 million and gross annual revenues of $10 million. Trabzon is considering building a smaller, second plant. Financial Times quoted in James M. Dorsey, Turkish soccer club pioneers new funding strategy, The Turbulent World of Middle East Soccer, August 14, 2012, http://mideastsoccer.blogspot.com/2012/08/turkish-soccer-club-pioneers-new.html
47. Ibid.
48. Ibid.
49. James M. Dorsey, 'Islamist Power Politics Threaten Clean-Up of Turkish Soccer', *The Turbulent World of Middle East Soccer*, May 11, 2012, http://mideastsoccer.blogspot.com/2012/05/islamist-power-politics-threaten-clean.html.
50. Justin Vela, 'Turkey Hearing Casts Spotlight on Gulen', *The Daily Star*, December 15, 2011, http://www.dailystar.com.lb/News/Middle-East/2011/Dec-15/156924-turkey-hearing-casts-spotlight-on-gulen.ashx#axzz2FFDk0Mh7.
51. Ibid Dorsey.
52. Ibid.

References

Akin, Yigit. 'Not Just a Game: The Kayseri vs. Sivas Football Disaster'. *Soccer and Society* 5, no. 2 (2004): 219–32.
Balci, Kerim. 'Galatasaray Enters the EU in Copenhagen', *Hurriyet Daily News*, May 19, 2000, http://www.hurriyetdailynews.com/default.aspx?pageid=438&n=galatasaray-enters-the-eu-in-copenhagen-2000-05-19.
Battini, Adrien. 'Reshaping the National Bounds through Fandom: The UltrAslan of Galatasaray'. *Soccer & Society* (2012), doi:10.1080/14660970.2012.730771.
Berita Satu. *Politik sepakbola Arifin dan Bakrie* [The Politics of Football Between Arifin and Bakrie], http://www.beritasatu.com/ekonomi/8817-politik-sepakbola-arifin-dan-bakrie.html (accessed November 29, 2012).

Bola magazine. 'Helen of Troy, PSSI, dan Politik' ['Helen of Troy, PSSI, and Politics'] in *Bola.net*, April 25, 2012. http://www.bola.net/editorial/helen-of-troy-pssi-dan-politik.html (accessed November 29, 2012).

Colombijn, Freek. 'The Politics of Indonesian Football'. *Archipel* 59 (2000): 171–200.

Dorsey, James M. 'Debt fuels Turkish Soccer but Threatens Country's Economic Growth.' *The Turbulent World of Middle East Soccer*, January 1, 2012, http://mideastsoccer.blogspot.com/2012/01/turkish-soccer-crisis-dents-erdogans.html.

Dorsey, James M. 'Galatasaray Plans to Seek Listing For Some Assets'. *The Wall Street Journal*, November 14, 2000.

Dorsey, James M. 'Islamist Power Politics Threaten Clean-Up of Turkish Soccer'. *The Turbulent World of Middle East Soccer*, May 11, 2012, http://mideastsoccer.blogspot.com/2012/05/islamist-power-politics-threaten-clean.html.

Dorsey, James M. 'Istanbul Club Spurs Change in Turkey's Soccer World – Galatasaray Hopes to Float Shares'. Forms Plan for Stadium, Complex, November 4, 1996.

Dorsey, James M. 'Turkish Soccer Club Pioneers New Funding Strategy'. *The Turbulent World of Middle East Soccer*, August 14, 2012, http://mideastsoccer.blogspot.com/2012/08/turkish-soccer-club-pioneers-new.html.

Emrence, Cem. 'From Elite Circles to Power Networks: Turkish Soccer Clubs in a Global Age, 1903–2005'. *Soccer & Society* 11, no. 3 (2010): 242–52.

Financial Times quoted in James M. Dorsey. 'Turkish Soccer Club Pioneers new Funding Strategy'. *The Turbulent World of Middle East Soccer*, August 14, 2012, http://mideastsoccer.blogspot.com/2012/08/turkish-soccer-club-pioneers-new.html.

Goldblatt, David. *The Ball is round, A Global History of Soccer*. New York: Riverhead Books, 2006.

Inilah.com. '*Guncangan Politik Dalam Sepakbola Indonesia*' ['Political Tremor in Indonesian football']. http://bola.inilah.com/read/detail/1774387/guncangan-politik-dalam-sepakbola-indonesia (accessed November 29, 2012).

Kompas. '*Jauhkan Sepak Bola dari Politik!*' ['Keep the Football Out of Politics'] http://bola.kompas.com/read/2011/01/14/18134356/Jauhkan.Sepak.Bola.dari.Politik (accessed November 29, 2012).

Koran Baru. *Bakrie Biang Keladi Kehancuran Sepakbola Indonesia?* [Is Bakrie the Culprit of the Indonesian Football Disaster?] http://koranbaru.com/bakrie-biang-keladi-kehancuran-sepakbola-indonesia/ (accessed November 29, 2012).

Kozangolu, C. 'Beyond Edirne: Football and the National Identity Crisis in Turkey'. In *Football Culture and Identities*, ed. G. Armstrong and R. Giulianotti, 117–26. London: MacMillan, 1999.

Natakusumah, Arief. *Drama Itu Bernama Sepak Bola: Gambaran Silang Sengkarut Olah Raga, Politik, Dan Budaya* [This Drama is called Football: A Chaotic Illustration of How Sports, Politics, and Culture Intersects]. Jakarta: PT Elex Media Komputindo, 2008.

'No end to the chaos', *World Soccer*, December, 2011: 38.

Okezone. *Menpora: Rekonsiliasi, Solusi Terbaik Kisruh PSSI* [Youth and Sports Minister: Reconciliation, the Best Solution for PSSI Conflict] http://bola.okezone.com/read/2012/03/21/51/597744/menpora-rekonsiliasi-solusi-terbaik-kisruh-pssi (accessed November 29, 2012).

Ramage, Douglas E. *Politics in Indonesia: Democracy, Islam and the Ideology of Tolerance*. London: Routledge, 1995.

Semino, E., and M. Masci. 'Politics is Football: Metaphor in the Discourse of Silvio Berlusconi in Italy'. *Discourse and Society* 7, no. 2 (April 1996): 243–69.

Skala News. 'Timnas Jadi Lumbung Pencitraan Parpol?' [National Team has become the tool for Political Parties to Create Good Image?], *Skala News*, http://skalanews.com/baca/news/8/0/89733/politik/timnas_jadi_lumbung_pencitraan_parpol__.html (accessed November 29, 2012).

Statistik Sosial Budaya. Jakarta: Badan Pusat Statistik, 2009.

Suara Merdeka. 'Pro-Kontra Ramadhan Pohan Jabat Manajer Timnas' ['Pros and Cons on Ramadhan Pohan's Position as the Manager of the National Team'], http://www.suaramerdeka.com/v1/index.php/read/sport/2012/04/30/16234/Pro-Kontra-Ramadhan-Pohan-Jabat-Manajer-Timnas (accessed November 29, 2012).

Tempo. '*Kompetisi dengan Spesialis Blunder dan Kado Penalti*' ['A Competition with Confusion and Penalty Gift'] http://majalah.tempointeraktif.com/id/arsip/2011/01/24/LU/mbm.20110124.LU135733.id.html (accessed November 29, 2012).

Tempo. 'La Nyalla Tantang Timnas PSSI Lawan Timnasnya,' http://www.tempo.co/read/news/2012/08/10/099422526/La-Nyalla-Tantang-Timnas-PSSI-Lawan-Timnasnya (accessed August 18, 2012).

Tempo. 'SBY: PSSI Jangan Sibuk Berantem!' http://www.tempo.co/read/news/2012/03/05/099388061/SBY-PSSI-Jangan-Sibuk-Berantem (accessed August 20, 2012).

Tempo. 'Timnas Versi La Nyalla Incar Riedl atau Bendol', http://www.tempo.co/read/news/2012/08/10/099422529/Timnas-Versi-La-Nyalla-Incar-Riedl-atau-Bendol (accessed August 18, 2012).

Tribun News. '*Staf Khusus Presiden Sindir Kunjungan Timnas ke Rumah Ical*' ['Presidential Expert Staff Criticizes the National Team's Visit to Ical's House'], *Tribunnews.com*, http://www.tribunnews.com/2010/12/21/staf-khusus-presiden-sindir-kunjungan-timnas-ke-rumah-ical (accessed November 29, 2012).

Van Limbergen, K., Colaers, C. and Walgrave, L. 'The Societal and Psycho-Sociological Background of Football Hooliganism'. *Current Psychology* 8, no.1 (Spring 1989): 4–14.

Vela, Justin. 'Turkey Hearing Casts Spotlight on Gulen', *The Daily Star*, December 15, 2011, http://www.dailystar.com.lb/News/Middle-East/2011/Dec-15/156924-turkey-hearing-casts-spotlight-on-gulen.ashx#axzz2FFDk0Mh7.

Yahoo. '*Persoalan Kongres PSSI Dinilai Sudah Masuk Ranah Politik*' ['The PSSI Congress has entered the political arena'] http://id.berita.yahoo.com/persoalan-kongres-pssi-dinilai-sudah-masuk-ranah-politik-073609113.html (accessed November 29, 2012).

'Hamlet without the Prince': understanding Singapore–Malaysian relations through football

Charles Little

London Metropolitan Business School, London Metropolitan University, London, UK

> In January 2012, a Singaporean football team returned to the Malaysian Super League for the first time in 17 years. Those years of exile (caused by the Football Association of Singapore's withdrawal from Malaysian football in 1995) were the most recent manifestation of the long-standing sporting and political tensions across the Causeway. Since Singapore's expulsion from Malaysia in 1965, the two neighbours have had a tumultuous relationship, marked by frequent squabbles caused by economics, personality and race. This paper analyses the political relationship between the two countries through the prism of football. It shows how the game has acted as a mirror of these wider tensions, and has itself been a source of political disputes. Among the key findings of this paper are that footballing tensions predated the ill-fated merger between the two nations and that, despite the mutual antipathy, the two states are locked together in an inescapable inter-dependence.

Introduction

The turn of 2012 saw stories about football dominating the sports pages of Singapore's newspapers. This might not seem unusual, given the local passion for the sport. However, these stories were not the usual fare of the English Premier League (EPL), UEFA Champions League or even the increasingly popular La Liga from Spain. Instead, domestic football was gaining a rare turn in the spotlight.[1] The catalyst for this attention, almost unprecedented for at least a decade, was the forthcoming return of a Singaporean football team to the Malaysian Super League for the first time in 17 years. The Malaysian Super League, as the successor to the old Malaya Cup competition, was seen by many as the spiritual home of Singaporean football and the debut of the LionsXII (as the new team was billed) was keenly anticipated.

Despite the fond memories many held towards the old competition, it had also been the site of bitter and acrimonious debate between Singapore and Malaysia. The years of exile after 1994 caused by the Football Association of Singapore's (FAS) withdrawal from all Malaysian domestic football in 1995 were only the most recent manifestation of the long-standing sporting and political tensions across the Causeway. Prior to 1994, Singapore had twice withdrawn from the competition, whilst it had been expelled on another two occasions. These footballing disputes mirrored the political rivalries between the two nations. Since Singapore's expulsion from Malaysia in 1965, the two neighbours have had a tumultuous relationship marked by frequent squabbles rooted in issues of economics, personality and race.

This article analyses the political relationship between the two countries through the prism of football. It shows how the game has acted as a mirror of these wider tensions, and, on occasion, has itself been a source of political disputes. Among the key findings of this paper are that footballing tensions predated the ill-fated merger between the two nations (and perhaps can be seen as having foreshadowed the almost inevitable break-up of the union). More fundamentally, the paper argues that the enduring sporting links reflect the fact that, despite the mutual antipathy, the two states are locked together in an inescapable inter-dependence.

Cross-Causeway football

Organised football arrived in Singapore in the late 1880s, and the Singapore Amateur Football Association (SAFA) was established in 1892. Although initially the preserve of European settlers, the sport quickly gained a following within the Malay and Chinese communities. Cross-Causeway competition began in 1894 when an all-European team from the Singapore Cricket Club travelled north to Johor to meet an all-Malay Johor Football Club XI.[2] Sporting rivalries took on an organized form after 1921, when the visiting warship HMS Malaya donated two cups (one for association football and the other for rugby) for competition between the states and colonies of the region. Singapore dominated this competition in the years up until the outbreak of the Second World War, reaching every final and winning the cup on 13 occasions.[3]

The first signs of rancour in the relationship arose in 1950, when a dispute over both the control of the sport and finances led SAFA to break from the Football Association of Malaya (FAM) and seek direct affiliation with FIFA as an independent governing body.[4] Singapore had been a member of FAM since that body was first formed in 1926, and was the driving force in this association during its early years. It provided FAM's first secretary and four of its first six presidents. From 1940 onwards, however, the bulk of administrators were based in peninsular Malaya[5] and there was a feeling that the Kuala Lumpur-based FAM did little to promote the sport in Singapore and saw Singapore as little more than a cash cow.[6]

Despite withdrawing from FAM, FASA believed that it would still be entitled to enter the Malaya Cup, arguing that the rules of the competition specifically guaranteed Singapore's involvement.[7] FAM, for its part, rejected this argument and took the line that Singapore's continuing participation in the Cup was conditional on affiliation. The debate rumbled on throughout 1950 and into 1951, leading the President of SAFA, W. McGregor Watt, to argue that 'to exclude Singapore from the Malaya Cup competition is analogous to Hamlet being played without the Prince'.[8]

Watt's words, this article will argue, reflect the reality of Singapore–Malaysian football relations, not just in 1951, but in their entirety. Both parties gained significant benefits from the relationship (however much either party was uncomfortable with this reality), and there is a strong element of mutual dependence. Participation in the Malaya Cup provided Singapore with access to regular high-level competition which drew fans and gave vibrancy to its domestic football. On the other hand, Singapore brought much needed financial rewards to Malayan football.

Eventually, a compromise was reached whereby SAFA agreed to affiliate with FAM, although with conditions attached. SAFA stated that 'we will abide by all of the bye-laws of FAM for the running of the Malaya Cup competition but we do not consider ourselves bound by any other rule, regulation or bye-law of FAM', and it maintained its affiliation to FIFA.[9] Although this proved a temporary solution to the problem, it failed to address the underlying issues and effectively sowed the seeds for later conflict.

It is important to note that this debate about the place of Singapore within Malayan sport mirrored the ongoing political negotiations about the post-independence future for the two colonies, and particularly, the place of Singapore within any wider Malayan Union. The key stumbling block was the racial composition of the two territories; Malays comprised the largest ethnic group in Malaya, whereas Singapore had a substantial Chinese majority. If the two territories were combined, however, it would have resulted in an overall Chinese majority. This was unacceptable to Malay political leaders, who thus blocked any notion of the two territories uniting. This was era of the Emergency (the communist uprising in Malaya), and there were also major race-riots in both colonies. Thus, when the Federation of Malaya became independent in 1957, Singapore remained outside it.[10]

Alongside these wider political and social tensions, the old debates about the relationship between the two football associations were still unresolved. These were revived in March 1957 when FAM demanded that Singapore accept affiliation 'like any other state or settlement', which was specified to mean abiding by all bye-laws of FAM, or else they would be excluded from both the Federation and the Malaya Cup.[11] The catalyst for this ultimatum was another dispute over finances.

Beyond the financial rivalries between Singapore and Kuala Lumpur, it is clear that personal acrimony between Singaporean and Malayan officials exacerbated, or perhaps even caused, the crisis. An editorial in the *Straits Times* claimed that there was 'no doubt that a clash of personalities is the root of the present evil', whilst the President of FAM accused Singapore's officials of acting in a 'high-handed' manner, which had 'irritated and annoyed FAM'.[12] What is particularly interesting here is how this discourse, specifically allegations of Singaporean 'arrogance' in dealing with their Malayan counterparts, reflects what would become one of the enduring traits of Singapore–Malaysian relations (both in politics and in football[13]).

However, there were also signs that the shadow of the wider political situation was never far away. A FAM spokesman noted that 'a break must come eventually as the two territories would soon attain independence and could not carry on as one [sporting] unit much longer', whilst the *Straits Times* noted that 'the real point, perhaps, is that with the political changes impending this split was inevitable'.[14]

At this point, it needs to be noted that there is a danger in automatically investing sporting disputes with a deeper political meaning, especially given the often abrasive personalities of some sports administrators. In the case of South-East Asia, however, sports administration was often intertwined within the wider political process. Nowhere was this better encapsulated than through Tunku Abdul Rahman, who was President of FAM from 1951 until 1974, and was latterly, President of the Asian Football Confederation. Rahman was also the Father of Malayan Independence, having led the United Malays National Organization since 1951 and become the first Prime Minister of the newly independent state (remaining in the position until 1970).[15]

Rahman was by no means merely a figurehead sporting administrator. Despite his heavy political commitments, he took a hands-on role within FAM. This was particularly evident during the debate over Singapore's involvement in the Malaya

Cup in 1957. Rahman chaired the key meetings and even offered to travel to Singapore to seek a resolution to the crisis.[16] Rahman would not prove to be an exception to the linkages between sport and the state in Malaysia, and subsequent leaders of FAM had strong ties with the political system. As well as the involvement of Federal politicians, Douglas also notes the extensive involvement of members of various Malay royal families in sports administration. The Sultans of Malaysia's component states were frequently active within their respective State football associations and a number of them would take a central stage in later disputes involving Singapore.[17]

Such political linkages could also be found in Singapore. Soh Ghee Soon, president of SAFA from 1957 to 1963, was elected as an MP for the Liberal Socialist Party (a small opposition party within Singapore's Legislative Assembly) in June 1957.[18] As in Malaysia, the links between sport, particularly football, and political actors would remain constant from this point onwards. When the People's Action Party (PAP) took power in 1963, they asserted control over SAFA, and have continued to take a key role in appointing its leadership. Oon notes that FAS operated under 'direct government supervision', and nothing that the association did after 1963 can therefore be seen to have occurred without at least the tacit approval of the Singapore government.[19]

Returning to the events of 1957, the debate rumbled on, but eventually an extraordinary meeting of FAM voted by 10 votes to three that Singapore would be excluded from the Malaya Cup unless it accepted full affiliation. There was not uniformity in the opposition, with three states, including Selangor (ironically Singapore's greatest on-field rival in the Malaya Cup), opposing the exclusion. Selangor's representative returned to a familiar metaphor in arguing that 'Without Singapore, the Malaya Cup will be like Hamlet without the Prince of Denmark'.[20]

However, unlike in 1950, there was to be no reprieve, and in 1958 Singapore was absent from the Cup for the first time in the competition's history. The exclusion proved to be short-lived, however, and the following year FAM voted to allow Singapore to reenter the Malaya Cup on an invitational basis. There appears to have been concessions from both sides, with the reconciliation started by a letter from SAFA asking for the ban to be overturned. This was taken as a gesture of conciliation and was accompanied by Singapore's withdrawal of their previous financial demands, although they did not agree to affiliation to FAM. Rahman took the leading role in persuading FAM to accept Singapore back into the Cup. However, FAM very publically stressed that Singapore's participation would be reviewed on a yearly basis suggesting that there was still an undercurrent of tensions.[21]

The footballing relationship was overtaken by wider political events, which saw Singapore and Malaya merge into the new nation of Malaysia in 1963. This was mirrored in football, with the FAS affiliating to the renamed Football Association of Malaysia as a state association. There is no space here to fully analyse the period of Singapore's political incorporation into Malaysia and the dissolution of the relationship. Ultimately, the merger was undermined by mutual suspicions and by differing notions of what the new state would actually entail. Underpinning this conflict were the enduring challenges of race, power and political representation, which had been apparent since the 1940s. Fundamentally, Singaporean and Malay visions of the new Malaysia were different, and in fact, mutually incompatible.[22]

The dissolution of the political union between Malaysia and Singapore did not have any immediate impact on the football pitch. The annual Merdeka tournament opened just five days after the separation and the Malaysian XI continued to field Singaporean players in its starting line-up. Despite the political separation, the football authorities considered that 'for the time being, Singapore is an affiliate of the Football Association of Malaysia, and as the Merdeka tournament is a friendly affair, there is no need to make any changes at this stage'.[23] The newly-renamed FAS sought reaffiliation with FIFA, which was provisionally granted in September 1965.[24]

Despite its political exit from Malaysia and its affiliation with FIFA as an independent national federation, there was no immediate discussion about Singapore's continuing involvement in the Malaysia Cup. The sporting authorities of both countries were happy to allow the status quo to continue – which, of course, had been in existence since before the short-lived political union. Singapore continued to compete in football's Malaysia Cup in 1966 and the same pattern was replicated in most other sports (including cricket, badminton, hockey and tennis). The only voice of dissent appears to have been the Selangor Rugby Union, which unsuccessfully called for Singapore's exclusion from rugby union's Malaya Cup in 1966. For the most part, however, the political split did not alter the existing sporting environment.[25]

This calm was shattered on 16 May 1968, when the Straits Times ran a short Stop Press item under the headline 'S'pore Out' which noted that 'The F. A. of Singapore announced last night that they have decided to withdraw from the Malaysia Cup and FAM Cup competition'.[26] Given the magnitude of this decision, it would be expected that there would be significant discussion of the decision in the media, but this was not forthcoming.[27] This reflects one of the problems of writing history in Singapore. The PAP government have exercised strict control over Singapore's domestic media resulting in a lack of press freedom. Newspapers usually take a pro-government line, and often do not delve too deeply into controversial matters. Additionally, there is a lack of plurality in the press, which again precludes the airing of dissenting viewpoints.[28] Nor is there free and open access to government archives,[29] and none of the key actors in this decision have written on their own roles in these events.[30]

What is clear is that the decision to withdraw was taken at a political level. As mentioned earlier, FAS had been under the control of the PAP since 1963, and was acting under the government's direction. Inche Othman Wok, the Minister for Social Affairs, had foreshadowed the decision in January of 1968, when he criticised Singapore's continuing participation in Malaysian domestic sporting competitions, arguing that it lowered the interest of players on the national team and was responsible for lowering the standard of football in Singapore.[31] After the withdrawal, Wok argued that 'FAM and Malaysia Cup championships are domestic competitions for the states of Malaysia and not an international competition between sovereign states'. He described the tournament as 'irrelevant to Singapore's new situation' and 'a wasteful, enervating and ridiculous exercise in which achievements are meaningless and defeats humiliating and bad for morale'.[32] Wok's decision to withdraw Singapore from the Malaysia Cup did not receive universal agreement within Singapore. Indeed, there were even some within the PAP government who opposed the move. The most prominent of these was the MP Lenny Rodrigo, who had been appointed to lead FAS at the time of the withdrawal. Rodrigo urged Wok to reconsider, but to no avail.[33]

Singapore's withdrawal from the Malaysia Cup in 1968 was, however, fundamentally different from the other cases considered within this article. There was no real dispute between either of the parties, and little rancour. Even Wok did not want a complete break with Malaysian football, merely a readjustment of the relationship. The letter from FAS to FAM announcing their withdrawal from the Malaysia Cup called for the establishment of new tournaments between the two nations, but between their national men's and under-23 teams rather than Singapore continuing to compete against Malaysian state teams.[34] FAM and Rahman urged Singapore to reconsider, but ultimately accepted the decision in a diplomatic manner.[35]

Singapore's attempt to go it alone did not last long, and in December 1969, FAS asked FAM to return to the Malaysia Cup. Essentially, Singaporean football could not afford to go it alone, and FAS faced a significant financial shortfall. It was estimated that withdrawing from the Cup cost it $40,000 in lost revenue. The root cause of this was the inability to develop the local inter-club league to rival the popularity of the Malaysia Cup.[36]

Despite Singapore having abruptly exited the Malaysia Cup mid-season in 1968, they were readily welcomed back into the competition by FAM. Perhaps the most obvious reason for this was economics as Singapore's involvement in the Cup had, since at least the 1950s, brought significant financial returns to FAM and the Malaysian states. Given that most State football associations were suffering from financial problems (Perak lost $8400 in 1968 and Malacca $7000[37]), the return of Singapore provided hopes of arresting this decline.

Relations deteriorate

Singapore was now back in Malaysian football, but the sporting relationship remained strained by tensions. Although Singapore qualified for the finals series in its return season, events surrounding the second leg of the semi-final against Kelantan in Kota Bahru showed that Singapore's place in Malaysian football was far from cosy. The match ended in an embarrassing 8–0 loss for Singapore, but it was the repercussions of this match that were most telling. Following the match, Singapore's Minister of Culture prohibited the screening of a replay of this match on national television, citing the 'humiliating actions against the Singapore players'.[38]

If banning the screening of the match seemed an excessive reaction, it paled in comparison with FAS' response. In September of 1970, it wrote to FAM asking that they are not be required to play any future matches in Malaysia's East Coast states. For a team that had just returned to Malaysian football after a self-imposed exile, dictating where they would or would not play seemed a remarkably bold request. Perhaps even more surprisingly, however, FAM appeared to give serious consideration to this request. Given the seriousness of the move, it is surprising that it was given relatively little coverage in the press. In particular, the reasons for Singapore making the request were never elaborated upon, apart from a comment that 'Singapore players were not happy with the crowd's behaviour [in Kota Bharu]'.[39]

The lack of any further coverage of such a significant development gives rise to an impression that something was being deliberately obscured and not talked about. This would be in tune with many of the other wider political tensions between Singapore and Malaysia, where the issue of race has always been the elephant in the room. As Lee has argued 'race is very important and many will argue, the determining factor in Malaysia-Singapore relations. Very few aspects of such relations can be fully understood without at least considering race as an underlying factor'.[40]

There is certainly reason to suspect that race was a factor in Singapore's request to avoid playing on the East Coast. Kelantan, along with neighbouring Terengganu, was the most-ethnically Malay of all the Malaysian states.[41] It is therefore not surprising that it was these two states that had been most resistant to Singapore's political incorporation into Malaysia, specifically because of fears that Singapore's Chinese population would undermine the political dominance of Malays.[42] Given such a landscape, there are strong indications of underlying racial tensions.

However, there is a danger in assuming that race lay behind all of the sporting tensions between the two states. A wider analysis of sporting tensions between the two nations reveals that individuals and actors involved in key decisions did not always act in ways that reflected their ethnic heritage. For example, when Singapore was excluded from the Malaya Cup in 1957, the Malayan Chinese FA was one of the parties to vote in favour of Singapore's expulsion, whereas the Malayan Malay FA had abstained on the issue.[43] Moreover, the key architect of Singapore's withdrawal from Malaysian football in 1968 had been the ethnically Malay Inche Othman Wok.[44]

Events six years later would again show that Singapore's place in Malaysian football was not universally favoured. Again, it was to be a match on the East Coast that sparked the controversy.[45] The crisis developed out of the semi-finals of the Malaysia Cup, which had pitted Singapore against Pahang. Singapore won the first leg 6–0 at home, and Pahang looked to have little change of overturning the result in the return fixture. The Sultan of Pahang thought otherwise and took over as coach for the match.[46] This match finished in a nil-all draw, but was more notable for the tactics employed by the home side, which were diplomatically described as 'robust' in one report. Another report was more direct, claiming that 'the Pahang team gave a convincing impersonation of a lynch mob', and there were claims that Singaporean players were kicked in the chest, stamped upon and spat at by their opponents. The Singaporean team required a police escort to leave the stadium, and it is little surprise that the atmosphere at the after-match was described as 'strained'.[47]

Despite the acrimony of the match, it initially appeared that there would be no long-term consequences. It was only four months later that the Pahang made the shock demand that Singapore be permanently expelled from the Malaysia Cup. Pahang's anger stemmed from an unexpected source – a British football magazine had carried a photo of the violence during the match. This fact was reported back to the Pahang FA by a Malaysian living in the UK leading it to declare that 'we feel that it has tarnished the good image of our state and also of our leader the Sultan'. Pahang's response was to call for Singapore to be excluded from Malaysian Cup.[48]

However, Pahang's proposal was not supported by FAM or any of the other states (some of whom threatened to withdraw from the competition themselves if Singapore were expelled). Despite Pahang's exhortation that its fellow states not allow money to come before national pride, finances played a vital role in securing Singapore's position. Almost half of the gate receipts that FAM received from Malaysia Cup matches were generated from matches involving Singapore, and a trip to Singapore was lucrative for Malaysian state teams.[49] Pahang reacted to

FAM's refusal to exclude Singapore by withdrawing from the Malaysia Cup in 1977, returning in 1978.[50]

Although Singapore survived this affair, it wasn't so lucky five years later, when it found itself excluded from the Malaysia Cup for three years. The circumstances that led to this expulsion were remarkably similar to those of 1976. Again, they stemmed from the fall-out surrounding a Malaysia Cup semi-final, and again, there were claims from the Malaysian side that the local sultan had been insulted. This time, however, the aggrieved state was Johor, and this time FAM backed the call to exclude Singapore.

What is perhaps most interesting about the whole dispute is that, certainly to the eyes of an outside observer, it appears to be caused by incredibly petty issues (again mirroring many of the wider political disputes between the two neighbours[51]). Johor's chief complains were; Johor officials were not treated well during the first match in Singapore; Singaporean officials had disrespected the Sultan of Johor by taking his seats in the stadium prior to the return encounter; the Singapore team had refused to attend the post-match dinner; there was unfair reporting of Johor's hospitality in the Singapore press[52]; and Singapore had displayed arrogance in announcing ticket sale details for the final before the semi-final against Johor had been played.[53]

Quite how these seemingly minor issues could escalate into a three-year sporting exile for the Singapore team says a lot about the depths to which Singapore–Malaysia relations had sunk by this period. What is particularly noteworthy about the entire incident, however, is the degree to which the discourse surrounding the dispute mirrored the wider political tensions between the two nations. Particularly, a key element of Johor's complaint was that Singapore's officials had treated Johor in an arrogant fashion.[54] Such claims of Singaporean arrogance became a cornerstone of many of the political disputes between the two countries. Writing as early as 1978, Bedlington argued that Singapore was overly 'abrasive' in its relationship with Malaysia claiming that 'for several years Singapore adopted a posture of what can only be termed arrogance towards her neighbours, caring little for their national susceptibilities',[55] and these views have been shared by several other writers.[56]

While Malaysia commonly blamed Singaporean arrogance for problems in the bilateral political relationship, Singapore often suggested that Malaysia's own attitudes were at the heart of the problems. Jealously and resentment at Singapore's post-separation success were perceived to lie behind many of Malaysia's grievances. For instance, Mauzy and Milne note that 'Malaysia exhibits considerable resentment at Singapore's economic accomplishments and resentment at being adversely compared to Singapore', while Leifer suggests that it had 'never been forgiven [by Malaysian politicians] for its trumpeted internationally-renowned success'.[57] Such claims seem to be reflected in many of the footballing controversies. It is notable that Johor's calls for Singapore's expulsion in 1981 and those from Pahang in 1976 came in the context of defeats at the hands of Singapore in semi-finals. It is hard not to detect some element of sour grapes in the responses of these Malaysian states. Additionally, Singapore's acrimonious exit from the Malaysia Cup in 1994 came in the season that it had secured a League and Cup double (winning the Malaysia Cup for the first time since 1980) adding further fuel to this suggestion.

Why Singapore was excluded in 1982 rather than 1976 is not entirely clear, and was not apparently linked to any obvious aggravating factors in the bilateral political relationship.[58] Perhaps it may have been more a reflection of Malaysian domestic issues, and the power of its component states. While Pahang was a relatively peripheral state, both geographically and politically, Johor is the second most populous state in the Federation.

Singapore remained excluded from the Malaysia Cup until 1985. Their return did not remain peaceful for long, and in 1986, their position was again challenged. While previous disputes had mirrored wider tensions between the two states, this incident marked the direct extension of these political tensions into sport. The catalyst for this controversy was a state visit to Singapore in November 1986 by Israeli President Chaim Herzog. Singapore had long maintained close ties with Israel, but the visit was controversial with its Muslim neighbours. However, while Indonesia and Brunei were satisfied to respond to the visit with largely symbolic diplomatic protests, the reaction from Malaysia was explosive. Exacerbated by Prime Minister Mahathir's own championing of anti-Zionism as a political vote-winner, Malaysia unleashed a massive political firestorm. This was coupled by widespread, and in some cases, violent public protests across the country, which led Leifer to conclude that the issue had brought Singapore's 'relations with Malaysia to their lowest ebb since constitutional separation in August 1965'.[59]

Malaysia responded to the Herzog visit with a variety of measures including bans on Singapore sports teams competing in Malaysia. Singapore was asked by FAM to pull out of Charity Shield match in Kuala Lumpur in late November and a provisional ban on all Singaporean participation in Malaysian football was imposed the following January. Singapore was thus excluded from the Sultan's Gold Cup (a competition for ethnically Malay players) and the Presidents Cup (Under-21).[60] However, the Malaysia Cup was not scheduled to begin until the following June, which gave time for tensions to diminish. In mid-March, Singapore's ban was lifted with FAM declaring that 'we have done our part in getting the message across'.[61]

Singapore may have ultimately retained its place in the Malaysia Cup, but it was becoming clear that the constant turmoil surrounding its presence was taking its toll on spectator interest. Despite Singapore riding high in the League, only 8200 fans turned out for a home clash against Armed Forces in 1987.[62] The wider political relationship between the two countries was also becoming increasingly toxic. The Herzog crisis proved to be a portent for a deterioration of relations, and the 1990s brought a new nadir to the relationship. Alongside the ongoing hostility over water supply, the countries clashed over matters ranging from a territorial dispute over the island of Pedra Branca through to Malaysian ownership of railway land in Singapore.[63]

Up until this point, footballing relations between the two countries had merely mirrored wider political tensions. In 1994, however, issues arising from the Malaysia Cup themselves became a source of cross-Causeway tension. As the Singapore team was on its way to collecting a league and cup double in the competition, a serious match-fixing scandal was uncovered. Although match-fixing proved to be endemic across the entire competition, Malaysian administrators and politicians put the blame on Singapore for not doing enough to investigate football gambling in the island state. They threatened to exclude Singapore from the league if it could not demonstrate its commitment to tacking the problem. Additionally, FAM demanded that Singapore pay it an additional levy of 15% of all gate takings (on top of an existing levy of 20%).[64]

Singaporean football administrators had long been resentful of the economic demands that FAM placed upon them for the right to compete as 'guests' in the league. This article has already shown that the tensions of the 1950s had a strong financial dimension, and these resurfaced in the early 1980s when FAM sought to increase the levy that Singapore paid them. In 1985, and again in 1991, there were suggestions that Singapore might not be able to afford to remain in the Malaysia Cup because of these demands. Fuelling this anger was the belief that Singapore was already more than paying its own way in the competition, given the revenues that it generated. In 1990, for instance, gate receipts from matches in Singapore were over three times greater than those from the nearest Malaysian state team, and provided almost 40% of all revenue.[65]

The demand for the increased levy was essentially a device to force Singapore to withdraw from the League (which was the stated desire of a number of the State FAs) and it proved successful in this aim. In February 1996, amid an atmosphere of mutual enmity, FAS announced its withdrawal from the Malaysia Cup.[66] As with previous Singaporean withdrawals from Malaysian football, there were some who welcomed the opportunity to develop Singapore's own national league. Mindful of the problems that had befallen previous efforts to develop a viable national league, FAS invested time and money developing a new competition. The new league, billed as the S-League, kicked off in 1996 and featured eight fully professional clubs backed by a slick marketing and promotions campaign.[67]

Singapore's return to the Malaysian League

Given the enmity of cross-Causeway relations in the mid-1990s, and the determination of Singaporean officials to create their own footballing framework, it seemed certain that the split of 1995 would prove terminal. That Singapore returned to the Malaysian League in 2012, then, was somewhat of a surprise. That this was able to happen was due to both a changed political situation, but more importantly, due to issues surrounding both countries domestic football leagues.

Singapore's return was made possible by a marked improvement in the cross-Causeway bilateral relationship that had developed since the mid-2000s. Partially this was due to new leadership in both countries. Not only did this bring fresh perspectives to the relationship, but it overcame the clashes of personalities that had exacerbated previous bilateral conflicts.[68] Mahathir was succeeder by Abdullah Ahmad Badawi in 2003 (who was in turn replaced by Najib Abdul Razak in 2009), whilst Lee Hsien Loong took over as Singaporean Prime Minister in 2004. Under their leadership, there was a 'normalization' of ties between the two countries. Some of the previous disputes were resolved, and new challenges were managed in a much more cordial fashion.[69]

Whilst the improved political landscape provided the opportunity for a footballing rapprochement, it was ultimately issues within the sport itself that dictated the final outcome. The football associations of the two countries had begun discussions about a possible Singaporean return to the Malaysian League as early as 2005, but despite cordial relations, this did not eventuate.[70] It was only the calamitous state of both leagues in the early 2010s that put the item back on the agenda. By then, football was facing serious problems in both countries, and it was hoped that Singapore's return to the Malaysia Cup might prove a panacea to at least some of these problems.

Singapore's desire to create its own league structure had proved fruitless. Although the S-League drew reasonable crowds in its first season, attracting an average of 3486 spectators per match, it was unable to sustain these figures in subsequent seasons. Newly formed clubs were unable to engage with their local communities, and by 1998, the league average was down to 2239. Many of the component clubs also struggled with 2003 seeing the withdrawal of two clubs and the merger of two others.[71] The league then entered an even more serious decline. Despite match tickets costing a maximum of only S$6 (approximately US$4.90) the average attendance had dropped to just 944 by 2011.[72] Given a national population of over five million, these figures are particularly damning and marked little improvement upon the 700-plus crowds that the semi-professional National Football League had achieved in 1991.[73]

Things were no rosier in north of the Causeway. Despite efforts to revitalize the league, including allowing club sides to compete alongside the State associations, interest in domestic football was waning. On the opening day of the Malaysian Super League's 2010 season, the country's largest English-language newspaper devoted only half a page of coverage to the league (out of a total of 11 pages of sports coverage). The fact that the subtitle of that sparse coverage was 'New Malaysian League tipped to be lacking in fan appeal again' further reflected the sport's problems.[74]

As in Singapore, attendances at matches were poor. During the 2009 season, the average attendance across the Super League was just 3377 spectators per match, a 20% drop from the previous season (and substantially lower than the average of 8271 that the league had drawn between 1989 and 1991[75]). The league average also hid extreme disparities between clubs. Whilst some state representative teams like Kedah, Kelantan, and Selangor continued to draw five-figure crowds, other teams were struggling. Kuala Muda Naza FC were forced to withdraw from the league that season after drawing fewer than 200 fans per home match, and there were reports that one match drew fewer paying spectators than there were players.[76]

It is not the intention of this article to suggest the decline in interest in the two local leagues was solely due to Singapore's absence from Malaysian football. Both competitions have numerous weaknesses, including poor management at clubs and ongoing concerns about match-fixing.[77] What can be said, however, is that Singapore's absence from the Malaysian league weakened public interest in local football in both countries at the very time it was facing its most serious external challenges.

The most significant of those challenges lay in the form of growing public interest in overseas football, particularly the EPL. The twin drivers of satellite television and the increasing economic prosperity of the two countries made them a particular target for profit-seeking EPL clubs at the very time that Singapore withdrew from the Malaysian league. Manchester United and Liverpool were particular favourites and have been regular visitors to the region, as have other EPL clubs. Manchester United's match against a Malaysian XI at Kuala Lumpur in 2009 drew 85,000 spectators (more the entire attendance [61,415] across all 182 matches of Malaysia's second-tier Premier League that same season[78]). South-East Asia has developed into an important commercial market for EPL clubs with Manchester United operating branches of their club Megastore in Kuala Lumpur and on Singapore's famous shopping stretch of Orchard Road in 1999. This can also be seen in the decision of many major local companies (such as Malaysia's Air Asia and Singapore's Tiger Beer) to focus their sports sponsorship on EPL clubs rather than their own domestic leagues.[79]

English football dominates local media coverage of sport.[80] The same 9 January 2010 edition of the *Star* that gave only half a page of coverage of the start of Malaysia's own domestic league devoted four pages (including its back page) to the EPL, and another page to the Spanish and Italian leagues, and it has been a similar process in Singapore.[81] Local clubs struggle to compete against this global competition, losing spectators and sponsors to their global rivals. In its first year of its existence, the S-League was forced to reschedule matches from their regular evening kick-off time to early afternoon in order to avoid a clash with a Premier League match that was being broadcast live on local television, and it continues to be viewed as a second-rate competition by the majority of local football fans.[82] It was this global challenge and the stagnant state of both local domestic leagues, that brought Singapore back into the Malaysian League.

Conclusions

Despite what many authors claim, this study refutes the suggestion that the enduring tensions between Singapore and Malaysia are solely a product of the bitterness caused by Singapore's expulsion from Malaysia in 1965. This argument has been made most recently [2010] by Saravanamuttu, who claims that 'Singapore's "Malaysia period", 1963–65, was clearly the source of what observers have termed the historical baggage that plagues relations up till today',[83] and this view has been echoed by a number of other authors.[84]

This analysis of footballing relations highlights, that this '1965 factor' is overstated. Serious tensions had existed between Singapore and Malaysian sports administrators since at least the end of the Second World War, mirroring exactly the contemporaneous debate about the place of Singapore within a post-independence Malaya. Singapore's exclusion from the Malaya Cup in 1958, just as the decision not to include Singapore in the 1957 Federation, were not due to any residual ill-feeling, but because of deep and fundamental incompatibilities between the two parties. Football also shows that the merger itself did not suddenly bring about a rise in tensions. Indeed, not only did it take two years for Singapore to exit the Malaysia Cup after the dissolution of the merger, but this would prove to be by far the least acrimonious of any of the footballing splits since 1950. Given this evidence, there is a need to revisit any claims that the events of 1965 alone are responsible for the ensuing relationship.

The thesis being argued in this paper is supported by a number of authors working in the field. These have highlighted that Singapore's incorporation into Malaysia in 1963 was not so much the problem in itself, but rather an attempt (albeit ultimately unsuccessful) to address the underlying incompatibility between a Chinese-dominated Singapore and a Malay-majority Malaya. Tai, in what is probably the most in-depth study of the politics of the merger, argues that 'the seeds of dissention had indeed been sown earlier [prior to 1963] when the deal was being worked out'.[85] Similarly, Baker, in what is perhaps the most succinct analysis of the merger, notes that it was ultimately the 'triumph of hope over reality'.[86]

Secondly, and perhaps most significantly, analysing Singapore–Malaysia relations through the prism of football highlights a fundamental truth about this relationship. W. McGregor Watt's argument in 1951 that 'to exclude Singapore from the Malaya Cup competition is analogous to Hamlet being played without the Prince' has been shown to be prescient. The 61 years that have passed since he made that statement have shown that football in one country is weaker without a partnership with the other. The recent entry of the LionsXII to the Malaysia Super League is just the latest confirmation of this essential truth. Singapore's efforts to develop its own domestic league have repeated flattered to deceive, whilst this article has shown how badly Malaysian football needs Singapore.

However, this article argues that Watt's reasoning has a resonance far beyond football. What this case study helps to show is that, despite all of the mutual antagonism and loathing, the two nations are locked into a state of mutual interdependence. Whilst this is true of football, it is equally relevant in the economic, social and political spheres. Writing just four years after demerger, Gullick commented on the difficulties of writing a separate history of Malaysia without reference to Singapore:

> How does one deal with a territory which until 1945 was as much a part of Malaya as any other; was then set on a path of separate evolution for almost 20 years; then brought into the new Malaysia of 1963 only to be expelled for unruly behaviour in 1965. Even on the sidelines, Singapore continues to cast a shadow and it cannot be ignored.[87]

Nothing that has happened since Gullick wrote those words has challenged their continued relevance.

As Shiraishi has concluded in his recent [2009] collection on the topic of Singapore-Malaysia relations, 'despite the fraught nature of Malaysian–Singapore relations … both countries have been economically dependent on each other' and 'cooperation rather than rivalry is becoming more important'.[88] He might just as accurately have concluded that 'without Singapore, [Malaysia] will be like Hamlet without the Prince of Denmark [and vice versa]'.

Notes

1. See, for example, *New Paper on Sunday*, December 11, 2011, 52–53 and *Straits Times*, December 16, 2011, D1–D2.
2. Horton, 'Complex Creolization', 94–96; Netto, 'Football: Origins and the Domestic Game', 50; *Singapore Free Press*, November 19, 1894, 3 and *Straits Times*, September 4, 1899, 2.
3. Aplin and Quek, 'Celestials in Touch', 82–85.
4. *Singapore Free Press*, October 7, 1950, 6.
5. Siebel, 'Soccer', 119–121.
6. *Singapore Free Press*, October 9, 1950, 7.
7. *Straits Times*, October 12, 1950, 12.
8. *Singapore Free Press*, October 30, 1950, 7 and April 5, 1951, 7.
9. *Straits Times*, February 17, 1951, 2 and *Singapore Free Press*, May 8, 1951, 7.
10. Lau, *A Moment of Anguish*, 1–10.
11. *Straits Times*, March 19, 1957, 14.
12. *Straits Times*, Match 28, 1957, 14 and July 8, 1957, 14.
13. See the discussion surrounding Singapore's expulsion from the Malaysia Cup in 1982 later in this article for an analysis of this point.
14. *Straits Times*, March 23, 1957, 13 and March 26, 1957, 14.
15. Siebel, 'Soccer', 121 and Sheppard, *Tunku*, 128–131.
16. *Straits Times*, October 12, 1957, 14.
17. Douglas, 'Sport in Malaysia', 172.
18. Drysdale, *Singapore: Struggle for Success*, 174.
19. Oon, 'Government Involvement in Sport in Singapore', 142–154.

20. *Straits Times*, July 8, 1957, 14.
21. *Straits Times*, February 16, 1958, 19; April 22, 1958, 14; April 25, 1958, 14 and April 27, 1958, 18.
22. Lau, *A Moment of Anguish*; Bakar, 'Seeds of Separation'; Tai, *Creating Greater Malaysia* and Lee, *The Singapore Story*.
23. *Straits Times*, August 10, 1967, 21.
24. *Straits Times*, September 28, 1965, 17.
25. *Straits Times*, May 5, 1966, 17.
26. *Straits Times*, May 16, 1968, 19.
27. There was some follow-up commentary, but none of this probed the decision in any depth. For example, *Straits Times*, May 17, 1968, 22.
28. George, 'History Spiked', 264–280 and Yen, 'The Mass Media', 288–311.
29. For the challenges historians face in gaining access to government records in the region, see Ang, 'Writing Diplomatic History', 171–181.
30. The key figure in the decision, Inche Othman Wok, did not comment on his role in the decision in his autobiography. Wok, *Never in My Wildest Dreams*.
31. *Straits Times*, January 23, 1968, 21.
32. Robert, *The Malaysia Cup*, 60 and *Straits Times*, June 5, 1968, 23.
33. *Straits Times*, June 5, 1968, 23 and Official Programme, Merlion Cup 1984, unpaged [National Archives of Singapore, NA 1172].
34. *Straits Times*, June 8, 1968, 23.
35. *Straits Times*, July 13, 1968, 23.
36. *Straits Times*, May 21, 1968, 20 and Official Programme, Merlion Cup 1984.
37. *Straits Times*, March 8, 1969, 16 and December 18, 1969, 21.
38. *Straits Times*, July 9, 1970, 18.
39. *Straits Times*, September 18, 1970, 29 and September 21, 1970, 23.
40. Lee, 'Malaysia-Singapore Relations', 219.
41. Saw, *The Population of Malaysia*, 72.
42. Cheah, *Malaysia: The Making of a Nation*, 92.
43. *Straits Times*, July 8, 1957, 14.
44. Lee, *The Singapore Story*, 641.
45. In the interim there was another match, again on the East Coast, that was marred by claims of violence against the Singapore team. That 1974 clash against Terengganu at Kuala Terengganu led to letters in the *Straits Times* calling for Singapore to withdraw from the Malaysia Cup. *Straits Times*, April 21, 1974, 21 and April 27, 1974, 26.
46. *Straits Times*, July 27, 1976, 1.
47. *Straits Times*, July 25, 1976, 28; July 26, 1976, 29; July 27, 1976, 1 and July 31, 1976, 27.
48. *Straits Times*, November 5, 1976, 35 and November 11, 1976, 23.
49. The FAM was entitled to over 17% of the takings at all matches, whilst visiting teams received 25%. *Straits Times*, October 29, 1976, 30; November 5, 1976, 35 and December 29, 1976, 29.
50. *Straits Times*, October 13, 1977, 29.
51. Jeshurun notes that 'outsiders in the region have never stopped asking themselves or their Malaysian and Singaporean friends how such seemingly petty issues always seen to lead to a contretemps between the two countries'. Jeshurun, *Malaysia: Fifty Years of Diplomacy*, 297.
52. This complaint did not refer to the Singaporean press as a whole, but to just one story in the newly-established *New Nation* tabloid. That article had accused the Johor FA of poor hospitality and 'shabby' and 'shocking' behaviour towards Singaporean officials at the match. *New Nation*, May 25, 1981, 21.
53. *Straits Times*, November 21, 1981, 39 and December 2, 1981, 35.
54. Johor's letter to the FAM concluded 'the Singapore team must be made to realise that they are a guest team and as such must have the characteristic of the same. They should not be arrogant, proud and boastful toward their neighbour i.e. the Johor team'. *Straits Times*, December 2, 1981, 35.
55. Bedlington, *Malaysia and Singapore*, 247–248.
56. Hass, 'Mass Society', 169; Leifer, *Singapore's Foreign Policy*, 24 and Rahin, *Singapore in the Malay World*, 182.

57. Mauzy and Milne, *Singapore Politics*, 177 and Leifer, 'Israel's President in Singapore', 344–345.
58. The years between 1976 and 1981 are generally regarded as one of the least acrimonious periods of relations between the two countries. Lee, 'Malaysia-Singapore Relations', 222–223.
59. Leifer, 'Israel's President in Singapore', 341–352.
60. *Straits Times*, December 5, 1986, 43; January 31, 1987, 1; February 1, 1987, 20 and February 4, 1987, 21.
61. *Straits Times*, March 15, 1987, 22.
62. *Straits Times*, September 4, 1987, 39.
63. Saravanamuutu, *Malaysia's Foreign Policy*, 288–292 and Sidhu, 'Malaysia-Singapore Relations Since 1998', 76–78.
64. *Straits Times*, January 12, 1995, 31 and January 27, 1995, 37.
65. Robert, *The Malaysia Cup*, 110; *Straits Times*, May 24, 1985, 47 and *Players!*, September/October 1991, 22.
66. *Straits Times*, January 17, 1995, 31; February 1, 1995, 32 and February 26, 1995, 2.
67. *Straits Times*, February 23, 1995, 31 and S-League, *The S-League Handbook: Season*, 1996.
68. Jeshurun, *Malaysia: Fifty Years of Diplomacy*, 297.
69. Sidhu, 'Malaysia–Singapore Relations', 75–92 and Saw and Kesavapany, *Singapore-Malaysia Relations*, 6–15.
70. Saw and Kesavapany. *Singapore-Malaysia Relations*, 53–54.
71. *Straits Times*, August 4, 1998, 33 and *Today*, November 19, 2001, 34.
72. Osman, 'Football Attendance'.
73. *Players!*, March/April 1991, 2.
74. The *Star's* main English-language rival, the *New Straits Times*, provided equally scant coverage, devoting less than one of its eleven pages to the League. Again, its headline ('Gloomy outlook for Super League') and story were focused on the League's problems. *Star*, January 9, 2010, S46–S55 and *New Straits Times*, January 9, 2010, 30–40.
75. Benson and Sim, 'The Demand', 137.
76. Star, 'Poor Turnout May Force'; Samuel, 'Poor Fan Turnout Forces' and Rowe, *Global Media Sport*, 99.
77. Little and Nauright, 'Globalization and Development in Sport', 198–203.
78. Star, 'Poor Turnout May Force'.
79. Little and Nauright, 'Globalization and Development in Sport', 198–203.
80. Little, 'Association Football, Southeast Asia', 193–194.
81. *Star*, January 9, 2010, S46–S55.
82. Little, 'Association Football, Southeast Asia', 193–194.
83. Saravanamuutu, *Malaysia's Foreign Policy*, 286.
84. Ganesan, *Realism and Interdependence*, 56 and Rahim, 'Singapore-Malaysia Relations', 39.
85. Tai, *Creating Greater Malaysia*, vii.
86. Baker, *Crossroads*, 323.
87. Gullick, *Malaysia*, cited in Lau, 'The National Past', 49.
88. Shiraishi, 'Introduction', 3.

References

Ang, Cheng Guan. 'Writing Diplomatic History: A Personal Journey'. In *The Makers and Keepers of Singapore History*, ed. L. Seng and L. Khium, 171–81. Singapore: Ethos Books, 2010.

Aplin, Nick and Quek Jin Jong. 'Celestials in Touch: Sport and the Chinese in Colonial Singapore'. In *Sport in Asian Society: Past and Present*, ed. J.A. Mangan and Fan Hong, 65–98. London: Frank Cass, 2002.

Bakar, Mohamad Abu. 'Seeds of Separation'. In *Across the Causeway: A Multi-Dimensional Study of Singapore-Malaysia Relations*, ed. Takashi Shiraishi, 52–79. Singapore: Institute of Southeast Asian Studies, 2009.

Baker, Jim. *Crossroads: A Popular History of Malaysia and Singapore*. Singapore: Times Books, 1999.

Bedlington, Stanley. *Malaysia and Singapore: The Building of New States*. Ithaca, NY: Cornell University Press, 1970.
Cheah, Boon Kheng. *Malaysia: The Making of a Nation*. Singapore: Institute of Southeast Asian Studies, 2002.
Douglas, Stephen. 'Sport in Malaysia'. In *Sport in Africa and Asia: A Comparative Handbook*, ed. Eric Wagner, 165–82. Westport, CT: Greenwood Press, 1989.
Drysdale, John. *Singapore: Struggle for Success*. Singapore: Times Books, 1996.
Duke, Vic, and Liz Crolley. *Football, Nationality and the State*. Harlow: Longman, 1996.
Ganesan, N. *Realism and Interdependence in Singapore's Foreign Policy*. London: Routledge, 2005.
George, Cherian. 'History Spiked: Hegemony and the Denial of Media Diversity'. In *Paths Not Taken: Political Pluralism in Post-War Singapore*, ed. Michael Barr and Carl Trocki, 264–280. Singapore: NUS Press, 2008.
Hass, Michael. 'Mass Society'. In *The Singapore Puzzle*, ed. Michael Hess, 151–94. Westport, CT: Prager, 1999.
Horton, Peter. 'Complex Creolization: The Evolution of Modern Sport in Singapore'. In *Europe, Sport, World: Shaping Global Societies*, ed. J. Mangan, 77–104. Frank Cass, London, 2001.
Jeshurun, Chandran. *Malaysia: Fifty Years of Diplomacy 1957–2007*. Kuala Lumpur: The Other Press, 2007.
Lau, Albert. 'The National Past and the Writing of the History of Singapore'. In *Imagining Singapore*, ed. Ban Kah Choon, Anne Pakir and Tong Chee Kiong. Singapore: Times Academic Press, 1992.
Lau, Albert. *A Moment of Anguish: Singapore in Malaysia and the Politics of Disengagement*. Singapore: Times Academic Press, 2001.
Lee, Poh Peng. 'Malaysia-Singapore Relations: A Malaysian Perspective'. In *Malaysia and Singapore: Problems and Perspectives*, ed. Azizah Kassim and Lau Teik Soon. Singapore: Singapore Institute of International Affairs, 1992.
Lee, Kuan Yew. *The Singapore Story: Memoirs of Lee Kuan Yew*. Singapore: Prentice Hall, 1998.
Leifer, Michael. 'Israel's President in Singapore: Political Catalysis and Transnational Politics'. *The Pacific Review* 1, no. 4 (1988): 341–52.
Leifer, Michael. *Singapore's Foreign Policy: Coping with Vulnerability*. London: Routledge, 2000.
Little, Charles. 'South East Asia'. In *Routledge Companion to Sports History*, ed. S. W. Pope and John Nauright. Oxford: Routledge, 2009.
Little, Charles. 'Association Football, Southeast Asia'. In *Sports Around the World*, ed. John Nauright and Charles Parrish, 193–94. Santa Monica: ABC-Clio, 2012.
Little, Charles, and John Nauright. 'Globalization and Development in Sport: Perspectives from South East Asia'. In *Development in Asia: Interdisciplinary, Post-neoliberal and Transnational Perspectives*, ed. Derrick Nault. Boca Raton: Brown Walker Press, 2009.
Mauzy, Diane, and R.S. Milne. *Singapore Politics Under the People's Action Party*. London: Routledge, 2002.
Netto, Terence. 'Football: Origins and the Domestic Game'. In *The Encyclopedia of Malaysia: Volume 15 (Sports and Recreation)*, ed. Ahmed Hamid. Singapore: Archipelago Press, 2008.
Ooi, Keat Gin. 'Politics Divided: Malaysia-Singapore Relations'. In *Across the Causeway: A Multi-Dimensional Study of Singapore-Malaysia Relations*, ed. Takashi Shiraishi, 27–51. Singapore: Institute of Southeast Asian Studies, 2009.
Oon, Desmond. 'Government Involvement in Sport in Singapore, 1959–1982'. PhD thesis, University of Queensland, 1984.
Osman, Shamir. 'Football attendance: Not all bad news'. *Channel News Asia*. http://www.channelnewsasia.com/stories/sportsnews/view/1185686/1/.html.
Rahim, Lily Zubaidah. 'Singapore-Malaysia relations: Deep-Seated Tensions and Self-Fulfilling Prophecies'. *Journal of Contemporary Asia* 29, no. 1 (1999): 38–55.
Rahim, Lily Zubaidah. *Singapore in the Malay World: building and breaching regional bridges*. Abingdon: Routledge, 2009.
Robert, Godfrey. *The Malaysia Cup*. Singapore: 2A Publications, 1991.

Rowe, David. *Global Media Sport: Flows, Forms and Futures*. London: Bloomsbury Academic, 2011.

S-League. *The S-League Handbook: Season 1996*. Singapore: Singapore Professional Football League Private Limited, 1996.

Samuel, Eric (2009) 'Poor Fan Turnout Forces Kuala Muda Naza to Quit Super League'. *The Star*. http://thestar.com.my/sports/story.asp?file=/2009/11/25/sports/5174767&sec=-sports.

Saravanamuutu, Johan. *Malaysia's Foreign Policy: The First Fifty Years: Alignment, Neutralism, Islamism*. Singapore: Institute of Southeast Asian Studies, 2010.

Saw, Swee-Hock and K. Kesavapany. *Singapore-Malaysia Relations: Under Abdullah Badawi*. Singapore: Institute of Southeast Asian Studies, 2006.

Saw, Swee-Hock. *The Population of Malaysia*. Singapore: Institute of Southeast Asian Studies, 2007.

Sheppard, Mubin. *Tunku: His Life and Times: The Authorized Biography of Tunku Abdul Rahman Putra al-Haj*. Petaling Jaya: Pelanduk Publications, 1995.

Shiraishi, Takashi. 'Introduction'. In *Across the Causeway: A Multi-Dimensional Study of Singapore-Malaysia Relations*, ed. Takashi Shiraishi, 1–10. Singapore: Institute of, Southeast Asian Studies, 2009.

Sidhu, Jatswan. 'Malaysia-Singapore Relations Since 1998: A Troubled Past – Whither a Brighter Future'. In *Malaysia's Foreign Relations: Issues and Challenges*, ed. Ruhanas Harun, 75–92. Kuala Lumpur, University of Malaya Press, 2006.

Siebel, Norman. 'Soccer'. In *Who's Who in Sports in Malaysia and Singapore*, ed. T. Dawson, 119–121. Petaling Jaya: Who's Who in Sports, 1975.

Star. 'Poor turnout may force FAM to lift ban on foreigners'. *The Star*. http://thestar.com.my/sports/story.asp?file=%2F2010%2F5%2F20%2Fsports%2F6298921&sec=sports.

Tai, Yong Tan. *Creating 'Greater Malaysia': Decolonization and the Politics of Merger*. Singapore: Institute of Southeast Asian Studies, 2008.

Wilson, Peter, and Benson Sim. 'The Demand for Semi-Pro League Football in Malaysia 1989–91: a panel data approach'. *Applied Economics* 27 (1995): 131–8.

Wok, Othman. *Never in My Wildest Dreams*. Singapore: Raffles, 2000.

Yen, Chen Ai. 'The Mass Media, 1819–1980'. In *A History of Singapore*, ed. E. Chew and A. Lee, 288–311. Singapore: Oxford University Press, 1991.

The otherness of self: football, fandom and fragmented (sub) nationalism in Bengal

Madhuja Mukherjee

Department of Film Studies, Jadavpur University, Kolkata, India

>This paper examines the significance of football cultures and its mythical histories in Bengal. I specifically consider the recent social developments and its complex relation to global media, in order to comprehend the density of our contemporary everyday. By narrating the accounts of the local clubs, which developed through colonial encounters, this paper tackles the *affect* produced in the playing fields or outside. Therefore, through an exploration of the set of parallel values attached to the clubs and its public displays, this paper shows the processes via which 'differences' are produced because of a series of *displacements*. Moreover, while fan cultures in Bengal have been marked with violence, the peculiar fan-following of the national teams of Brazil and Argentina demonstrates complicated strands of history. In brief, with reference to the histories of football in Bengal, this paper comments on the patterns of myth-making and fan cultures.

Introduction

This paper examines the import of football cultures and the (mythical) histories of the game in Bengal (East India), by closely looking into the wide range of public behaviour connected to the sport. In relation to this, I consider the social developments of the post-colonial nation and the location of football within media networks in order to comprehend the meaning of football in our political everyday.[1] However, the subject of televised and sponsored sport events is taken as backdrop in an attempt to examine the massive popularity of the game and specific fan ethos in Bengal. From this perspective, the paper relocates the question of club football in Bengal within the framework of world football to understand the connections between particular (sub) nationalist fervour and global sport events. By narrating the history of the local clubs, which emerged through fervent encounters with the colonial regime as well as through the disparate moments of post-colonial conflicts, this paper reads into the socio-political implications of the emotional acts performed in the playing fields. Briefly, with reference to the histories of football in Bengal, this paper focuses on its allegorical meaning and the function of fan cultures.

While Mohun Bagan (established in 1889) is remembered for defeating the (English) East York Regiment in 1911, the chronicles of East Bengal (established in 1920), as well as their entrenched mutual rivalries bifurcated by issues of community, language and locations, present an intricate mesh of historical narratives that problematize the very idea of binaries and issues of identity politics.[2] Hence, through a thorough exploration of the set of parallel values attached to these clubs, and by considering its public displays, this paper illustrates the processes via which 'differences' are produced through a series of *displacements* rather than any direct and telling recognition with a cause. Arguably, in such cases, the mass identification with a club is produced through a stream negations (i.e. enemy's enemy is my friend), and as Amir Ben Porat shows 'produces a fan's identity,' and for 'certain conspicuous reasons, the emotional experience of football fandom seems most critical'.[3] The devotional aspect of the fans, which is also narrated by Boria Majumdar and Kausik Bandyopadhyay, is the basis of this paper.[4]

While club football in Bengal has inspired popular films, novellas, short stories, songs and theatrical performances,[5] the popularity of the game is clearly premised on a succession of historical events including incidents of oppressions during the colonial rule followed by the partition of Bengal (/India) in 1947, Bangladesh war in 1971 and the problem of immigration, as well as political acrimony between the Communist Party of India (Marxist) and the party currently in power in Bengal, along with a host of trivia, together with distinct local practices like the choices of food from either sides of Bengal, and the shifting association of East Bengal with Brazil (since Mohun Bagan played against Cosmos and the legendary Pele in 1977). Therefore, through a series of *negations* (for instance, East Bengal had lost to Mohun Bagan in 1977, but Mohun Bagan could not defeat their opponent), the adversary of 'our' adversary became discreetly identifiable. In reality, fan cultures in Bengal have problematical accounts and have been marked with much violence and bloodshed, culminating into the death of 13 fans during a match in 1980. Moreover, the peculiar fan-following of the national teams of Brazil and Argentina amongst the local Bengali people (and celebrations by the neighbourhood or *para* clubs) demonstrates further complications, as well as the political links between post-colonial countries and the shared histories of the Global South. This tendency effectively remarks on the ramifications of the frenzy around international football. Thus, besides providing a historical overview of club football in Bengal, I would particularly study the function fandom as well as the *affect* re-produced through the media when South American teams from Brazil and Argentina fight for the FIFA World Cup and (equally) socially backward groups in Calcutta clash with each other by taking up different sides.[6] The structures of displaced (sub) nationalist commitments become imperative in the context of global flows, and as I look into social history, public cultures, media, politics and the periphery of *affect*.

Growing up Bengali

It may be necessary for an uninitiated reader to known that Bengal is a province located in the eastern region of India. Calcutta/Kolkata, the capital of Bengal, was also the capital of the country during the colonial period (until 1911). Furthermore, until the Independence, Bengal comprised both East Bengal (now Bangladesh) and West Bengal. There are further local complexities pertaining to matters of geo-politics, differences and similarities as well as cultural histories, but we are circumventing that, to arrive at a larger field which entails other uncertainties. Therefore, this paper principally deals with the metaphorical meaning of football in Bengal, and its knotty associations with political-cultural histories. I wish to study sports in the context of social arena, in which politics itself is apparently being played out, and therein make meaning of how sports may both support and subvert issues of identity politics.

Myth No.1: As a child, the photograph of 'some' Brazilian football player named Pele, in my family album, always intrigued me. Why was my cousin sticking his head out from behind this black man? Later, I was also given a five-rupee note, on which Pele had done his signature. As well, I was told that this was extremely valuable. Thus, I would often try to copy (the value of) this strange word 'Pele', which was written conspicuously on Mahatma Gandhi's face (the watermark on Indian currency). Clearly, the significance of Pele and the game would become momentous to me only at a later stage in life.

Myth No. 2: The local team Mohun Bagan plays against Cosmos in 1977. On the given day, it rained heavily, therefore, it was feared that the match might be called off. There was the buzz that Pele will not play on this muddy field. Nevertheless, he did not dampen the spirits of the Calcutta people, and the over-joyed crowd gave a 'thunderous' welcome as Cosmos and Mohun Bagan players arrived at the field. While Cosmos scored the first goal (at 17th minute), Mohun Bagan equalized the score at the very next minute. Thereafter, at the 23rd minute, Mohun Bagan scored a second goal, thus in reality got lead in the match. At the last minutes of the first half, Cosmos created pressure on Mohun Bagan and almost scored twice. Pele took a magnificent thirty-yard free kick though Mohun Bagan's Sivaji Banerjee pulled off an equally great save. The first half ended with the game in favour of Mohun Bagan. In the second half, thus, Mohun Bagan played in a defensive way. Pele took another brilliant free kick and got Chinaglia to take it up, but Chinaglia failed to score. Eventually, in the 17th minute, Mohun Bagan conceded a penalty and Chinaglia made it 2–2, as a consequence the match ended in a draw.[7]

Notwithstanding this, the man with an outstanding record failed to score against a home team and Cosmos made it 2–2 only through (the advantage of) penalty, was sort of taken up by the fans of the opponent teams. Eventually, the following myth was circulated, and became quite popular. First, Pele never came to India. Secondly, it was perhaps the well-known theatre artist Shanti Gopal (popular for playing Comrade Lenin, Comrade Stalin et al), who was masquerading as Pele in the fields. Consequently, the question of 'Shanti Gopal' beating the famous Mohun Bagan players like Sivaji Banerjee, Gautam Sarkar, Shyam Thapa, Habib and Subrata Bhattacharya et al, does not arise.

And, other myths: We all grew up reading Moti Nandy's (Bengali) novellas and short stories published and re-published as *Striker* (1972), *Stopper* (1973), etc., which depicted the mythical rise of the local footballer amidst much politick-ing. As well, films like *Mohun Baganer Meye* (/'The Girl from Mohan Bagan', Dir. Monu Sen, 1975) and *Dhanyi Meye* (/'Brava Girl!' Dir. Arabindo Mukherjee, 1971), which are repeatedly telecast on TV, constitute our collective memories.[8] Actually, such random local stories illustrate that football is perhaps not a game as in 'sports'. Clearly, football in Bengal is a culture, and is a powerful allegory of the nation and its fragments. Indeed, football as a cultural phenomenon is deeply attached to our uneven modernities, and specific (regional) political histories (see Figure 1).[9]

Figure 1. Photograph of Pele (in India, 1977), from the family album.

'Ghoti-Bati' and the ball as (Foucault's) pendulum

The history of Indian football has been read in tandem with the colonial rule and the British initiative in the Colleges (in St. Xavier's College, Presidency College, Bishop's College, etc.).[10] Writing about 'Calcutta Soccer', Moti Nandy suggests that the Army had brought the game to India and the acquaintance of unwitting Bengalis with it was somewhat accidental. Nandy elaborates on how:[11]

> [t]he first Indian football club, the Wellington Club, was set up in 1884 by none other than Nagendraprasad ... The same year, Nagendra married into the Shobhabazar Raj family, and at once used his new influence to found the Shovabazar Club.

Additionally, Bengali teams started playing against English teams; and in time, football became an essential tool through which the brown natives could be westernized. Thus, the 'football project' (like the educational drives, by Macaulay (1835)) became a decisive one through which the ever-flagging morale of the Indian people could be effectively lifted. This making of the 'man' was a part of a larger project, with far reaching implications especially because, through the early nineteenth-century, the British attempted to portray the Indian male as effeminate. Indira Chowdhury in her seminal work has discussed the nuances of the production of a weak masculine figure, as well as the responses to it (which were deeply 'cultural').[12] While by and large the Bengali male were interpellated into this notion of effeminacy and frailty, several nationalist leaders including Bankim Chandra Chattopadhyay, Nabagopal Mitra, Swami Vivekananda et al., became instrumental in producing an alternative (virile) image of the young Bengali. Thus, forceful physical exercises (*byam*) became one of the ways in which such stereotyping could be contested.[13] Nevertheless, physical sports like wrestling and bodybuilding could not adequately mobilize the masses. A popular film like *Rajat Jayanti* (Dir. P.C. Barua, 1939) in a comic mode criticizes such projects of the Bengali elite. In the film, the very refined protagonist (Rajat) practises homoeopathy and desperately hopes to gather enough courage to propose to the heroine (Jayanti). In the process, Barua ridicules the task of masculinization of young Bengalis (who are ironically referred to as *purush singha*/'Male' as in Lion).[14]

Seemingly, the great nationalist missionary Vivekananda played a significant role in inspiring millions to take up football as a larger nationalist project.[15] Kausik Bandyopadhyay explains how after Nagendra Prasad (Sarvadhikari) the game was popularized extensively in Bengal.[16] Bandyopadhyay shows the manner in which football became a 'cultural weapon'. Bandyopadhyay describes how, 'Nagendra Prasad's organizational effort was followed by enthusiastic Bengalis .... As a result, football clubs emerged in different localities and suburbs of Calcutta in the late 1880s...'.[17] Indeed, through the 1880s and 1890s, football emerged as a compelling form of political–cultural game, and by the early twentieth century, it became an integral part of the popular ethos. While the Indian Football Association (IFA) was formed in 1882, the institutionalization of the Mohun Bagan club in 1889 was apparently the most important event of Indian football history.[18] Clearly, the successive victories of Mohun Bagan at the turn of the twentieth century[19] resulted in a greater achievement when the team (comprising barefooted players, largely from the east of Bengal) defeated the powerful British teams in the July of 1911, and won the IFA shield. A crowd of about 80, 000 gathered near *Maidan* (field) on the fateful day. The people, as suggested by Bandyopadhyay,[20]

> became obsessed with the dream of beating the ruling British at their own national game. The dream became a reality when Mohan Bagan defeated the East Yorks team 2–1 in the historic final of 29 July 1911.

While the corelation between football, nationalist fervour and topics of masculinity have been discussed in other contexts, in this paper, I would exclusively deliberate on the significance of the *affective* qualities of the game, particularly in which barefooted Indians took the mighty English. Thus, the political–cultural effects of 1911, as well as the transactions between history and myth-making, become crucial within this framework.[21] As evident through several scholarly researches, the game quickly became a cultural phenomenon and was enthusiastically supported by slang, jokes, quarrels, fist-fights, other physical gestures/caricatures etc., on the field; as well, such ardent involvements were accompanied with violent outbursts like taking off or tearing off one's clothes, burning posters, brick-braking, etc. In short, football in Bengal evoked extreme and passionate engagements and brought together Bengalis from all walks of life (officers, clerks, and labourers alike) onto this contested field. Boria Majumdar and Kausik Bandyopadhyay in their book-length study bring up the historical perspectives and the pattern in which Bengal emerges as the crucial playground where larger nationalist missions are played out.[22] In due course, Mohun Bagan's victory at the IFA shield final became one of most powerful legends of nationalism. According to Kausik Bandyopadhyay:[23]

> The trend of bare-foot on field battle against European civil and military teams was set in the context of political agitation and social unrest that grew in response to the partition of Bengal in 1905. The so-called Swadeshi [nationalist] age from 1905–1911 was incidentally the age of Mohun Bagan in Bengal football ... Mohun Bagan achieved some stunning victories against strongest of European sides during this period of stirring up mass imaginations ...

Consequently, the romantic Bengali blockbuster *Saptapadi* ((Dir. Ajar Kar, 1961) set in the context World War) uses this background to produce a rather dense love story between a Christian Anglo-Indian girl and a Bengali Brahmin boy (both doctors). While the theme of the film dwells on the communal (dis)harmony, in which the puritan father disallows his son to marry the illegitimate daughter of a British officer, Krishnendu (the protagonist, played by the all-time popular Bengali star Uttam Kumar), eventually, converts to Christianity and abandons his community. Nevertheless, the gusty Rina Brown (the female lead, played by the enigmatic Suchitra Sen) suffers from guilt, betrays their love and becomes an alcoholic. After a long separation and much suffering, the characters eventually meet in (an undefined) war zone and live happily ever after. Two scenes from this film become significant within the structure of this paper. First, the scene where Rina and Krishnendu perform for a college programme (the Shakespearean drama, *Othello*) and evidently fall for each other during the performance of the English play, and more importantly the second one, in which they meet for the first time, during a football match. The possibility of using the football ground as a setting for the hero and heroine to meet in an otherwise romantic film becomes meaningful only when we perceive that Krishnendu – barefooted – is fighting against the heavily booted White men, and Rina is cheering for the White team. Indeed, this is no football at all; this scene distinctly represents the import of football within nationalist narratives, and the ways in which Bengalis have been romancing the ball since 1911. Clearly, football in Bengal has wrought social structures and sometimes the vice versa (see Figure 2).

Nevertheless, the broad framework of football and nationalism becomes somewhat problematic as we explore the historical narratives of the three major football

Figure 2. The bare-footed footballer in *Saptapadi* (DVD, frame grab).

clubs in Bengal, namely Mohun Bagan, East Bengal and Mohammedan Sporting Club.[24] Especially crucial are the circumstances of social 'differentiation', as opposed to the ways in which football may be described as the tool of 'unification'. This tendency is especially perceptible in the post-colonial period, at the times when football was apparently being performed on the messy political grounds. Indeed, the outline that joins nationalist fervour with football becomes somewhat faint in due course. Thus, while by the late nineteenth century football was a distinguished tool to represent Bengali masculinity and an evocative icon of resistance, in the later period, the Mohun Bagan team was repeatedly accused of elitism and discriminations. In fact, the East Bengal club was founded in 1920, after the alleged prejudices against them (especially against Sailesh Basu) by the *Bhadralok* club Mohun Bagan.

Yet, this was in view of the fact that many of players in the Mohun Bagan team were in actuality from the East Bengal region (as well from the suburbs); nevertheless, that players from East Bengal were seemingly denied their due recognition, resulted in the setting up of the club. As a matter of fact, as the name signifies, the club became a formidable device that reinstituted the 'East Bengali' sense of self-esteem and pride. In 1925, East Bengal was promoted to First Division level amidst a series of controversies. Furthermore, the Mohammedan Sporting Club, established in 1891, emerged as a formidable team after winning the Calcutta Football League for five consecutive years between 1934 and 1938. In time, Mohammedan Sporting and East Bengal clubs turned out to be extremely popular and influential, emerging as mass teams, and thus, strategically withdrew from League matches (in 1939) in protest against IFA's contemptuous attitude towards them. In 1940, Mohammedan Sporting won the IFA shield, while East Bengal won their first league match in 1942 and the IFA shield in 1943. Football, to use Bandyopadhyay's,[25] 'was a site for inclusion and for exclusion then, as the game was shaped by the often contradictory forces of colonialism'.

Nevertheless, this chronicle of 'differentiation' has its own fuzziness as well. Therefore, it was not improbable for players from different regions to play for either East Bengal or Mohun Bagan. In fact, the legendary defender of Mohun Bagan team, Gostho Paul, hailed from east of Bengal (Faridpur District), and in time became a heady symbol of fragmented (sub) nationalism. All the same, in the post-colonial period, especially during 1949–53, football in general, and East Bengal club in particular, became truly potent symbols of refugee problems. In time, *Maidan* became the site where disparate cultural and political groups fought out their respective histories of suffering. Both Boria Majumdar and Kausik Bandyopadhyay, respectively, have conducted significant researches on histories of such group formation and have demonstrated the modes in which such differences are not based on any one (definite) historical event.[26] Using vernacular sources, they demonstrate the ways in which football becomes a forceful public culture. For instance, *Manasi* (journal) published verses, which may be translated as the following:[27]

> We've scored against the whites; it's a triumph of the Bengalis/The air is filled with songs of rejoicing/The motherland will never forget today's victory/Hail! Hail! Mohun Bagan; you have played very well …

Indeed, an in-depth study of the popular debates on East Bengal–Mohun Bagan rivalry, published in the popular and influential dailies, illustrate the processes of compartmentalization (see Figure 3).[28]

Figure 3. The statue of Goshto Paul in the Maidan Area.

Clearly, despite what the Paul Demio and others suggest, the acrimony between Mohun Bagan and East Bengal did not possibly have any 'ethnic' issue per se.[29] For instance, Mohun Bagan's players in the much discussed match of 1911 were, in reality, mostly from East Bengal. Therefore, one would like to propose that the conditions through which the clubs became iconic are correlated to the course of myth-making and larger nationalist discourses, and not merely to any specific historical fact. In short, this ambiguity is certainly a (/our) reality, though it may not be necessarily true. For instance, *Ghoti* is a slang which generally means people from regions of West Bengal, who have settled in and around Calcutta. *Ghoti* is therefore, to put it simply, a derivative of the *Bhadralok*, who have lost much of their elitism.[30] Similarly, *Bangal* is a colloquial term singifying people from Bangladesh; however, it also implies the refugee in post-colonial contexts. *Bangals* apparently lack taste, education and sophistication. The *Bangal* thus could mean a person from Bangladesh, a refugee as well as an 'uncultured' (loud) person and even a fool. *Ghoti* too should be seen as a poor cousin of the *Babu*, while *Bati* is another slang meaning children born out of mixed cultures. Note, that none of these have ethnic and/or religious connotations, thus, the emphasis is on the problems of culture, class and regional differences (including dialects, ritualistic practices, etc.). Albeit, such apparent animosity become telling with the partition of Bengal, and with millions of refugees pouring in as shown in the film *Chinnamul* (/'Rootless', Dir. Nemai Ghosh, 1950).

The unending queues of refugees became perceptible with the partition of Bengal. It began in as early as 1946 with violence in Calcutta, Bihar and in the districts of East Bengal. This led to the migration of 14,000 East Bengalis. After the partition in 1947, 2, 58,000 migrants sought shelter in West Bengal. This increased by 5, 90,000 people in 1948, and 1, 82,000 people in 1949.[31] Many of the migrants had some pre-partition links of kinship (or of occupation) with Calcutta. Nevertheless, though some of the refugees had a source of earning, many more waited at the iconic thoroughfare – at the Sealdah railway stations – to take a train to a non-existent future. From the city of the *Babus*, Calcutta was refigured as the city of refugees/*Bangals*, while immigration continued ceaselessly through the 1950s. The arrival of the refugees forced the city *Bhadralok* to look at Calcutta and its burgeoning urban problems from a different perspective. However, unlike the working-class migrants from the neighbouring states, the *Bangal* migrants were extremely vocal about their political rights,[32] and gradually aligned themselves with the Left politics.

In this context, cinema becomes an important visual evidence of the changing cityscapes.[33] For instance, *Chinnamul* that was an Indian People's Theatre Association's collective effort, addressed the problem of the immigration. The film is regarded as the solitary cinematic document of partition and refugee problems. It begins in a leisurely pace and, thereafter through an evocative montage, shows the fear and trauma of partition. While the masses remain somewhat unsure of the meaning and implications of Independence and partition, eventually families migrated to Kolkata leaving behind their homes and land, and as filmmaker Ritwik Ghatak would put it, by abandoning an entire landscape and their manners of speaking as well, to traverse onto unknown territories and a new cityscape.[34]

In the film, after a series of difficulties, the family of the protagonist (Srikanta) would go on to live in a mansion they captured (along with other families). The film ends with the death of Srikanta's pregnant wife after the birth of their son. However, partition perhaps also meant a new beginning through violence and pain, as another young boy of the family looks at the picturesque city from their terrace, and is in awe by its scenic qualities. The hostile conditions thus truly opened up new possibilities. In this context, two popular narratives the *Striker* and the *Stopper* by the eminent Bengali writer Moti Nandy become important. For instance, Prasun, the protagonist in *Striker* tells his mother that, 'football is fairy tale for him'. Nandy shows the poverty-stricken conditions in the city and the ways in which sports, other than education, become an effective tool for social mobility. As well, the intra-club politics and the moral degradation in the post-partition period, are highlighted in these engaging accounts of the youth, and that of the young nation striving to produce its own reminiscent history.

While Nandy also writes about the ways in which the game becomes a part of the nationalist discourse, the fanfare around football is the basis of this paper. Clearly, years immediately after the partition (1949–53) belonged to the East Bengal team in terms of victories at higher-level tournaments. The Famous 'Five Pandavas'[35] or the forward line of East Bengal, namely Vengkatesh, Apparao, Dhanraj, Ahmed Khan and Saleh became heroes in own their rights, though as their names reveal that most of them came from southern regions of the country (and were not Hindus despite the fact that, Hindu–Muslim bitterness remains a crucial element of *Bangal* sub-nationalist politics).[36] Thus, the ruthless politicization of the game, as well as its the 'indigenisation', clearly comments on the histories of football in Bengal and in India; as well as on the mobilization of the youth (especially from suburban areas) along with the mass mobilization of youth within larger political movements. It is within this background of mass movements that we discuss the vehemently aggressive fan cultures. For instance, the fighting at the IFA shield final in 1947 resulted in police firing and the abandonment of the match. Thus, the shield final of 1950 took place under massive police protection. Eventually, the nature of the game became so violent that, from this time onwards, IFA decided to host league and shield matches under police protection. In way, *Maidan* or the playing fields became a proxy nation, in which the struggles over the land, in real and metaphorical sense, were being played out. The situation apparently was so severe that the then Chief Minister of Bengal, Dr. B. C. Roy, who himself was the icon of modern Bengal, suggested change of names of the clubs (which had communal overtones).

A popular film of the period like *Mohun Bangan er Meye* shows such rivalry in a comic vein. In this film, the respective fathers – of the bride and the groom – support disparate teams. Bearing the mythical connotations of the respective teams, the father figures disapprove of the match. Especially interesting is the role essayed by the comedian Robi Ghosh, who acts as a vendor and supplies material (like stone chips and brick pieces), which are useful in the killing fields. In a particular song sequence, the heavily bandaged comic figure comments on the issue. Another film from this time, *Dhanyi Meye*, illustrates the passion and presents the processes of the localization of the game. Briefly, the film shows the indigenization of the game, the obsessions and the dire conditions of the local (village) teams, and also elaborates on the means through which a suburban team contests a team from Calcutta. Furthermore, within its comic mode, the film shows the diverse forms of subversive resistance, which include cheating and coercion (like forced marriage) in order to retain the prestige of village (named 'Harbhanga'/literally brittle bones, though, apparently inspired by Darbhanga). As well, the film includes an evocative song regarding the king of games or football.[37]

The appropriation of football into local myths, thus, highlights the reformulations of the colonial game and those of the rules of ethics; and in fact, presents larger conflicts and dissonances within the nation and at the margins. Note that, while the peak period of popularity of the game was during 1930s–1950s, and unto 1970s, these were also the fundamental moments of historical transformations, marked by the establishment of Communist Party of India (in 1925), as well as mass sufferings during the Second World War (1939–1945), resulting in one of most devastating man-made famine (in 1943), deaths and more deaths during nationalist movement which was at its height after the commencement of Quit India Movement (in 1942), followed by riots (especially in 1946), partition of Bengal/India (in 1947), the inflow of refugees through the 1960s, scarcity of food and Left agitations (like the '*Khadya Andolan*' during 1959) in Bengal, formation of United [Left] Front (in 1967), Bangladesh war (1971) and the eventual setting up of the Left Front Government in 1977.[38] Therefore, one may argue that the excessively violent fan culture in Bengal, in reality, stems out from the intensities of politics discontents.

Indeed, with establishment of East Bengal club in 1920, and rise of Mohammedan Sporting Club in the early thirties, questions of football and pan-nationalism get deeply fractured, fragmented and complicated. In effect, one of the issues that appear to become problematic is that football is an 'emblem of nation formation'. Precisely, football appears to be the 'symbol of fragmentation' and fragmented histories. Furthermore, what becomes evident as we examine club rivalries in Bengal are the ways in which football functions as a game of identity politics and social segregation. For instance, as we analyse the Mohun Bagan–East Bengal binary, by connecting it to the *Ghoti-Bangal*, *Chingri-Ilish* (fish/food habits) dichotomies, or even further to Trinamul Congress–CPIM rancor, what in actuality becomes apparent are the ruptures within the post-colonial nation-state.[39] Therefore, if *Bangal* is a caricature of the East Bengalis residing in the colonies of South Calcutta, then the *Ghoti* too is a slang that describes the petty lives of the middle-class *Babus* striving for sunlight and water in their overcrowded mansions in North Calcutta.[40] Consequently, the 'inconsequential' strifes between East Bengal and Mohun Bagan became more and more grave and far-reaching after the partition. While violence on the field was a major concern for the government through 1950s, this was apparently further intensified after the Bangladesh war in 1971. Therefore, with the entry of more and more immigrants during this time, the stature of clubs and the game also rose meteorically.

Nonetheless, the actual politicization of the game is crucial within this context. For example, while the Communist Party of India gained acceptance in Bengal through its massive field work during the great famine, the party became deeply involved with the refugee cause and did extensive welfare activities in building the refugee colonies in and around Calcutta. Therefore, the refugees from East Bengal would align with the Left, and on a popular level that they – and the unemployed youth in particular – would also find a noble cause through East Bengal's victories is but obvious. Especially, with the growth of aggressive Naxalite Movements in Bengal, and its bloody after effects on the Calcutta streets, the violent ethos was easily transported to the playing fields.[41] This to a great extent meant a sub-division of the fans on the political lines, as well as certain overlap of ideologies, which would further complicate the conditions. For example, back in 1970s, it was not impossible for an educated, middle-class, CPIM supporter to back Mohun Bagan (particularly if he/she was originally from the regions of West Bengal). This condition, however, would become more and more muddled in 1980s, with the (then) opposing Trinamul Congress Leader Ms. Mamata Banerjee taking up the cause of the unfortunate death of the 16 Mohun Bagan fans and marking it as the day of yearly mourning.[42] It is in this context that this paper explores the function of emotion and *affect* on political grounds and on football fields.

During this time, spectator behaviour went through considerable shifts, while the affection for the clubs was expressed in extreme and almost hysteric ways. Therefore, queuing-up had a symbolic meaning since people started queuing up for everything including tickets of an ordinary derby match, and the public hysteria over minor issues, and consequent bloodshed on the streets, seem like an externalization of the political frenzy of the period. For instance, in 1975, East Bengal defeated Mohun Bagan by 5–0. After the fourth goal was scored, a Mohun Bagan supporter had a heart attack. Moreover, a 25-year-old man was so dejected that he committed suicide, after leaving a note which said that 'he would be reborn – with vengeance – and as better footballer'. In 1977, Mohun Bagan's defeat in league matches caused more suicides, though they later won other trophies in the same year and thereafter played the famous Cosmos, mentioned earlier.

The public behaviour of fans changed considerable through 1978–1979, and this in a sense culminated into the violence of 16 August 1980, in which 13 people (from the Mohun Bagan stands) died on the field, and three more in the hospital. This tragedy, which left thousands injured, caused further political injuries. This was clearly a case of gross mismanagement, as well as a political crisis. While clashes between local rival teams like those between Manchester United and Chelsea, UK (despite the fact leading players often shift teams) are not uncommon, football seems to serve specific political functions in the Bengal context. Therefore, after the present chief Minister Mamata Banerjee (then a fire-brand opposition leader) took up the cause of the deceased fans, and marked this incident as an occasion of yearly public mourning, besides intensifying the cultures of public displays of affection, this also produced further ruptures within club rivalries giving it a certain fixed political identity.

Meanwhile, through the late 1980s and 1990s, with the rise of satellite TV (and live telecast of FIFA matches, which brought glimpses of world-class football to the Bengalis)[43] and the meteoric rise of the popularity of cricket after the World Cup victory in 1983 (as well, the waning of the popularity of national games like Hockey), the shift from yearly winter test matches to (televised) one-day Internationals etc., relocated club football in Bengal within the media networks of global flows; hence, as a consequence, the local football clubs lost much of their intensities.[44] This period experienced the successive decline of the popularity and frenzy around local-club football due to other reasons, including victories of the Goan team at the national level and with the visual experience international football (after TV became a household thing post-Asiad games in 1982), resulting in the untimely

Figure 4. Writing on the wall: Graffiti of the Brazilian flag in Calcutta by Gopal Nagar Club.

retirement of the die-hard fans in Calcutta.[45] Arguably, Calcutta football has now entered its third phase of *post-nationalism* and *post-fandom*, after its fervent nationalist and hyper sub-nationalist conditions.[46] Thus, at the time when the magician of the playing fields, Diego Maradona, arrived at Calcutta in December 2008, the very exhausted hero appeared like a walking symbol of lost narratives.[47] It is within this framework that the final section of the paper argues about the significance of the popular associations between Indian and Latin American football teams (see Figure 4).

Colours of affection and disrupted (sub)nationalism

This comparison between international football teams from Brazil and Argentina (which have won the FIFA World Cup in the years 1958, 1962, 1970 and 1994, as well as in 1978 and 1986, respectively) with the local Bengal teams is not based on the histories of the three nations and its peripheries. Certainly, there are certain historical commonalities between post-colonial/'third-world' nations; however, focusing on the 'politics of affect', I would like to mention how a Left political culture, that aspired to produce an environment of Internationalism (by connecting the third world nations, as well as by recreating the narratives of revolutionary countries like Argentina, Cuba and so on, and through the retelling of the movements lead by Che Guevara and others);[48] in time, succumbed to the populist parametres.[49] Moreover, the mass consciousness of other nations did not necessarily come from the history classes, but by and large through a convoluted process of mythical stories (available through popular biographies for instance) and via fragmentary images (published in newspapers). In this connection, one may mention the Brazilian crime film *City of God* (Fernando Mei relles, 2002), which shows the growth of organized crime in the city. Narrated by Rocket the protagonist, who is an aspiring photographer (and one of the few survivors), the film tells the story of the city of God (a suburb of Rio de Janerio) between 1960s and 1980s. Presenting his memory about the ways in which a systematic structure of crime is formed and begins to control the small town, the film starts off with the flashback sequence and presents a local/street football match. While the football game is not directly linked to the main plot, nor is it developed effectively, this opening sequence in curious way underlines everyday practices, as well as the hushed histories and unaccounted memories of smaller nations (though large territories), along with the volatile political conditions of the Global South. The political-cultural environment within which the game football may become a popular symbol of self-wroth in countries like Brazil becomes critical from this perspective.[50] As a matter of fact, the local adaptations of an imperial game are crucial in the fashion in which, first, football was initially associated with nationalist fervour and, secondly, the manner in which the game often turned violent and therefore eventually highlighted certain deep ruptures within nationalist frameworks. Multiple issues like the subject of the sporting body; implications of the sweat, blood and bodily gestures; as well as the subjects of spaces, landscapes, classes and communities and the mobilization of the disposed, all seem to be rolled into one to produce a common myth called football.

Thus, one may return to Myth No: 1. Indeed, in 1977, Mohun Bagan eventually won IFA Shield, Durand Cup, Rover's Cup and Bordoloi Trophy. This winning of the triple crowns (while East Bengal had won the league matches) was followed by Mohun Bagan playing the legendary Cosmos. A Mohan Bagan follower reports:[51]

> This year Mohun Bagan players got the great opportunity to play against the Football King Edson Arantos Jo Nasimanto – Pele. Kolkata football lovers got the chance to see some of the famous international footballers like Mike Dillon, Kith Edi, Toni Field and Terigarbet of England, Ramon Mifin of Peru, Giorgio Chinaglia of Italy, Carlos Alberto and Nelsi Morez of Brazil, Erol Yasin of Turkey, Ditomir Dimitri and Toni Donlich of Yugoslavia including Pele. The historical match was played on 24th September of this year in Eden Gardens. About 80,000 spectators gathered on that in Eden gardens …

While rain had dampened the weather, spirits were not dampened and Mohun Bagan defended themselves against the mighty players though as we know, the game was a draw. This, by certain kind of curious calculations and through a series of negations, conspicuously meant that the East Bengal supporters at that time would support Brazil since Pele had played against Mohan Bagan. Nevertheless, such typical fan cultures are in actuality supported by fluid movements of the players and supporters as well.

In the era of Global TV, cultural values appear eclectic and, thus, as Richard Peterson has shown (in the context of music), people may have disparate and even contradictory likings as well as divided notions of belonging.[52] For example, at present, both Mohun Bagan and East Bengal have players from Nigeria and other countries, and these players often change teams. Moreover, within a rigid structure of binaries, the understanding that an East Bengal fan till date would support Brazil may or may be true. This could be because, on one hand, Brazil suffered a dry patch during the eighties and, on the other, Argentina became popular through its FIFA World Cup victories during this time; additionally, regular TV telecast of the FIFA World Cup during the said period reproduced (dedicated) fans of international teams. Thereafter, the 1980s generation, as it were, grew up without knowing what it exactly meant to see Pele play on the rainy day or the mass hysteria over a goal. Such deep sense of belonging which has been arguably produced through the 'political uncertainties and social depression' of the 1970s was reshaped in a different order through TV programming and daily telecast of sports.[53] The cultures of fandom produced by TV ushered in a shift from *active participation* on the playing fields to somewhat *passive viewership* performed in the living rooms. Thus, the present mediated condition basically creates a decentred spectacle, and infinite fan cultures as opposed to the more focused (in time and space) expressions of the fans in the field. A contemporary fan may thus be interested in football, food and films with equal zeal. The 'post-fan', according to Redhead, approaches the game knowing that it is 'just a game', and perhaps, if it has not been on TV, it has had not happened at all.[54] The new fan, therefore, is not obsessed with live attendance at the stadium or is not willing to sacrifice his/her life (or life style) over an ordinary derby match. The fan now may be described as the consuming body in the era global media.

And yet, specific historical contexts disturb such speculations as well. For instance, interviews with local club members (of 47 Pally, Ramgarh, Calcutta) demonstrate certain shifting commitments with football.[55] Born in the year 1986, Baaptu is an ardent East Bengal fan, and as a child, he encountered football through the televised highlights of the FIFA World Cup matches. Prior to this, he had heard of Maradona, but watching him score the goal converted him into a follower of the Argentina team. In 2010, the club put up huge screens to enable the local people watch the FIFA World Cup finals. They gathered children, painted their faces in blue and white strips, gave them jerseys and hung Argentine flags in their own locality. A popular Bengali TV channel had telecast the club's programmes. Curiously, during our conversations, Baaptu could neither understand the impact of Brazil nor its ambiguous relationship to East Bengal. Being a footballer himself (who earlier played for the local Kumartuli club, but is now in service), Maradona remains his sole inspiration; though, at the time when he (sometimes) goes to the derby matches, he always records them on his cell phone and circulates the media files amongst his friends. Another glaring example of contemporary fan cultures could be the vandalization of the luxury resort named Vedic Village, located in the Calcutta, during August, 2009. Apparently, two local (*para*) rival football teams were enraged and unhappy regarding the results. Thereafter, a more or less benign fight quickly turned enormously violent, as one group chased by another, sought refuge in the Vedic village. The place was eventually burnt down by the huge mob of about seven-hundred people and the incident immediately opened up a series of contradictions imbedded in the processes of post-colonial developments, followed by the recent rapid post-liberalization growth in Calcutta. Clearly, football becomes a dynamic process through which peoples of 'developing nations' can make sense of their own histories, and may intervene through disparate (and sometimes violent) forms of cultural enunciations.[56]

Acknowledgement
Subhransu Roy and Meghdut Rudra.

Notes
1. A different version of this paper was presented at the National Seminar on 'Latin America and Indian Modernities: Self, Exile, Revolution', organized by the Department of Comparative Literature, Jadavpur University, Calcutta, in March 2011.
2. Especially see Sen 'Wiping the Stain Off the Field of Plassey' in which Sen tackles the 'two strands' of the debates on Indian football and society; as well see Majumdar and Bandyopadhyay ' Ghati-Bangal on the Maidan' for a thorough analysis of the club rivalry in Bengal. Also see Bandyopadhyay 'The Nation and Its Fragments', for a study of the Mohammedan Sporting club, and his consistent argument regarding the non-communal/non-religious, yet culturally different position of the clubs.
3. Porat, ''Football fandom', 218.
4. See Majumdar and Bandyopadhyay 'Ghati-Bangal on the Maidan'.
5. See Roy 'Moti Nandyr Kamalye Football'.
6. The following blog mentions how since 1958 fans in Bengal followed the trajectory of Brazil, and it also mentions the anti-colonial ethos, which connects the Latin American countries to India/Bengal. http://www.indianfootballnetwork.com/blog/2011/10/12/kolkata-and-its-passion-for-latino-football/ (accessed October 24, 2012).
7. Visit the fan site www.mohanbaganclub.com for evocative retelling of past victories including the 1905 and 1911 matches, as well as the match with Cosmos. http://www.mohunbaganclub.com/memory_lane_view.php? id=Mw== (accessed September 9, 2012).
8. *Striker* was also filmed in 1978 by Archan Chakraborty.
9. Also see Majumdar 'The Politics of Soccer' for a historical overview.
10. 'Ghoti-Bati' are colloquial expressions, to be explained later. *Foucault's Pendulum* is a reference to the well-known novel by Umberto Eco, published in 1989, in which The Plan/game becomes a reality.
11. Nandy, 'Calcutta Soccer', 317.
12. Chowdhury, *The Frail Hero and Virile History* and Sinha *Colonial Masculinity*.
13. See Gupta, 'Cultures of the Body in Colonial Bengal'. Also note that, the relations between nationalist endeavours and bodily cultures are also connected with other public

cultures and religious festivals including Durga Pujas. Thus, the Simla 'Byam' Samiti (North Calcutta) organizes one of the most popular Durga Pujas in Calcutta.
14. The general category *Bhadralok* is best understood as the 'English Educated Urbanized Gentlemen' whose class, caste, and communal identities were often displaced on to the realm of education and culture. While, they were basically 'educated' to serve the colonial power (in Macaulay's famous words (1835) 'English in taste' and 'Indian in blood'), in the course of time, the *Bhadralok* emerged as a forceful and influential group that resisted colonial exploitations. However, the 'Babu culture' is different from this. It was largely shaped through negotiations with the West that combined somewhat haphazardly with the residual *nawabi* (princely) culture. Moreover, the term *Babu* had many meanings and was added to a name like the pre-fix 'Mister'.
15. Chowdhury, at the International Conference on 'Sport and the Nation' in January 2012 (held at Jadavpur University, Calcutta) mentioned that, there is no historical evidence to support this; nevertheless, one should not overlook the cultural value of this powerful myth.
16. See Bandyopadhyay 'The Nation and Its Fragments'.
17. For instance, National Association, Town Club, Kumartuli, Chandannagar Sporting, Chinsura Sporting came up during this period. Moreover, the Rajas and the princely states, patronized the game with equal zeal. The Sovabazar Raj family, Bhukailas and the Lahas as well as the Maharajas of Coochbehar, Mahisadal and Burdwan supported the cause. See Bandyopadhyay, 'Nationalist Consciousness', 7.
18. Also see Bandyopadhyay '1911 in Retrospect'.
19. The club successively won the Cooch Behar Cup in 1904–1905, as well, the Gladstone Cup in 1905. Also, the Gladstone Cup in 1908 and Cooch Behar Cup in 1907; between 1906 and 1908 it won the Traders Cup.
20. Bandyopadhyay, 'The Nation and Its Fragments', 380.
21. See Sarkar, *Writing Social History* and the function of rumour in historical projects. Therefore, it is not surprising that the Calcutta footballers refused to wear shoes until 1959 (also see Nandy 'Calcutta Soccer').
22. Majumdar and Bandyopadhyay *Social History of Indian Football*.
23. See Bandyopadhyay, 'Nationalist Consciousness', 10.
24. Chatterjee in his paper on 'Football and the Politics of Identity in Colonial Calcutta' presented at the International Conference on 'Sport and the Nation' in January 2012, at Jadavpur University, elaborated on the histories of Mohammedan Sporting club.
25. Bandyopadhyay 'Nationalist Consciousness', 9.
26. Bandyopadhyay's book length work *Scoring off the Field*, is a mammoth addition to this study.
27. From Majumdar, 'The Vernacular in Sports History', 107–25.
28. Also see Sen 'Wiping the Stain Off the Field of Plassey'.
29. See Dimeo ' Football and Politics in Bengal'.
30. See Sarkar, *Writing Social History* and his discussions on the City, 159–85.
31. Reference Sarkar, *Modern India, 1885–1947*.
32. Nevertheless, ironically, in most cases their dialects were suppressed and ridiculed.
33. Also see paintings on this period by Chittoprasad and Somnath Hore.
34. See Ghatak, *Chalachitra Manush Ebong Aro Kichu*.
35. Drawing clearly from the epic *Mahabharat*, in which the exiled Pandavas brothers fight for their land, the idea that the Pandavas are the just group conducting the *Dharma Yudh* (fighting for ideology) against the mighty Kauravas, was also referred to in other popular texts, including a teenaged thriller series named 'Pancha (Five) Pandavas'.
36. See Chatterjee *Bengal Divided*.
37. Also see Gooptu 'Peculiarities of Soccer in Bengali Cinema'.
38. Note, in the same year the National [Indira] Congress lost out at the Centre, during the post-Emergency elections.
39. Chatterjee *Our Modernity* and *A Possible India*.
40. A recent Bengali film *Herbert* (Dir. Suman Mukhopadhyay, 2006) addressed the mutations of the Kolkata cityscape, and acknowledged the heterogeneity of our urban landscapes. More recently, *Sthaniya Sambaad* (Dir. Moinak Biswas and Arjun Gourisaria, 2010) analyses this historical trajectory of development, along with the brutal changes.

Referring back to Ghatak, and shooting in south Kolkata, Biswas and Gourisaria illustrate the everyday of refugee lives, and its vitality despite the instances of under-development.

41. Films by Mrinal Sen namely *Kolkata 71* (1972) and *Padatik* (1973) as well as those by Satyajit Ray, namely *Pratidwandi* (1970) and *Jana Aranya* (1975) remark on this volatile political situation.
42. It must be noted that, politicians in Bengal have been regularly accused of 'politicising' the game. See letter written by Amal Datta addressed to the then Chief Minister Jyoti Basu (as quoted by Kausik Bandyopadhyay 'Social Conflict, Club Rivalry and Fan Culture: Ghoti-bangal in Bengal Football,' 26).
43. Also see Nandy 'Calcutta Soccer'.
44. Refer to Featherstone, *Global Culture, Nationalism, Globalisation and Modernity* for further discussion on global flows.
45. See Kapadia 'Triumphs and Disasters' on the economy and economics of football. As well, note that, Mohun Bagan and East Bengal are at present, supported by brewery companies.
46. See Hughson et al., *The Uses of Sports*.
47. Also see *Maradona* (Dir. Emir Kusturica, 2008).
48. I am especially referring to the Left populist projects like the blood donation camps, and the setting up of Marxist literature stalls during Hindu festivals. Also see Left Word Books publications.
49. Here I am considering the activities of Subhash Chakraborty, the erstwhile Transport Minister as well as Sports and Youth Services Minister of the Left Front Government, and the ways in which he planned popular programmes like 'Hope 86' to raise funds. Chakraborty was also instrumental in inviting Maradona to Calcutta. See a critical review of Chakraborty's activities by a popular daily on- http://www.telegraphindia.com/1080426/jsp/frontpage/story_9190343.jsp (accessed November 23, 2012).
50. Guilianotti, *Football: A Sociology of the Global Game* for discussion of Latin American football.
51. From www.mohanbaganclub.com (accessed August 9, 2012).
52. Peterson *Creating Country Music*.
53. See Mehta, *Television in India*.
54. See Redhead, *Post-fandom and the Millennium Blues*.
55. Note that this particular club, reflecting a common tendency, also followed the IPL cricket matches especially at the time when the Bengali cricketer Saurav Ganguly was involved. 47 Pally also organizes Durga Puja. The interviews were conducted during 2012.
56. Alternately, the huge investments into games as in case of FIFA World Cup in 2010 or the Beijing Olympics in 2008 have inspired artists across the world (like Harun Farocki's 'Deep Play'), who have produced large scale media art.

References

Bandyopadhyay, Kausik. '1911 in Retrospect: A Revisionist Perspective on a Famous Indian Sporting Victory'. *The International Journal of the History of Sport* 21, nos. 3–4 (2004): 363–83.

Bandyopadhyay, Kausik. '"The Nation and Its Fragments": Football and Community in India'. *Soccer & Society* 9, no. 3 (2008): 377–93.

Bandyopadhyay, Kausik. 'Nationalist Consciousness and the Supporting Identity: Football in Swadeshi Bengal', *in 90 Minutes* 1, no. 1 (2009): 5–20.

Bandyopadhyay, Kausik. 'Social Conflict, Club Rivalry and Fan Culture: Ghoti-bangal in Bengal Football', *in 90 Minutes* 2, no. 1(2010): 9–33.

Bandyopadhyay, Kausik. *Scoring Off the Field: Football Culture in Bengal, 1911–80*. New Delhi: Routledge, 2011.

Chatterji, Joya. *Bengal Divided, Hindu communalism and partition, 1932–1947*. Cambridge: Cambridge University Press, 1994.

Chatterjee, Partha. 'A Possible India', in *The Partha Chatterjee. Omnibus*, New Delhi: OUP, 2002.

Chatterjee, Partha. *A Princely Impostor? The Kumar of Bhawal and the Secret History of Indian Nationalism*. Delhi: Permanent Black, 2006.
Chinnamul. Directed by Nemai Ghosh. Kolkata: Desha Pictures, 1950.
Chowdhury, Indira. *The Frail Hero and Virile History*. Delhi: OUP, 1998.
City of God. Directed by Fernando Mei relles. Brazil: Andrea Barata Ribeiro and Mauricio Andrade Ramos, 2002.
Dhanyi Meye. Directed by Arabindo Mukherjee. Kolkata: Sree Productions, 1971.
Dimeo, Paul. 'Football and Politics in Bengal: Colonialism, Nationalism, Communalism'. *Soccer & Society* 2, no. 2 (2001): 57–74.
Featherstone, Mike, ed. *Global Culture, Nationalism, Globalisation and Modernity*. London: Sage, 1999.
Ghatak, Ritwik Kumar. *Chalachitra Manush Ebong Aro Kichu* ['Films, People, and Something More']. Calcutta: Dey's Publishing, 2007.
Gooptu, Sharmistha. 'Peculiarities of Soccer in Bengali Cinema'. *Economic and Political Weekly* 40, no. 1 (2005): 67–71.
Guilianotti, Richard. *Football: A Sociology of the Global Game*. Oxford: Polity, 1999.
Gupta, Abhijit. 'Cultures of the Body in Colonial Bengal: The Career of Gobor Guha'. *The International Journal of the History of Sport* 29, no. 12 (2012): 1687–700.
Herbert. Directed by Suman Mukhopadhyay. Kolkata: Ripples Production (in association with Tritiya Sutra Films), 2006.
Hughson, John David Inglis and Marcus Free. (ed.). *The Uses of Sports, A Critical Study*, London: Routledge, 2005.
Jana Aranya. Directed by Satyajit Ray. Kolkata: Indus Films, 1975.
Kapadia, Novy. 'Triumphs and Disasters: The Story of Indian Football, 1889–2000', *Soccer & Society* 2, no. 2 (2001): 17–40.
Kolkata 71. Directed by Mrinal Sen. Kolkata: D. S. Pictures, 1972.
Majumdar, Boria. 'The Politics of Soccer in Colonial India, 1930–37: The Years of Turmoil'. *Soccer & Society* 3, no. 1 (2002): 22–36.
Majumdar, Boria. 'The Vernacular in Sports History'. *The International Journal of the History of Sport* 20, no. 1 (2003): 107–25.
Majumdar, Boria, and Kausik Bandyopadhyay. 'Ghati-Bangal on the maidan: Subregionalism, club rivalry and fan culture in Indian football'. *Soccer & Society* 6, no. 2–3 (2005): 210–26.
Majumdar, Boria, and Kausik Bandyopadhyay. *Social History of Indian Football, Scoring to Survive*. New York: Routledge, 2006.
Mehta, Nalin, ed. *Television in India, Satellites, politics, and cultural change*. Oxon: Routledge, 2008.
Mohun Baganer Meye. Directed by Monu Sen. Kolkata: Kalimata Productions, 1975.
Nandy, Moti. 'Calcutta Soccer', in *Calcutta, The Living City*, ed. Sukanta Chaudhuri. Vol. II. New Delhi: OUP, 2005, 316–320.
Padatik. Directed by Mrinal Sen. Kolkata: Mrinal Sen Productions, 1973.
Peterson, Richard. *Creating Country Music: Fabricating Authenticity*. Chicago, IL: Chicago University Press, 1997.
Porat, Amir Ben. 'Football Fandom: A Bounded Identification', in *Soccer & Society* 11, no. 3 (2010): 277–90.
Pratidwandi. Directed by Satyajit Ray. Kolkata: Priya Films, 1970.
Redhead, S. *Post-fandom and the Millennium Blues*. London: Routledge, 1997.
Roy, Paramita. 'Moti Nandyr Kamalye Football' [Football as penned by Moti Nandy], *90 Minutes* 1, no. 4 (2009): 65–72.
Sarkar, Sumit. *Modern India, 1885–1947*. Delhi: Macmillan India Ltd., 1984.
Saptapadi. Directed by Ajar Kar. Kolkata: Alocchaya Productions, 1961.
Sarkar, Sumit. *Writing Social History*. Delhi: OUP, 1997.
Sen, Dwaipayan. 'Wiping the Stain Off the Field of Plassey: Mohun Bagan in 1911'. *Soccer & Society* 7, no. 2–3 (2006): 208–32.
Sinha, Mrinalini. *Colonial Masculinity: The Manly Englishman and the Effeminate Bengali in the Late Nineteenth Century*. Manchester, NH: Manchester University Press, 1995.
Sthaniya Sambaad. Directed by Moinak Biswas and Arjun Gourisaria. Mumbai: Black Magic Motion Picture Pvt. Ltd, 2010.

'Hope for the win and hope for the defeat': constructions of South Korean identity and the 2010 FIFA World Cup

Miyoung Oh

Department of Sport, Sheffield Hallam University, Sheffield, UK

This article critically examines South Korean identity with a case study of the 2010 FIFA World Cup. Since identity is constructed through commonalities shared by group members and also through difference created by the 'Other', this article aims to explore the double-edged nature of identity construction. Smith claims common traditions, history, cultures and memories as key components in the formation of national identity with an emphasis on ethnicity. This article seeks to examine South Koreans' attempts to establish or maintain such commonalities to come to terms with who they are. Conversely, Hall suggests that identity is constructed through the 'Other'. In this regard, an examination of South Korea's relationships with its neighbouring countries, notably North Korea and Japan, is requisite. The 'Othering' processes of these countries are similar and dissimilar in many aspects. This article aims to explore these processes by focusing on the intricate workings of ethnic and postcolonial identities in the construction of South Korean identity.

Introduction

Smith claims that a sense of national identity helps people define and locate their individual selves in the world. In other words, 'through the prism of the collective personality and its distinctive culture' and 'through a shared, unique culture', people come to understand 'who they are'.[1] Defining the 'collective personality' of a nation is invariably a complex matter. South Koreans' distinctive culture and their coming to terms with who they are also defy a simple account. South Koreans are proud of their five-thousand–year-old national history, through which they have demonstrated their peace-loving, harmonious, humble and hard-working nature.

While South Koreans become distinguished on the basis of qualities such as these, the confrontation with North Korea compels one to consider additional insights into South Koreanness. Since the partition of the Korean peninsular into South and North Koreas in 1948, 'South' Korean identity, which was previously non-existent, had to be created and has since been defined primarily by not being 'North' Korean. It is, however, never clear-cut due to the ethnic ties between South and North Koreans. All these points to the intersection of national and ethnic identities, which provide the foundation for 'pan-Korean identification', which I discuss elsewhere.[2] This in turn explains South Koreans' support for North Koreans in international sporting events. In addition, as typically depicted as aggressive and antagonistic towards South Korea (and former united Korea) in South Korean history, Japan is paramount in its influence on the construction of South Korean identity. Japan invaded Korea repeatedly throughout history and colonized it for 35 years in the early twentieth century. Moreover, contemporary political controversies between South Korea and Japan surrounding the ownership of an inhabited island Dokdo and Japan's history books have solidified Japan as a foe. Furthermore, Japan helps South Koreans confirm their ethnic ties with North Koreans, which is often manifested through their support of North Korea in international sport competitions.

International sporting events provide an important platform to unearth people's understanding of themselves and their nation through their collective dreams, values and fears. Since their creation in the late nineteenth and early twentieth century, international sporting contests have compelled people to locate themselves and their nation in the wider world beyond their own and (re)construct their collective identities in the global context.[3] The FIFA World Cup, in this regard, offers an arena to investigate the construction of national identity, since the tournaments bring out and foreground people's emotions, hopes and anxieties. In particular, the 2010 FIFA World Cup Finals held in South Africa offered a unique opportunity to investigate the character of South Korean identity in that, while South Korea and Japan took part in it as two frequent participants in the Finals, it was North Korea's first appearance since 1966, thereby commanding intense media interest worldwide. With the three countries' participation, the tournament helps explore South Korea's fears, pride, disappointment, dreams and hopes in relation to its neighbours. Identity is constructed through commonalities shared by group members and simultaneously through difference created by the 'Other'. This article aims to examine the ways in which South Koreans produce shared memories and also differentiate themselves from North Koreans and the Japanese, specific to the 2010 World Cup Finals. This will in turn illuminate how they come to terms with who they are and the character of South Korean identity.

Methods

This article explores South Koreans' subjective perceptions of who they are and who they want to become. In particular, it critically examines individual accounts of common features that bind them together of being South Korean. It also uncovers their views of North Korea and Japan, all of which display the way they construct their national identity. Accordingly, qualitative methods were deemed most appropriate and specifically, focus group interviews were employed for the study. The interview participants were identified through 'networking' or 'snowball technique', which usually starts out with contacting the researcher's friends and/or acquaintances, who then recruit a specified number of people as participants who conform to certain specified characteristics.[4] The characteristics for the current study were being ethnically Korean men and women in their 20s and 30s with interests in football. Five group interviews, totalling 18 individuals, were conducted in Seoul, South Korea, during the 2010 World Cup. The participants consisted of all ethnically Korean males and females aged between 25 and 39. All of them were also enthusiastic about the World Cup Finals and had followed the previous Finals. The interviews were carried out in quiet meeting rooms available in cafes or participants' companies, and lasted between an-hour-and-a-half and two-hour. The participants' identities are disguised in this article to honour their rights to privacy.

Construction of national identity: group membership

Weeks and Hetherington suggest that identities are fundamentally about belonging.[5] If so, one can have numerous groups, affiliations or communities that s/he feels or establishes a particular sense of belonging to. One notable community is the nation. In fact, because of immense influence the nation has exerted on the modern world, the nation has been 'one of the most discussed concepts in modern social and political thought'.[6] However, conceptualizing the nation has become notoriously difficult and evasive because nations exist in a great diversity of forms and configurations, constantly changing and reinventing themselves.[7] Nevertheless, endeavours to theorize the nation have been ceaseless in academia as have debates around national identity.[8]

Identity is commonly argued to be double-edged. That is, it requires commonalities shared by group members and simultaneously difference created by the 'Other'. In arguing this, Hall argues that Englishness necessitates the existence of the 'Other' such as the French and the German, and their allegedly associated characteristics,[9] thereby, stressing the significance of the 'Other' in identity formation. Similarly, Triandafyllidou maintains the double-edged character of national identity. She asserts that, on the one hand, national identity emphasizes 'a set of common features that bind members of the nation together' and on the other hand, it underlines difference, through which a nation seeks to differentiate itself from the 'Other'.[10]

Anderson's well-known definition of the nation as 'an imagined community' is one that focuses on common features shared amongst group members.[11] According to him, individual cognition of imagination, through the aid of media technologies and capitalism, enables members of a community to confirm that same or similar life styles, traditions, customs and daily routines are observed, adhered to and replicated amongst people residing in different locations. This confirmation plays a vital role in convincing them that they collectively form a community, which is a nation. Smith also foregrounds the importance of shared sense of history, traditions, memories and myths as fundamental components of the nation.[12] Both Anderson and Smith heed attention to the significance of commonalities in the formation of the nation, and yet they differ in many regards, one of which is Smith's emphasis on ethnicity. He claims that memories, myths, symbols and traditions of the dominant ethnie come to represent the nation, finding their places in the consciousness of the majority of the population, thereby contributing to the construction of national identity.

Shared 'selected' memories and construction of South Korean identity

The interviewees' narratives demonstrate their conscious and deliberate efforts to construct their national identity in a particular manner. One such occasion is through their selective memories. The 2002 World Cup, which was co-hosted by South Korea and Japan, is cherished by all the interviewees as a historic moment in the (re)making of South Korean identity. They are proud of street celebrations and electrifying festival atmospheres, which shook many corners of the nation throughout the 2002 Finals, and indeed, all of the participants associate the 2002 event with positive images such as fun, harmonious, dynamic, cheerful, friendly and glorious. Moreover, many interviewees connect these spirits to South Korea's ancient traditions, customs and way of life, thus maintaining the historical roots of these qualities. A female participant, Jaelim, represents one such voice. Fondly recalling her 2002 memories, she asserts that 'we [South] Koreans have always been generous, dynamic, peace-loving and fun-loving. It is in our DNA'. In her mind, the images of street parties and high-spirited festivities during each World Cup tournament are manifestations of 'who we have always been'.

Additionally, the 2002 World Cup is unanimously treasured by the interviewees, due to the achievement of the South Korean football team. South Korea was an unexpected semi-finalist, and to some this had a meaning transcending success in football. A female interviewee, Sungyun, seeks to locate the significance of the success in a wider context. South Korea underwent economic crisis, which hit Asia hard in the late 1990s, and this is when she was studying in Canada. She remembers vividly the sense of despair, humiliation and hopelessness she felt back then. She recalls, 'Our currency and our national reputation plummeted, and I was so terrified, confused and humiliated'. The 2002 World Cup came to the rescue. South Korea successfully hosted the global event, and furthermore, the South Korean squad advanced to the semi-finals. For Sungyun, the 2002 event is meaningful and precious because 'just coming out of such a national disaster and humiliation, it showcased national solidarity and potential to ourselves and the world'. The 2002 tournament turned her into a football fan and she has since been following the national team, emotionally attached to them, identifying their successes and failures as her own. This explains why she personally felt embarrassed and dejected when Argentina saw South Korea off by a defeat of 4-1 in South Africa in 2010.

Smith maintains that 'it is because we know that our interests, indeed our very identities and survival, are bound up with the nation, that we feel such devotion to the nation'.[13] Jaelim's and Sungyun's narratives beg similar questions. What makes members of a nation feel that their own destiny is intimately bound up with that of their nation's? How can this deep sense of identification be explained? Smith argues that the concept of the nation is 'felt, and felt passionately, as something very real, a concrete community',[14] which assures our own place in the world. The World Cup helps Jaelim and Sungyun to *feel* the nation, which may otherwise remain abstract and also helps them come to terms with who they are and their place in relation to other South Koreans and also to the world.

As noted above, interview participants paint their 2002 memories overwhelmingly favourably. They also highly praise the national team's performance in the 2010 World Cup, where South Korea advanced to the second round. Interestingly, in their narratives, some World Cup Finals are conspicuously absent: the ones prior to 2002 and the 2006 German tournament. This suggests the political dimension of identity construction. It is not an exaggeration to claim that South Koreans' interests in football and the World Cup sparked largely in 2002, when South Korea co-hosted the Finals with Japan. In this regard, widespread disinterest in football before 2002 may account for the absence of interviewees' comments relating to the World Cup up to 1998. However, it is striking that the 2006 event also escapes their attention. The South Korean team did not fare well in Germany as they were sent packing in the first round. That the interviewees 'neglected' the 2006 event is an understatement as there was a conscious effort on their part to forget that tournament. Identity is constructed through deliberate inclusion and exclusion, therefore, this 'forgotten' World Cup plays a crucial role in constructing South Korean identity. When pointed out about their silence on the German World Cup, the interviewees blamed the national team's poor performance for it. A female participant, Taemin, justifies the absence of any mentioning of the 2006 tournament in her enthusiastic World Cup story by claiming that '[there was] so much contrast to the previous one' referring to the success in 2002. Changsoo, a male interviewee, also rationalizes his silence by posing a question, 'Why do we bring it up? Why do we want to talk about something we didn't do well?' The 2006 World Cup is 'forgotten' or 'unspeakable' because it failed to repeat the triumphs of the previous World Cup and tarnished their glorious 2002 World Cup memories. It can be then interpreted as their attempt to protect their own self- and national esteem and remain proud, successful and glorious. Interviewees' conscious efforts to 'un-recognize' the pre-2002 Finals and the German World Cup are a demonstration of identity politics.

All these stories about football, offered by interviewees, unravel the process of a nation-making: the construction of national narratives of South Koreanness. Smith asserts that symbols, myths, routines, values and memories, customs and traditions make up the complex community of the nation.[15] On the other hand, Hobsbawm's conceptualization of the nation is intricately related to 'invented traditions'.[16] He argues that today, 'old' traditions are expected to be replaced with 'new' traditions more rapidly than in the past, when they appear no longer adequate or appropriate. The World Cup Finals provide opportunities to reinforce 'old' national symbols, routines, values and memories, and also create 'new' ones.

Many interviewees remark how they enjoy the World Cup, what routines and practices they usually perform and in what ways those are uniquely South Korean. How did South Koreans entertain themselves and support their national team before 2002? Interestingly, no one seems to remember, and their football and/or World Cup stories and memories invariably begin with the 2002 Finals. The 'Be the Reds' T-shirts, which since 2002, has been established as the 'national' uniform that South Koreans wear in international sporting scenes is a case in point. Most interviewees fondly recall purchasing the T-shirts for themselves and their family and friends. The T-shirt appears to be a 'must-have' item for them, which confirms their active identification of being South Korean and their emotional attachment to the nation. So are gigantic screens that are set up in major cities across the nation during the Finals, the subsequent public congregations, the festivities and street celebrations, all of which have become 'new' World Cup traditions since 2002. Joori, a female professional, for example, has been an ardent fan of such public spectatorship and street parties since 2002. During the 2010 World Cup, she and her husband in the 'national' uniform with their faces decorated with national symbols frequented City Hall Plaza, one of the main public viewing points in Seoul and entertained themselves day and night whenever South Korea played. She enthuses how mesmerizing and addictive it is to sing and chant with tens of thousands of South Koreans in support of the national team, and how intoxicating it is to join street parties afterwards. She is eager to explain how in joining the crowd she feels free, uninhabited and individualistic, and at the same time a sense of collective identity as South Korean.

Experiences and images such as these have been told and retold over the years across the nation through people's narratives and various media outlets. Along the way, some 'old' symbols, routines and practices have been reemphasized or repackaged as authentically South Korean, and some 'newly invented' components have been introduced as distinctively expressive of South Koreanness. Together, they have become solidified as South Koreans' way of life at each World Cup Finals, seeping into their consciousness about who they are or who they have become individually and collectively. As noted above, interviewees' identities are partly built upon their historical sense of customs, traditions, rituals and memories. Simultaneously, 'invented' traditions play a crucial role in the construction of modern-day South Korean identity. The FIFA World Cup is thus a significant platform, in which the 'old' and 'new' symbols and rituals are played out and practiced, which greatly contributes to the construction of South Korean character, morality and capabilities, and which helps South Koreans to come to terms with their identity in relation to other South Koreans and the world.

North Korea as 'an enemy unable to hate' – blurring boundaries of group membership

As discussed above, national identity requires commonalities that are shared by members of the nation. The assertion of in-group commonalities as integral ingredients of national character, however, is a complex one for South Korean identity. It is because much of South Koreans' national history, traditions, memories and customs are shared by North Koreans. Sarup underscores the process of labelling as one element of identity construction.[17] People attach certain labels to others, which have an effect on both parties involved. South Korea's latest Defence White Paper officially labels North Korea as its enemy. Nevertheless, due to the five-millennia-long history of the two Koreas as a united nation, many South Koreans' perceptions of North Koreans are incongruent with the government's official designation. As revealed through this study, North Korea is commonly viewed in familial terms such as 'a sister country' (Jungeun) or 'a family that is temporarily separated' (Sooji). Thus, one commonality the majority of the interviewees share is their emotional attachment to North Koreans.

Smith claims that ethnicity is a powerful force that binds people together.[18] For symbols, customs, routines, habits, rituals and traditions to be able to mobilise people, he argues, they have to resonate with the majority of the population. That is, symbols, way of life, history and traditions of the dominant ethnic group come to represent the nation, and a sense of cultural intimacy becomes a powerful driving force that binds people of various classes and interests. As such, ethnic ties are a basis for a sense of cultural intimacy, which is integral to the formation of a nation. This is a useful theoretical tool that helps analyse South Koreans' emotional ties to North Koreans and their concerns for North Koreans' well-being.

On the other hand, due to the petitioning of the Korean peninsular in 1948, much of South Koreans' memories and stories of North Korea defines it as South Korea's 'Other', which has been influential in constructing South Korean identity. Hall notes that the presence of the 'Other' is essential in the meaning-making processes as it provides the vital ingredients to create 'difference'.[19] In other words, it is the 'difference' that marks, signifies and carries meaning, which is produced by the 'Other'. Similarly, Barker emphasises the role of the 'Other' in identity formation when he asserts that 'what we think of as our identity is dependent on what we think we are *not*'.[20] Furthermore, in her analysis of national identity, Triandafyllidou foregrounds the role of 'significant others', from which the in-group members become distinguished and form solidarity, and from which the nation seeks to differentiate itself.[21] This implies that 'national identity has no meaning per se'; instead, 'it becomes meaningful in contrast to other nations'.[22] According to her, 'others' become significant when they are perceived as threat to a nation's survival, identities, distinctiveness, authenticity and/or independence; thus, they influence the development of a nation's identities. As Triandafyllidou argues, each nation has more than one nation or ethnic group that becomes its significant other, and for South Korea, one such significant other is North Korea. Hence, interrogating the part North Korea has played since the division in 1948 is vital in understanding what constitutes South Koreanness and what it means to be South Korean because North Korea clarifies what South Koreanness is not and what South Koreans are not.

How the 'Other' is represented is, then, the key to identity formation. On this, Said directs attention to political and ideological manufacturing of images of the 'Other'.[23] Underscoring the West's political and ideological construction and manipulation of stereotypes of the Orient as the 'Other', he asserts that the West has done so in order to create its own identity. He argues that notions of racial hierarchies emerged at the same time as Euro Western colonialism, such as Britain and France, but more significantly, ideas about the physical, mental and sexual status of non-Europeans were set against definitions of whiteness. In other words, 'the Orient has helped to define Europe (or the West) as its contrasting images, idea, personality, experience',[24] and thus, depicting the Orient in a particular way is an effective way of constructing the identity of the West. Applying Said, it can be argued that the contemporary popular stereotypes of 'the Arab' as irrational, menacing, untrustworthy and dishonest function to construct the West as having opposite qualities, which enables it to claim racial, moral and political superiority. This highlights that in the business of representations, power plays a key role. Said also points out the West's comprehensive and concerted efforts to produce and disseminate 'discourses' on stereotypes of the Orient and the way in which those stereotypes have become known as the 'reality' of the Orient in the West, shaping an understanding of the Orient as the 'Other'.

A strong sense of ethnic ties to North Koreans is found in the majority of interviews. It is telling in part because the interviews took place only five months after the Cheonam incident. In March 2010, a torpedo reportedly fired by a North Korean submarine sank a South Korean navy ship, Cheonam, causing 46 causalities. As one of the deadliest incidents between the two Koreas since the end of the Korean War in 1953, it has evoked in South Koreans a deep sense of grief and resentment towards North Korea. Political tension on the Korean peninsula had sharply risen since the conservative Lee Myung-bak administration came into power in South Korea in December 2007. In stark contrast to the two previous governments, the Lee administration has taken hard-line policies in its dealings with the North, which has led to frosty relations between the two Koreas politically and economically. In such political climates, the Cheonam incident has added another layer of antagonism towards North Korea.

It was in this particular context when the 2010 World Cup Finals were hosted in South Africa, and when the interviews for this research were undertaken. Yet, the interviewees lend great support for the North Korean football team taking part in the World Cup. Most of the interviewees display their political and intellectual maturity by distinguishing the politics from ordinary North Koreans, who they perceive as victims of North Korea's dictatorship. A female participant, Junga, emphatically labels the Cheonam incident as 'political' and firmly holds North Korean leadership accountable for it. In her eyes, however, North Korean footballers and ordinary North Koreans are a completely different matter. Accordingly, she separates them from North Korea's political leaders and their politics. She is assertive that the Cheonam attack did not change her views on North Koreans and that she still feels emotionally connected to them. It is this sentiment that she uses to justify her support for North Korea at the 2010 World Cup.

A male interviewee's account for his support of North Korea is equally compelling and shines light on the complexity of South Korean identity. The great majority of South Korean men must undertake military service for about two years. At the time of the interview, it has been only a few years since Namsoo completed his military obligation. In the interview, he recalls receiving an emergency text message from the army immediately after the Cheonam incident took place. He recounts that the message stated that he might be called into the army, if the tension between South and North Koreas was to escalate. He had to comply, otherwise he would be sent to prison for disobedience. He also recalls training sessions, which he had to attend on Wednesday evenings while on military service. In one session, he and his comrades were questioned as to who South Korea's main enemy was, to which most people including him named the USA, only to be corrected. They were told that it was North Korea. Despite such 'education' for two years, he admits that he is 'gravitated to watch their [North Korean] games and support them'. He adds that 'it's not just me. All of my [male] friends are like me. They all support North Korea'. He then remembers how distressed and sorry he felt for North Korea while watching the team crushed by Portugal by 7-0. He finds it difficult to rationalize his emotional attachment to North Korea, but says he cannot help it. Just like Junga quoted above, he claims that the Cheonam incident does not and should not define the relationship between South and North Koreas. For him too, it was all political and had nothing to do with ordinary North Koreans.

Most of the interviewees claim that they have never considered North Korea the 'Other' despite the official view of it as South Korea's enemy. Sarup maintains that identities are influenced by events or actions in the past and consequences of these and that they are also influenced by how these events or actions are interpreted retrospectively.[25] In arguing this, he emphasizes the co-existence of determining forces beyond individuals' control and individual agency as a critical element of identity construction. The Cheonam incident as a historic event, offers an opportunity to interview participants to rethink their perceptions of North Koreans, and moreover, their own identities in relation to them.

Furthermore, Smith claims that a sense of national belonging compels people to recognize that their destiny is bound up with that of their nation. It is understandable, then, that Yura feels personally humiliated when South Korea lost to Argentina by a big margin, 4-1. Surprisingly, she insists that she felt the same degree of humiliation when North Korea was defeated 7–0 by Portugal. This experience has confirmed her personal belief that 'we [South and North] are the same people'. She further confesses that 'however mean and malicious they are to us, I feel very sympathetic for them [North Koreans]' because 'we [South and North Koreans] are one family, one nation'. Her sense of identity, which is inclusive of North Koreans, is grounded upon the long history shared by the two Koreas. In her own words, 'the past 60 years of the separation is nothing because we [South and North Koreans] had spent much longer together as one people, one nation'. This historical root forms the basis of her perceptions of who she is and who North Koreans are to her, which makes it impossible for her to view North Korea as the 'Other'.

The majority of interviewees' support for the North Korean team was based on their sense of history, traditions, myths, memories, cultural intimacy and most crucially, ethnic ties to North Koreans, and confirms 'pan-Korean identification', which I discuss elsewhere.[26] This identification evokes pan-Korean nationalism and produces pan-Korean identity. As such, it expands South Koreans' available identity choices. On the other hand, this research also reveals that North Korea is simultaneously perceived as the 'Other', which serves to articulate South Koreanness. It also shows interviewees' claims for moral, cultural, economic and political superiority, which distinguishes them from North Koreans.

During the 2010 World Cup, there were media and public allegations concerning the North Korean squad's safety. Some media outlets have reported that harsh punishment awaits the coaches and the players, if they perform poorly at the tournament. Indeed, in South Africa, the North Korea's records were dismal with three defeats in the first round: 2-1 to Brazil, 7-0 to Portugal and 3-0 to Côte d'Ivoire. Many interviewees appear genuinely concerned about the wellbeing of the North Korean team. A female participant, Eunjung, is troubled by the speculation that as punishment, they may be sent to Aoji coal mine in North Korea, which is notorious for physical and mental abuse and hardship. Another interviewee, Younghee's comment sheds further light on her sense of identification with North Koreans. She recounts that she stopped watching the North Korea vs. Portugal game at 4-0 as she found it too heartbreaking to watch any longer. She says that she was in tears and felt extremely sorry for the players. She is disturbed by media suggestions that they may be severely punished for their poor results. She also names the infamous Aoji coal mine as their potential destination once they return to North Korea. Some other participants express their worries about North Korean players' allegedly poor nutrition, health and training regimes. For example, Yuna wonders 'if they are well fed', a concern that would almost certainly never be raised in relation to South Korean players and those from the West. What is assumed here is extreme poverty and famine, which stereotypically defines North Korea in South Korea's and the West's popular discourses.

In these narratives, North Korean society is depicted as irrational, barbaric, threatening, dangerous, inhumane, intolerant, poor and poverty-stricken. By portraying it as such, South Korea is implicitly defined as being rational, reasonable, civilized, cultured, safe, humane, understanding, healthy and wealthy. This is a powerful way of claiming South Korea's moral, cultural, economic and political superiority. In his argument on Orientalism, Said maintains that Orientalism is a discursive 'reality' in which the actual Orient is absent and rather presented by the West.[27] Significantly, this emphasizes one's power to narrate and block those of others from emerging.[28] On a similar note, actual North Korea is absent in popular discourses of North Korea, which is almost entirely produced by non-North Korean media. Thus, what has been feeding the interviewees' imagination is the non-North Korean media's speculations with respect to the destiny of the North Korean squad. These, in turn, function to construct South Korean identity in a way that it is meaningfully different from, and superior to, that of North Korea.

'I want Japan to lose no matter what': Japan and postcolonial identity

As discussed above, ethnic ties, history, traditions and cultures are binding forces that compel interview participants to feel attached to North Koreans, and at the same time, North Korea serves to construct South Koreanness by helping them articulate who they are not. Japan plays a similar role to that of North Korea in that it helps South Koreans define their identities as not being Japanese. Resentment and antagonism towards Japan prevail amongst many South Koreans and mobilize them to stand together against the 'old' foe. Hall's theorization of the relations between the past and the present offers an insight into the understanding of post-colonial consciousness. He considers identity a 'production', which is never complete, always in process, and is always constituted within representation.[29] Representation of historical relations between (former united) Korea and Japan is responsible for instilling in South Koreans hostility and a sense of bitterness towards the neighbouring country. Specifically, South Koreans are taught that throughout (Korean) history, Koreans encountered numerous invasions from Japan, against whom they fought and defended their people, culture and nation. They are taught that during the Japanese annexation in the early twentieth century, Koreans were forcefully united to preserve their language, traditions, ethnicity and culture and that many sacrificed their lives to regain the sovereignty of their nation. Japan is thus South Korea's 'significant other', in Triandafyllidou's term,[30] who had threatened to extinguish Korea and Koreans from the global map and history. In these fights, Koreans were united, helping to explain interviewees' emotional connection to North Koreans.

Furthermore, the popular perception of Japan as an enemy has become intensified in South Korea over recent years because of a series of political controversies between the two countries triggered by Japan's claim of ownership of an uninhabited island Dokdo, located in East Sea. This, along with its distortion of colonial history, is argued to reveal its unapologetic attitudes towards atrocities it committed on Koreans (and other Asians) during its colonial rule. For these reasons, Japan is undoubtedly perceived as South Korea's 'significant other', helping South Koreans come to terms with who they are and who they want to become. Said claims that 'past and present inform each other, each implies the other and... each co-exists with the other. Neither past nor present ... has a complete meaning alone'.[31] Historical accounts of relations, along with current political controversies, between South Korea and Japan enable South Koreans to see themselves with pride as peace-loving people, who have never invaded other nations, as honest and responsible with integrity, resilient, nationalistic and respectful of other nations, all of which are antithetical to the meaning of Japan and being Japanese.

History and contemporary political conflicts between South Korea and Japan offer a glimpse into the majority of interviewees' resentment and fierce rivalry with Japan in and beyond sport. Unlike her sentiment towards North Korea, Minhee declares that ambiguity has no place in defining what Japan is and pronounces it as 'our arch enemy and perennial rival'. North Korea frequently provokes South Korea, exemplified by the Cheonam attack. Yet, most interviewees refuse to antagonize North Koreans. On the other hand, Japan's provocations, such as its challenge to South Korea's sovereign power on Dokdo and its glossing over the colonial past, are perceived very differently. Keesuk, a male participant, defends his resentment by insisting that 'while North Korea provokes the South Korean government, Japan provokes South Korean people. This is the difference between them. The Japanese wind us up and get on our nerves'.

Most interviewees' competitive edge over Japan has its roots, which they share collectively under the name of being South Korean. Doyun's account and sentiment represent their voices. She locates her animosity and rivalry primarily in the colonial history. She explains, 'because we were colonised, we always try to overcome a sense of inferiority to Japan'. Japan is, for her, a nation that invokes in her 'a sense of inferiority'. Here, she is identifying the humiliation of her nation as her own as if it were an indelible scar in her on a personal level. This conveys a deep sense of identification with her nation which Smith emphatically stresses as an integral element that constitutes a nation.[32] Accordingly, for Doyun, South Korea's triumphs and Japan's losses in international sporting events are symbolic showcases of her nation's superiority over Japan. For this reason, she has nervously watched most of Japan matches and rejoiced at its defeats. At the 2010 World Cup, South Korea failed in the second round ahead of Japan's attempt to reach the quarter-final stage against Paraguay. Accordingly, it was crucial for Doyun that the Japanese team should fail too, which it did eventually. Another interviewee, Taemin, watched this game with tens of thousands of people at Jong-ro, one of the major public viewing points in downtown Seoul. She recalls that virtually everyone at that place went wild with joy when Japan missed the crucial penalty shootout and lost the match. Doyun, Taemin and many other interviewees profess that they had no wishes to see Japan as the sole Asian participant in the quarter-final stage.

Sugden and Tomlinson argue that 'the place and meaning of football in a society can vary widely'. 'It is', they claim, 'open to cultural and political forms of appropriation. It can mean different things in different places'.[33] South Korea's records in international football, as well as those of Japan's, have been closely monitored and analysed by interviewees, since they interpret them as an indicator of their nation's superiority over Japan. Arguably, South Korea's records excel those of Japan. Since the mid-twentieth century, South Korea has dominated Asian football and formed a degree of football supremacy in the region.[34] In addition, South Korea has represented Asia in eight times at the FIFA World Cup Finals: in Switzerland in 1954, Mexico in 1986, Italy in 1990, America in 1994, France in 1998, Germany in 2006, South Africa in 2010, and as a co-host in 2002. This makes South Korea one of the most frequent World Cup Finals participants. It is not only this number that bolsters interviewees' national pride. It is also the fact that South Korea holds some of Asia's best records in international football: a semi-finalist at the FIFA U-20 World Cup in 1983 (known as World Youth Championship till 2005) and the World Cup Finals in 2002.

With these records, as Manzenreiter and Horne point out, 'the consciousness of being Asia's football powerhouse is still prevalent among large parts of the population in South Korea'.[35] Such consciousness enables a male participant Namsoo to proudly declare that 'Japanese football is inferior to ours. It is a league behind us'. Most participants admit that they are relieved to see South Korea's World Cup Finals record remained intact in South Africa so that they could retain a sense of supremacy over Japan. Archetti claims that success at international sporting events symbolizes something special for a nation and that it is hailed as a 'landmark for a nation's capability and potential not only in football but also in other spheres'.[36] FIFA also emphasizes 'its significance as a barometer of international relations'.[37] If football, indeed, serves as a 'landmark for a nation's capability and potential' and a 'barometer of international relations', it could suggest that with great capability and potential South Korea assumes leadership in Asia's international relations. Furthermore, this could mean much more since it potentially symbolizes the inversion of power relations between the former colonizer and colonized. Vidacs argues that victories of the former colonised nation over its former colonizer could signify the inversion of power relations between them, although temporarily.[38] This helps in explaining the rivalry between England and India and England and Ireland in sport. South Korea did not play Japan in South Africa in 2010, but the interviewees' ardent interests in Japan's matches and their hopes for its losses can be interpreted as their desire for symbolic inversion of power relations between the two countries and to demonstrate their national superiority to the Japanese, the world and themselves.

During the 2010 World Cup, the South Korean media have promoted the 'pan-Asian identification' by promoting Japan's success as Asia's pride. Prior to South Korea's defeat in the round of 16, the media entertained the potential possibility of having two Asian teams, South Korea and Japan, in the quarter-finals, which is unprecedented in World Cup history. After South Korea's fall, Japan was portrayed, by some media, as Asia's hope and pride. Such favourable media depictions of Japan shock and displease many interviewees. Jaesun is astonished to hear about a media report that South Koreans wish for Japan's progress to the quarter-finals. She is suspicious of the report and refuses to believe it. She then defines it as media propaganda, which is far removed from most South Koreans' sentiments. Otherwise, she is unable to comprehend the report. Another interviewee, Joori, reluctantly concedes that Japan's success may be Asia's pride, but she firmly declares that 'I personally do not want to see it. I do not want Asia's reputation to be elevated by Japan. I rather it isn't'. Hall maintains that our cultural identity can be understood in terms of 'positioning', produced by the narratives of the past, and concludes that it is only from this that the trauma of the colonial experience can be properly comprehended.[39] This research unravels participants' post-colonial consciousness as being integral to their identity, and the production of interplay between history, culture and power.

Conclusion

This research has revealed how history, cultures, customs and memories form the foundation for national identity. These research findings may seem to suggest that South Korean identity is static, fixed and complete. However, it should be clarified that interviewees expressed a variety of opinions of South Koreanness, North Korea and Japan, many of which suggested fluidity of South Korean identity, which warrants further research. In this article, nevertheless, focus has been on the 'Othering' processes in relation to North Korea and Japan, and this means that what is presented throughout the article is not exclusive in interviewees' perceptions of these countries. Indeed, Said asserts that cultures are far from being unitary or monolithic and they assume more 'foreign' elements and differences than they consciously exclude.[40] In fact, foreign cultures in contemporary South Korean society, are so deeply imbedded that it is hard, if not impossible, to distinguish them from allegedly 'authentic' South Korean culture. Also, their impact on the society is immeasurable. All of this inevitably affects the character of South Koreanness. In this regard, Hall's claim for cultural identity as 'becoming', as well as of 'being', which undergoes constant transformation,[41] is illuminating. Today, South Korea is multicultural with over a million foreign employees and numerous foreigners settled or naturalized for varied reasons, who have established and normalized 'new' ways of life, 'new' practices and 'new' customs in society, which in turn modifies the characteristics of South Koreanness. Similarly, interviewees' views of North Korea and Japan were diverse. Many participants expressed strong ethnic ties to North Koreans and antagonism towards Japan, but some of them did not share such unambiguous, straightforward perceptions and sentiments, as they considered North Korea as their 'significant other' and Japan as their major political and economic ally. Needlessly to say, South Korea's relations with North Korea and Japan are in constant re-making in relation to socio-cultural and political environments. This significantly affects the nature of South Koreanness. As Hall claims, identity is thus a process or a journey, and is never complete.

Notes

1. Smith, *National Identity*, 17.
2. Oh, *Sport, Nation, Nationalism;* 'Eternal Other Japan'.
3. Maguire, *Global Sport*.
4. Arber, 'Designing Samples'.
5. Weeks, 'The Value of Difference' and Hetherington, *Expressions of Identity*.
6. Bairner, *Sport, Nationalism and Globalisation*, 2.
7. Triandafyllidou, 'National Identity and the "other"'.
8. Anderson, *Imagined Communities*; Gellner, *Nations and Nationalism*; Hastings, *The Construction of Nationhood;* Hobsbawm, 'Introduction: Inventing traditions'; *Nations and Nationalism Since 1780*; Smith, 'Towards a Global Culture?'; *National Identity; Nationalism and Modernism* and Triandafyllidou, 'National Identity and the "other"'.
9. Hall, *Representation*.
10. Triandafyllidou, 'National Identity and the "Other"', 599.
11. Anderson, *Imagined Communities*.
12. Smith, *Nationalism and Modernism*.
13. Smith, *Nationalism and Modernism*, 140.
14. Smith, *Nationalism and Modernism*, 140.
15. Smith, *Nationalism and Modernism*.
16. Hobsbawm, 'Introduction: Inventing Traditions'.
17. Sarup, *Identity, Culture and the Postmodern World*.
18. Smith, *Nationalism and Modernism*.
19. Hall, *Representation*.
20. Barker, *Cultural Studies: Theory and Practice*, 195.
21. Triandafyllidou, 'National Identity and the "Other"'.
22. Triandafyllidou, 'National Identity and the "Other"', 599.
23. Said, *Orientalism*.
24. Said, *Orientalism*, 2.
25. Sarup, *Identity, Culture and the Postmodern World*.
26. Oh, *Sport, Nation, Nationalism*; 'Eternal Other Japan'.
27. Said, *Orientalism*.
28. Said, *Culture and Imperialism*.
29. Hall, 'Cultural Identity and Diaspora', 222.
30. Triandafyllidou, 'National Identity and the "Other"'.
31. Said, *Culture and Imperialism*, 4.
32. Smith, *Nationalism and Modernism*.
33. Sugden and Tomlinson, 'Football and FIFA', 195.
34. Lee, 'The Development of Football in Korea'.
35. Manzenreiter and Horne, 'Global Governance', 18.
36. Archetti, 'In Search of National Identity', 214.
37. Sugden and Tomlinson, 'Football and FIFA', 175.
38. Vidacs, 'The Postcolonial and the Level Playing-Field'.
39. Hall, 'Cultural Identity and Diaspora'.
40. Said, *Culture and Imperialism*.
41. Hall, 'Cultural Identity and Diaspora', 225.

References

Anderson, Benedict. *Imagined Communities*. London: VERSO, 1983.
Arber, Sara. 'Designing Samples'. In *Researching Social Life*, 2nd edition, ed. Nigel Gilbert G, 58–82. London. Sage, 2001.
Archetti, Eduardo P. 'In Search of National Identity: Argentinian Football and Europe'. In *Tribal identities: Nationalism, Europe, Sport*, ed. J. A. Mangan, 201–219. London: Frank Class, 1996.
Bairner, Alan. *Sport, Nationalism and Globalisation: European and North American Perspectives*. Albany, NY: State University of New York Press, 2001.
Barker, Chris. *Cultural Studies: Theory and Practice*. London: Sage, 2000.
Gellner, Ernest. *Nations and Nationalism*. New York, NY: Cornell University Press, 1983.
Hall, Stuart. 'Cultural Identity and Diaspora'. In *Identity: Community, Culture, Difference*, ed. Jonathan Rutherford, 222–237. London: Lawrence & Wishart, 1990.
Hall, Stuart. *Representation: Cultural Representations and Signifying Practices*. London: Sage, 1997.
Hastings, Adrian. *The Construction of Nationhood: Ethnicity, Religion and Nationalism*. Cambridge: Cambridge University Press, 1997.
Hetherington, Kevin. *Expressions of Identity: Space, Performance, Politics*. London: Sage, 1998.
Hobsbawm, Eric. 'Introduction: Inventing Traditions'. In *The Invention of Tradition*, ed. E. Eric Hobsbawm and Terence Ranger, 1–14. Cambridge: Cambridge University Press, 1983.
Hobsbawm, Eric. *Nations and Nationalism Since 1780: Programme, Myth, Reality*. Cambridge: Cambridge University Press, 1990.
Lee, Jong-Young. 'The Development of Football in Korea'. In *Japan, Korea and the 2002 World Cup*, ed. John Horne and Wolfram Manzenreiter, 73–88. London: Routledge, 2002.
Maguire, Joseph. *Global Sport: Identities, Societies, Civilizations*. Cambridge: Polity Press, 1999.
Manzenreiter, Wolfram, and John Horne. 'Global Governance in World Sport and the 2002 World Cup Korea/Japan'. In *Japan, Korea and the 2002 World Cup*, ed. John Horne and Wolfram Manzenreiter, 1–26. London: Routledge, 2002.
Oh, Miyoung. '"Blood is thicker than water": South Korea and its "Other" North Korea'. In *Sport, Nation, Nationalism: Proceedings of 8th ISHPES Seminar and International Conference on Social Science and Sport*, ed. T. Pavlin, 307–322. Ljubljana, Slovenia: Fakulteta za sport, 2008.
Oh, Miyoung. '"Eternal Other Japan: South Koreans" Post-colonial Identities'. *International Journal of the History of Sport* 26, no: 3 (2009): 371–389.
Said, Edward W. *Orientalism*. London: Penguin Books, 1978.
Said, Edward W. *Culture and Imperialism*. New York, NY: Vintage Books, 1993.
Sarup, Madan. *Identity, Culture and the Postmodern World*. Edinburgh: Edinburgh University Press, 1996.
Smith, Anthony D. 'Towards a global culture?'. In *Global Culture: Nationalism, Globalisation and Modernity*, ed. Mike Featherstone, 171–192. London. Sage, 1990.
Smith, Anthony D. *National Identity*. London: Penguin, 1991.
Smith, Anthony D. *Nationalism and Modernism*. London: Routledge, 1998.
Sugden, John, and Alan Tomlinson 'Football and FIFA in the Postcolonial world'. In *Sport and Postcolonialism*, ed. John Bale and Mike Cronin, 175–196. Oxford: BERG, 2003.
Triandafyllidou, Anna. 'National Identity and the "Other"'. *Ethnic and Racial Studies* 21, no: 4 (1998): 593–612.
Vidacs, Bea. 'The Postcolonial and the Level Playing-Field in the 1998 World Cup'. In *Sport and Postcolonialism*, ed. John Bale and Mike Cronin, 147–158. Oxford: BERG, 2003.
Weeks, Jeffrey. 'The Value of Difference'. In *Identity: Community, Culture, Difference*, ed. Jonathan Rutherford, 88–100. London: Lawrence & Wishart, 1990.

South Asia and South-East Asia: new paths of African footballer migration

Gerard A. Akindes*

Department of Sports Administration, Ohio University, Athens, OH, USA

> Today, playing football can be considered a global practice, a universal reference that transcends cultures and nations. Football players' global mobility exhibits some aspects of the worldwide dimension of the culture of the game. Quantitative data (along with academic analysis and studies of the contemporary migration) rank Africa as the third-largest exporter of footballers. Such data explain the magnitude of the exodus and the migratory routes in light of Africa's colonial history and world economic disparities. Although the colonial and neocolonial approaches to analysing the migration of African footballers remain valid, Asian trajectories of the African players' migrations have emerged and suggest different frames of analysis. This article (after reviewing African football migration factors, such as the colonial connections and the 'push and pull' factor) examines the particularities and the impact that the Asian paths of migration have had on the emergence of the semi-peripheral football economy located in South Asia and South-East Asia.

Introduction

The cultural and economic dimensions of the labour migration of African footballers are often studied from a colonial and neocolonial perspective. Indeed, African footballer labour migration can be explained by Africa's historical connections with Western Europe (Africa's former colonizers).[1] Although it remains relevant to use colonial and neocolonial legacies to analyse the migration of African footballers, new routes and dimensions of the migrations have emerged in the late 1980s and early 1990s. For example, Abhishek[2] estimates that 400 African players are currently playing in India. Today, African footballers are employed in many South and South-East Asian countries, such as Vietnam, Indonesia, India, Singapore, Cambodia and Thailand. Leagues' and clubs' websites in these countries contain evidence of a consistent presence of players of African descent in their organizations. This paper intends to add to the studies of the south–north migration of African footballers, the more recent south–south routes leading to South and South-East Asia.

This article introduces several significant historical factors of the sport, such as the European diffusion of football in Africa and Asia, and the shaping of modern football system. What will follow is an explanation of the mechanisms and supply channels bridging Africa and Asia, which facilitate the recruitment of African players. Included is an account of the experiences of the players, and an idea of how these new paths of migration can be articulated with the existing paths. The conclusion proposes that the emergence of semi-peripheral economies in the modern world system (in addition, the economic growth of the European football) is shaping a 'modern football world system', with a distinct timeline from Wallerstein's[3] 'long sixteenth century'. Despite much significant relevance, the modern world system of Wallerstein does not completely capture the whole complexity of the migration of African footballers moving from peripheral football spaces to a no-less peripheral one in South and South-East Asia.

The diffusion of football in South and South-East Asia
This section offers an overview of the introduction and diffusion of football in India, Indonesia, Vietnam, and Thailand. Magee and Sugden[4] illustrate that the global diffusion of football occurred from the Europe to the rest of the world, Africa, South America, Central America, Asia, Oceania and North America. Europeans were instrumental in introducing football in Asia, just as they did in Africa. As in Africa, the diffusion of football to Asia happened essentially through colonial institutions, such as armies, missionaries and schools. In Asia, the exposure and adoption of football also was due to European traders.

The colonial inheritance of football is recognized in India, Malaysia and Indonesia. As mentioned by Novy Kapadia,[5] football was introduced in India by missionaries and the British army during colonial rule. The British introduced football in Malaysia along with other Western sports.[6] By the same token, the Dutch colonials introduced the game to the local population in Indonesia. In Indonesia (the former Netherland Indies), the role of the Netherland (the former colonizer) in the diffusion of football came through institutions and organizations, such trading firms, the army and civil servants.[7] Colombijn[8] states that 'the introduction of football to Indonesia followed the Netherlands pattern in remarkable detail'.[9] India, Malaysia, Vietnam and Indonesia adopted football very much in the same way as Africa did. The early adopters of football in these countries were Europeans and the local populations (mainly elites in contact with colonial institutions). From the late nineteenth century, football clubs emerged in India, run by the local population.[10] In Indonesia, organized football clubs and leagues were dominated by Europeans, but had local players, and these clubs were in place by the early twentieth century.

India, Malaysia, Vietnam and Indonesia exemplify the colonial introduction and diffusion of football in South and South-East Asia from the late nineteenth century and early twentieth century. In countries, such as Thailand (with a limited colonial past), local people who had lived in Europe introduced football in their home country. Kookannog[11] believes that the son of King Rama V and his subjects brought back football from England in the early twentieth century. In China, the introduction of football came from Hong Kong and disseminated through high schools and universities.[12]

No matter the method, football in Asia arrived through the Europeans' influences. Although in Africa, colonization constitutes the essential total of the history of football in the continent, the period of its introduction and the diffusion from elite to grassroots in Africa is comparable to what evolved in South and South-East Asia. Alegi[13] describes the role played by the European-built railroads in the diffusion of football in Africa, and Alegi reinforces the similarity between Asia and Africa's early experience with the sport. In both regions, the nineteenth century and early twentieth century are the periods of the first contact with European-import football. This is the time of the creation of the first teams and leagues in several areas of Asia and Africa.

On the world stage, Asia and Africa also shared some historical similarity on a very limited performance level. For a long time, African and Asian nations' qualification for the FIFA World Cup was tight. Only one country between them could have a chance to represent both continents. In fact, the FIFA World Cup system of qualifiers contributed to limiting the presence of African and Asians teams at the World Cup. The already independent nations and members of FIFA of Asia and Africa had to qualify only one team after play-offs with a European team. Examples of this situation include Egypt (in 1934), the Dutch East Indies (in 1938) and today Indonesia.[14] Mills and Dimeo[15] indicate that the British presence on the FIFA committee denied India an invitation to participate in the 1950 World Cup; Kapadia[16] justifies India's absence by a lack of foreign exchange currency and the challenge of a long sea trip! Regardless of the real reason of India's non-appearance at the World Cup in 1950, Indian football was active and performing at the Olympics and other Asian competitions. Clearly, India experienced an early, significant international experience and success at the Olympics. Kapadia[17] maintains that India qualified for the Olympics until 1960, finished fourth in the football tournament in 1956, and won the gold medal in the Asia Games in 1962. Among other South and South-East Asian countries, India had an early international presence and relative success.

India's Olympic performances coincided with the end of European colonial rule in Africa, the emergence of African nations and the establishment of Africa's national federations and leagues. From the 1960s, and from the independence of most African nations, those nations joined FIFA and were engaged in an exorable ascension for global recognition. Despite India's early presence on the international football scene, and despite the first participation of the Dutch Indies in the FIFA World Cup, the evolution of South and South-East Asian football showed limited signs of ascension.

From the historical evolution of football in the two geographical areas, nothing from the post-independence time could have predicted that today South and South-East Asia could have become one of the main destinations of African footballers at the end of the twentieth century. South and South-East Asia's capacity to attract African footballers was the least foreseeable possibility, considering the colonial period, the first years of independence and the prevalence of colonial connections in defining migration patterns and routes.

The traditional route of African football labour migration
Colonial past

As argued in several studies,[18] colonial strings are a significant factor of migration of African footballers. Darby et al.[19] contend that colonial and neocolonial ties significantly define the flow of African footballers' migration. From the early 1960s independence years, a majority of African countries (England, France, Belgium and Portugal) have been the prominent destinations of African footballers in Europe.[20]

Although Arthur Wharton, in 1886, is recognized as the first African in European football, the migration of African footballers is more of a post-World War II phenomenon. The colonial era of African footballers' migration revealed talented players, such as the Senegalese Raoul Diagne, the Moroccan Larbi Ben Barek and the Mozambicans Eusebio and Coluna. From 1945 to 1962, there were 117 North Africans playing in France's professional league.[21] Prior to the 1960s, Sub-Saharan Africa was not well represented. In France, Northern Africans made up the majority of African migration. Nevertheless, there were also West African players from Côte d'Ivoire, Mali, Senegal, Benin and Cameroon.[22] The colonial tendency of African football migration was also visible in Portugal, where players from Mozambique, Angola, Guinea Bissau and Cape Verde were recruited by Portuguese clubs. Although Marion Coluna and Eusebio da Silva Ferreira are the best-known players of the early post-war migration, many African players from Portuguese colonies were recruited from Africa. In 1951, for example, Miguel Arcanjo from Mozambique was playing for Porto in Portugal.[23]

The significance of colonial ties for the recruitment of athletic labour remained significant beyond the era of independence. Despite political independence and the creation of national football leagues affiliated to FIFA, African footballers continued to migrate to Europe for a professional career. After independence, the colonial patterns of the migration continued. France, Portugal, and Belgium leagues continue to employ African players from their former colonies. Among the former colonial states, only England had a limited influx of African players from their former colonies. Although England been a former colonizer, and also had the first recorded black football player, African players' presence in England remain marginal until factors such as FIFA geopolitics, media deregulation and the Bosman law transformed the European football economy and geopolitics.

Until the 1980s, the post-independence football in Africa had a limited global presence beyond a few world-class players, such as Eusebio da Silva and Salif Keita. After Egypt first participated in the World Cup in 1934, there was no other African team present until 1970. Except for a few individuals (playing mostly in France, Portugal and Belgium), African football teams had limited world value and scant recognition on the football world stage. By mid-1980s, due to a combination of new factors, African football gained more presence, attention and recognition on the world stage. Darby et al.[24] explain the transformation as a result of the growing profile and status of African national teams from mid-1980s. Darby[25] suggests that FIFA's president, Joao Havalange (elected in 1974), and his effort to promote football outside Europe and Latin America was a contributing factor to the raising profile of African football. Indeed, the good performance of African youth national teams at FIFA's 'Under-20' and 'Under-17' World Cups, which were established under Havalenge's presidency, were also contributing factors to the rising status of African football. The fresh profile of African football led to what Darby describes as the 'new scramble for Africa'.[26] The flow of African footballer migrants drastically increased and has continued to rise.

The increase presence of African footballers in Europe coincided with unrelated factors. These factors included both the Bosman ruling and broadcasting deregulation in most European countries. In 1995, the Bosman ruling deregulated the football labour market and led to a rise of foreign players moving to England, Italy, Germany, France and Spain. They moved to the biggest leagues in Europe. During the season 2008–2009, Radio France International[27] listed 670 African players in 10 European countries' first- and second-division leagues. These lists also show that West African countries (principally Nigeria, Ghana, Cameroon, Senegal and Côte d'Ivoire) are the main suppliers of footballers to European leagues. According to Poli,[28] these five countries account for 54% of the African football diaspora in Europe. The global space of the migration of African footballers is not tempered by the dominance of the geographic West of the African continent. The legal and technological transformations that occurred in television broadcasting of football provide an incontestable global dimension to the migration of African footballers.

Broadcasting deregulation and the competition for acquisition of broadcasting rights by media groups injected a substantial amount of money in most of European leagues through broadcasting rights revenues. Magee and Sugden[29] (Sugden and Tomlinson 1998; Magee and Sugden 2002, 421–437) applied Wallerstein's[30] 1974 economic world system model to the concept of world football. The researchers looked at the resulting economic power of European football, the role and position of Europe in diffusing football, and the destination of football labor migrants. Their analogy is illustrated in Figure 1.

The model illustrated by Figure 1 is Wallerstein's modern world system, with the concept of core, semi-periphery and periphery adapted to football global diffusion and football labour global migration. As illustrated in Figure 1, the regions of Asia, South, Central and America are located at the semi-periphery when Africa is located at the dependent periphery. Asia and North America are respectively positioned in the periphery/semi-periphery for their football performance, and the core for their contemporary global economic stature. Figure 1 also illustrates the diffusion of football from the core Europe to the semi-periphery and periphery. While the football labour migration flows from the periphery and semi-periphery to the core with additional flows between the semi-periphery and the periphery.

From George Weah in the 1990s, to the more recent stars, Didier Drogba and Samuel Eto'o, African footballers have (through migration) gained recognition and global exposure. In addition to such African global stars, worldwide credibility for African football has been gained by the performance of a few national teams at the FIFA World Cups in 1990, with a quarter final played by Cameroon in 1990, Senegal in 2002 and more recently Ghana in 2010. The progressive building of African football through its migrants and national teams' performances justifies positioning Africa at the world model periphery instead of in the impoverished and dependent periphery. Moreover, the migration of African players towards South and South-East Asia operates more from one periphery to another periphery. The following section

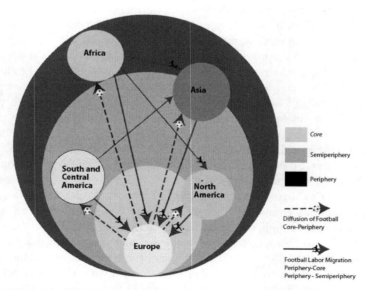

Figure 1. The global diffusion of football and football labour migration.
Source: Magee and Sugden (2002, 428).

explains the determining factors of the football labor migration from Africa to South and South-East Asia.

South and South-East Asian path to African labour migration
Geographical trends

Football history in Asia and Africa experienced similar patterns until the era of independence. Initially, there was colonial and European introduction of the game and limited FIFA World Cup participation by the continents. The exception would be two South and South-East Asian (Indonesian) teams in 1934 and later qualification (without participation) of India in 1950. Following the boycott of the 1966 FIFA World Cup by Africa and Asia, the two continents obtained their own World Cup representatives. Since then, Sub-Saharan African countries (unlike South and Southeast Asia) have qualified for several FIFA World Cups (winning 'under 17' and 'under 20' competitions). In fact, Thailand and Malaysia participated in the FIFA 'under 20' as a host country and Indonesia qualified once in 1979, having reached the final of the tournament. An assessment of the two geographical regions (based on national teams' performances) shows a contrasting post-independence football achievement on the world stage. African national teams and players have achieved more on the international scene than their counterparts in South and South-East Asia. Despite the Asians' limited achievements on the world stage of football, South and South-East Asian countries have attracted a noticeable African football labour force since the mid-1990s. As Poli[31] observes, several dozens of African players perform in South and South-East Asia countries, such as India, Thailand, Singapore, Indonesia, Bangladesh and Cambodia. There is no database of how many African players are there across South and South-East Asia. However, valuable information about the origin of African players can be located in leagues' cross information from league and teams' websites, combined with news articles and interviews with officials or journalists. Figure 2 represents a sample of African nationalities playing in Bangladesh, India, Indonesia and Vietnam.

Figure 2 was constructed by studying the various teams' rosters accessible on the leagues' websites. There were 108 players playing within Bangladesh, India, Indonesia and Vietnam in 2010. Only in Cambodia, it is estimated that about 30 African players were listed in various teams' rosters in 2012 (Interview Andrew). According to Ezra Kyrill Erker, in Thailand,

> Almost every TPL (Thai Premier League) team has at least one African player on its books, and some have half a dozen-players … Africans are still highly valued by the clubs – with over thirty African players currently on the books of TPL teams and dozens more in the lower leagues.[32]

If one were to add the number of African players in Singapore, Thailand, and Nepal, there would be an even higher number of players officially performing in South and South-East Asia. Eighteen African nationalities are represented in various leagues, especially players from Cameroon, Nigeria, Ghana and Liberia.

European migration routes of players have been well researched and established through the factors of colonial legacy and pull and push.[33] But less studied are the South and South-East Asian routes. It is not well examined, for example, why there is a dominance of certain nationalities who display particular factors and specificities in regard to recruitment and supply channels.

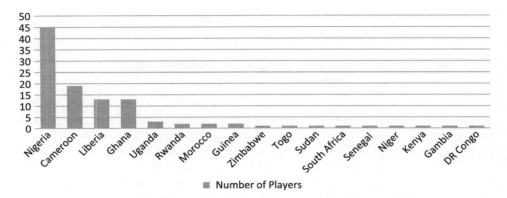

Figure 2. Number of African players per country in Bangladesh, India, Indonesia and Vietnam.

Players' origin and supply channels

This section analyses the recruitment supply channels of African players. It is interesting to see the recruitment of African players in countries like Indonesia, India and Cambodia. Looking at these countries provides a way to understand the supply channels of South and South-East Asian leagues, and the trajectories of the players leaving Africa to play in South and South-East Asia.

In 1938, Indonesia was the first Southeast Asian nation to play the FIFA World Cup. In 1956, Indonesia qualified for their first and only Olympic football tournament, in Melbourne. In the 1970s, Indonesia was ranked as one of Asia's leading football nations.[34] In spite of these early successes and their 1991 win of the South-East Asian Games, Indonesia is not ranked high in football among the Asian nations. In October 2012, Indonesia was 170 on an FIFA ranking.[35] That ranking is lower than in 1993, when foreign players were allowed in the league. [The Indonesian league, started in 1993 allowed in foreign players.[36]] African players started to play in Indonesia shortly after the football borders were opened to non-Indonesian players. Roger Milla, the legendary player from Cameroon, was one of the first African players to play in Indonesia. Roger Milla joined the Indonesian league after participating in his last FIFA World Cup in the USA in 1994. Emmanuel Mabaoang Kessack and Roger Milla were the first African and Cameroonians to play in Indonesia.[37] This is a good illustration of one of the early supply channels of African footballers in Asia: the presence of these two players in Indonesia and Jules-Denis Onana, a former Cameroonian international. In fact, many African players are recruited on the recommendation of another player already playing or who had already played in the league. De Latour,[38] discussing the recruitment and trajectories of African players in Asia, argues that the trajectories are more independent and self-driven, with the support of a coach or an agent.

So, there are some differences in the recruitment paths for players heading to Asia, compared to those heading to Europe. The 'official' paths are those methods of recruitment defined by rich and well-established European professional clubs. These recruitment methods include academies with joint-ventures in Africa, and the constant scouting of African competitions. Recruitment to Asia does display, however, a similarity with the unofficial and illegal migration of African players in Europe.

The recommendation-type supply channel remains a strong method to recruit players. Following Milla, Maboang and Onana, many Cameroonian players have played (and continue to play) in the Indonesian Super League. One of them explains that before his retirement, he was approached to be a consultant in recruiting African players.[39] Being himself from Cameroon facilitated the recruitment of other Cameroonians in Indonesia. Cameroonians are the largest contingent of African football migrants officially employed in Indonesia. Having a Cameroonian FIFA-accredited agent contributes to reinforcing the Cameroon–Indonesia route to professional football. The country of origin of the pioneers, such as Roger Milla, played a determinant role in establishing the origin and the trajectory of the players from Cameroon to Indonesia.

In Malaysia, the recruitment of African players resumed in 2011, after the 2009 closing of the country's football borders to foreign players.[40] The recruitment channels of Malaysia are very similar to the ones existing in Indonesia. A player who moved to Malaysia in 2010 with a student visa, and hoped to be recruited, describes how he relied on other players and an African agent with connections in Malaysia to find a team and to sign a contract.[41] He stated that 'many nationalities are present in Malaysia, but Nigerians and Cameroonians represent the majority'.[42] According to the same player, many of the footballers leave their countries without any real connection in Malaysia and without any agent to represent them. Upon their arrival with a tourist visa, their quest for a club begins. Unfortunately, the method of being recruited by an agent and a good resume (including national team caps or playing time in Europe) seems to be extremely random. The Malaysian supply channels of African players include agents, recommendations and freelance players travelling from their home countries with the hopes of generating enough interest in local clubs for a contract. The supply route to India (similar to the supply routes between Cameroon–Indonesia and Cameroon/Nigeria–Malaysia), thus, depends on personal chains of supply.

India has a long history with African players. In fact, their first African player, Chima Okerie, was from Nigeria and arrived in India in the mid-1980s.[43] Over the years, more Nigerian players followed. Nigerians are the most represented African nationality in the I-league (the Indian professional football league).

The presence of higher number of Cameroonians in Indonesia and Nigerians in India is certainly due, in part, to the prevalence of the recommendation method and the early recruitment of players from a certain origin. Nevertheless, other supply channels, facilitated by football agents, help to supply African players to South and South-East Asia football clubs. For example, Arunava Chaudhuri[44] believes that the professionalization of the Indian league has favoured recruitment through agents. Former players, initially recruited with the help of agents, are today FIFA-licensed agents as well. They are actively involved in recruiting for the Indonesian league. The sports agency Mutiara Hitam, Sport & Management, is an example of an agency with African agents involved in recruiting African players. FIFA-licensed agents can provide a more official and safer recruitment channel that benefits the young African players engaging in professional football career and the clubs recruiting them. Former players remain in the host country and will become agents facilitating the recruiting of other African players from their home country or other African countries. In addition to the official licensed agents, agents with no FIFA credentials operate as well in South and South-East Asia, and they contribute to spontaneous and unofficial supply channel.

In fact, many players across South and South-East Asia either follow agents with no license and who are ethically questionable, or fly to the countries where friends and acquaintances are already in place, just hoping that they will be recruited. In Cambodia, a football analyst relates the situation:

> They come directly from their home country in the main, lured sometimes by agents or simply their friends who are already here. There is also a lot of movement of players from Thailand, where there are more clubs and therefore more opportunities for trials.

One Cameroonian agent said that 'out of forty players officially under contract and playing for a team, there are fifty others in the street without contract and means for living'.[45] A similar pattern is observed in Cambodia, where the players stick around, form an unofficial team to play friendly matches against the local clubs, hoping to make an impression for a contract. Some come just to look around and leave.[46] In addition to the number of players listed and playing in official clubs, the supply of African players appears higher than the demand in most leagues. Singapore does have a non-limit foreign players' league. But Asian clubs under the Asian Football Confederation can have only four foreign players on the field, with absolutely one being Asian, for international club competition. The spontaneous (or not) footballer migration often generated by unscrupulous agents and unemployed football migrants is a known fact in the Africa–Europe migration. The similar pattern just described is an Asian version of the same European problem, which has comparable legal and social implications.

The spontaneous supply channel leads to players commuting from league to league, due to induced unemployment or underemployment.[47] Chaudhuri[48] describes these individuals as freelance players, who may join the Indian league from Thailand, Singapore or other Asian countries. African 'freelance footballers' or 'commuters' exhibit an extraordinary capacity for adaptation. This ability to be versatile also characterizes the supply channel currently in place between African footballers and South Asian/South-East Asian leagues.

Regardless of the supply channels used, African footballers in Asia, since their early involvement in the late 1980s and early 1990s, have made their mark in various South Asian and South-East Asia leagues. Players such as Onana (in Indonesia) and Chimokeri (from Nigeria, in India) remained after their careers in their host country to pursue their post-football careers. As Chaudhuri[49] explains, 'Many of them never go back. A lot of players from the late 1980s are still around. Some of them left, and try to come back'. An agent acknowledges the cultural and social similarities of the host country (such as the food and the climate) that facilitate the integration of African footballers to the host society and community. Their capacity to regroup and form 'African communities' helps to ease their adaptation. They may also enjoy a comparatively lower cost of living[50] Emmanuel, a former player who is now an agent in Thailand, agrees that food and climate similarities are a positive factor of adjustment for African players.[51]

Thus, the spontaneous supply channel has led to some African footballers achieving successful careers. To travel this path, players have had to be mobile, adjustable and tenacious to obtain contracts. But the spontaneous method for gaining work in South and South-East Asia has also led to legal and social complications.

Legal challenges

As previously mentioned, many hopeful players arrive in Asia with no guarantee of a contract. They may have arrived through personal means or through unscrupulous agents. According to an African agent in Indonesia,

> Many players arrive in Indonesia without the fundamentals and may sign a first contract; but they won't be able to fulfill the expectations, and they will quickly be out of contract ... They will be confronted with immigration problems comparable to the ones existing in Europe; but from here, Africa is eighteen hours away.[52]

His comment describes the precariousness of African footballers caught in an immigration problem in faraway Asia, compared to players stuck in the same way in Europe. A few dramatic stories expose the less-enviable side of African footballers' adventures in South and South-East Asia.

Louis-Paul Mfede is a former international player from Cameroon who played two World cups in 1990 and 1994. He was jailed in Indonesia for overstaying past five years on his visa.[53] Mfede's case illustrates a problem relevant to a migrant footballer, post-career. For the younger players, the 'illegal' status may start before the signing of any hypothetical contract. In fact, there are numerous stories about young migrant players abandoned by agents without a contract, money or a return ticket home from South or South-East Asia. Owen Slot, a reporter for the British *Sunday Times,* presented the stories of one Ghanaian and two Nigerians abandoned by an agent in Cambodia, with no means to return home.[54]

The number of African players in South and South-East Asia without a contract and in an illegal status is substantial. According to the agent's estimation, there are more players failing to obtain a contract than players with a contract.[55] In another example, Cochrane[56] says that in Cambodia, there are dozens of African players, practising on a field, hoping to get a contract one day.

Every year, all the supply channels contribute to the increasing migration. Although the spontaneous supply channels remain the most problematic, the inherent insecurity characterizing footballers' careers expose African players to the harsh consequences of a failure far from their home countries. In spite of the risk and numerous failures, Africans continue to find their way to South and South-East Asia in the hope of having a football career, when such a career had not seemed possible at home or in Europe.

The determining factors of the migration

As has been shown, due to a combination of factors, African footballers have risen in world recognition, and a demand was created for them in the South and South-East Asia nations. Asians succeeded in attracting African footballers to their leagues. There are several reasons for the migration of young African players to South and South-East Asian leagues.

Athleticism and experience

From the mid-1990s, the desire of South and South-East Asian leagues to improve the playing standard of their leagues contributed to the recruitment of foreign players. The athleticism and experience of African players are two reasons why they are valued. Cochrane[57] (citing Andy Brouwers) states,

> While the African players come to Cambodia seeking fame and fortune, they've helped boost the standard of the game ... They just have more experience, they are more physically strong, and they usually form the spine of any of teams they play for, so we're talking central defender, central midfield, central striker, and so they have a big influence on the games.[58]

The positive contribution of African players to the game is not shared by all. A former coach of the Cambodia National team, Scott O'Donnel, argued that foreign players dominated their Cambodian counterparts with their physical strength and athleticism ascendant.[59] With more nuances, Chaudhuri[60] acknowledges the technicality of some African players, and then he also mentions the physical strength and presence of African players in India.

Despite some reservations about the technical level or superiority of African players, the African players' physical and technical qualities remain determining factors in their recruitment by South and South-East Asia football leagues. The players' experience is a significant element of recruitment.

Several African players with long international experience took advantage of the demand created by some leagues with resources (such as India, Indonesia, Malaysia, and Vietnam). Pioneers migrants, such as Roger Milla, Jules-Denis Onana (in Indonesia), Chimokeri (from Nigeria), and Felix Aboagye (from Ghana, in India), met a demand for talented African footballers. The creation and professionalization of South and South-East Asia leagues and their development quickly expanded the demand beyond experienced, renowned players. Young African players, in quest of professional football careers elsewhere than Europe, found alternative destinations in South and South-East Asia. However, the supply has overtaken the demand now. Malaysia has closed its border to foreigners, while other leagues have introduced a number of restrictions. African supply channels, driven by unscrupulous agents, continue to send young players to Asia. But the demand appears limited by the size of most football organizations and constrained by the groups' economic resources.

So, although the migration continues, the supply exceeds the demand today. Cochrane[61] maintains that there are possibly only 30 positions available in the league for more than 100 African players expecting a contract. In the same way as the situation occuring in Europe, African players wanting to be part of South and South-East Asian leagues create a large pool of unemployed players who remain on the margin of the official leagues, hoping for a contract.

Economic disparity

There is an important economic differential factor that cannot be overlooked. In 2007, in African leagues, the average pay was €2200 Euros ($2792).[62] In most Sub-Saharan African countries, in fully professional leagues with a steady income for players is not the norm. For example, Darby[63] notes that the average salary of players in the Ghanaian premier league is between $100 and $300, with the possibility to win bonuses.

In contrast, the best players in Indonesia can earn up to $80,000. According to the African agent in Indonesia, in Vietnam, some salaries reach $200,000 – $300,000. These numbers are corroborated by Eric Bui, a football journalist, who states that 'The average salary is US$4000–7000 per month. Best-paid got around US$ 10,000 or more per month. Local players got at most 4000 per month but they got much better signing fee because of their fame'.[64]

Thus, in a few leagues – Indonesia (ISL), Malaysia (MSL), Singapore, Thailand, Vietnam (V-league) and India (I-league) – there is a substantial economic incentive for African players to migrate from Africa. The financial gain to migrate towards some of the richest of these leagues is therefore evident. Additional incentives to migrate are the quality of the practice and game facilities, the professionalism of the league, the expertise of the clubs' management and a favourable tax system.

Additional disparities and mobility

If some Asian leagues and their best clubs have an economic advantage over most Sub-Saharan leagues, it must be pointed out that Bangladesh, Laos and Cambodia do not offer better salaries. Yet, these regions host a substantial number of African players.[65] Commenting on the Cambodia league, Cochrane states that 'lucrative deals simply don't exist. The best any player in Cambodia can hope for is a contract with one of the ten premier league clubs receiving accommodation, food, and a few hundred dollars a month'.[66] The conditions in Cambodia, as described by Cochrane, are very similar to what a decent African league in Senegal, Cameroon, or Côte d'Ivoire can offer their players. Why, then, do these teams have an appeal for young African players? Ebenezer Abbey, one of the pioneers of the Asia supply channel from Ghana, (Adjei 2005) explains that 'There are agents who now consider Asia a good football hub; so if I do well here, there is every chance that I can get a big move to Europe'.[67] Although some South and South-East Asia countries' teams do not provide great income, young players are enticed by the locations, and the players hope to use Asia as a stepping stone to European teams. For many African footballers in quest of a professional career, South and South-East Asia represent an opportunity that could be a transition. Two Ghanaian players in India put it this way:

> Money is not the parameter. A lot of teams in African countries, like Algeria and Egypt, pay more than the Indian clubs. But we are thinking two or three years down the line. If we play in India, we might get noticed more, and it could be easier to go to Europe.[68]

Very few cases, however, have demonstrated any such transit hub role of South and South-East Asia leagues. Christian Bekamenga (from Cameroon) represents one of the most recent successful transitions from Asia to a first-division league in Europe. In fact, Bekamenga, after playing two years in Indonesia and a year in Malaysia, was recruited by the FC Nantes in France Ligue 1. He then got his first national team cap of Cameroon after a few months.[69] Bekamenga's story may nourish hope for many young African players working in Asia. The story also provides an enticing narrative to recruiting agents for players hoping to reach European leagues through South and South-East Asian contracts.

Unfortunately, Bekamenga's example is exceptional. There are hurdles blocking the potential movement of players from Asian leagues to Europe. For example, the Asian leagues have lack of media exposure. Further, their national teams and clubs have a low ranking in the global football world. Thus, Asia as a platform for a European career is more a mirage or dream for young African players than a consistent reality. The most common migration of African players in Asia actually occurs among the South and South-East Asian leagues. So the career mobility is horizontal and trans-Asian for the majority of African players reaching the South and Southeast Asia football market.

Despite the limited movement of African players from Asia to Europe, the Asian transnationalism of African football labour in South and South-East Asia contributes to supporting the increasing globalization of the modern world of football labour. Today, agents, clubs and players operate in various interconnected geographical spaces. The African players' labour transnationalism makes them 'actors of globalization' in the football players' labour market. As previously mentioned, the globalized football industry can be viewed as a model. This model of football world systems follows Wallerstein's[70] economic model of modern world systems.

The modern world football system

Wallerstein[71] defines the term *modern world system* as a single structure with a core, a semi-periphery and a periphery. This economic theory proposes that this system emerged from the mercantile expansion of Europe during the 'long sixteenth century' and the colonialism era that followed.

World football has comparatively recently evolved in a similar manner to Wallerstein's model. In fact, as played today, football in Africa and Asia is one of the unattended results of the mercantile and colonial expansion of Europe during the 'long sixteenth century'. The diffusion of the game in Asia and Africa came about through missionaries, colonial armies, colonial schools, and European traders. Football diffusion was essentially an unplanned consequence, not intended by the colonial rulers as a way to extract labour or money. Only France and Portugal adopted and conducted early labour extraction with players like Larbi Ben Barek and Eusebio, who played as European citizens when their countries of origin were still, respectively, Morocco and Mozambique. Consequently, framing migrations of African footballers through the modern world system requires a 'time adjustment', because football as world system is a more recent phenomenon. The construction of a core, semi-periphery and periphery has occurred due to a combination of factors.

Paradoxically, the construction of the football world system (including its migration patterns) followed the full integration of Africa and Asia into the FIFA's World System.[72] The growing status of African football on the world stage through FIFA World Cup and 'under 17' and 'under 20' World Cup was a significant factor in establishing a football periphery. Although the history of African football, narrated by Alegi[73], positions African teams on the world stage in the early 1960s, he identifies the early 1980s as the turning point of African football in the era of commercial football. Darby's[74] description of 'the new scramble for Africa' explains how the active recruitment of African footballers by scouts (and later on through football academies) established the active peripherization of African football.

The influx of money in European leagues, induced by a broadcasting-rights economy, contributed to shaping a football world system with a core, a semi-periphery and a periphery. Darby[75] tempers the application of Wallerstein's economic modern world system to the FIFA's world system. However, the economic growth of European football (as well as the FIFA), resulting from broadcasting rights revenues, has reshaped the football world system around leagues, clubs and confederation economic power. The increasing commodification of football provides an economic shape to the world model, setting up a system that influences and determines the supply channels of African football migration.

Financial and economic factors (such as players' wages, playing facilities, standing, and professionalization of leagues and clubs' management) constitute the most prominent and visible factors of differentiation between the core, semi-periphery and periphery of the modern football system. Consequently, these factors are contributing elements to players being 'pulled' from the least affluent leagues (the periphery) to the richest one (the core). The migration of African player towards South and South-East Asia presents equivalent patterns. As mentioned by the African agent in Indonesia,[76] Indonesia and other South-East Asian countries are nations with well-managed clubs and leagues and good facilities. As mentioned, there is a significant wage difference that exists between Sub-Saharan Africa and several countries, such as India and Indonesia. The economic disparity establishes Sub-Saharan Africa in the peripheral space of the modern football world system. The financial difference alone explains much about African footballers' migration towards Asia.

The role played by income in defining periphery, semi-periphery and core is discussed by Wallerstein.[77] In devising his economic model, he explained that factors such as wages and value add to define the core, the periphery, and the hegemony of the core. Amin describes the periphery economy as dominated by an 'over developed' export sector, with a small manufacturing sector for mass consumption (as cited in Martinussen[78]). Furthermore, Amin argues that the capacity to compete in the world market determines nations' positions in the world system. These explanations by Wallerstein and Amin of their economic world model help to draw a parallel with the world football model.

There is no viable sport industry in most Sub-Saharan African countries (or at least a limited one). Yet football academies in those countries train hundreds of young players. There are no local sports teams to employ these trained players at regular and competitive salaries. In Wallerstein's economic model, these players are equivalent to an 'over developed' export sector, with a small manufacturing sector for mass consumption. The incapacity of Sub-Saharan African leagues and clubs to absorb all the players trained by all types of academies thus positions South and South-East Asia as viable alternatives to the competitiveness of the European market.

Wallerstein's modern world system provides a pertinent framework with which to analyse the migration of African footballers towards South and South-East Asia. However, this model does not explain the full situation of world football today, where African players also move towards the least affluent and weaker leagues of South and South-East Asia. The influx of Africans in other peripheral leagues and economies suggests additional analytical frameworks at play.

Conclusion

The migration of African footballers towards South and South-East Asia since the mid-1990s is a significant and invisible facet of the overall migration of African players. There are a noteworthy number of African players in Indonesia, Singapore, Cambodia, Laos, Bangladesh, and Vietnam. Although Nigerians are mentioned, as being by far the largest nationality represented, Cameroonians and Ghanaians are also well represented. But overall, players from more than 15 African countries are in South and South-East Asia for a football career.[79] With pioneers such as Roger Milla (in Indonesia), Chimokeri (from Nigeria), and Aboagye (from Ghana), the supply channel of African players to these countries continued. African players have become an integral component of the football history and landscape of their host countries; many of them now have a post-career in the host country, such as being a coach or an agent. They have become citizens integrated into the host society. Despite the socio-economic challenges, the distance and the limited opportunities, African players continue to travel to South and South-East Asia hoping for a football career unreachable in Europe or unavailable in their home country.

The capacity of South and South-East Asian leagues to attract African players establishes the peripheral position of African football in the world football system, in which Europe represents the core. Despite the higher performance of Sub-Saharan football leagues and their rising ranking on the world football stage, the area is still undermining its youths. The region's limited league professionalization, overall low playing level and poor management has condemned trained youth interested in a professional football career to become either a legal or an illegal exile. African football players in South and South-East Asia demonstrate the global value and affordability of a labour commodity mass-produced on the continent by all types of football academies. But there areonly limited professional outlets for these young players. Their dream of a football career at any cost, anywhere in the world, has facilitated the 'mining' role of (at best) legitimate agents and (at worst) unscrupulous agents. Such agents often lead these youth to peripheral football leagues in other lands having less limitation and regulation than Europe. This situation leaves many players without a contract and resources, not wanting to return home in failure. Moreover, as stated by the African agent in Indonesia, 'Africa is eighteen flying hours away, and being able to go back home is not always a choice'.[80] With migration towards either Europe or South and South-East Asia, there is a considerable pool of talented players lost for African football. Despite their high profile, Sub-Saharan African domestic footballers appear rooted at the periphery of the football world system with an export-oriented culture.

Notes

1. Darby et al., 'Football Academies', 145; Bale and Maguire, *The Global Sports Arena*; Alegi, *African Soccerscapes* and Magee and Sugden,'The World at their Feet', 426.
2. Abhishek, 'African Players Add'.
3. Wallerstein, *The Modern World-System*.
4. Magee and Sugden, 'The World at their Feet'.
5. Kapadia as cited in Dimeo and Mills, *Soccer in South Asia*, 17.
6. Ahmad Kamaluddin Megat Daud Megat, 'Sport Management Movement in Malaysia'.
7. Colombijn, 'The Politics of Indonesian Football'.
8. Ibid.
9. Ibid., 174.
10. Dimeo and Mills, *Soccer in South Asia*, 17.
11. Kookannog, 'A Study of Football Teams'.
12. Jinxia and Mangan, 'Football in the New China'.
13. Alegi, *African Soccerscapes*.
14. Crouch, *The World Cup*.
15. Dimeo and Mills, *Soccer in South Asia*, 1.
16. Kapadia, as cited in Dimeo and Mills, *Soccer in South Asia*.
17. Ibid.
18. Darby et al., 'Football Academies'; Bale and Maguire, *The Global Sports Arena*; Alegi, *African Soccerscapes*; Magee and Sugden,'The World at their Feet' and Raffaele Poli, *Les Migrations Internationales Des Footballeurs*.
19. Darby et al., 'Football Academies'.
20. Darby, 'The New Scramble for Africa'.
21. Alegi, *African Soccerscapes*, 179.
22. Ibid.

23. Ibid.
24. Darby et al., 'Football Academies'.
25. Darby, 'The New Scramble for Africa'.
26. Ibid., 236.
27. Dreyfus, 'Tous Les Africains De L1'.
28. Poli, 'African Migrants in Asian and European Football', 1011.
29. Magee and Sugden, 'The World at their Feet'.
30. Immanuel Maurice Wallerstein, *The Modern World-System*.
31. Poli, 'African Migrants in Asian and European Football'.
32. Erker, 'For African Footballers'.
33. Darby et al., 'Football Academies'.
34. FIFA, 'Indonesia: FIFA Goal Programme'.
35. FIFA, 'FIFA Coca-Cola World Ranking—Indonesia'.
36. Colombijn, 'The Politics of Indonesian Football'.
37. Phone interview with a Cameroonian agent in Indonesia on April 4, 2010.
38. De Latour, 'Joueurs Mondiaux, Clubs Locaux', 65.
39. Phone interview with a Cameroonian agent in Indonesia on April 4, 2010.
40. Daryl, 'Malaysia to Kick Out All Foreign Footballers'.
41. Phone interview with a Cameroonian player (without a contract in Malaysia) on November 17, 2012.
42. Ibid.
43. Ghoshal and Aabhas, 'Foreign Players Get their Kicks in India'.
44. Phone interview with Arunava Chaudhuri on April 2, 2010.
45. Phone interview with a Cameroonian agent in Indonesia on April 4, 2010.
46. Phone interview with a Cameroonian agent in Indonesia on April 4, 2010.
47. Poli, 'African Migrants in Asian and European Football'.
48. Phone interview with Arunava Chaudhuri on April 2, 2010.
49. Ibid.
50. Phone interview with a Cameroonian agent in Indonesia on April 4, 2010.
51. Erker, 'For African Footballers'.
52. Phone interview with a Cameroonian agent in Indonesia on April 4, 2010.
53. Binyam, 'Emmanuel Maboang Kessack'.
54. Owen, 'The Dream that Turned'.
55. Cochrane, 'The Pitfalls of a Football Career in Cambodia'.
56. Ibid.
57. Ibid.
58. Ibid.
59. Redahan, 'Expatriate Games'.
60. Phone interview with a Cameroonian agent in Indonesia on April 4, 2010.
61. Cochrane, 'The Pitfalls of a Football Career in Cambodia'.
62. Andreff, 'The Economic Effects.
63. Paul Darby, *Ghanaian Football Labour Migration: Preliminary Observations* Birkbeck Sport Business Centre, http://www.sportbusinesscentre.com/images/WladimirAndreffPresentation, Birkbeck Sport Business Centre Research Paper Series, May 1, 2008.
64. Phone interview with a Cameroonian agent in Indonesia on April 4, 2010.
65. Phone interview with a Cameroonian agent in Indonesia on April 4, 2010; Adjei, 'Breaking Asian Barriers'.
66. Cochrane, 'The Pitfalls of a Football Career in Cambodia'.
67. Adjei, 'Breaking Asian Barriers'.
68. Patwardhan, 'Africans Kicking in Indian Football'.
69. Songo'o et Bekamenga avec les Lions RFI.
70. Wallerstein, *The Modern World-System*.
71. Ibid.
72. Darby, *Africa, Football, and FIFA*.
73. Alegi, *African Soccerscapes*.
74. Darby, 'The New Scramble for Africa'.
75. Darby, *Africa, Football, and FIFA*.
76. Phone interview with a Cameroonian agent in Indonesia on April 4, 2010.

77. Wallerstein, *The Modern World-System*.
78. Martinussen, *Society, State, and Market*.
79. Erick Bui cites the following nationalities in Vietnam: Nigeria, Ghana, Ivory Coast, Cameroon, Uganda, Kenya, Malawi, South Africa, Zimbabwe, Zambia, Cape Verde, and Togo.
80. Phone interview with a Cameroonian agent in Indonesia on April 4, 2010.

References

Abhishek, Roy. 'African Players Add Extra Kick to Indian Football'. *Little About*. http://www.littleabout.com/Sports/african-players-add-extra-kick-indian-football/88605/

Adjei, Michael Oti. 'Breaking Asian Barriers'. *BBC*, 2010, http://news.bbc.co.uk/sport2/hi/football/africa/4298202.stm.

Alegi, Peter. *African Soccerscapes: How a Continent Changed the World's Game*. Athens: Ohio University Press, 2010.

Andreff, Wladimir. 'The Economic Effects of *Muscle Drain* in Sport'. Birkbeck Sport Business Centre. http://www.sportbusinesscentre.com/images/WladimirAndreffPresentation, Birkbeck Sport Business Centre Research Paper Series, May 1, 2008.

Bale, John, and Joseph A. Maguire. *The Global Sports Arena: Athletic Talent Migration in an Interdependent World*. London: F. Cass, 1994.

Binyam, Junior. 'Emmanuel Maboang Kessack: Mfédé Sortira De Prison'. *Cameroon-Info Net*, 2006, http://www.cameroon-info.net/stories/0,17279,@,emmanuel-maboang-kessack-mfede-sortira-de-prison.html.

Boniface, Pascal. *Football & Mondialisation*. Paris: Armand Colin, 2007.

Bromberger, Christian. *Football: La Bagatelle La Plus Sérieuse Du Monde*. Paris: Bayard Éditions, 1998.

Cochrane, Liam. 'The Pitfalls of a Football Career in Cambodia'. *Radio Australia*, 2010, http://www.radioaustralia.net.au/connectasia/stories/201005/s2907437.htm.

Colombijn, Freek. 'The Politics of Indonesian Football'. *Archipel* 59, no. 1 (2000): 171–200.

Crouch, Terry. *The World Cup: The Complete History*. rev ed. London: Aurum, 2006.

Darby, Paul. 'The New Scramble for Africa: African Football Labour Migration to Europe'. *Sports History Review* 3 (2000): 217–44.

Darby, Paul. *Africa, Football, and FIFA: Politics, Colonialism, and Resistance*. London: F. Cass, 2002.

Darby, Paul, Gerard Akindes, and Matthew Kirwin. 'Football Academies and the Migration of African Football Labor to Europe'. *Journal of Sport & Social Issues* 31, no. 2 (2007): 143–61.

Daryl. 'Malaysia to Kick Out all Foreign Footballers'. *The Off Side*, 2008, http://www.theoffside.com/world-football/malaysia-to-kick-out-all-foreign-footballers.html.

De Latour, E. 'Joueurs Mondiaux, Clubs Locaux. Le Football d'Afrique En Asie'. *Politique Africaine* 118 (2010): 63–84.

Dimeo, Paul, and James Mills. *Soccer in South Asia: Empire, Nation, Diaspora*. London: F. Cass, 2001.

Dreyfus, Gerard. 'Tous Les Africains De L1'. RFI. http://www.rfi.fr/sportfr/articles/092/article_55066.asp.

Erker, Kyrill Ezra. 'For African Footballers, the Grass is Greener in Thailand'. *Bangkok Post*, 2012, http://www.bangkokpost.com/news/investigation/288910/for-african-footballers-the-grass-is-greener-in-thailand.

FIFA. 'FIFA Coca-Cola World Ranking – Indonesia'. *FIFA*, 2012, http://www.fifa.com/associations/association=idn/ranking/gender=m/index.html.

FIFA. 'Indonesia: FIFA Goal Programme'. *FIFA*, 2013. http://www.fifa.com/associations/association=idn/goalprogramme/index.html.

Ghoshal, Devjyot, and Aabhas Sharma. 'Foreign Players Get their Kicks in India'. *Business Standard*, 2012, http://www.business-standard.com/india/news/foreign-players-get-their-kicks-in-india/403648/.

Jinxia, Dong, and J. A. Mangan. 'Football in the New China: Political Statement, Entrepreneurial Enticement and Patriotic Passion'. *Soccer and Society* 2, no. 3 (2001): 79.

Kalfa, David. 'Songo'o Et Bekamenga Avec Les Lions'. *RFI*, 2008, http://www.rfi.fr/actufr/articles/104/article_71661.asp.

Kapadia, Novy, as cited in Dimeo, Paul, and James Mills. *Soccer in South Asia: Empire, Nation, Diaspora*. London: F. Cass, 2001.

Kookannog, Thanadesh. *A Study of Football Teams' Management in a Competition of the Sixth Thailand Provincial Football League Division*. Master thesis. Thailand: Mahidol University, 2006.

Magee, J., and J. Sugden. 'The World at their Feet: Professional Football and International Labor Migration'. *Journal of Sport & Social Issues* 26, no. 4 (2002): 421–37.

Martinussen, John. *Society, State, and Market: A Guide to Competing Theories of Development*. London; Atlantic Highlands, NJ: $bZed Book; Halifax; Pretoria: Fernwood Pub.; Hrsc/rgn, 1997.

Megat Ahmad Kamaluddin Megat Daud. 'Sport Management Movement in Malaysia'. *Asian Sport Management Review* 1, no. 1 (2007): 21–31. https://docs.google.com/viewer?url=http://e-jasm.jp/docs/aasm/asmr01.pdf.

Owen, Slot. 'The Dream that Turned into Living Nightmare for Lost Boys of Africa'. *Sunday Times*, October 27, 2007. http://www.timesonline.co.uk/tol/sport/football/article2748770.ece.

Patwardhan, Deepti. 'Africans Kicking in Indian Football'. *Rediff India Abroad*, 2008, http://www.rediff.com/sports/2008/jan/14africans.htm.

Poli, Raffaele. *Les Migrations Internationales Des Footballeurs: Trajectoires De Joueurs Camerounais En Suisse*. Neuchâtel: Editions Centre International d'Etude du Sport, 2004.

Poli, Raffaele. 'African Migrants in Asian and European Football: Hopes and Realities'. *Sport in Society* 13, no. 6 (2010): 1011.

Poli, Raffaele, and Loic Ravenel. *Annual Review of the European Football Players' Labour Market*. Neuchâtel: Centre International d'Etude du Sport, 2007.

Redahan, Eoin. 'Expatriate Games: Foreign Footballers Feature Heavily in the Cambodian Premier League, But Is Their Presence Constructive or Destructive?' *Cambodia Daily*, 2008, http://www.camnet.com.kh/cambodia.daily/story_month/Oct-09.htm.

Wallerstein, Immanuel Maurice. *The Modern World-System*. New York: Academic Press, 1974.

Twenty years of development of the J-League: analysing the business parameters of professional football in Japan

Harald Dolles[a,b] and Sten Söderman[c]

[a]Molde University College, Molde, Norway ; [b]Centre for International Business, School of Business Studies, Economics and Law, University of Gothenburg, Gothenburg, Sweden; [c]School of Business, Stockholm University, Stockholm, Sweden

> By considering the implementation, as well as the immediate and sustainable success of the Japanese professional soccer (hence: football) league (J-League) during its first two decades as a neglected research example, we apply the 'network of value captures' research framework to the Japanese context. This research framework identifies and describes the business parameters of professional football by the following dimensions: (1) the product and its features; (2) various customer groups; and (3) the future vision of the club as central to different levels of strategy aggregation. The outcome of this research provides insight into the management of football in Japan by revealing different practices compared to Europe e.g. in target customer groups, in associated product marketing and merchandizing and in distribution of media revenues. The success story of the J-League also contributes to an increasing international awareness of Japanese football, its players and its fans.

Introduction: Soccer (football) in Japan

When the idea of the J-League began to materialize in the late 1980s, the prospect of a professional soccer (hence: football) league in Japan received limited national and practically no international attention. Moreover, one might argue that football already had been played in Japan for more than a century without establishing a self-sustaining basis, not being able to attract substantial audiences and the national team did make any big impact on international tournaments (besides winning the bronze medal at the 1968 Summer Olympics in Mexico City). The story is told that football entered Japan already in 1873 by means of a British naval commander who was teaching at Tokyo's naval academy and who started kicking a ball around with students between drills. Football then spread slowly via academic institutions. The first national championship was held in 1921, and shortly thereafter the foundation of the Japanese Football Association (JFA).

Compared to baseball in Japan (the Japanese professional baseball league was established in 1935), however, football held a minor position of importance in Japanese sports, as even the Japanese football championship, the Emperor's Cup, was contested almost exclusively by college and college old-boy teams.

Nonetheless, Waseda University's victory in the 1963 Emperor's Cup was the last of its kind for a college in Japan because Japanese firms of the 1950s began to form sports teams to improve morale and to help employees identify with their employer. By moving towards mass consumption, company sport began to be broadcast more extensively on TV. Surpassing the goal of merely uniting employees, the purpose of sports teams became to advertise on TV and in newspapers. To increase their competitiveness, players were scouted especially for these teams, which led to the out recruiting of college football, and paved the way for first non-university win of the Emperor's Cup by the Furukawa Electric company team in 1964. During the following decades, football in Japan only survived because of the supporting framework of corporate sports; however, it never acquired a competitive edge to enable it to challenge the dominant positions of professional baseball, golf and sumo.

The incorporation of the J-League in 1991 and the opening match on 15 May 1993 between Verdy Kawasaki and Yokohama Marinos at the National Olympic Stadium in Tokyo were intended to change sporting culture in Japan. Foreign ideas about the various ways in which football should be governed, structured, played and consumed were gradually institutionalized within Japanese sports during this process.[1] McDonald et al. state in their analysis that the L-League adapted practices to fit with Japanese cultural and social patterns.[2] The Economist described the J-League's instant success as a puzzle.[3] It is 'an exceptional case of creating a whole new market out of the blue – totalling a cumulative flow of JPY 472 billion [5.4 bn US$, added by the authors] over the first ten years' as argued by Hirose.[4] Light and Yasaki highlight the J-League as an outstanding success, 'attracting crowds that could not previously have been dreamt of for football in Japan.'[5] The J-League is said to be the basis for the Japanese national team's qualification for the last four World Cups, reaching the knockout stages in two of those tournaments and winning the Asian Football Confederation's Asian Cup a record four times.[6] We might conclude the success story of the J-League as an incredible period of growth for football in Japan – from amateur to the knockout stages of a World Cup in 20 years. The development of professional football in Japan therefore provides a promising area for research which, to date, has not been extensively covered outside Japan.

The article starts with the twentieth anniversary of the J-League and takes its success during their first two decades as a neglected research example, with it structured as follows: after identifying the research gap, we apply a conceptual network of value captures for professional team sport management for analysis. This framework will be used to highlight distinctive features of the J-League's establishment and practice. In the last chapter, we will conclude how the changes associated with the establishment of the J-League have changed the international attractiveness of Japanese football.

Development of football in Japan
Most of the existing literature in English on the J-League has been provided by journalists,[7] insiders, like the former coach of the Japanese National Team,[8] or practitioners.[9] While there are a few case surveys available,[10] most of the academic research in the field takes a sociological approach. For example, previous studies by Light and Yasaki[11] and Sugimoto[12] analyse the promotion of the J-League as a

community-based sport for the future development of all sports in Japan. The studies also promote the idea that sport might simply be an opportunity to interact socially and to identify oneself as belonging to a specific group of fans.[13]

Shimizu contrasts the behaviour of the supporters of the Urawa Red Diamonds team – the largest fan group in the J-League – with other football supporting cultures in Europe.[14] Among the supporters in Japan, women are much more present in the football arena than is the case in Europe. As such, Manzenreiter addresses the conjunctions of football, masculinity and gender relations in Japanese society in his research.[15] By conducting two surveys on J-League games, Sumino and Harada analysed the relationship between affective experience at the arena in Japan, team loyalty and intention to attend further matches.[16] In a similar attempt, Nakazwa et al. categorized Japanese fans into three segments according to J-League attendance.[17] The relationship between new team entry in the J-League and the options of team identification or brand switching by fans is examined by Harada and Matsuoka.[18] A socio-linguistic approach is taken by Ophüls-Kashima in research explaining the history of names, team emblems, team songs and mascots of Japanese football clubs.[19]

Existing research on the globalization of football might be placed within ethnosociology when examining the cultural meanings attached to social changes involving the rise of football in North-East Asia and its development in Japan.[20] The impact of both the Japanese sports lottery (toto) in 2001 and the 2002 FIFA World Cup on the development of the J-League is examined by Funk et al.[21] The use of public sport facilities in Japan and the planning, construction and operation of the football World Cup arenas in Japan are analysed by Manzenreiter[22] and Nogawa and Toshio.[23]

The existing body of work on the J-League's business system and impact can be categorized as descriptive and explorative. For example, Takahashi et al. explores the financial structure and business parameter of J-League clubs.[24] Hirose reflects on the design process and the costs of establishing a professional league.[25] To him, the initial success of the J-League owed a great deal to high mass media exposure deriving from media reporting, not simply from advertising. Football itself was marketed in Japan as a 'new, improved product, now on sale', in the mould of a marketing principle well known to Japanese marketing professionals.[26] Manzenreiter, however, suggests causal links between the success of J-League's clubs and sponsoring engagements by firms as well as the support by local communities are responsible for the J-League's success.[27] 'Community pride' also constituted one of seven contributing factors quoted by Mahony et al., where the overall focus was on spectator motives and an attempt to measure influence on the behaviour of J-league audience.[28] Ōsumi[29] and Matsouka et al.[30] reported on J-League team identification and satisfaction and the reasoning behind match attendance. Manzenreiter and Horne also identified the fan's capability and willingness to spend on football and those consumer products advertised through the game as the economic base for professional football in Japan.[31] However, they conclude that 'reducing the role of spectators to pure consumers would do injustice to the complexity of motives and objectives that draw people into football support.'[32]

From the literature review, three main limitations in the current state of management research regarding Japanese football were identified. Firstly, the findings of those research streams have neither been systematically consolidated into a framework nor validated by means of a broader empirical survey. Secondly, given its economic impact, the business perspective in the development of football in Japan still needs to be addressed in further research, thus challenging existing 'westernized' assumptions how the football business should be organized and managed. Thirdly, Japanese football is increasingly becoming part of the global network of interdependency chains in the football business, therefore adding further dimensions to the research on sport as a global business.

Methodology

The development of our network of value captures, as a framework for research, is built upon empirical literature analysis on stories of success or failure of professional football clubs. In addition, to confirm the analysis we requested comments from football club managers, football associations' officials and sport management experts during 32 semi-structured interviews. Some comments were very general in nature or related to fundamental concerns about the cases and models we used or the assumptions we made. Other comments were more specific and very detailed in nature. We responded to the more general, broad-based comments, concerns, and issues in order to develop a general framework that can be applied in investigating a professional team sport setting in general, and more specifically, the football industry.

The network of value captures for professional team-sport club management, as introduced and applied to football in the next section, benefited much from the discussion succeeding its initial presentation at the Academy of International Business 2005 annual meeting and the circulation of the subsequent working paper.[33] All the comments received have led to a revised version of the research framework.[34] This framework was presented and further discussed at various conferences and workshops, thus involving practitioners from the football industry as well as academics in the field. The network of value captures in team-sport management presented in the next section is an extension and revision of the earlier version and reflects the development in the football industry. It also incorporates the changes suggested by Dolles and Schweizer in regard to football services and the relationship between clubs.[35] An application of the initial framework on the development of the Japanese professional football league has been made by Dolles and Söderman[36] and was discussed at research seminars at Chuo University and Waseda University in Tokyo, with the JFA as well as with two representatives from Japanese football clubs.

The network of value captures as research framework

It is not one single product, service or entertainment that are offered in professional team sports, that could be termed as the competitive scope of a football club, the league or a football association. It is therefore the managerial task to evaluate, change, bundle and utilize the club's resources (value captures). Our understanding of value captures is based on Barney's conceptualization of resources and sustained competitive advantage.[37] A football club's resources can only be a source of competitive advantage when they are valuable and recognized by the customer, as stated by Dolles and Söderman.[38] Resources are considered to be value captures when they enable a football club to implement strategies (value capturing activities) that improve its efficiency and effectiveness. Valuable football club resources possessed by a large number of competing clubs cannot be sources of sustained competitive advantage if a club is not differentiating upon them. A football club only enjoys a competitive advantage when it is implementing a unique value-creating strategy combining bundles of valuable club resources (value captures) recognized and accepted by the customer (by the customer's groups). Our research framework therefore builds upon three dimensions suitable to analyse professional football at three levels – the club, the league and the football association: (1) the product and its features, (2) the customers, (3) the business process, strategic vision and intent.

Product offerings: Football is not one single product, service or entertainment that a football club offers. We can consider the following possible offerings, termed value captures: (1.A) team; (1.B) sporting competitions; (1.C) club; (1.D) players; (1.E) football services; (1.F) event, facilities and arena; (1.G) merchandise, and (1.H) other commercial activities. The arrows in Figure 1 indicate that all value offerings are interlinked and might also be considered as bundles of a club's value captures.

Value capture 1.A: *Team* A variety of models have been proposed and explored in the literature on organizational behaviour and personnel psychology to understand work team effectiveness in various industry settings.[39] In a team sport setting it is obvious that eleven skilled players do not necessarily comprise a winning team. A team with superior physical ability alone cannot beat an opponent that has good technique and a carefully planned strategy. Furthermore, without

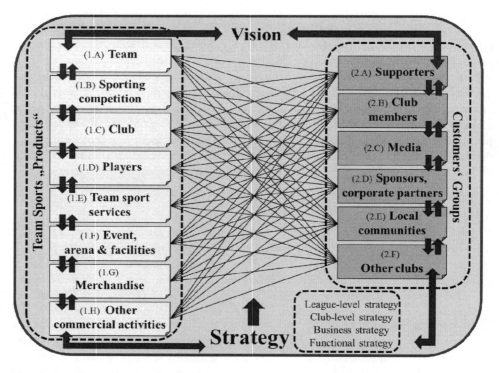

Figure 1. The network of value captures in professional football. Source: Dolles and Söderman, *Analyze Competitive Advantage*, p. 327.

adequate training and performance techniques, even the most well intentioned teams fail to win the match.

Value capture 1.B: *Sporting Competitions* Football as a team sport also requires coordination among the contesting teams because the game involves at least two distinct teams. Revising the arguments for the necessary institutional features of a league,[40] we prefer to change perspective and to focus on the following elements of sporting competitions, (1) Distribution: How to schedule matches or tournaments. (2) Hierarchy: What are structural pathways for players and teams to progress and regress. (3) Multiplicity: How many leagues should be at the same level of hierarchy. (4) Membership: What are the conditions under which a team enters and exits a league. (5) Governance: How are league rules decided and enforced as well as controlling of the economic behaviour of its members handled. (6) Labour: What is the structure of the transfer market and how to determine the level of compensation to players, coaches and managers.

Value capture 1.C: *Club* Hosting a winning team has a dual meaning for professional sports organizations. Not only must the players on the sporting team be able to give their utmost to the cause of winning, but the financial and organizational structure behind it must also work closely to ensure that its business goals will be achieved (thus referring to the contextual factors of team effectiveness and the necessary prerequisites for league membership, see 1.A and 1.B).

Value capture 1.D: *Players* Players and their development are of prime concern to football managers. Football clubs send out their scouts to discover young players in the region and to sign contracts with them, as some of them might later find their way to a professional team. Driven by the rise in transfer fees of players, and the increase in value of young players, professional football clubs began operating Youth Academies.

Value capture 1.E: *Football services* Football services are considered a rather new development in the commercial activities of a club and cover three different areas.[41] First, the idea of a one-stop-shop for all club related services and merchandizing products (refer also to value capture 1.G). Second, the establishment of Football Youth Academies as a service to recruit and retain talented young players (refer also to value capture 1.D and 1.F). Third, specialized tailored services offered as a development programme for other football clubs, coaches and players all over the world.

Value capture 1.F: *Event, Arena and Facilities* A football match is intangible, short-lived, unpredictable and subjective in nature. It is produced and consumed by the spectators in the arena at the same time, mostly with a strong emotional commitment from the fans. In recent years those football matches have been transformed into media events for the benefit of millions of spectators, few of which have the chance to watch the match in the arena. Such mediatised events affect even the arena they are attached to, attaining the power to transform ordinary places into extraordinary sites.

Value capture 1.G: *Merchandise* One of the key ingredients of the business of football is its local character, yet one that participates in a global football market; this presents special challenges to marketing the brand. Simply put, the brand is standing for everything about a football club, from the team to its players, which is communicated by the name and related identifiers (football merchandise). Football merchandise means goods held for resale but not manufactured by the football club, such as: flags and banners, scarves and caps, training gear, jerseys and fleeces, etc.

Value capture 1.H: *Other Commercial Activities* Chadwick and Clowes explored brand extension strategies by Premier League football clubs, by examining factors which have led clubs to consider extending their product lines and their brands further. They concluded as the key consideration for both clubs and their supporters that there is a clear and obvious link between the club's brand and the extension.[42]

Customer groups: Why do supporters choose one team over another? Cost is certainly not the sole argument in the football business for fans, whereas fun, excitement, skilled players, regional embeddedness might be all good reasons for supporting a team. The bottom line may be the corporate culture of the football club as the underlying culture helps to determine the value that consumers place on the football club; however, we need to recognize that every customer integrates multiple markets. Consumers want different offerings at different times under different circumstances. Consequently, the variety of offerings creates a broader consumer approach in football by addressing (2.A) spectators and supporters (fan base), (2.B) club members (club membership), (2.C) media, (2.D) sponsors and corporate partners, (2.E) local communities, and (2.F.) other clubs. The arrows in Figure 1 indicate that all customer groups are interlinked and also be considered as bundles of a club's value captures.

Value capture 2.A: *Supporters* When it comes to 'sales' in the football business, the supporters, with regard to ticket sales and merchandizing, create the main attention. According to Fisher and Wakefield, fan motivation and subsequent behaviour goes beyond the record of the team and, at times, seems unrelated to performance.[43] Fan motivation and behaviour vary depending upon the type of fan. For our purposes, we adopt a slightly different classification by introducing the 'psychic distance' dimension, defined as factors that make it difficult to understand the local embeddedness of a club: local fans vs. international fans.[44]

Value capture 2.B: *Club Members* The football club, as host of their teams, wants to have a sustainable stock of members, which requires an iterative approach between the product and the customer. Such approaches are covered in the vast literature on interactive marketing[45] and on relationship marketing[46] (Bühler & Nufer 2010; Gummesson 2002).

Value capture 2.C: *Media* With regard to income in professional football, the media is the other main customer—or the main sales channel. The importance of football for the media business can be seen in the increasing amounts of money paid for broadcast rights to the national league or for events like the FIFA World Cup as well as the growth in the number of sports-oriented broadcasting networks.[47] Rowe notes that sport and TV have become mutually and internationally indispensable.[48]

Value capture 2.D: *Sponsors and Corporate Partners* Football is a natural area for sponsorship as it carries very strong images, has a mass international audience and appeals to all classes.[49] Each sponsored event is capable of reaching differently defined audiences.[50]

Value capture 2.E: *Local Communities* The relationship between football clubs and their communities has been subject of debate and discussion in political circles and in academic research.[51] Morrow and Hamil argue that a football club's community is made up of two dimensions: 'first, a direct community of supporters and, second, a wider notion encompassing people and groups who can be affected either directly or indirectly by the existence and operation of a football club within a particular space, usually geographical.'[52] The focus on the relationship between football clubs and their local communities is also to some extent debt driven, when communities serve as a lender of last resort in times of financial trouble for football clubs.

Value capture 2.F: *Other Football Clubs* Other football clubs are of prime importance when it comes to player transfers as well as lending players, as mentioned in the discussion of value capture (1.D). Additionally, by introducing football services as a value capture (1.E), we might consider other football clubs – amateur as well as professional clubs; national as well as international – also as potential recipients of football services. And on the regional level, clubs are collaborating in player development in youth teams by providing football services in exchange.

The highest and broadest level business objective is the *vision of the club* (**3. A**). This is a statement of broad aspiration, as it deals with where the club hopes to be in the future. This is not about winning the next game, it is the attempt by the club management to define where it expects the club to be at a later point in time: to win the championship; to stay in the league; to make profit; or to go international. With the exception of merchandizing, the football business lacks the option of producing and storing inventory for future sale, as the main characteristic of football is its ambiguity and the uncertainty of the outcome of a game.

In order to reach the goals attached to the vision of where the club should be in the future, what kind of *strategies* should be applied? **(3.B)** Strategies can be articulated for different activities within the club, where the lowest level of aggregation is one specific task, while the highest level of aggregation encompasses all activities within the club. A logical extension of this distinction is the league level strategy.

The analysis of the J-League's development

By applying the research framework outlined in the previous section we will

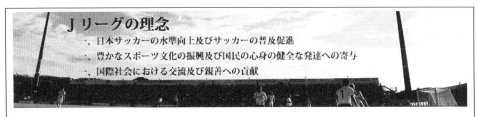

J-League Ideology

- To raise the level of Japanese football and promote the diffusion of football.
- To foster the development of sporting culture, to assist in the healthy mental and physical growth of Japanese people.
- To contribute to the international community though friendship and exchange.

highlight the key characteristics of professional football in Japan and analyse how the J-League is organized and developed in Japan. We begin by introducing the *strategic vision* and *objectives statements* (3.A) of the J-League:[53]

Linking the *vision* (3.A) with *strategy* (3.B), the *national team* (1.A) and the *fan base* (2.A) the 'JFA Declaration' (see Figure 2) demonstrates the Japanese midterm objectives of the JFA to be achieved by 2015 and the long-term vision on the promotion and development of football in Japan to be fulfilled by 2050.[54] After being ranked 43rd in the old FIFA ranking in 1993, the JFA was ranked No. 58 in the new FIFA world ranking and advanced to No. 24 in the men's rankings in 2012.[55] Making their sixth straight appearance in the Football World Cup and becoming world champions in Football in the final round played in Germany in

Figure 2. The JFA declaration. Source: Japanese Football Association, *JFA Declaration*.

2010, the Japanese women's national team 'Nadeshiko Japan' is the most successful Asian team in women's football and the JFA is already ranked as No. 3 in the women's world ranking.[56]

By interlinking the strategic *vision* (3.A) with the *team* (1.A) and *all customer segments* (2.A to 2.F), one major difference to football in Europe becomes obvious when comparing the mission statements. Popular enthusiasm for football in Japan is tied to the success of the national squad, compared to club teams in Europe. 'The national team will be good if the local teams are good, the local teams will be good if they are well supported locally, and local support will be strong if the national team does well'.[57]

Another particularity of Japanese football becomes apparent by connecting different *levels of strategy* (3.B), *sporting competition* (1.B), as well as *media* (2.C) and *corporate partners* (2.D). The main objective for the J-League during the first decade since its establishment was to survive due to the extreme simplicity of its contracts, organizational structures, and substantial investments in marketing.[58] The J-League markets itself as an autonomous, non-profit organization, like the Championnats of France and the German Bundesliga. The striking difference is that most of the decisions concerning sponsorship and licenses were dealt in the beginning centrally by the management of the J-League, whereas in Europe, the clubs are responsible for their own corporate partners. In its first few seasons, the J-League and its *member clubs* (1.C) had to cooperate to survive in a country where football was overshadowed by baseball, sumo and golf. If the football clubs were to settle their own sponsorship deals (2.D) and TV contracts (2.C) from the start, many teams would have left the J-League with financial problems.[59] By having contracts, sponsorship deals and TV rights all decided centrally, the J-League achieved to accumulate larger sums of money, which have been distributed equally among its member teams. This synchronized effort at equitable financial support and public exposure/marketing aimed to increase support for football in Japan as a whole, as opposed to just the top teams of the league. Following in the footsteps of the North-American sport system (like the NFL or the NBA), this was believed to achieve higher competitiveness by giving equal growth opportunities for each individual team. The US influence on the J-League is also visible in the franchise system of all football merchandise, such as kits, balls, refereeing equipment, nutrition (soda) drinks and all other imaginable *merchandise* (1.G).

The J-League started with a clear belief that the only way to gain the all-important support of the general public in the beginning was to create a true 'home-town' system with a close mutual commitment between the football club and the local people (interlinking strategic *vision* (3.A), *club* (1.C), *fans* (2.A) and the *local community* (2.E)). Opposing the North-American sport system and basing themselves on the German tradition, the J-League founders wanted to create the sort of atmosphere where local people are passionately involved in the fortunes of the home club. Equally, they tried to avoid the franchise type of sports league organization that is common in the USA, where a team's home depends on the preference of the legal owner. This *hometown-base* (2.E) is still a condition of J-League membership:

> The J. League wants its member clubs to serve as fully integrated members of their local community. Each club promotes sporting development in its designated hometown area. The hometown concept is for each club to be a self-sufficient entity based

on the combined support of local citizens, administrators and companies, functioning and growing as a community gathering point and symbol. Each club is therefore called after its hometown area with the addition of a moniker of its own choosing.[60]

One major challenge by establishing the hometown concept was that *club membership* (2.Bn had to be defined within Japanese society. In most European countries, football is organized through clubs, with active members taking part as amateurs in competition, and non-active members. In Japan, however, this was not common. Influenced by the American system, Japan's football was solely provided previously by companies on the one hand, and schools, colleges, and universities on the other hand.

When analysing the *structural features* (1.B) of the J-League, it started with 10 *clubs* (1.C) in a single league in 1991 that implemented a two-division system in 1999 (see Table 3 in the conclusion section for the development). As of 2012, the twentieth anniversary season, the number of football clubs had risen to 40 (18 in J1, 22 in J2) with even more football club's seeking admission. A Club Licensing Administration was established in 2011 as a follow up to the regular participation of Japanese club teams to the Asian Football Confederation's Champions League. Due to the expansion strategy, the concept of promotion and relegation is in flux. For example, the two top teams in J2 have been promoted to J1 without any relegations in 2004. In fulfilling the club's obligations to the J-League organization, Japanese professional football clubs will also not drop down from the second J-League as is the case across Europe. Additionally, a J-League 2 club, even if it qualifies on the pitch, can only be promoted if it satisfies the formal requirements for entry to J-League 1.[61]

Linking *club* (1.C), *merchandise* (1.G), *fans* (2.A) and *corporate partners* (2.D) during the initial years of the J-League, the founders targeted people who played and enjoyed football and who were passionately involved in the action on the pitch. Match attendance included not only families – there was not so much as a hint of the hooligan tendency that keeps young women and children away from visiting the arena in Europe – but also teenage girls and office ladies, who came to cheer on individual players. Still – and different from the football watching audiences in Europe – female and family attendance dominate the scene in Japanese football arenas (Ref. to Tables 1 and 2). Creating a football supporting culture was one of the major tasks of the first decade of the J-League. For this purpose and different to European practices, associated *product marketing and merchandizing* (1.F) is centralized in the J-League. 'The unified marketing system allowed consistent pricing, design and quality, ensuring responsible trademark management and equal

Table 1. Fan attendance in J-League matches – gender and age.

Age	Total (in %)	Male (in %)	Female (in %)
18 or below	5.9	6.1	5.5
19–22	6.1	5.7	6.6
23–29	14.1	12.8	16.1
30–39	29.4	29.5	29.2
40–49	26.3	27.8	24.0
50 or above	18.3	18.1	18.6

Note: $N=16,222$; Average Age: 38.2 years.
Source: Nakazawa et al., *J. League Spectator Survey*.

Table 2. Fan attendance in J-League matches – Attendance distribution.

	Attend for myself (in %)	Attend with friend(s) (in %)	Attend with family (in %)	Other (in %)
Total	15.3	35.6	52.8	3.3
Male	21.1	33.8	47.5	3.3
Female	5.7	38.5	61.1	3.5
Age				
18 or below	4.8	46.9	52.3	3.4
19–22	9.3	59.6	29.2	5.9
23–29	13.9	56.6	28.3	6.0
30–39	16.3	37.2	51.6	3.0
40–49	16.8	24.8	63.4	2.3
50 or above	17.3	20.5	66.0	2.5

Note: N=16,227.
Source: Nakazawa et al., *J. League Spectator Survey*.

exposure for each club'.[62] This strategy reflects the fundamental principle of the founders of the J-League that all teams should have an equal chance of exposure and an equal share of the merchandizing revenue. In the same vein, the J-League practices a method of distributing *media revenues from broadcasting rights* (2.C) equally to all J-League teams irrespective of performance,[63] challenging prevailing European practices in professional soccer (and even other sports, like baseball, in Japan).

Conclusion: creating a new market for football in Japan and Asia

The network of value captures constitutes a number of paths for a club, the league or the football association to enter when succeeding in this growing industry. Without a local *fan base* (2.A) and *local revenues* (2.E) a *football club* (1.C) or a professional league cannot expect to survive and prosper beyond its market of origin. The twentieth anniversary of the J-League provides a good opportunity to look back at what has been achieved towards the development of football in Asia. During the first two decades, the J-League's establishment has been the catalyst for the growth of football in Japan and, when comparing globally, few other countries can boast such a rapid improvement in team sports. And, during those two decades the J-League not only expanded in terms of teams but also fans attraction and revenues (see Table 3).

Attracted by the huge potential market and the growing popularity of football in Japan, Europe's top football clubs, like Manchester United, Real Madrid, FC Barcelona and FC Bayern Munich pay increasingly regular visits to Japan to play friendly matches. By means of follow up and service to their Japanese fans, a Japanese language version of the clubs' website is frequently available, which also allows them to purchase official club products online (linking the *friendly match* (1.F) with the *fans* (2.A) and the *merchandise* (1.G)). However, the problem still remains how to convert this attention of foreign clubs into sustainable revenue streams for Japanese football.

Table 3. J-League – development of match attendance and revenues.

Year	No. of clubs	J-League 1 total match attendance (no. of spectators)	J-League 1 average match attendance (no. of spectators)	J-League 2 total match attendance (no. of spectators)	J-League 2 average match attendance (no. of spectators)	J-League 1 + 2 total match attendance (no. of spectators)	Income from broadcasting rights (in million Yen)	Income from J-League sponsorship (in million Yen)	Income from J-League merchandizing and licencing (in million Yen)	Total J-League revenues (in million Yen)	Total revenue distribution to J-League clubs (in million Yen)
1993	10	2,235,750	17,976			3,235,750	1093	2310	3601	8892	8460
1994	12	5,173,817	19,598			5,173,817	2190	2961	3587	10,031	8028
1995	14	6,159,691	16,922			6,159,691	2214	2799	2543	10,400	7363
1996	16	3,204,807	13,353			3,204,807	1187	4681	934	8301	5385
1997	17	2,755,698	10,131			2,755,698	2056	4106	473	8016	5127
1998	18	3,666,496	11,982			3,666,496	2189	4032	234	7994	4779
1999	(J1: 16/J2: 10)	2,798,005	11,658	827,217	4596	3,625,222	2386	3281	277	7546	4362
2000	(J1: 16/J2: 11)	2,655,553	11,065	1,340,820	6095	3,996,373	2221	4018	237	8009	4624
2001	(J1: 16/J2: 12)	3,971,415	16,548	1,505,722	5703	5,477,137	2461	3876	593	8520	5212
2002	(J1: 16/J2: 12)	3,928,215	16,368	1,806,392	6842	5,734,607	4815	3521	697	11,148	7223
2003	(J1: 16/J2: 12)	4,164,229	17,351	2,084,185	7895	6,248,414	4818	3902	739	11,454	7667
2004	(J1: 16/J2: 12)	4,551,695	18,965	1,904,172	7213	6,455,867	4978	4281	682	11,789	7681
2005	(J1: 16/J2: 12)	5,742,233	18,765	1,975,340	7482	7,717,573	4905	4005	668	11,718	6959
2006	(J1: 16/J2: 13)	5,597,408	18,292	1,998,648	6406	7,596,056	5341	4347	723	12,712	7532
2007	(J1: 16/J2: 13)	5,834,081	19,066	2,034,543	6521	7,868,624	5278	4201	680	12,342	7196
2008	(J1: 16/J2: 15)	5,875,865	19,202	2,227,570	7072	8,103,435	5323	4624	613	12,845	7027
2009	(J1: 16/J2: 18)	5,809,516	18,985	2,903,607	6326	8,713,123	5197	4729	698	12,776	7066
2010	(J1: 16/J2: 19)	5,638,894	18,428	2,290,082	6696	7,928,976	4851	4523	588	12,372	7351

Source: J-League, *Balance Sheet*; J-League, *People Attending*.

To strengthen their position, Japanese football clubs also target the international market. For example, the collaborative agreement between Urawa Red Diamonds and Germany's FC Bayern Munich plays a significant role in their strategy to become one of the best-known Japanese team in Europe. This partnership was signed in 2006 aiming at, e.g. (1) playing team friendlies against each other in both countries (1.B); (2) sharing scouting information (1.D, 1.E); (3) accepting each other's players for training and the development of exchange systems for youth players (1.D, 1.E); (4) mutual merchandizing support (1.G).[64] J-League matches are frequently attended by international scouts from clubs in Europe, North and South America looking for *Japanese players* (linking 1.D with 2.F). At the league level, the North-American Major League Soccer (MLS) appointed an Asian scouting coordinator based in Tokyo, who will be looking to open a bigger door for players to come through to play their trade in MLS. To help with fostering relationships in Japan, the two leagues also committed to share best practices[65] (covering the value captures 1.B, 1.D, 1.E and 1.H). Similar agreements have also been signed between the J-League and European leagues, e.g. the Bundesliga, or even between tournaments. In 2012 it was announced that the Gothia Cup – the largest youth football tournament in the world played annually in Gothenburg (Sweden) with teams from more than 100 nations – has signed a three-year cooperation agreement with the JFA and the J-League. The agreement states that the football club receiving the award for best youth team in Japan – Best Academy Club Award – will send its team for boys at the age of 16 to participate in the Gothia Cup.[66]

One of the key ingredients of the business of football is its simultaneously global and local character. The J-League has continued to provide a good competitive environment but it is the experience of international football that has raised the standard in Japan. There are still foreign players in the J-League, but not of the level as in the beginning of the J-League when players such as Bazil's Zico and Germany's Littbarski played in Japan. Those former superstars made a big impression on Japan's young players at that time and contributed greatly to the J-League's soaring popularity. Today, the J-League is attractive for non-Japanese *players* (1.D), especially from Asia, and Japanese players are increasingly making careers in the top clubs all over the world. By itself, more than 10 Japanese players have moved to Germany's Bundesliga after the World Cup in South Africa, underlining not only Japan's newly accomplished status in the global world of football, but also helping to banish old European perceptions that Asian players cannot make it in top European leagues. Furthermore, due to foreign players from Asia in the J-League and the resulting increase in popularity of Japanese Football in Asia outside Japan, the J-League initiated negotiations with authorities from four Southeast Asian nations (Thailand, Indonesia, Vietnam and Malaysia) to broadcast Japanese football free of charge on terrestrial TV[67] (2.C). In pursuing the project and to boost its profile in Asia further, the J-League also intends to place itself as part of the 'Cool Japan' brand initiative by the Japanese Ministry of Economy, Trade and Industry,[68] which promotes Japanese creative industries for expansion into overseas markets.

Notes

1. Dolles and Söderman, *Implementing a Professional Football League*.
2. McDonald et al., *Spectator Sport Industry*.
3. Economist, *Goal!*.

4. Hirose, *The Making of*, 38.
5. Light and Yasaki, *Rekindling of Regional Identity*, 40.
6. Darnbrook, *Success of the J-League*.
7. E.g. Chubachi, *J.League's New Goal*; Darnbrook, *Success of the J-League*; Hara, *Professional Soccer in Japan*; Moffett, *Japanese Rules*; Ōsumi, *Happiness*, Tsuboi and Yaki, *Databook*.
8. Troussier, *Passion*.
9. Hirose, *The Making of*; Hirose, *J-League Managment*.
10. E.g. Harada and Ogasawara, *Sport Management*; Light and Yasaki, *Winds of Change*; Manzenreiter, *Japan and Football*; Probert and Schütte, *Japan Scores in Soccer*; Takahashi et al., *Sports Management*.
11. Light and Yasaki, *Breaking the Mould*; Light and Yasaki, *Rekindling of Regional Identity*.
12. Sugimoto, *School Sport*.
13. Also Ōsumi, *Happiness*.
14. Shimizu, *Soccer Fans*.
15. Manzenreiter, *Crisis of Masculinity*; Manzenreiter, *Reconstruction of the Gender Order*.
16. Sumino and Harada, *J.League Fans*.
17. Nakazawa et al., *Segmenting J.League Spectators*.
18. Harada and Matsuoka, *New Team Entry*.
19. Ophüls-Kashima, *Japanese Club Names*.
20. E.g. Close and Askew, *Globalisation and Football*; Horne, *Sakka*; Horne, *Football in Japan*; Horne, *Professional Football*; Horne and Bleakley, *Development of Football*; Manzenreiter, *Japan and Football*; Manzenreiter, *World Sports*; Manzenreiter and Horne, *Football Goes East*; Manzenreiter and Horne, *Playing the Post-Fordist Game*; Nogawa and Maeda, *Japanese Dream*.
21. Funk et al., *Impact of the National Sports Lottery*.
22. Manzenreiter, *The Benefits of Hosting*.
23. Nogawa and Toshio, *Mega-Events*.
24. Takahashi et al., *Sports Management*.
25. Hirose, *The Making of*; Hirose, *J-League Managment*.
26. Watts, *Soccer Shinhatsubai*.
27. Manzenreiter, *Japan and Football*.
28. Mahony et al., *Behaviour of J-League Spectators*.
29. Ōsumi, *Happiness*.
30. Matsuoka et al., *Interaction Effects*.
31. Manzenreiter and Horne, *Playing the Post-Fordist Game*.
32. Manzenreiter and Horne, *Playing the Post-Fordist Game*, 574.
33. Dolles and Söderman, *Ahead of the Game*.
34. Dolles and Söderman, *Network of Value Captures*.
35. Dolles and Schweizer, *Advancing the Network*.
36. Dolles and Söderman, *Implementing a Professional Football League*; Dolles and Söderman, *Learning From Success*; Dolles and Söderman, *Professional Football Management*.
37. Barney, *Sustained Competitive Advantage*.
38. Dolles and Söderman, *Learning From Success*, 233.
39. I.e. Campion et al., *Relations Between Work Teams*; Gladstein, *Groups in Context*.
40. E.g. as developed by Noll, *Organization of Sports Leagues*; Smith and Westerbeck, *Sport Business Future*.
41. Dolles and Schweizer, *Advancing the Network*.
42. Chadwick and Clowes, *Use of Extension Strategies*.
43. Fisher and Wakefield, *Group Identification*.
44. Dolles and Söderman, *Analyze Competitive Advantage*.
45. Adler et al., *Getting the Most*.
46. Bühler and Nufer, *Relationship Marketing*; Gummesson, *Total Relationship Marketing*.
47. Gratton and Solberg, *Sport Broadcasting*.
48. Rowe, *Global Love-Match*; Rowe, *Media and Sport*.
49. Ferrand and Pages, *Image Sponsoring*.

50. Javalgi et al., *Awareness of Sponsorship*; Meenaghan and Shipley, *Media Effect*; Söderman and Dolles, *International Sponsorship*, Söderman and Dolles, B*eijing Olympic Games*; Thwaites, *Football Sponsorship*.
51. E.g. Bale, *The Changing Face*; Jaquiss, *Mutualism Rules*.
52. Morrow and Hamil, *Community Involvement*, 1–2; Morrow, *Business of Football*.
53. J-League, *About J-League*.
54. Japanese Football Association, *JFA Declaration*.
55. FIFA, *World Ranking*.
56. FIFA, *Women's World Ranking*.
57. Probert and Schütte, *Japan Scores in Soccer*, 15; also Horne and Bleakley, *Development of Football*; Horne and Manzenreiter, *The 2002 World Cup*; Troussier, *Passion*.
58. E.g. Harada and Ogasawara, *Sport Management*; Moffett, *Japanese Rules*.
59. Personal interview by the authors with a JFA representative.
60. J-League, *Home Towns*.
61. J-League, *Conditions for J1, J2*.
62. Probert and Schütte, *Japan Scores in Soccer*, 8.
63. Horne and Bleakley, *Development of Football*.
64. Urawa Red Diamonds, *In the World*.
65. Major League Soccer, *MLS expands*.
66. Gothia Cup, *Gothia Cup*.
67. Chubachi, *J.League's New Goal*.
68. Cool Japan Advisory Council, *Creating A New Japan*.

References

Adler, Paul S., Avi Mandelbaum, Vien Nguyen, and Elizabeth Schwerer. 'Getting the Most Out of Your Product Development Process'. *Harvard Business Review* 74, no. 2 (1996): 134–52.

Bale, John. 'The Changing Face of Football: Stadiums and Communities'. In *The Future of Football: Challenges For The Twenty-First Century*, eds. John Garland, Dominic Malcolm and Mike Rowe, 91–101. London: Frank Cass, 2000.

Barney, Jay. 'Firm Resources and Sustained Competitive Advantage'. *Journal of Management* 17, no. 1 (1991): 99–120.

Bühler, André, and Gerd Nufer. *Relationship Marketing in Sports*. Oxford: Butterworth-Heinemann, 2010.

Campion, Michael A., Gina J. Medsker, and A. Catherine Higgs. "Relations Between Work Team Characteristics and Effectiveness: Implications for Designing Effective Work Groups". *Personnel Psychology* 46, no. 4 (1993): 823–50.

Chadwick, Simon, and Jeff Clowes. 'The Use of Extension Strategies by Clubs in the English Football Premier League'. *Managing Leisure* 3, no. 4 (1998): 194–203.

Chubachi, Shinichi. 'J. League's New Goal is Tapping Southeast Asian Markets', *Asahi Shimbun*, January 7, 2012. http://ajw.asahi.com/article/asia/AJ201201070001 (accessed November 20, 2012).

Close, Paul and David Askew. 'Globalisation and Football in East Asia'. In *Football Goes East. Business, Culture And the People's Game in China, Japan and South Korea*, eds. Wolfram Manzenreiter and John Horne, 243–56. London: Routledge, 2004.

Cool Japan Advisory Council. *Creating a New Japan: Tying Together "Culture and Industry" And "Japan and the World"*. Tokyo: Ministry of Economy, Trade and Industry, 2011.

Darnbrook, James. 'The Success of The J-League Mirrors The Success of Japan The Country'. http://www.worldsoccer.com/blogs/337671 (accessed November 26, 2012).

Dolles, Harald and Sten Söderman. 'The Network of Value Captures in Football Club Management: A Framework to Develop and Analyze Competitive Advantage in Professional Team Sports'. In *Handbook of Research on Sport and Business*, eds. Sten Söderman and Harald Dolles, 367–95. Cheltenham: Edward Elgar, 2013.

Dolles, Harald and Sten Söderman. 'Implementing a Professional Football League in Japan – Challenges to Research in International Business'. *DIJ Working Paper* no. 05/6, German Institute for Japanese Studies, 2005.

Dolles, Harald and Sten Söderman. 'Ahead of the Game - The Network of Value Captures in Professional Football'. *DIJ Working Paper* no. 05/5, German Institute for Japanese Studies, 2005.

Dolles, Harald and Roger Schweizer. 'Advancing the Network of Value Captures in the Football Business: The Everton Football Club Case'. Paper presented at the European Academy of Management 10th Annual Meeting, Rome, Tor Vergata University, May 19–22, 2010. http://www.euram2010.org (accessed June 20, 2010).

Dolles, Harald and Sten Söderman. 'Learning From Success: Implementing a Professional Football League in Japan'. In *Sport as a Business: International, Professional And Commercial Aspects*, eds. Harald Dolles and Sten Söderman, 228–50. Houndmills: Palgrave Macmillan, 2011.

Dolles, Harald, and Sten Söderman. 'The Network of Value Captures: Creating Competitive Advantage in Football Management'. *Wirtschaftspolitische Blätter Österreich [Austrian Economic Policy Papers]* 55, no. 1 (2008): 39–58.

Dolles, Harald, and Sten Söderman. 'プロ・サッカーのマネジメントにおける経済価値獲得のネットワーク―日本プロ・サッカー・リーグ発展の分析―' [The network of economic value captures in professional football management: Analyzing the development of the Japanese professional soccer league]. Shōgaku Ronsan. *The Journal of Commerce* 40, no. 1–2 (2011): 195–232.

Economist (US). 'Goal! Says Japan. Soccer is Challenging Baseball's Grip on the Japanese Imagination'. *Economist*, October 22, 1994, 109.

Ferrand, Alain, and Monique Pages. 'Image Sponsoring: A Methodology to Match Event and Sponsor'. *Journal of Sports Management* 10, no. 3 (1996): 278–91.

FIFA. 'FIFA/Coca-Cola Women's World Ranking'. http://www.fifa.com/worldranking/rankingtable/women/index.html (accessed November 26, 2012).

FIFA. 'FIFA/Coca-Cola World Ranking'. http://www.fifa.com/worldranking/rankingtable/index.html (accessed November 26, 2012).

Fisher, Robert J., and Kirk Wakefield. 'Factors Leading to Group Identification: A Field Study of Winners and Losers'. *Psychology and Marketing* 15, no. 1 (1998): 23–40.

Funk, Daniel C., Makoto Nakazawa, Daniel F. Mahony, and Robert Thrasher. 'The Impact of the National Sports Lottery and the FIFA World Cup on Attendance, Spectator Motives and J. League Marketing Strategies'. *International Journal of Sports Marketing and Sponsorship* 7, no. 3 (2006): 267–85.

Gladstein, Deborah L. 'Groups in Context: A Model of Task Group Effectiveness'. *Administrative Science Quarterly* 29, no. 4 (1984): 499–517.

Gothia Cup. 'Gothia Cup to Collaborate With the Japanese Football Association'. http://www.gothiacup.se/eng/2012/05/gothia-cup-to-collaborate-with-the-japanese-football-association/ (accessed November 15, 2012).

Gratton, Chris and Harry Arne Solberg. *The Economics of Sport Broadcasting*. London: Routledge, 2007.

Gummesson, Evert. *Total Relationship Marketing: Rethinking Marketing Management*. Oxford: Butterworth-Heinemann, 2002.

Hara, Takeo. 'J.League – Professional Soccer in Japan'. *Nipponia*, no. 18 (15. September) (2001): 1–4.

Harada, Munehiko, and Hirotaka Matsuoka. 'The Influence of New Team Entry Upon Brand Switching in the J-League'. *Sport Marketing Quarterly* 8, no. 3 (1999): 21–30.

Harada, Munehiko, and Etsuko Ogasawara. スポーツ・マネジメント[Sport Management]. Tokyo: Taishukan, 2008.

Hirose, Ichiro. 'The Making of a Professional Football League'. In *Football Goes East. Business, Culture And the People's Game in China, Japan and South Korea*, eds. Wolfram Manzenreiter and John Horne, 38–53. London: Routledge, 2004.

Hirose, Ichiro. Jリーグのマネジメント―「百年構想」の「制度設計」はいかにして創造されたか [J-League Management: How the Organzational Plan of the One Hundered Year Vision Was Created]. Tokyo: Tōyō Keizai Shinpōsha, 2004b.

Horne, John. '"Sakka" in Japan'. *Media, Culture and Society* 18, no. 4 (1996): 527–47.

Horne, John. 'Professional Football in Japan'. In: *Japan At Play. The Ludic And The Logic of Power*, eds. Joy Hendry and Massimo Raven, 199–213. London: Routledge, 2002.

Horne, John and Derek Bleakley. 'The Development of Football in Japan'. In *Japan, Korea and The 2002 World Cup*, eds. John Horne and Wolfram Manzenreiter, 89–105. London: Routledge, 2002.

Horne, John. 'Football in Japan: Is 'wa' All You Need?'. In *Football Culture: Local Contests and Global Visions*, eds. Gerry Finn and Richard Giulianotti, 212–29. London: Frank Cass, 2000.

Horne, John, and Wolfram Manzenreiter, eds. *Japan, Korea and The 2002 World Cup*. London: Routledge, 2002.

Japanese Football Association (JFA). 'The JFA Declaration 2005'. http://www.jfa.or.jp/eng/declaration2005/index.html (accessed November 22, 2012).

Jaquiss, Kevin. 'Mutualism Rules: The Community in Football. Introduction to Model Rules For a Football Community Trust'. In *The Changing Face of the Football Business: Supporters Direct*, eds. Sean Hamil, Jonathan Michie, Christine Oughton, and Steven Warby, 51–6. London: Frank Cass, 2001.

Javalgi, Rajshekhar G., Mark B. Traylor, Andrew C. Gross, and Edward L. Lampman. 'Awareness of Sponsorship and Corporate Image: An Empirical Investigation'. *Journal of Advertising* 23, no. 4 (1994): 47–58.

J-League. 'Jリーグについて' [About J-League]. http://www.j-league.or.jp/aboutj/ (accessed November 22, 2012).

J-League. 'Home towns and club names'. http://www.j-league.or.jp/eng/jclubs/ (accessed November 22, 2012).

J-League. 'Conditions for J1, J2 And Affiliate Membership'. http://www.j-league.or.jp/eng/jclubs/ (accessed November 22, 2012).

J-League. 'Jリーグの収支' [J-League Balance Sheet]. http://www.j-league.or.jp/aboutj/document/documents.html (accessed November 22, 2012).

J-League. '大会別入場者数' [Number of People Attending Matches]. http://www.j-league.or.jp/aboutj/document/pdf/attendance.pdf (accessed November 22, 2012).

Light, Richard, and Wataru Yasaki. 'J League Football and the Rekindling of Regional Identity in Japan'. *Sporting Traditions* 18, no. 2 (2002): 31–45.

Light, Richard, and Wataru Yasaki. 'Breaking the Mould: Community, Education and the Development of Professional Football in Japan'. *Football Studies* 6, no. 1 (2003): 37–50.

Light, Richard, and Wataru Yasaki. 'Winds of Change for Youth and Children's Sport in Japan? A Case Study of the Kashima Antler's Football Development Program'. *Asian Journal of Exercise and Sport Science* 1, no. 1 (2004): 63–74.

Mahony, Daniel F., Makoto Nakazawa, Daniel C. Funk, Jeffrey D. James, and James M. Gladden. 'Motivational Factors Influencing the Behaviour of J-League Spectators'. *Sport Management Review* 5, no. 1 (2002): 1–24.

Major League Soccer (MLS). 'MLS Expands International Scouting Network'. http://www.mlssoccer.com/news/article/mls-expands-international-scouting-network (accessed November 26, 2012).

Manzenreiter, Wolfram. 'Japan und der Fußball im Zeitalter der technischen Reproduzierbarkeit: Die J. League zwischen Lokalpolitik und Globalkultur' [Japan and Football in the Age of Technical Reproducibility: The J. League Between Local Policy And Global Culture]. In *Global Players. Kultur, Ökonomie und Politik des Fußballs*, eds. Michael Fanizadeh, Gerald Hödl, and Wolfram Manzenreiter, 133–58. Frankfurt/Wien: Brandes & Apsel/Südwind, 2002.

Manzenreiter, Wolfram. 'Japanese Football and World Sports: Raising the Global Game in a Local Setting'. *Japan Forum* 16, no. 2 (2004): 289–313.

Manzenreiter, Wolfram and John Horne (eds.). *Football Goes East. Business, Culture and The People's Game In China, Japan And South Korea*. London: Routledge, 2004.

Manzenreiter, Wolfram. 'Fußball und die Krise der Männlichkeit in Japan' [Football And the Crisis of Masculinity in Japan]. In *Arena der Männlichkeit: Über das Verhältnis von Fußball und Geschlecht*, eds. Eva Kreisky and Georg Spitaler, 296–313. Frankfurt/Main: Campus, 2006.

Manzenreiter, Wolfram. 'Football in the Reconstruction of the Gender Order in Japan'. *Football & Society* 9, no. 2 (2008a): 244–58.

Manzenreiter, Wolfram. 'The 'Benefits' of Hosting: Japanese Experiences From the 2002 Football World Cup'. *Asian Business and Management* 7, no. 2 (2008b): 201–24.

Manzenreiter, Wolfram, and John Horne. 'Playing the Post-Fordist Game in/to the Far East: The Footballisation of China, Japan and South Korea'. *Football & Society* 8, no. 4 (2007): 561–77.

Matsouka, Hirotaka, Packianathan Chelladurai, and Munehiko Harada. 'Direct and Indirect Interaction Effects of Team Identifiction and Satisfaction on Intention to Attend Games'. *Sport Marketing Quarterly* 12, no. 4 (2003): 244–53.

McDonald, Mark, Toru Mihara, and JinBae Hong. 'Japanese Spectator Sport Industry: Cultural Changes Creating New Opportunities'. *European Sport Management Quarterly* 1, no. 1 (2001): 39–60.

Meenaghan, Tony and David Shipley. 'Media Effect in Commercial Sponsorship'. *European Journal of Marketing* 33, no. 3/4 (1999): 328–47.

Moffett, Sebastian. *Japanese Rules. Why the Japanese Needed Football and How They Got It*. London: Yellow Jersey Press, 2002.

Morrow, Stephen. *The New Business of Football: Accountability and Finance in Football*. Houndmills: Palgrave Macmillan, 1999.

Morrow, Stephen and Sean Hamil. 'Corporate Community Involvement by Football Clubs: Business Strategy Or Social Obligation?'. *Stirling Research Papers in Sports Studies* no. 1, University of Stirling, 2003.

Nakazawa, Makoto, Munehiko Harada, Junya Fujimoto and Yoshio Takahashi. 'J. League Spectator Survey 2010'. http://www.j-league.or.jp/eng/data/index_02.html (accessed November 28, 2012).

Nakazawa, Makoto, Daniel F. Mahony, Daniel C. Funk, and Sumiko Hirakawa. 'Segmenting J. League Spectators Based on Length of Time as a Fan'. *Sport Marketing Quarterly* 8, no. 4 (1999): 55–65.

Nogawa, Haruo and Mamiya Toshio. 'Building Mega-Events. Critical Reflections on the 2002 World Cup Infrastructure'. In *Japan, Korea and The 2002 World Cup*, eds. John Horne and Wolfram Manzenreiter, 177–94. London: Routledge, 2002.

Nogawa, Haruo, and Hiroko Maeda. 'The Japanese Dream: Football Culture Towards the New Millennium'. In *Football Cultures and Identities*, ed. Garry Amstrong and Richard Giulianotti, 223–33. Houndmills: Macmillan, 1999.

Noll, Roger. 'The Organization of Sports Leagues'. *Oxford Review of Economic Policy* 19, no. 4 (2003): 530–51.

Ophüls-Kashima, Reinold. 'Schiffe, Kirschblüten, Eichhörnchen und Hirschgeweihe. Die Struktur japanischer Vereinsnamen und die Konstruktion von Identität im japanischen Fußball' [Vessels, Cherry Blossoms, Squirrels and Deer Antlers. The Structure of Japanese Club Names And the Construction of Identity in Japanese Football]. In *Querpässe. Beiträge zur Literatur-, Kultur- und Mediengeschichte des Fußballs*, eds. Ralf Adelmann, Rolf Parr and Thomas Schwarz, 79–90. Heidelberg: Synchron Wissenschaftsverlag der Autoren, 2003.

Ōsumi, Yoshiyuki. 浦和レッズの幸福 [The Happiness of Urawa Reds]. Tokyo: Asupekuto, 1998.

Probert, Jocelyn and Hellmut Schütte. Goal! Japan Scores in Soccer. *INSEAD cases*. Fontainebleau: INSEAD, 1997.

Rowe, David. 'The Global Love-Match: Sport and Television'. *Media, Culture and Society* 18, no. 4 (1996): 565–82.

Rowe, David. 'No Gain, No Game? Media and Sport' In *Mass Media and Society*, ed. James Curran and Michael Gurevitch, 3rd ed., 346–61. London: Edward Arnold, 2000.

Roxburgh, Andy. 'The Technician Interview – Takeshi Okada'. *UEFA Newsletter for Coaches* 48 (2011): 2–5.

Shimizu, Satoshi. 'Japanese Soccer Fans. Following the Local and the National Team'. In *Japan, Korea and The 2002 World Cup*, eds. John Horne and Wolfram Manzenreiter, 133–46. London: Routledge, 2002.

Smith, Aaron C., and Hans Westerbeek. *The Sport Business Future*. Houndmills: Palgrave Macmillan, 2004.

Söderman, Sten, and Harald Dolles. 'Strategic Fit in International Sponsorship. The Case of the Olympic Games in Beijing 2008'. *International Journal of Sports Marketing & Sponsorship* 9, no. 2 (2008): 95–108.

Söderman, Sten, and Harald Dolles. 'Sponsoring the Bejing Olympic Games – Patterns of Sponsor Advertising'. *Asia Pacific Journal of Marketing and Logistics* 22, no. 1 (2010): 8–24.

Sugimoto, Atsuo. 'School Sport, Physical Education and the Development of Football Culture in Japan'. In *Football Goes East. Business, Culture and the People's Game in China, Japan and South Korea*, eds. Wolfram Manzenreiter and John Horne, 102–16. London: Routledge, 2004.

Sumino, Misaki, and Munehiko Harada. 'Affective Experience of J. League Fans: The Relationship Between Affective Experience, Team Loyalty and Intention to Attend'. *Managing Leisure* 9, no. 4 (2004): 181–92.

Takahashi, Yoshiaki, Hiroko Hayakawa, Harald Dolles, and Sten Söderman, eds. スポーツ・マネジメントとメガイベント: Jリーグ・サッカーとアジアのメガスポーツ・イベント [Sports Management and Mega Events: J-League Soccer and Mega-Sports Events in Asia]. Tokyo: Bunshindo, 2012.

Thwaites, Des. 'Professional Football Sponsorship – Profitable or Profligate?'. *International Journal of Advertising* 14, no. 2 (1995): 149–64.

Troussier, Philippe. *Passion*. Tokyo: The Japan Times Press, 2002.

Tsuboi, Yoshinari and Tatsuya Yaki. J1. J2 完全詳細データ: /全チーム/全選手/全リーグ戦 [J. League Kanzen Databook 2002]. Tokyo: Kanzen, 2002.

Urawa Red Diamonds. 'In the World. FC Bayern Munich Partnership'. http://www.urawa-reds.co.jp/english/club-in_the_world.html (accessed November 26, 2012).

Watts, Jonathan. 'Soccer shinhatsubai. What are the Japanese Consumers Making of the J. League?'. In: *The Worlds of Japanese Popular Culture: Gender, Shifting Boundaries And Global Cultures*, ed. Dolores P. Martinez, 181–201. Cambridge: Cambridge University Press, 1998.

Latin America, football and the Japanese diaspora

Jorge E. Cuéllar*

American Studies and Film Studies, Yale University, New Haven, CT, USA

> It is much less of a novelty today that Asian footballers play amongst the best in Europe's top flight. Some footballers, however, have had career paths through equally important clubs in Latin America like Santos, Guaraní and Pachuca. Due to different social and political dynamics of Latin American culture and their relationship to waves of Asian immigration, the presence of Asian players in Latin American football speaks to the unique history of Asian peoples and the growing commercial necessity of football clubs to appeal to diasporic communities as integral parts of multicultural societies. This essay aims to open up a discussion on how the Japanese diaspora connects to sports culture in Latin America. By exploring the careers of players Kenji Fukuda and the Japanese-Brazilian Rodrigo Tabata among others, this piece contributes to studies on diaspora and sport, on how capital, commercialization, and nationalism function in relation to Latin America's Nikkei.

Introduction

> Today, every soccer player is a playing advertisement. In 1989, Carlos Menem played a friendly game wearing the shirt of the Argentine national team, along with Maradona and the rest. On television it was hard to tell if he was the President of Argentina or Renault, whose enormous logo he wore on his chest.   Eduardo Galeano[1]

At one level, club football functions as a way to engender community, competition and provide entertainment for groups of people from a specific geographic area, ethnic identity or politico-ideological position as exemplified in the abundance of teams that have been born out of factories and unionization efforts alongside national projects for industrialization.[2] Leading to the growth in popularity in the hearts and minds of the masses of workers, the football club has and continues to be an important and sizable part of the leisure time of the labouring classes. While there exist many factors such as taste, class, and education that contribute to the importance of community-centred sports that contribute to peoples' allegiances to a particular club or national team within diverse sporting practices, it is no surprise that football has simultaneously been at the center of state-building projects through its utility in serving the needs of nationalism as well as, albeit to a lesser degree, political and social movements.[3] With its close relationships to trade unions, religious organizations, as well as educational institutions, football has been a key component to the negotiating of identity, class and ideology in contemporary societies especially in the nations of Latin America.

In what follows, I argue that the globalization of football and the changing dimensions of the football club amidst global capitalism are central to the understanding of neoliberal multiculturalism as the dominant organizing logic of society in Latin America. Unearthing these issues, I find evidence for my assertion in the recent phenomenon of both native and migrant Asian, specifically Japanese, football players opting to play in Latin American football leagues in places like Mexico and Brazil as opposed to those of Europe or Asia. In examining these examples, I find a host of intersecting issues that football and the football club can help to untangle around questions of Asian identity, politics, capitalism, and its relationship to conceptions of the national in Latin America.

The political ideology of fútbol

Football is instrumental in the performance of politics as can be historically tracked through the grand public gestures of Brazil's Getúlio Vargas, Argentina's Juan Domingo Perón as well in quite different situations such as in the mediation of ethnic tension amidst the 1970 FIFA World Cup qualifying stages in what became known as the Salvadoran-Honduran Football War.[4] From the inception of the sport in the schoolyards of the British Empire, football has functioned as an event of special social significance at the intersection of cultural exchanges that due to regional and local specificity can arguably, supersede the dominant narratives and myths of the nation.[5] Above all, however, it is the commercial interests of footballing clubs and the governing structures of the sport at the international, national, and club levels that dictate the role football plays in the communities in which they are embedded today. For Vargas and Perón it meant appealing to the people through demonstrating their relationship to their fellow citizen's daily experience with which they really had nothing in common; for the Salvadoran and Honduran governments, football served as a convenient distraction to escalate a long-standing border dispute. In the experience of Africa, we also learn that the adoption of sports such as soccer, rugby, and cricket became agents of modernization introduced by colonial administrators, important features of the foreign apparatuses for social control.[6] While not wholly new, I am attempting to re-highlight here the view that larger political goals and concerns are always central to the performance and business of sports.

In contradistinction, in contemporary Europe it appears that 'politics' has been seemingly drained out of a sport which has today become dominated by the huge sums of money that are thrown around to artificially create competition and rivalry. Seemingly, politics in sport as such has taken a step back in the epoch of global capital, deemphasized in ways common to historical moments past. Millions of dollars in player transfers and weekly wages bring the best and brightest talents from around the world to compete in the European domestic leagues. In doing so, European teams elevate the marketability of themselves and their leagues domestically and abroad, in many cases mirroring the diversity of the society at large to open the sport to unincorporated local and global consumer-subjects making the sport further porous and relatable, effectively cementing its position as the leader in the game. While these processes of ethnic inclusion via sport are not without their share of contradictions such as racism, classism, homophobia, hypermasculinity and other ills that affect the game, the superseding rationale for diversifying the people's game is and has always been in the interests of capital.

It is precisely in this way that multicultural societies like those that compose the audiences of the most visible leagues in the world such as England's Premier League, Italy's Serie A, Spain's La Liga and others, make concerted efforts to draw upon and negotiate the various communities they interact with (as players, investors, fans, consumers, etc.) via a multitude of platforms (e.g. television, radio, print and online), all the while asserting a distinct character and culture to congregate around the club those people who represent a financial benefit to the organization. Important to the development of the global enterprise that is the modern-day football club, the gathering of talent from foreign countries such as North and Latin America, Asia, Oceania, the Middle East and Africa becomes a way for these organizations to draw the attention and capital of people around the world towards their leagues, their clubs and their national economies (e.g. through tourism, television contracts, apparel sales, and so on). In short, football has gone through a multifaceted and comprehensive process of commodification as a response to the requirements of global capitalism to include and market to new groups of people both domestically and abroad, making clubs transnational mega-businesses with global needs and interests in courting foreign audiences and capturing emergent markets.

A recent Forbes article on 'The Business of Soccer' that ranks the top 10 richest clubs in the world argues that the current financial state of the football club is proportionate to its identification as a global object of consumer exchange. 'Look closer and it becomes clear that the wealthiest clubs have a big advantage over their competitors because they are global brands, which allows them to generate more revenue outside their home market from sponsorships, merchandise and broadcasting'.[7] Too many players to name, here we can think of the masses of Latin American players that have moved to Europe after being bought by large European clubs, traditionally a process that rising stars must eventually make on the road to becoming the world's best; lack of infrastructure and local investment in Latin American countries forces players to move to Europe. The new commodity form, the football player, echoes what Marx teaches us about the nature of wealth, 'capital comes out of circulation, enters into it again, preserves and multiplies itself within its circuit, comes back out of it with expanded bulk, and begins the same round ever afresh'.[8] Pointing to the ever-expanding nature of capital, the football club as a global institution has similarly followed suit in globalizing its image and presence around the planet. Recognizable in all corners of the globe from inland China to the open-air marketplaces of El Salvador, teams like Real Madrid CF, FC Barcelona, Juventus and Manchester United are familiar staples of top-flight football fandom worldwide.

Looking at football in this mode allows us to better comprehend how its transformation has opened new spaces or capital 'flows' as a result of financial globalization, bringing along with it, reformulations and new sensibilities with regard to culture and race – encapsulated by the rhetoric of 'fair play' and the more recent campaigns such as the 'say no to racism' mission promoted by FIFA.[9] Inverting what is normally understood in relation to racism and its intimate relationship to the successes of extractive capitalism towards justifying economic discrimination or exploitation in relation to social others, the role of Japanese in the Latin American context provides a much more nuanced snapshot to understanding this phenomenon as related to processes of cultural homogenization and rather cosmetic responses to national and social contradictions. Couching our thinking about the Latin American football club, capital and the relationship of Asian and Japanese players to this set of concerns allows us to see a complication of the conventional social pyramid as well as clarifying the role of sport as a politicized cultural space and form.

This essay concerns itself with the phenomenon of Japanese footballers that have chosen to ply their trade in leagues atypical for Asian players like those of Latin America, specifically in Brazil and Mexico. I aim to explore this occurrence by embedding it into a larger framework and narrative of transnational commodification of football coupled with the increasing cultural demand to diversify domestic leagues to increase interest in local competitions. Simultaneously and as part of the nature of exploring this subject, I will look towards Brazilian players (both ethnically Japanese and otherwise) who have elected to play in the Japanese J-League, placing careful focus on those Latin American athletes who have also opted to represent Japan in international competitions. Addressing issues and concerns present in both literatures regarding the Japanese and Brazilian diasporas, this piece aims to understand football as cultural labour and investigate the way that Asian migration and its expression in Latin American culture can help elucidate some developments of the oft-contradictory role of football in the societies of Latin America.[10] Situating my analysis at the intersection of sport, nationalism, and globalization,[11] the role of Japanese players in Latin America explains with exemplary detail the process of commercial globalization as multidirectional and multilayered, a phenomenon that situates consumers alongside the reigning cultural and economic logic of liberal societies, in other words, neoliberalism and multiculturalism.[12] Following sociologist Barry Smart, 'in the context of a wide-ranging analysis of the consequences associated with the global implementation of neo-liberal free-market economic policies, sport was described as "the most important thing in the world"'.[13] It is from the point of re-centering sports into the conversation on globalization, as Smart suggests, that I take as the energy for this study.

Brazil, Mexico and the *Nikkei*

Looking specifically at the Campeonato Brasileiro Série A (Brazilian Serie A) and the Primera Division Mexicana (Mexican First Division, recently renamed Liga MX), one can immediately see the reflection of the general culture of society expressed on the football pitch. This 'field' is not only representative and inclusive of competition and the intersecting of various social practices, but rather also a meeting point for ideologies, politics and the expressions of cultural sensibilities, prejudices and aspirations.[14] As evidenced in the practices of populations around the world from Africa to Oceania, Latin America is no different. As a purveyor and instrument of multiculturalism, the football club negotiates and helps to designate the valences of cultural pluralism in the civic sphere. It attempts to reproduce tropes of the nation to accent and coincide with perceptions regarding the gradual refashioning of social relations and cultural practices. In the (re)presentation of Asian players in Latin America, many of whom are not only talented and capable of contributing to their teams in their own right, also operate as symbolic gestures both to entertain and re-imagine a civil society inclusive and demonstrative of changing sociocultural and ethnic idioms.

The role of the Japanese player at a club like Pachuca in Mexico represents not only the pragmatic day-to-day operation of a football club seeking financial solvency and the ability to display a strong squad come matchday, but can and often functions as a meeting point of sociocultural logics that rearticulate the nation, reinscribing meaning into the mundane experiences of the everyday as seen through diverse expressions of fandom.[15] By mobilizing fandom to support a particular club due to the specific names on their roster, organizations are able to bring in a variety of new aficionados into the game along with their purchasing power, making their teams much more lucrative enterprises. Due to the novelty of having a Japanese player form part of a Latin American club football team, it draws people to come out and see how the player fares amongst a competition primarily composed of nationals and other Latin Americans. That being said, it is not only the novelty and problematic place of the 'Asian' in Latin American popular culture and sporting practices that is on display here, but rather an underlying rationale that is attempting to engender a space at once more vibrant economically and culturally in its moving beyond stale understandings of the nation, raising the question of who composes it, and of course, who is able to represent it in the most national of activities for most Latin Americans – organized football.

According to scholars of the Japanese diaspora, the *Nikkei*, or Brazilians of Japanese descent, reside primarily in the city of São Paulo whose history speaks to the way they have been generally understood in the racial hierarchy upon which Brazil is organized. Unsurprisingly, a place where white is deemed preferable and superior in real economic terms, the Japanese have thought themselves part of the privileged middle and upper-middle class strata of Brazilian society due to their economic successes and lighter complexions when compared to Brazilian mestizos and Afro-Brazilians who are considered to be at the bottom of the socio-economic ladder due to their undesirability and perceived backwardness to the concealed nation-state goals of whitening Brazil through the explicit possession of whiteness.[16] Typically of the most economically dynamic sectors of the country with businesses in the import/export sector, Japanese-Brazilians represent a sizable portion of the general purchasing power of Brazil, not only in the sense that they are able to introduce capital into local football clubs such as São Paulo FC or Santos FC, but they also become avenues into bringing foreign interest and capital into the sphere of the footballing organizations as well.

Realizing this, clubs have attempted to court the interest of those sectors of society by nurturing talent from those ethno-racial communities. Japanese-Brazilians such as Rodrigo Tabata,[17] playing as an attacking midfielder for Santos FC, is an expression of a peculiar cultural-capitalist logic to include people from mixed race backgrounds and perpetuate the idea of Brazil as a racial utopia. Pragmatically, however, Tabata is an example of the way a football club can nurture creative talent and simultaneously move forward in articulating a set of changing cultural and ethno-racial actualities of Brazilian society. The highlighting of Japanese-Brazilians can be seen as a move by the clubs to redefine the harmony of the racial democracy that is Brazil, whilst simultaneously taking into account the importance of the production and consumption power of East Asia, one whose 'football capital' has exploded in the last decade through the successes of the Japanese national football team, the hosting of the 2002 FIFA World Cup in Korea and Japan, and of course, the representation of their countrymen in top leagues throughout the globe at clubs such as Borussia Dortmund, Manchester United, and Internazionale Milano.

Race and collective identity

Reconsidering the ideological role of the football club in society begins to open up questions regarding the differential reception of sporting practices in their relation to specific class fractions. Popularly conceived and understood by scholars as 'the people's game', the unrepentant rise of commercialization within football as its singular incentive has shifted club teams to aspire to become universally recognized brands, forgetting to nurture much of their local support – the football club itself has become globalized. However, as the club also operates as the cultural mediator par excellence for the ritual competition between social sub-groups, the football club seeks to establish the fluidity or lack thereof between 'sporting cultures' of social classes in a given society; internationally, football clubs function almost exclusively as symbolic capital carrying commodities in terms of their display of knowledge for individuals through a kind of cosmopolitanism or as components for the performance of diasporic identity.

For Brazilian society, one rooted in its unique racial and cultural hierarchies, conceives of football in a much different way than say those in the Mexican context. Putting these two side-by-side allows us to see the varied ways in which the football club makes use of players to articulate its own vision of society, one imbued with specific ideological and political intent. In this way, the role of the football club to society is of course, diachronic, yet seeks with some exceptions, to congeal disparate elements into a unified whole, for example, under the banner of nationalism. Following the formulations of Antonio Gramsci and Louis Althusser, football, like other convergent social sites of emotional and cultural identification, aims to influence public opinion and perception (think here of a conversion of values) for the more efficient extraction of capital, leading to a transformation of culture and of sociality itself.[18] Whether it is a Mexican nationalism centred on mestizaje and what José Vasconcelos articulated as the 'cosmic race', reigning racial theories about Latin America and Mexico in particular have never considered the Asian as being a formative part of any dominant national-cultural identity.

In Brazil, theories and mythologies about its own 'racial democracy' underpin the way institutions like the football club function in society. For example, the thought of Brazilian sociologist Gilberto Freyre speaks to the possibilities of Brazilian society to move beyond the regressive categories of race, many of which are still prevalent in places like the USA. Moreover, Afro-Brazilians are, at least in sporting practice, seen as integral components of the body politic of Brazil, one whose expression could be seen in the discourse around the team fielded by Brazil in the 1938 World Cup in France as well as in the majority of their celebrated icons which include Pelé, Sócrates, Garrincha, to more contemporary phenoms such as Roberto Carlos, Ronaldo, Ronaldinho, all the way to present-day hopeful, Neymar. As Tiago Maranhão writes, 'football plays an evident role in the construction of a collective subjectivity in relation to the Brazilian nation'.[19] Taking this formulation one step further into the near-present, the role of Japanese-Brazilians is increasingly becoming part of this process in developing and enlarging the 'collective subjectivity' of Brazilian society, not without its issues such as interminority racism and its manifestation in the, borrowing from Adorno, 'aggressive, barbaric, and sadist' character of spectator sporting cultures.[20]

Nationalizing the foreign

Inversely, there are many Brazilian footballers playing in Asian leagues such as Japan's J-League and the quickly rising Chinese Super League. Composing a sizable number of foreigners from a single country playing in Japan's professional league, Brazilian participation in the J-League demonstrates the important transactions and connections extant between Japan and Brazil both resulting from histories of migration through its importance as a passageway for capital. For example, Kazuyoshi 'Kazu' Miura's days as a teenager playing with Brazilian side Santos FC, Palmeiras, and Coritiba FC. We can also point to Masakiyo Maezono's 1998 season with Santos and in the following year, Goiás EC. Immersed within this global exchange, former FC Tokyo striker with a deft left-footed touch, player Kenji Fukuda remains unique in his multinational career, exemplifying the movement of football from Japan to Latin America.[21]

Fukuda is perhaps most emblematic for his career spanning multiple countries such as Spain, Paraguay, Greece, Mexico, and his native Japan. Considered as a part of Japan's 'lost generation' of footballers, because of the quick rise of younger talent from country as well as from the diaspora that overshadowed players like him, Fukuda found himself with limited playing opportunities in a Europe that became much more interested with younger players of the so-called 'golden generation' which included players like Shunsuke Nakamura and the prolific Yasuhito Endo. Studying Fukuda's play in Mexico and Paraguay allows us to see how his ethnic (and phenotypical) uniqueness serves an important role in the performance and presentation of the club to its fans and teammates.[22] Fukuda's career helps us to understand the phenomenon behind his travels to Mexico, as well as to Paraguay with Club Guaraní from Asunción,[23] by indicating to the demands on him professionally but also as a result of his uniqueness for being culturally legible as Asian to Latin Americans. For the season 2004–2005, after a less-than-stellar stint with Club Guaraní, Fukuda signed for Mexican club Pachuca as reinforcement for their run at the South American tournament Copa Libertadores to which they had qualified the previous season. Playing primarily for the reserve team, Pachuca Juniors, Kenji impressed with a whopping 12 goals in 19 appearances, instantly becoming a fan favourite. His transfer, while directly important to the winning of a tournament and maintaining the team competitive within the national league, had other effects that address the larger interest of diversifying, ethnically, the footballing culture of the country.

Speaking to the importance of players bridging the ethnocultural gap between Latin America and Asia, there have been other examples of players moving to Latin America after wooing by Mexican football organizations to sign for their squads.[24] Although the commonplace of this practice in Mexico is very rare, it is important to recognize the emergence of Asian players in the country as a new practice in managing the football club amidst globalizing forces. Under the aegis of neoliberal capitalism and its multicultural sensibility, the owners and managers of Latin American football clubs now identify the importance of Asian players as contributing to on-pitch and off-pitch activities. As footballers routinely engage in publicity actions for charities, community centres, benefits and so on, the presence of a foreign player from Asia not only represents the inclusionary space the club itself is trying to cultivate, but also showcases an image of diplomacy, of tolerance and of respect for ethnic others, again, following Marx & Engels, generating a global culture of cosmopolitanism.²⁵ Football clubs like Pachuca invest many resources in raising the profile of the team on the international stage. Echoing these sentiments journalist Fernando Vanegas' piece in Mexico's *El Mural* reads:

> The contracting of the Japanese [Fukuda] could be seen from its merchandising side, after all, his entire country has been following his moves when he played in Paraguayan football and now that he is at Pachuca the club will be recognized as well, reaching the level of internationalization that the directives want the team to be identified by, as 'the team of Mexico'.²⁶

It is clear that footballing organizations find it to be one of their chief concerns to make the club a profitable business endeavour. Certainly, this means that the criteria for purchasing players rests not only on their abilities, but also on the complex of other functions, largely symbolic and sentimental, that they serve to fan communities both global and local.

Another example of Japanese footballers in Mexico is the 2010 signing of youngster Minori Sato by club Puebla FC. Sato is a midfielder who has under-18 experience with the Japanese national team. The first Japanese player for Puebla FC, Sato was similarly touted as being the first step in the 'global' project of Puebla FC in raising its profile nationally and abroad as well as advancing the belief that Nipponese football has demonstrated significant progress since the last World Cup.²⁷ Expressed by their own communication team, Puebla FC understands the relevancy and heightened profile that comes from having a foreign player join the organization. Sato not only provides reinforcement for the team with talent in his own right, but also adds a cultural flair that draws in capital, fans and attention – the implications of his participation at Puebla reside in the changing national culture of football in Mexico.

More recently, we have seen Yuto Ono, a Japanese winger on loan to Celaya FC from Necaxa FC in the headlines as he is currently attempting to help Celaya win ascendancy into Mexico's First Division. In an interview made with Ono by the Mexican sporting website, *Once Titular*, he is asked about whether people in Japan talk about his playing in Mexico to which Ono replies, 'Mexican football is not famous in Japan. The football in Japan is very different to Mexico's, yet in Japan people do not know of Mexican football'.²⁸ Establishing the connections necessary to attract talent, attention, and capital to Latin American football, the experiences of Kenji Fukuda and Rodrigo Tabata among the many other players mentioned speak to a relatively recent phenomenon that makes use of the tumultuous histories among Latin Americans and Asians. Alongside its contradictions, the cultural sensibilities and economic hopes inculcated into footballers represent the multifaceted and contradictory forms of cultural and economic globalization spotlighted around footballing institutions and their aspirations for global visibility.

Conclusion

As Immanuel Wallerstein suggests, we should try to understand peoplehood for what it is – 'in no sense a primordial or stable social reality, but a complex clay-like historical product of the capitalist world-economy', one in which sports as the preeminent leisure practice of most Latin American countries is an essential part. It not only functions as a disseminator of narratives of the nation, of regional identity, or of local-neighborhood affiliation, it also plays an important role in determining the reception and legibility of different kinds of people to others within the civic sphere. In a complication of the 'common concerns' of people whose authority was found in the powerful institutions of society such as the church, the company, the university, and of course, the football club, Wallerstein suggests that we concern ourselves with peoplehood, that is, social and cultural identities and ethnicities, as intimately connected with the vacillations and idiosyncrasies of global capitalism.[29] The experience of Asian footballers in Latin American leagues not only elucidates the contradictory role that many of these players take on, but also offers us ways to envisage and critique the complex forms of racialization that coincide in ordinary leisure activities like professional football.

The opening Galeano passage to this essay points us in a similar direction as well; it is not only the advertisement worn by the corporate football club on the chest, back, sleeves, and shorts of the players that signifies, but also the actual embodiment of identity that is being paraded around the football pitch. In the same ways that other institutions have progressed to allowing women and minorities into their ranks, so too have football clubs diversified their personnel to better and perhaps more productively (e.g. financially) work in developing their organizations, growing their fan base and realizing more triumphs.

The multicultural rationality that is part and parcel of neoliberal globalization flattens cultural difference and obfuscates asymmetric power relations that condition all aspects of lived experience, which of course includes leisure activity. Cultural theorist Stuart Hall reminds us that, 'Cultural identities are the points of identification, the unstable points of identification or suture, which are made, within the discourses of history and culture. Not an essence but a positioning'.[30] A subjectivity that is fostered around the opening up of society's dominant cultural codes, the arrival and seemingly increasing footprint of Asian players in Brazilian or Mexican football leagues directs us, in some ways, to reconsider Ernesto Laclau's suggestion that it is by a process of 'dislocation' that modern societies are today organized. Laclau's proposition gains an edge when juxtaposed with the notion of neoliberal multiculturalism as it leads us to question whether there really is a possibility of new subject positions or 'new ethnicities' so to speak, to emerge independently from the ceaseless flux of capitalism.[31] Posing this question, gets us to a more nuanced understanding of culture, one where sporting practice as an integral part of modern Latin America clarifies the metamorphosing meanings and values implicit and explicit in particular ways of life.[32]

Acknowledgements

I would like to express my greatest appreciation for, above all, my father who instilled in me a love for football and to all of those family and friends who have served as interlocutors throughout this project.

Notes

1. Galeano, *Soccer in the Sun and Shadow*, 95.
2. I am thinking here of AC Milan, Spartak Moscow, as well as English clubs such as clubs Manchester United, West Ham United and Arsenal which were originally workers terms. For more on this point see Simon Inglis' *The Football Grounds of Great Britain* (1996).
3. Referring here to Pierre Bourdieu's analysis in *Distinction* (1987), he maintains the relevance of class to the symbolic hierarchy or 'field' of power relations that undergird

the accumulation of cultural and educational capital, or taste. Critical to the main argument in his book, this process takes the shape as a 'class habitus', the practice-unifying and practice-generating principle from which class conditionings originate.
4. For more on Vargas and Perón, see Tony Mason's chapter on '*Fútbol* and Politics' in *Passion of the People? Football in South America*, London: Verso Books, 1995.
5. It should be noted here that even the physical space of the stadium and its usual multipurpose use for political rallies, public gatherings and celebrations, evoke football in a tangential way by cohabiting the perhaps sacred space of ritualized national sporting practice.
6. Ndee, 'Sport as a Political Tool', 183. For an example of this process, the psychological, social and political dimensions of sport, see James, *Beyond a Boundary*.
7. Wallerstein, 'The Construction of Peoplehood' in Balibar & Wallerstein, *Race, Nation, Class: Ambiguous Identities*, 85. Schwartz et al., 'The Business of Soccer'. See also a more recent BBC article crowning Manchester United as the most valuable football club in the world second only to Real Madrid CF and FC Barcelona, http://www.bbc.co.uk/sport/0/football/17769654 (accessed October 16, 2012).
8. Marx, 'The General Formula for Capital', 88–9.
9. FIFA outlines its campaigns for social responsibility in 'FIFA Against Racism'.
10. Yamanaka, 'I Will Go Home, But When?'.
11. Denning, 'Globalization in Cultural Studies' 351–2. Globalization, an expansive term, is mobilized here in both the colloquial mode but perhaps most specifically as Denning defines it, 'Globalization names a process, an epoch, a discourse, a promise, a threat, a way of looking at the "world"'. He goes on to say that it points to 'the corrosive force of the market against the protectionism of the nation; the promise or threat of cheap commodities, a world culture, a world civilization in the image of…capital'.
12. Harvey, *A Brief History of Neoliberalism*, 3. Harvey defines neoliberalism as having the following characteristic from which I position my argument, referring to market exchange, he writes that it is 'an ethic in itself, capable of acting as a guide to all human action, and substituting for all previously held ethical beliefs', it emphasizes the significance of contractual relations in the marketplace'. 'Multiculturalism' is understood here as that cultural logic happening alongside the economic and social reforms of neoliberalism (e.g. understanding changing racial hierarchies).
13. Smart, 'Not playing Around', 6.
14. Bourdieu elucidates the notion of 'field' as both a field of forces and a field of struggles in *The Field of Cultural Production*.
15. Here I am thinking about the complex of conversations, organized chants, YouTube videos, blog posts and other kinds of commentary that, when thought about cohesively, illustrate a process of congealment and coherent appreciation that ascribes social value to an object, in this case, individual footballers and clubs.
16. Daniel, *Race and Multiraciality*.
17. Tabata, born 1980 in Araçatuba, Brazil had his most successful stint for Santos FC from 2006–2008. At his current 32 years of age, he now plays in Qatar for Al-Rayyan Sports Club (since 2010).
18. Rochon, *Culture Moves*, 55–6.
19. Maranhão, 'Apollonians and Dionysians', 514.
20. Davis, 'Gender, Class, and Multiculturalism', 40–2. I am working with the notion that 'neoliberal multiculturalism' is simultaneously pluralistic and particularistic. For more on Adorno's thoughts on sports, see the essay 'Education After Auschwitz', 197–198.
21. Fukuda, born 1977 in Niihama, Japan has played on many teams in his international career. He has worn the shirts of Paraguay's Guaraní, Mexican teams Pachuca and Irapuato, as well as Liga BBVA teams Castellón, and Numancia. He currently plays for Ehime FC in Matsuyama, capital of the Ehime prefecture in Japan.
22. Briseño, 'No viene el aire'. This piece describes some of the ways that Fukuda relates to his teammates, primarily being the target of jokes. His teammate, Mexican Christian Hernández says, 'He has more nicknames than anyone else in the whole of Mexican football, I think every one of us has given him one or two. Like Jackie Chan, "ojitos de regalo", and loads more. The ones he understands he laughs along, but for others he does not he still laughs for the sake of compromise. We give him a hard time out of respect so there will be no conflict amongst us'.

23. It is important to note that Fukuda is not the first Japanese footballer to play in Paraguay. This title belongs to Japan international midfielder Nozomi Hiroyama who played with Asunción team Club Cerro Porteño and was the first Japanese to score in the Copa Toyota Libertadores, 2001. See 'Los únicos japoneses que jugaron la Libertadores'.
24. The Daily Yomiuri (Tokyo), 'Fukuda latest to join exodus, lands in Paraguay'. Fukuda's agent and friend, Roberto Sato, is Paraguayan with Japanese heritage, a fact that likely made it easier for Fukuda to begin a career in Paraguay and hispanophone Latin America.
25. Szerszynski and Urry, 'Cultures of Cosmopolitanism'. For Marx and Engels' original formulation see *The Manifesto of the Communist Party* (1952) in which they express the following, 'The need for a constantly changing market chases the bourgeoisie over the whole surface of the globe. It must settle everywhere, establish connexions everywhere … the bourgeoisie has through its exploitation of the world market give a cosmopolitan character to production and consumption in every country … The individual creations of individual nations become common property. National one-sidedness and narrow-mindedness become more and more impossible', 46–47. Addressing the foreclosing of nationalism and racism traditionally conceived by Marx and Engels provides insight into understanding the values embedded in the sports environment of the present.
26. Vanegas, 'Tomas más vitaminas'. For more information see, 'Ficha el Pachuca a japonés para la Libertadores'. Unless otherwise noted, all translations are my own.
27. Minori Sato, born 1991 from Gunma, Japan is, according to the official website of Puebla FC the second Asian player in history to join a top Mexican club. See Comunicación y Prensa Puebla F.C., 'Minori Sato se vincula con el Puebla F.C. por las próximas cuatro temporadas'.
28. 'Yuto Ono espera jugar en primera division'. Ono is considered to be only the second Japanese player to play in Mexico.
29. Wallerstein, 'The Construction of Peoplehood', 85.
30. Hall, 'Cultural Identity and Diaspora', 53.
31. Laclau, *New Reflections on the Revolution of our Time*, 40. The notion of 'new ethnicities' comes from Stuart Hall's reflections on the emerging racialisms in Britain in the 1980s alongside neoliberal economic reform.
32. Williams, 'Analysis of Culture', 58–9.

References

Adorno, Theodor W. *Critical Models: Interventions and Catchwords*. Trans. Pickford, New York: Columbia University Press, 1998.
Balibar, Étienne, and Immanuel Wallerstein. *Race, Nation, Class: Ambiguous Identities*. London: Verso Books, 1991.
Bourdieu, Pierre. *The Field of Cultural Production*. New York, NY: Columbia University Press, 1994.
Briseño, Miguel Angel. 'No viene el aire'. *Palabra*. Marcador, Pág. 4 Edic. 8 N°2587, December 29, 2004, LexisNexis Academic, accessed November 20, 2012.
Comunicación y Prensa Puebla FC. 'Minori Sato se vincula con el Puebla F.C. por las próximas cuatro temporadas'. http://www.pueblafutbolclub.com.mx/int-not.php?id_noticia=233
Daily Yomiuri, The (Tokyo). 'Fukuda latest to join exodus, lands in Paraguay'. *The Daily Yomiuri*. January 17, 2004, LexisNexis Academic, accessed November 25, 2012.
Daniel, G. Reginald *Race And Multiraciality in Brazil And the United States*. University Park, PA: Pennsylvania State Press, 2006.
Davis, Angela Y. 'Gender, class, and Multiculturalism: Rethinking "Race" Politics', in *Mapping Multiculturalism*, ed. Avery Gordon and Christopher Newfield (Minneapolis MN: University of Minnesota Press, 1996), 40–8.
Denning, Michael. 'Globalization in Cultural Studies: Process and Epoch'. *European Journal of Cultural Studies* 4, no. 3 (2001): 351–64.
Douglass, Mike and Glenda S. Roberts. 'Japan in a global age of migration', in *Japan and Global Migration: Foreign Workers and the Advent of a Multicultural Society*, ed. Mike Douglass and Glenda S. Roberts (London: Routledge, 2005), 2–35.
El Universal. 'Ficha el Pachuca a japonés para la Libertadores'. *El Universal*. Deportes, December 23, 2004, http://www.eluniversal.com.mx/notas/260842.html

Fédération Internationale de Football Association (FIFA). 'FIFA Against Racism: A Decade of Milestones'. FIFA.com. http://www.fifa.com/aboutfifa/socialresponsibility/news/newsid=1384919/index.html.

Galeano, Eduardo, and Mark Fried. *Soccer in Sun and Shadow*. London: Verso Books, 2003.

Hall, Stuart. 'Cultural Identity and Diaspora', in *Identity: Community, Culture and Difference*, ed. J. Rutherford (London: Lawrence And Wishart Ltd., 1993), 222–37.

Harvey, David. *A Brief History of Neoliberalism*. Oxford: Oxford University Press, 2007.

Laclau, Ernesto. *New Reflections on the Revolution of Our Time*. London: Verso Books, 1990.

Maranhão, Tiago. 'Apollonians and Dionysians: The Role of Football in Gilberto Freyre's Vision of Brazilian People'. *Soccer & Society* 8, no. 4 (2007): 510–23.

Marx, Karl. 'The General Formula for Capital', in *Capital: A Critique of Political Economy* (Moscow: USSR, Progress Publishers, 1887), 102–8.

Mason, Tony. *Passion of the People? Football in South America*. London: Verso Books, 1995.

Ndee, Hamad S. 'Sport as a Political Tool: Tanzania and the Liberation of Africa', in *Modern Sport: The Global Obsession*, ed. Boria Majumdar and Fan Hong (London: Routledge, 2007), 171–88.

OnceTitular. 'Yuto Ono espera jugar en primera division'. OnceTitular.com. http://www.oncetitular.com/mosno.php?nota=12181 (accessed September 1, 2011).

PasionLibertadores. 'Los únicos japoneses que jugaron la Libertadores'. PasionLibertadores.com. http://www.pasionlibertadores.com/noticias/Los-unicos-japoneses-que-jugaron-la-Libertadores-20120725-0005.html (accessed July 7, 2012).

Rochon, Thomas R., and Culture Moves. *Ideas, Activism and Changing Values*. Princeton, NJ: Princeton University Press, 1998.

Schwartz, Peter J., Paul Maidment, and Michael K. Ozanian. 'The Business of Soccer'. Forbes.com. http://www.forbes.com/2010/04/21/soccer-value-teams-business-sports-soccer-10-intro.html

Smart, Barry. 'Not Playing Around: Global Capitalism, Modern Sport and Consumer Culture', in *Globalization and Sport*, ed. Richard Giulianotti and Roland Robertson (London: Blackwell Publishing, 2007), 6–27.

Szerszynski, Bronislaw, and John Urry. 'Cultures of cosmopolitanism', *The Editorial Board of the Sociological Review* 50, no. 4 (2008): 461–81.

Vanegas, Fernando. 'Tomas más vitaminas; Club de Futbol Pachuca. Además de Borgetti, llegan el "Pollo" Salazar, Nelson Cuevas, Rodrigo Pérez y el nipón Kenji Fukuda'. *Mural*. Señor Futbol; Pág. 3 Edic. 7 N°2235, January 6, 2005, LexisNexis Academic, accessed November 26, 2012.

Williams, Raymond. 'Analysis of Culture', in *The Long Revolution* (Peterborough: Broadview Press, 2001), 57–88.

Yamanaka, Keiko. 'I Will Go Home, But When?: Labor Migration and Circular Diaspora by Japanese Brazilians in Japan'. In *Japan and Global Migration: Foreign Workers and the Advent of Multicultural Society*, ed. Mike Douglass and Glenda S. Roberts (London: Routledge, 2000), 123–52.

'A' is for Australia: New Football's billionaires, consumers and the 'Asian Century'. How the A-League defines the new Australia

Zoran Pajic

The School of Journalism, Australian & Indigenous Studies, Monash University, Melbourne, Australia

> Recent changes within Australian soccer reflect changes that have taken place in the wider Australian context. Equally, the changes in soccer in Australia and the world reflect significant trends, such as postmodern consumerism and globalization. Whilst soccer in Australia had long been derided as a platform for ethnic nationalism, its current utility is as a vital cultural, geopolitical and economic commodity for Australian 'engagement' with Asia. The government-sanctioned *Crawford Report* (2003) and the New Football Era bookend the evolution of Australian soccer for the 'Asian Century' and the transformation to a new, post-multicultural, post-industrial Australia. This paper questions the legitimacy of the New Football Era and whose interests were served in its implementation, and whether what has been lost will have consequences that will outweigh and outlive the promised Asian riches.

Introduction: the *Crawford Report* (2003) and the New Football Era

In 2005, the A-League promised a new course for soccer in Australia. Its foundation occurred as a culmination of factors with the single most important factor being the development and implementation of a Government-sanctioned review (commonly referred to as the *Crawford Report*). The report's findings, 'made after extensive consultation, accessing international advice and evaluating good practices', recommended a 'need for major structural change at national and state levels'. For change to occur, it would need 'the resolve of all, including federal, state and territory governments'. The implication was clear: the existing Old Soccer Era at the time was doomed, while the 'new' would become the current New Football Era.[1] What was not evident at the time, however, was the overall purpose for this change.

Ostensibly, the implementation of the report led to the change in the sport's nomenclature, its governing body and the league; the Australian Soccer Association would become Football Federation Australia (FFA), while the National Soccer League (NSL) would become the A-League. More deeply, however, the essence of the Australian game would also change. Aside from the changes to its governance and hierarchy, what changed was the controlling demographic of the sport, its culture and to whom the sport 'belonged' or who it represented. Australian soccer has since transformed enormously, from its status to its purpose, value and the way it is consumed. In the meantime, Australia itself has changed, from its economy, its self-perception, ambitions, its demographics and political landscape. As Mark Davis, in 2008, suggested, something 'fundamental in Australian life has changed. Something that goes to the core of how Australians understand themselves and their nation's democratic project. It's to do with the way the country has been managed over the past three decades, the orthodoxies accepted by both major parties, and the damage they've done to traditions, institutions and ways of life'. These changes would infiltrate even the most 'un-Australian' of aspects – Australian soccer, for it, according to Hallinan and Hughson, was part of the widespread 'cultural xenophobia' that entered public and cultural debate.

While Australia has recently confirmed its commitment in Asia, via the release of the Gillard-Labor government's *Australia in the Asian Century White Paper*, Australian soccer has been Asian since joining the Asian Football Confederation (AFC) in 2006.[2] In terms of regional and international integration – what is now referred to as 'football diplomacy' – Australian soccer has been ahead of the game. Despite its 'turbulent' past and continued adversity, soccer now stands central to Australia's standing in the 'Asian Century', promising to be a cultural, economic and geopolitical commodity. It is here that New Football's agenda is highlighted and with it the report's. Then again, soccer has long been the perfect window to Australia's crosscurrents.

For long, soccer's Eurocentricity was a reflection of Australia's, and hence perhaps its rejection. Likewise, New Football has become a reflection of what Australia has been during that era, as well as the imagination of who the new Australia wants to be. This newfound defining vision, however, omits the context of the game's evolution and promises to bring into question the legitimacy of both Australian soccer's and the country's principles of 'multiculturalism' and egalitarianism. In particular, the destabilization of the Old Soccer Era symbolizes not only the waning of its fundamental demographic within the sport but its deterioration and validity as a distinct identity within a new Australia. Rather than mere 'sporting' events, the New Football Era presents a glaring representation of reality and future within the new Australia.

'We are football': New Football, New Australia and the Asian Century

Historically, soccer served as a negative comparative instrument in the defining of 'Australia' and its insularity. During the post-war European migrant influx, the game served as a refining and re-defining mechanism for what was considered 'Australian'. During the NSL-*fin de siècle* period, soccer served to reaffirm how Australia imagined itself and in turn, how Otherness was perceived during a period of xenophobic anxiety.[3] The generalization of the game as being 'foreign', 'violent' and 'corrupt' extended and epitomized the feeling towards 'Others', those deemed as 'un-Australian'. During each period, the labels attributed to the game reflected the game's status as well as the status of its constituents. Thus, in its genesis it was equated with 'Britishness'.[4] Later, with the arrival of post-war European migrants ('new Australians', 'wogs', or 'ethnics' in the *fin de siècle period*), it was equated with 'Europeanness'[5] – as evident in use of the term 'wogball' – and the enduring definition of soccer as an 'ethnic game'. This characterization, however, although long challenged and existing, is evolving rapidly through the game's utility, through 'corporate assimilation', by government and business.

In its current guise as 'the world game', it reflects Australia's global ambitions and its longing to 'engage' with Asia during the 'Asian Century' in cultural, geopolitical and ultimately economic terms. With it, it also defines Australia's contemporary complexes of its location, identity, culture, representation, its ambitions and economic outcomes. Unlike Australia's main sporting codes of cricket, Australian rules football (AFL) and rugby league, soccer promises to showcase Australia to a truly international marketplace. Therefore, whilst perhaps not accepted as such previously, soccer is increasingly becoming indoctrinated as part of the Australian landscape, its rhetoric and psyche. The game's utility in nation building is also quickly becoming a symbol of a wider development of a new Australian cosmopolitan consumer and the values of a new Australia. Furthermore, it reflects Australia's post-industrial dilemma; its need for global standing, economic investment and return without traditional industry which has been substituted by service industries such as 'cultural events' or sports tourism. With the United Arab Emirates and Qatar in mind as major examples, Australia is not unique in this respect.

In relation to its post-industrial (and post-multicultural) predicament, Australian soccer's evolution emulates increasing 'corporate assimilation'[6] within Australia, as well as corporate bodies co-opting or acquiring commodities or institutions within a contradictory pretext, in turn dissolving its original associations. While 'multiculturalism' remains Australia's official ideology, soccer's experience in this country characterizes multiculturalism's paradoxes and its ambiguity. While multiculturalism continues to be associated and promoted with soccer, Old Soccer's experience has shown how the use of 'multicultural elements' can undermine Australia's rich and complex diversity to help define and augment a dominant monoculture. This corresponds with changing demographics, habits and the growing irrelevance of previous ideologies. In its consumption habits, Australia is increasingly becoming more international, its culture increasingly cosmopolitan yet simultaneously homogenized, due to its assimilation to the offers and influence of corporate Australia. Soccer, now as part of corporate Australia, is being employed as part of an evolving mainstream Australian culture and identity – itself with a new industry and economy, an evolving 'worldly' consumer culture.[7] Just as Australia seeks to present itself to the Asian riches, government and corporations are opportunistically using soccer to engage with what is already the world's biggest soccer market and what will quickly become the focus of global wealth.

In the post-industrial, post-Sydney 2000 Olympics era, soccer's importance in Australia is increasing as it is creating a new industry and opportunities for new hierarchies. Increasingly reliant on sporting events with global significance, Australia's attempts to involve itself within 'the world game' (entry into the AFC, the 2006 and 2010 FIFA World Cups, the failed 2018–2022 World Cup-hosting bids, the upcoming 2015 Asian Cup and the continuous evolution of the A-League) reflect Australia's new self-consciousness and need for inclusion with the world, the 'global event industry', foreign interest and investment, as well as its political and economic promotion to the world (and to itself) as a worthy, all-encompassing, progressive destination. Culturally, Australia is in need of cultural commodities, institutions and icons – whether sporting or otherwise – to illustrate its values and define a contemporary 'culture' to identity and call its own. The increasing popularity and credibility of soccer, as well as the fanfare and status surrounding the A-League signings of 'world stars' suggests that soccer is filling a void during the transition from Old to New Australia.

Soccer's cultural significance in Australia also lies in the culture and association it has left behind. Perhaps related to or consequential of the growing corporatization and homogeneity, is the increasing obliteration of ambivalence and sentiment for the purpose of nation building. The Old Soccer Era once provided a national stage for such behaviour and values to be expressed. For many groups, soccer was central to their expression and existence as something other than Australian. What this suggests is a further push towards 'Australian' homogeneity via the deterioration of an institution that promoted Otherness. This push towards homogeneity has not just occurred in soccer but also in other sports and broader culture.[8] As with multiculturalism, soccer perhaps was (or remains) authenticity's last bastion, while its rapidly evolving future (if ultimately unsuccessful), may serve as the remaining outpost of corporate or cultural dissidence.

Soccer's values within the new Australia – just as the 'quiet revolution' to new Australia took place – according to Mark Davis, did not 'happen by accident or through natural progression. Australia's conservative revolution took years of hard, focused work by determined, well-organized activists who built a network of think tanks, discussion groups and ginger groups, forged close links with government and the media, and lobbied to promote their cause with the indefatigable energy of true believers'. Some of those involved in this (conservative) Australian revolution were also present in its footballing equivalent.

'Project Sydney': the Del Piero experiment

After some turbulent moments in its short history, the A-League is now in its eighth season, and as every other season before it, the 2012–2013 installment had been billed as the biggest and most exciting to date. Much of that has been due to Sydney FC's signing of former Italy and Juventus great, Alessandro Del Piero (see Hassett's articles) – despite offers from other parts of the world, as described by Orlowitz. The signing of Del Piero serves as a metaphor for Australia's soccer reality and aspirations. His signing is what soccer has become to Australia: just as the A-League is banking on the likes of Del Piero as the international catalyst, Australia is banking on soccer and its international and economic bona fides to serve as the wave for its engagement with Asia.[9] His move to the A-League has apparently been 'big news' around the world. In Australia, the soccer media have dubbed his signing as the biggest thing to happen to the A-League.[10] The game's administrators claimed that this event has brought unprecedented attention to the A-League that will heighten the level of interest from media, investors and consumers.[11] Shortly after Del Piero's signing, the former English Premier League (EPL) journeyman and England international, Emile Heskey, signed for the Newcastle Jets while the newest A-League franchise, the Western Sydney Wanderers, signed former Japanese international, Shinji Ono.

According to Del Piero, (featuring in the *Australian Four Four Two* article) his decision for joining the A-League was due to his desire to continue his career and make a 'major contribution and help grow the game' in Australia. One imagines that his two-year deal, claimed to be $AUD2 million-per-season (from Sydney FC alone), would bear significance in his decision to sign for Sydney FC yet for someone of his standing, one imagines that the immediate financial aspect would seem somewhat trivial. If it is, as claimed by media reports (see, Gatt; Brooks), that he was offered contracts by bigger clubs, would they not have made significant – if not loftier offers? Del Piero, after all, has an enviable résumé as both a World Cup and UEFA Champions League winner with Italy and Juventus, respectively. Having played for the Turin club for 19 years, he holds *The Old Lady's* all-time goal scoring and appearances records. He is also listed as the third highest all-time goal scorer for the Italian national team. However, recent transfers by other 'big name' players to the USA, Russia, the Middle East and the Far East, suggest that big money is made in places other than Australia.[12] In that case, should one question how and why Australia and Sydney FC became a suitable option for Del Piero, a player that could have seemingly gone to any league in the world? And, likewise why the FFA and Sydney FC saw Del Piero as the perfect 'marquee signing' and the tag of the highest paid footballer in a country dominated by other football codes? For the most part, decisions like these are now an accepted orthodoxy in Australian soccer.

The signing of Del Piero is Australian soccer's attempt at replicating Los Angeles Galaxy's and Major League Soccer's (and since, Paris Saint-Germain's) signing of David Beckham. It represents not merely the signing of a player based exclusively on his footballing quality. Rather, it is the signing of a 'brand', an ambassador whose presence promotes the game and the interests of the game's administrators. Such a signing brings 'engagement' and hype. As recent events suggest, it can make ripples around the world and cause people to take notice of Australia as a soccer nation. The news itself serves as a cheap advertisement for all involved. In such an event, the player also brings an element of credibility to the sport and the league, albeit perhaps synthetic, providing a greater impetus for a growing soccer economy, and hence a shortsighted, hurried, opportunistic marketing ambition rather than a production of localized experience and expression. It is here that Australian soccer's and the A-League's dilemma lies – perhaps even epitomizing Australian provincialism; its lack (or declining stocks) of top-class home-grown players,[13] the league's ability to attract 'elite' players merely at the end of their careers, yet at the same time maintain its atmospheric ambitions – just as Australia's insularity remains despite its global ambitions and 'credentials'.[14]

In the case of Beckham, he was seen to have the capacity to bring traditionally 'non-football' people – the mainstream, in both the USA and Australia (as discussed by Jessica Carniel) – as well as a perceived sense of 'glitz' and 'glamour' to the league. Brands such as Beckham and Del Piero will attract those who are football-conscious, but more so they will attract those interested in the 'spectacle' for the simple exercise of entertainment instead of any other deeper or more complex connection or commitment. In each case, it represents an attempt to create a culture within the sport, implying its previous (or existing) culture was foreign or inferior (or non-existent). Perhaps much like the major Australian political parties, the A-League is reliant on hype and 'selling the message' due to this lack of connection or affiliation between players, franchises and consumers, which are its constituency. Seemingly, it is hype emanating from and commonly referred to by sporting administrators as 'engagement', that is one of the few points of connection, albeit a corporate connection. Within this, based on such marketing decisions, there is the inherent belief by the game's administrators (a further example of corporate assimilation) that they can create a (top-down) culture for the game, despite their hyperbole about 'grassroots'.

Unlike in most 'footballing' nations, in traditional terms, the A-League franchises are not 'clubs' with a long and evolved history. The clubs or their names – referred to as 'nebulous sobriquets' by Hallinan and Hughson – do not reflect any social group or class (let alone any 'ethnic' group) or any specific point of locality.[15] Most A-League team names are not concomitant terms. Instead, they offer little demarcation from detergent brand names. With a nod to George Orwell's, *Nineteen Eighty-Four*, 'Victory' is a favourite! And, unlike in most leagues around the world where the consumerist elements were introduced decades after the leagues and the soccer cultures were developed, the A-League is starting at the other end of the continuum. At this stage, because of this lack of credibility in the sociocultural and environmental tapestry, there is no direct or authentic affiliation with any particular aspect of the A-League. For the most part, this 'engagement' is imagined through the interpretation of foreign leagues – namely the EPL. Old Soccer, perhaps via the tyranny of distance and romanticism, represented an engagement with (and interpretation of) continental European soccer, whereas New Football is an Anglocentric perspective with an element of Asian consumer culture and organization. Consumers are affiliated to 'their' A-League team just as they are to an EPL team – the obvious difference being their physical presence. Perhaps replicating similarities in other codes or wider social trends, soccer in Australia has become a place to co-opt, re-live and replicate foreign, observed rituals without subscribing or embedding oneself in the actual foreign culture. In this case, sporting fandom and consumption, where the more you consume (financially and emotionally), the more you are entitled to feel 'a part' of it. Like Australia, despite a decreasing sociocultural parallel, there is an increasing engagement towards corporate symbols and citizenship though transaction.

The case of Del Piero reveals a constant need for hype – and with it an inherent dilemma that organic hype (or 'passion') within Australian soccer remains lacking. The signing of elite Australian players previously provided a level of hype. Recent events suggest that their influence is waning. Likewise, the enduring hype of the Socceroos is intermittent at best, usually peaking around qualifying campaigns or major competitions. The signing of international 'stars' has become the accepted and remaining point of hype for the A-League since Australian fans' recent criticism of Australia's returning stars. Del Piero's presence, on the other hand, is as much about the hype that is intended to bring back or convert the 'Old Soccer faithful' to the A-League as creating new fans. For one, Del Piero never played in the EPL.[16] Old Soccer's connection to Del Piero is significant not merely because he played in Serie A during its peak and global value, but more so because of his status within the Italian diaspora and his admirers in Asia. With Sydney having an estimated four million residents who claim Italian heritage, Sydney FC's decision seems rather more considered. On the other hand, his signing suggests an attempt by the FFA to reach into Asia and use his status and standing in places like Japan to attract visitors, viewers and investors, in turn claim to extend Australia's 'brand'.[17]

Judging by the media's reaction, his overall conduct and flashes of brilliance since signing for Sydney FC, Del Piero has become a significant marketing attraction. His life and football story is a near fairytale: growing up in modesty, his dream was to become a professional footballer, and playing most of his career at the highest level at one of Europe's bigger clubs. Even when 'Juve' was relegated to Serie B in 2006, he remained at the club despite being one of European soccer's biggest names. Described by the media as a 'gentleman' and a 'family man', his unpretentious and wholesome image makes for the perfect advocate of any commodity – even as a 'Wog'! His networking extends to other sporting stars, rock stars and celebrities. He seemingly has a PR entourage that promotes the 'ADP' brand globally. Del Piero's connection to Asia is no secret. He claims to have had an interest in Japan since he was a child. In Japan, where in 1996 he played in the Intercontinental Cup for Juventus, and in 2002 during in the World Cup for Italy, he is revered, with a fan club, website and blog included. According to reports by Orlowitz, and Carroll, months before he became a Sydney FC player, he reportedly had discussions with Japanese clubs and played in his second charity match, this time raising funds for victims of the 2011 earthquake/tsunami in Japan. He is said to have affiliations with a number of corporations around the world, including Adidas, who are also the official apparel supplier to Sydney FC. He is said to be a long-term supporter of numerous charities around the world.

It is then perhaps no surprise then that he refers his move to Sydney as 'Project Sydney'. But what cannot be overlooked or underestimated however is his expected capacity to attract those who have not been engaged by the A-League or have found it difficult to convert their support to the post-2005 era. This claim is perhaps epitomized by his quote (interestingly, he continues to refer to the game as 'soccer') in one of his early press conferences in Australia:

> I know it's a young league but I think about the Australian people, there are a lot of Italians who have immigrated. A lot of English, Greek, Croatian and the other Yugoslavian people. In everybody I think there is soccer blood and we hope to wake up that ...[18]

Del Piero is therefore the best and most-affordable Beckham-alternative, one that just happens to have an ethnic name. His appearance on the Australian soccer scene adds to the wider argument that New Football is trying to woo back Old Soccer. The creation of the newest A-League franchise, the Western Sydney Wanderers, also adds to that argument. From its name, to its location, its colours and its crest, its choice of players and their backgrounds, as well as the club's claims towards its ties to its 'multicultural community', it is all a clear reference to Old Soccer.[19] Similar arguments could also be made about another recent franchise, Melbourne Heart, as well as Special Broadcasting Service (SBS) Television's return to the fold as a soccer broadcaster.[20] If that premise is accepted, then New Football to some extent has conceded that it cannot succeed by ignoring Old Soccer. At the same time, whilst utilizing the old, it is doing it on its terms and conditions. Perhaps New Football has hitherto failed in its bid to 'unite the tribes',[21] as was promised, to create a completely new market audience, and ironically, if it is to succeed, will now partly rely on an audience it did its best to expel. Initially, it was assumed that those who loved soccer would make the transition to the A-League without resistance – hence to some extent, the initial 'one city-one team policy'. Many did, although there remains a conflict between the two eras, which resides online, on social media, non-elite soccer and, symbolically perhaps, in low elite-level match attendances.[22]

On the other hand however, the claim of Old Soccer being re-engaged perhaps reflects the power New Football now wields. Nearing its first decade in existence, it can afford to do this as it can be assumed that many Old Soccer patrons have somewhat lost engagement with Old Soccer clubs, who themselves, in many cases, are on their last legs. A recent development in Australian soccer has been the compilation and announcement of a National Competitions Review by the FFA – a review that will have similarities to the *Crawford Report*. While its intention is said to create an elite pathway for young players by creating links with elite clubs, it will undoubtedly draw the curtains on many remaining ethnic-backed clubs (whose era had been rubber-stamped as subordinate a decade ago) who will not have links with elite clubs.[23] The above examples reflect the contemporary Australian dilemma of 'commerce versus culture', as discussed by Davis. Whilst the new Australia has long seen commerce as the priority, it growingly relies on 'culture' in the form of sport and event hosting to create commerce.

While the highlight reel will suggest increasing crowd engagement, figures and improving quality of play, the low points of the New Football Era suggest a present as close to the past as it is to a future. Soccer, in Australia – or perhaps like Australia – remains on the precipice, unsure of what it represents. Its seemingly bright future invariably seems hampered by its dark past. While the Old Soccer Era for the most part was unprofitable, the NSL lasted for 27 years. It maintained this 'longevity' because of the 'ethnic factor'; there because of a perceived connection or intimacy between ethnic groups and soccer clubs – a 'culture'. Rightly or wrongly, clubs represented the ethnic group. Old Soccer and the NSL represented ethnic Australia, which begs the questions: 'what does New Football and the A-League represent?' And, how will they survive and become profitable to ultimately differentiate itself from soccer's past? While NSL soccer was deemed as inferior, its supporting infrastructure was no better. With that in mind however, and for all its unpretentiousness, for the consumer it was inexpensive and acquirable; a poor economy and unsurprisingly lossmaking – yet it survived for over a quarter of century. While its ethnicity was claimed as exclusionary, its affordability was its inclusivity. While New Football may be a more polished product, it is a costlier product. One point that may explain its perpetual 'potential status' has been the game's discerning consumers. In soccer, as with many other commodities, Australians tend to indulge in the foreign. In many cases, it is better value for money.

Early statistics suggest that the 2012–2013 A-League season will prove to be the most attended in its history. The signing of global marquee names has surely played its part, yet the long-term sustainability of the A-League and the future of New Football remain unclear. For the time being at least, both remain unprofitable. In that case, for how long will New Football remain unprofitable, and for how long will those administering it maintain their support without a return? For how long will the Australian government be its main investor? While billionaires such as Frank Lowy, Nathan Tinkler and previously, Clive Palmer, profess (or professed) to be 'football people' and lovers of the game, it is unclear how much of their own money they are investing – or losing – and for how long they will wait to reap the rewards. Regardless of their investment (relatively speaking), compared to their wealth and the amounts being invested into soccer by individuals, organizations and governments around the world, it is a miniscule amount. Also, what is not entirely clear is why they are investing into soccer in the first place – especially if they are not yet making a return. Ultimately, what is New Football's purpose for its numerous stakeholders?

In Australia, soccer is an inexpensive, speculative commodity for any investor. New Football's administrators attained the sport with little or no investment – for the most part, it relies on the taxpayer. The *Crawford Report* guaranteed that the sport's entitlement had changed to new hands with little debate or associated cost.

While clubs and players around the world are bought and sold for stratospheric sums, New Football's administrators acquired the whole sport and associated assets and rights – with significant participation numbers and loyal consumers – within this country for a pittance. Like any commodity, its value is expected to grow but when you pay nothing for it, it is hard to see a loss! The A-League promises investors' potential for significant gains in the future with minimum investment – the Asian future. While various investors may have varying reasons for the game to succeed in this country, it is the networking and engagement with Asia by Australia's business elite that is the ultimate drive. Whilst the big financial rewards, the large-scale investments in Australia are potential, based on population and market size, they are long-term goals and rely on the change of 'Australian culture' or its broader perception.

Globally, while some of its biggest clubs continue to amass huge debt, there are questions regarding soccer's profitability and sustainability. Where soccer is immensely profitable is in its association, its utility by individuals and corporations to attract consumers and viewers, to utilize its hype, support and loyalty to drive secondary investment where it can be made profitable. In Australia, while these gains are said to be dependent on converting the large numbers of participants, their peers, families and friends, the payday worth chasing for soccer investors sits in the prospect of selling the league and its clubs to abroad – namely Asia. As the purchase of Brisbane Roar and Sydney FC by Indonesian and Russian billionaires, respectively, suggests, the largest of incentives for Australian soccer and in particular A-League clubs, is to attract wealthy owners, firstly in the hope of an initial profit boost for the stakeholders; and secondly, with hope of further investment from wealthy owners to provide increased exposure and firepower on the transfer markets – in turn enhancing the league as a marketable commodity. The status of the existing 'salary cap' will ultimately determine this aspect. On the other hand, for the wealthy owners of A-League clubs, it perhaps represents commercial diversity if not significant income or exposure that they can utilize to gain a foothold in business prospects in Asia. In football prospects, it provides them with a bargain and credibility for future opportunities within a football portfolio.

Politics and billions: the justification for New Football

While references to the A-League remain far from ubiquitous even following the signings of luminaries such as Del Piero, being the elite antipodean soccer competition, mention of it is far more prominent than its predecessor, the NSL, whose enduring legacy remains as the justification of 'why change was needed'. It perhaps also epitomized the thought of 'what was wrong with soccer in this country' and in many ways what was deemed wrong with Australia: the perception that there was people and institutions deemed as un-productive, unwelcome and unwilling to assimilate, and thus 'un-Australian'. They (people and institutions) 'refused' to leave their loyalties and differences behind, and become 'Australian'. It was this 'rejection' that epitomized their un-Australianness. Likewise, their failure to assimilate to 'Australian' sports – and their loyalty to soccer – reiterated this, in sporting terms. Soccer served as the beacon of foreignness, in most cases, continental European foreignness and as something distinctly different to 'Australian'. Despite this, however, Old Soccer's administrators controlled what is only now being considered as a lucrative commodity in the Australian context, a significant and highly desired piece of real estate with a beachfront view to the Asian Century. Yet, they could not or weren't willing to utilize it to any broader potential.

It is somewhat absurd to discuss a league competition in Australia for a specifically Asian-focused journal when considering that soccer had gone from being deemed 'the Australian sporting antithesis' to the sport consciously being absorbed as being bone fide Australian, openly promoted by governments and organizations, that would allow Australia to become an 'Asian footballing nation' and play a central role for Australia in the Asian Century. From 'wogball', it is now a sport that has more participants than all the other football codes combined. Although still facing resistance, it is something that is increasing its credibility amongst fans and pundits as the next big thing – as a sporting and cultural commodity as well as a meaningful career path for future generations of Australians. While details and evidence of this are only now unfolding, early manifestations were put in place many years before that will continue to shadow its historical, contemporary and potential representation. Even more importantly, however, in terms of the future may be who Australian soccer will represent and how and what they will represent it as. While its future is and will certainly be Asian, its representation will be of a contemporary Australia, representative of the game's administrators and financiers' imaginations. With the implementation of the *Crawford Report* – and the subsequent loss (or disbandment) of the overwhelming and the most significant influence and representation, it begs the question of what soccer in Australia (and the A-League) represents. If the original representation is not represented, then can it ever be truly Australian, and considerate of the whole 'Australian' experience?

While references to the *Crawford Report* are even less common, it is the watershed moment that enabled these changes to take place; changes including who governed the game; to which purpose the game could be used, and how much one could charge for the game. But most significantly perhaps, serving the purpose of justification to the disbanding of the previous soccer establishment that would set all the other effects into place it became the extenuation of the current political and corporate dominance. Soccer's Asian aspiration and its evolving fortunes are all central to this justification. There are numerous plausible explanations for why references to the report remain elusive or irrelevant: for one, since 1993 there have been no less than three reviews into Australian sporting (two of which were on soccer) competitions by prominent businessman, David Crawford. Otherwise, perhaps as much as Australians love sport, they claim not to mix politics with one of the quintessential Australian criterions – sport. After all, it was soccer that was interpreted as being too involved in politics – ethnic politics, to be precise.

Overwhelmingly, when raised, the report represented the necessity for restructure and implementing managerial and administrative changes in the sport – changes deemed long overdue and holding back the sport from becoming a powerhouse on the Australian sporting landscape. It should be noted that the reasons or discussion for why Australia should care to play soccer, let alone reasons for striving to be successful at it, are elusive throughout – just as they are now an accepted orthodoxy evangelized by the game's loyal pundits. Those justifications would only later surface, leaving its implementation malleable. Perhaps as one of many paradoxes of soccer in this country, the report was deemed welcomed seemingly by all in sundry yet in many ways its 80-plus pages had nothing to do with the 'soccer' itself, but more about the 'corporate viability'. Specifically, however, the report presented a justification for change for those that harboured a desire, desperation or visualization for the sport to be something other and bigger than it was before – closer to the realization of foreign leagues seen on television. Essentially, despite their claims and concerns of ethnic politics, the overwhelming ethnic representation of soccer – the drive was, ironically, for Australian soccer to represent and replicate the values, images, rituals, the aesthetic, corporate and consumer elements of the behemoth of global football economy – European soccer – and its opportunity for power and wealth through a 'uniquely Australian' perspective.

The *Crawford Report* became the most recent effort to break the stranglehold of the existing demographic. Initially but lastingly, soccer's complex was perhaps due to its conflict with imagined 'Australian' ideals or character supposedly more openly endorsed by the more 'Australian' of sports. Then it was arguably the role of the media and politicians during the post-war 'soccer boom' period of the late 1940s to the early 1960s.[24] The *Bradley Report* (1990)[25] illustrated a revival of similar themes during the 1990s – perhaps the height of soccer's 'ethnic' perception and the most direct influence to the *Crawford Report*. The 2003 report and the A-League would become the most significant and successful efforts to break the stranglehold because it involved elements from within soccer or those who claimed to be 'genuine soccer people', as well as those from corporate Australia with close links to both government and FIFA – those such as Frank Lowy, the Australian game's lynchpin. It was perhaps the relationship between Lowy and John Howard, and the willingness of the Howard government to support and implement change that was also significant, particularly as FIFA rules (to some extent) restricted political interference in soccer's national governance.[26] The Lowy–Howard effect would mutually benefit the corporate and political sides. For Howard and his government, it would resolve one instance of wider issues of immigration, assimilation and the role of multiculturalism – he, according to Hallinan and Hughson 'argued for a return to a simplistic monocultural way of life steeped in nostalgic longing for the Anglo place that Australia supposedly once was'. Soccer, apparently, as an 'ethnic' sport could not be at home in this imagined Australia. The soccer example highlighted the inherent ambivalence of his government towards multiculturalism, a concept perhaps idealized by Australian soccer. For Lowy, it would present him with an international commodity that he could rule upon.

Conclusion: soccer, wogball, football and the beautiful game

The Old Soccer–New Football depicts the far bigger subject of the wider Australian social fabric, and remains as Carniel put it, a 'rich site for investigation, the exploration of which illuminates the nation's colonial and migrant past'. While it is conveniently revised or simplified due to its complexity and substance, much like a contested territory, soccer is both a 'dream and a nightmare', reflecting the conflicts between representations – the Anglocentric hegemony, and the Other (in this case, the European Other) – and the changes of its wider milieu. In Australia, this period has reflected a lessening influence of the European Other, the prevalence or legitimacy of this identity as something other than Australian along with commodities and institutions that were 'their' being co-opted or corporately assimilated into 'Australianess'. In the case of soccer, what was once foreign and ambivalent is increasingly becoming a trademark of a dominant host culture with little reference to its previous social, cultural and historical value because the outcome of the anticipated riches of the 'Asian Century' are deemed as being worth the expense. This form of 'creative destruction' as Bauman claimed glosses over and passes by the destruction of other forms of life and so obliquely the humans who practice them.[27]

Old Soccer presented old culture and old territory – how Australia imagined itself, that which is now redundant, and the 'cities (or rather suburbs) of fear'. Like the once urban working-class areas, soccer represented opportunity – opportunity for development, for gentrification, cultural/cosmopolitan change and ultimately economic change, themselves all reflections of wider global trends. Soccer was ripe for the picking as it represented culture, and culture according to Davis represents future, and as Carniel described it, a 'globally recognized and marketable brand' that can be used to market other brands. But to be implemented into a wider agenda, it was wrestled away; defined using what Davis referred to as 'judgmental social tags' such as foreign, violent and corrupt to reaffirm its 'un-Australianness'. Perhaps not unlike developers buying up 'desolate' property with bureaucratic and economic clout, Old Soccer was boarded up, demolished and re-built and claimed as a new object, much like the way Australia portrays itself as a worldly, cosmopolitan destination to be used for the agendas of those who pushed for the changes.

New Football created a new soccer hierarchy, a new culture, a new commodity for a new economy; a new industry reflecting the changing market in order to enter a greater geopolitical and economic reward – Asia. However, being part of what Davis called the 'radical conservative agenda', its context was not merely economic. This agenda operates 'at the level of culture', a 'hearts and minds campaign to change attitudes' towards 'work, business, government, rights, obligations and citizenship', transforming the 'webs of social relationships and obligations between citizens, government, public institutions and business into market relationships'. The A-League not only represents a change from Old Soccer to New Football, but rather the transition from old Australia to the economically reformed, neo-conservative, market populist, 'personally aspirational' new Australia made of anxieties and hopes. Therefore, to analyse the A-League, to accept and appreciate it, requires the analysis of the drive and justifications for the development of the A-League that is embedded in the creation and implementation of the *Crawford Report*. To accept it as a sporting outcome, one needs to consider its broader context including the cultural ramifications.

Like any league in the beautiful and imperfect society of soccer, the A-League says a great deal about the place it is embedded in. Like any league in the world, the A-League represents the imperfect and highly politicized and highly globalized environment – something not self-professed, but Australian nonetheless. It also goes a long way to narrate and to represent all the 'players' involved. From the onset, the A-League, created as many questions as it did answers. It destroyed and ignored as much as it created. Time will of course tell whether it was worth it and whose interests were being served. Critics would stress that broader analysis of the game has been suppressed or subordinated. If as Davis claims, culture is 'the glue that holds our understandings of place together; in culture, questions of shared memory, identity, tradition, aesthetics, utility and design come together', then this episode of Australian history has undermined the collective cultural representation.

On the flipside, its advocates would point to the new era's record: entry into Asia, consecutive FIFA World Cup qualifications, hosting of the 2015 Asian Cup and a 'vibrant' local competition. While it took away the Wog's remaining bastion on the national scene and repressed his identity, and brought the veracity of multiculturalism into question, it is continuously promoted as something Australian because of its global and multicultural claims. With all its opportunistic focus and 'engagement' towards the Asian Century, Australia has undermined its claimed ideals of democracy, egalitarianism and the 'fair-go'. By its focus to sell itself to what is perceived as the 'Asian gravy train', Australian soccer and the A-League provide their own ambiguity in terms of what it represents. Regardless of whether the 'Asian Century' delivers on its soccer promise in the short term, will what has been eroded culturally outweigh any economic benefits? More importantly, for the time being, if the A-League fails in its promised hype, what will become of Australian soccer, and what will Australia co-opt next? Referring to the 'Australian Dream', Davis states that the 'greatest losses are symbolic. In the name of reform, many of the traditions that made Australia a distinctive democracy have been lost. Lip service is paid to egalitarianism and the 'fair go', but the dream of a country where all are equal has ended'.

Notes

1. 'Soccer' in this paper will refer to the code in general, whilst 'Old Soccer' and the 'Old Soccer Era', and 'New Football' and the 'New Football Era' will differentiate the pre- and post-2005 eras, respectively.
2. Both Australia and New Zealand had made unsuccessful attempts to join the AFC in 1964.
3. Beilharz, quoted in Hallinan and Hughson, observed 'that through the 1990s a dominant frame of discourse emerged with "fear and loathing" of ethnic otherness at its core'. According to Hallinan and Hughson, soccer may have been 'removed from the Tampa Affair, the Border Protection Bill and the Cronulla Beach Riots on the scale of public alarm', but the 'unwillingness of Anglo-Australian sports fans to embrace domestic soccer over the years is a reflection of the cultural xenophobia now at the surface of public debate'.
4. As in British football, or British/Scottish association football.
5. More precisely by its 'Greekness', 'Italianness' and 'Croatness' as these three ethnic groups provided the most significant and enduring ethnic support for soccer in Australia – and particularly at the elite level prior to the A-League. Notably, non-elite or state league clubs in most Australian states remain 'ethnic-backed' clubs.
6. 'Corporate assimilation' represents the idea of corporate entities – distinct to national or cultural institutions, for example – influencing and defining a consumer, constituency, marketplace and/or an economy by their political, economic and cultural influence. In soccer's example, they are using a taxpayer-funded institution to peddle their interests. In post-tribal Australia, the role of such concepts has been filled by corporate equivalents – sporting brands, 'cultural brands' and corporate commodities in developing corporate identities. Whereas previously one's identity may have revolved around 'nationality', 'ethnicity' or one's social class, those concepts have been undermined or dissolved by corporate assimilation where one's identity is defined by his purchasing profile – his association and consumption of corporate products and brands. In the Australian context, while Old Soccer may have been the expression of one's (non-Australian) ethnicity or origin, consumption of New Football predominantly reflects the status and influence of corporate entities – New Football's governing body, its franchises and their corporate backers. In terms of ethnicity, Old Soccer provided the possibility for ambivalence for it allowed the harbouring of an identity that was not an official identity. The attempted acquisition of soccer in general, in both 'Australian' and corporate terms has near-negated soccer's existence in any other terms. The prospect of playing soccer in Australia without attribution or association to the FFA is almost non-existent. Unlike perhaps in other parts of the world where soccer has a true 'grassroots' context where it is played on the street in an unofficial capacity, soccer citizenship in Australia is increas-

ingly on a pay-to-play status through the New Football economy. Much like the 2012–2013 motto 'We Are Football' suggests, and not unlike their AFL counterparts, the FFA claims ownership of the whole game of soccer and its utility in Australia. It has been 'assimilated' into their (corporate) framework.

7. Within the last decade, Australian culture and its economy have changed drastically. While the spending power of Australians has increased during that time, as the recent influx (or in some cases the return) of European retailers and brands (fashion labels and motor vehicle brands, for example) would indicate, so too has their purchase options, http://www.ausstats.abs.gov.au/ausstats/subscriber.nsf/0/0BFA73E639A17B3CCA25732F001C9F7B/$File/41020_Purchasing power_2007.pdf. Recent years have also seen unprecedented numbers of Australians travelling throughout the world, http://abs.gov.au/AUSSTATS/abs@.nsf/DetailsPage/3401.0Sep%202012?OpenDocument. The increasingly redundant stereotyped 'Aussie' who followed the pre-prescribed 'Australian' trends of consumption is changing to a more cosmopolitan and 'worldly' consumer. Both on a cultural and economic level in Australia, soccer is being co-opted into this increasingly global consumer identity.

8. The rise of mainstream Australian coffee and 'foodie' culture or cosmopolitan Australian fashion also reflect this. Not unlike soccer, they have almost become quintessential Australian characteristics, whereas before were considered foreign, effeminate or inferior. When it comes to commerce, seemingly anything can become 'Australian'.

9. As the recently released government White Paper, unequivocally entitled *Australia in the Asian Century*, suggested, Australia's high standard of living and future prosperity is heavily dependent on its engagement with Asia. According to the report, 'the scale and pace of Asia's transformation is unprecedented and the implications for Australia are profound. Australia's geographic proximity, depth of skills, stable institutions and forward-looking policy settings place it in a unique position to take advantage of the growing influence of the Asian region'. In terms of sport, the White Paper argues that sport in the Asian century would serve as a 'powerful unifier'; strengthening connections with Asia; bridge language and cultural barriers and serve as a platform to build relationships. It argues that Australian sports are already taking advantage of the burgeoning Asian market, and that sport has the potential to leverage a range of benefits through better social, cultural and economic/trade relationships. The *Crawford Report*, in many ways, was the White Paper for Australian soccer in the Asian century. The institution of soccer and its administrators were at the forefront of the 'Asian Century' idea, because without Asian integration Australian soccer was seen as futureless, particularly after FIFA reneged on its promise to award Oceania Football Confederation, in which Australia was a part of, direct World Cup qualification. In some soccer circles, the White Paper was received with consternation for only making brief mention of the game's role and only after cricket's role. The Lowy Institute, however, continues to promote 'football diplomacy' and lobbies government and business for the potential of Australia's engagement with Asia through soccer, suggesting that the think tank is a significant stakeholder in this respect. The Lowy Institute (coincidentally also formed in 2003) had referred to the importance of football diplomacy in 2005 (see Bubalo, 'Football Diplomacy'); the FFA had made its submission to the *Australia in the Asian Century White Paper* in March 2011.

10. Staff Writer, 'Boungiorno Oz! Del Piero Signs'.

11. The first round of the 2012–2013 season broke records for both single-round attendances and average television viewers. 93,500 fans turned out across venues to watch the round's five matches. The previous record was 87,508. As for television audiences, an average of 108,000 viewers watched each match during round one. http://www.football-australia.com.au/news-display/record-breaking-weekend-for-hyundai-a-league/49843.

12. Tim Cahill recently signed a three-and-a-half-year deal with Major League Soccer's New York Red Bulls, where he is earning a minimum of US$3.5-million per season, making him the fourth highest paid player in the league. http://www.mlsplayers.org/files/October%201,%202012%20Salary%20Information%20-%20Alphabetical.pdf. Didier Drogba moved to Chinese Super League Club, Shanghai Shenhua F.C., where his weekly wage was around $300,000. http://www.bbc.co.uk/news/world-asia-18840348. Cameroon's Samuel Eto'o from Russian Premier League outfit Anzhi Makhachkala reportedly earns

close to $US30 million per season, making him one of the highest-paid athletes in the world. http://online.wsj.com/article/SB10001424053111903327904576526622339442518.html.
13. Brooks, 'Ageing Without Grace'.
14. In October 2012, Australia was admitted to the United Nations Security Council (http://www.theaustralian.com.au/national-affairs/foreign-affairs/australia-wins-seat-on-united-nations-security-council/story-fn59nm2j-1226498971111).
15. For the most part, they potentially serve as advertisements for major Australian cities. While not steeped in football tradition, A-League team names do illustrate a reference to European clubs: their names, colours and footballing terminology, such as 'FC' or 'United'. Much to the chagrin of Australian media, A-League supporter groups attempt to replicate the roles, behaviour, chants and the choreography of Continental (and Asian fan groups) (i.e. the 'Brigades', the 'Hordas' or the 'Ultras'). A-League franchises, much like Australia, reflect a hodgepodge of European heritage blended with corporate Australiana.
16. The recent release of player salaries by the MLS Players' Union shows that the highest paid players in the league have all previously and most recently featured in the EPL. This evidence suggests that either all the players who have joined the MLS from the EPL are perceived as 'better' players than those coming from other leagues, and are thus considered more valuable, or rather it is their EPL connection, and thus an increased television-based value that makes them more profitable in the MLS economy.
17. Hitherto, the 2012–2013 season has been shown in Hong Kong, Singapore, Myanmar, Italy, USA and the UK. http://www.footballaustralia.com.au/news-display/Recordbreaking-weekend-for-Hyundai-ALeague/49843. Initially, Del Piero was said to have been staying at the The Star casino, while Sydney FC's main shirt sponsor is an online flight- and hotel-booking company. Sydney FC's secondary sponsor, worn on the back of the strip, which reads 'sydney.com', is Destination NSW, a New South Wales government authority set up to 'support growth in the state's tourism and events sectors' http://www.destinationnsw.com.au/. The press conferences in which his signing (and re-signing) was announced were held at a Circular Quay building overlooking Sydney's Harbour. http://www.theage.com.au/sport/soccer/more-idol-chatter-as-star-italian-resigns-20130221-2eu96.html.
18. Brooks, 'Del Piero's "Project Sydney" underway'.
19. The first game of association football (in what was to become 'Australia' post-1901) occurred in 1880 involving a team called the 'Wanderers'. Western Sydney is seen as the 'heartland' of soccer (and rugby league), a place that boast significant 'grassroots' participation numbers, and a place where many of its current and former stars grew up. In recent years, it has become a battleground for competing footballing codes, with the AFL setting up the Greater Western Sydney Giants franchise before the Wanderers entered the A-League in 2012. Western Sydney had earlier attempted to field a side, known as the Sydney Rovers, but that proposal, despite attaining a license in 2009 and due to enter the competition in 2011–2012, was later rejected by the FFA due to 'funding concerns'. The FFA presently wholly owns the Western Sydney Wanderers.
20. The new television-rights deal between Fox Sports Australia and SBS means that, for the first time, the A-League will be shown live on free-to-air television. The new deal, which expires in 2016, is reportedly worth around $AUD160 million. http://www.smh.com.au/sport/a-league/sbs-to-show-live-aleague-as-part-of-new-160-million-tv-deal-20121119-29lb9.html. SBS is synonymous with both soccer and Otherness in Australia; renowned for its coverage of soccer as much as it is known for its status as a 'multicultural institution'. In some quarters, the term 'SBS' stood for 'Sex Before Soccer' – a reference to SBS's habit of screening of 'raunchy' late-night 'world movies' followed by soccer matches – or just 'Soccer Bloody Soccer'.
21. Upon making his entry on the soccer scene, former FFA boss, John O'Neill, famously remarked that his organization and the A-League would 'unite the tribes', which would serve as a short-lived catch-cry, mainly for those outside of soccer. The intent behind it might have been to 'end tribalism' in Australian soccer but its intention was clearly to remove the loyalty and attitudes associated between ethnicity and Old Soccer clubs. There was also a belief that loyalty to a corporate entity would become more significant

than any ethnic affiliation; that 'corporate assimilation' would prove to be more powerful that any 'cultural assimilation'. Another catch-cry that defined Old Soccer was 'the lunatics running the asylum'; the lunatics seemingly referred to the Wogs. Funnily enough, the aforementioned first game of soccer in Australia was said to have been played at a lunatic asylum.
22. Even the debate in nomenclature: soccer vs. football suggests which camp its user resides. 'Football' seems to be used by those in the FFA and New Football camps, or those battling the ambivalence of the word 'soccer' – whereas 'soccer' continues to be in prevalence amongst those who have been involved throughout in both eras. Otherwise, they are supporters of the other 'football' codes in the country.
23. 'National Competitions Review: summary of outcomes'. *Football Federation Australia*, May 2012. http://www.footballfedvic.com.au/index.php?id=816.
24. In *Soccer Boom: The Transformation of Victorian Soccer Culture 1945–1963* (2007), John Kallinikios provides evidence of the negative attitudes soccer faced, particularly in the print media, at the time. During the 1950s and early 1960s, soccer was 'framed in terms of ethnic identity when the Australian public was consumed by anxieties over the migrant presence'. Significantly, Kallinikios indicates that during this 'boom' soccer was already professional; clubs and administrators were not merely concerned with ethnic factors but were also interested in making the game profitable. Perhaps it is worth asking, 'if the game was already professional (relatively speaking) and there was a significant and loyal fan base, what was it that prevented it from becoming any more that it was (and realistically, made it far less than what it was then) over the next fifty to sixty years?'
25. Dr Graham Bradley's report into the game's standing and prospects suggested that soccer in Australia was widely a game only played by ethnic groups; that a change in the structure of the governing body, and changes within the NSL, the national team and future player base were needed. Most significantly, the suggestions, while attempting to make the game more national, were seen as an attempt to lessen the ethnic influence. This was epitomized by the decision in 1992 when ethnic club names across all levels were banned.
26. One of the reasons the FFA revoked Gold Coast United's A-League license was due to Clive Palmer's sarcastic use of the slogan 'Freedom of Speech' on the front of his team's shirts. The most fascinating aspect of Palmer's opposition to the current governance of soccer in Australia, both before and after his Gold Coast franchise lost its A-League license, was his rumored attempts to create a rival league and federation (known as Football Australia), as well as creating a review into the current running of the game by the FFA, entitled *National Public Inquiry into the state of football in Australia*. While Palmer's intentions may have been at least sardonic, the biggest irony and significance was that his actions mimicked and highlighted the processes by which the Frank Lowy-led administration formed its governance of soccer in this country. Unfortunately for Palmer, he perhaps did not have the political or corporate clout that Lowy enjoys. http://footballofaustralia.com/wp-content/uploads/2012/06/Football-Australia-Public-Inquiry-Final-Report.pdf.
27. Bauman, *Liquid Life*, 3. In Davis, *The Land of Plenty*.

References

'Australia in the Asian Century White Paper'. *Australian Government*. October 2012. http://asiancentury.dpmc.gov.au/sites/default/files/white-paper/australia-in-the-asian-century-white-paper.pdf.

Bauman, Z. *Liquid Life*. Cambridge: Polity, 2005.

Beilharz, P. 'Rewriting Australia: the Way We Talk About Fears and Hopes'. *Journal of Sociology* 40, no. 4 (2004): 432–45.

Brooks, R. 'Del Piero's "Project Sydney" underway'. *Espnfc.com*. http://espnfc.com/columns/story/_/id/1161746/rob-brooks:-alessandro-del-piero's-'project-sydney'-underway?cc=3436 (accessed September 17, 2012).

Brooks, R. 'Del Piero Kicks Off New Era for A-League'. *Espnfc.com*. http://espnfc.com/columns/story/_/id/1151486/rob-brooks:-alessandro-del-piero-begins-new-era-for-a-league?cc=3436 (accessed September 5, 2012).

Brooks, R. 'Ageing Without Grace'. *Espnfc.com*. http://espnfc.com/columns/story/_/id/1335754/a-league-angle:-ageing-without-grace?cc=3436 (accessed February 11, 2013).

Bubalo, A. 'Football Diplomacy'. *The Lowy Institute*. http://www.lowyinstitute.org/events/football-diplomacy-australias-engagement-asia-through-football#.UKvct7QK6fc.twitter (accessed November, 2005).

Carniel, J. 'Sheilas, Wogs and Metrosexuals: Masculinity, Ethnicity and Australian Soccer'. *Soccer & Society* 10, no. 1 (2009): 73–83.

Carroll, S. 'Del Piero Strikes in More Ways than One in Charity Match'. *Daily Yomiuri Online*, July 23. http://www.yomiuri.co.jp/dy/sports/T120722000961.htm.

Crawford, D. 'Independent Soccer Review: Report of the Independent Soccer Review Committee into the Structure, Governance and Management of Soccer in Australia'. *Australian Sports Commission*. https://secure.ausport.gov.au/__data/assets/pdf_file/0008/153818/Crawford_Report_2003.pdf (accessed April, 2003).

Davis, M. *The Land of Plenty: Australia in the 2000s*. Melbourne: Melbourne University Press, 2008.

'FFA Submission to the Australian in the Asian Century White Paper', *Football Federation Australia. March 2011.* http://asiancentury.dpmc.gov.au/sites/default/files/public-submissions/Football-Federation-Australia.pdf.

Gatt, R. 'Sydney FC Reportedly Offer Italian Legend Alessandro Del Piero $2 Million Deal to Ply Trade in A-League'. *Fox Sports Australia*. http://www.foxsports.com.au/football/a-league/sydney-fc-reportedly-offer-italian-legend-alessandro-del-piero-2-million-deal-to-ply-trade-in-a-league/story-e6frf4gl-1226461402737#.USxBzKCTNUQ (accessed August 30, 2012).

Hallinan, C. and Hughson, J. 'The Beautiful Game in Howard's 'Brutopia': Football, Ethnicity and Citizenship in Australia'. *Soccer & Society*, 10, no 1. (2009): 1–8.

Hassett, S. 'Del Piero to Sign with Sydney FC'. *The Sydney Morning Herald*. http://www.smh.com.au/sport/a-league/del-piero-to-sign-with-sydney-fc-20120831-255tw.html (accessed August 31, 2012).

Hassett, S. 'SBS to Show Live A-League as Part of New $160 Million TV Deal'. *The Sydney Morning Herald*. http://www.smh.com.au/sport/a-league/sbs-to-show-live-aleague-as-part-of-new-160-million-tv-deal-20121119-29lb9.html (accessed November 19, 2012).

Hassett, S. 'More Idol Chatter as Star Italian Re-signs'. *The Age*. http://www.theage.com.au/sport/soccer/more-idol-chatter-as-star-italian-resigns-20130221-2eu96.html (accessed February 22, 2013).

Orlowitz, D. 'Del Piero to Participate in J-League Charity Match'. *Goal.com*. http://www.goal.com/en/news/3688/japan/2012/07/16/3245313/del-piero-to-participate-in-j-league-charity-match (accessed July 16, 2012).

Staff Writer, 'Boungiorno Oz! Del Piero Signs – Official'. *Australian Four Four Two*. http://au.fourfourtwo.com/news/250078,buongiorno-oz-del-piero-signs-official.aspx (accessed September 5, 2012).

Australia, Asia and the new football opportunity

Chris Hallinan and Tom Heenan

School of Journalism, Australian and Indigenous Studies, Monash University, Australia

> After numerous attempts to join the Asian Football Confederation (AFC), Australia finally became a member in 2006 and was immediately re-designated from 'Oceanic' to 'Asian'. In examining the impact of this move, we contextualize it within Australia's broader economic and socio-cultural shift from its British roots to an increasing economic enmeshment with Asia. Australia's AFC membership coincided with football's corporatization locally, exemplified in the A-League's establishment. This altered the dynamics of identity politics in Australian football shifting the game at the elite level from its multicultural roots to a corporate assimilationist model and generating debate surrounding the very essence of multiculturalism. We show this move was a necessary precondition to Australia joining the AFC. We assess whether this complex interplay of politics, national identity and regionalism has facilitated any paradigm shift in Australian attitudes towards Asia; or was the move based on Australian football's opportunistic quest for bigger market?

Introduction

On 19 November 2012, the Football Federation Australia (FFA) announced a four-year, $AUD160 million television deal. Commencing in July 2013, the deal solidified the pay-television operator, Fox Sports, as the principal broadcaster of the A-League and Australia's international matches, including the World Cup qualifiers and the 2015 Asian Cup. But the deal also provided a foothold in the free-to-air television market. Australia's multicultural network, Special Broadcasting Services, secured the rights to televise one A-League game in the prized Friday night time-slot, as well as highlights packages and delayed broadcasts of all finals and internationals. At a time when football's major codes, rugby league and Australian rules, were pushing more of their games into the pay-television market, the FFA was keen to broaden the A-League's viewing base by entering its free-to-air counterpart.

In announcing the deal, the FFA chief executive, David Gallop, stated with a touch of hubris that '[t]he former sleeping giant of Australian sport is awake'. Gallop's mood was buoyed possibly by the A-League's near record attendances, Sydney F C's signing of the Italian great, Alessandro Del Piero, and rumours that the English legend, David Beckham, may have one final footballing fling 'downunder'. But the FFA Chairman, Frank Lowy, was more cautious. After declaring that it had been 'a bloody good day', Lowy let slip that he would have liked to secure more money from the deal. According to Lowy, the four-year deal secured the immediate financial futures of the 10 clubs, but left little room to increase 'the existing salary base arrangements' per club of $AUD2.48 million.[1] As a consequence, the A-League was unable to compete with the larger salary caps of Asian leagues resulting in playing-lists of lesser financial value than the more well-heeled Japanese, South Korean, Chinese and Saudi Arabian leagues. Indeed, the current £61 million market value of the A-League's list is dwarfed by the J-League's £215 million and the K-League's £160 million.[2] This position will not alter under the A-League's new television rights deal. But despite this, the deal was greeted with optimism. Though the FFA could not hope to attract the billion dollar plus figures secured by the National Rugby League (NRL) and the Australian Rugby League and the Australian Football League (AFL), the new broadcast arrangement was a marked increase on the original $AUD120 million seven-year-deal which the FFA signed with Fox Sports in May 2006.

The recent deal also marked a dramatic shift in the face of the Australian game. Football's corporatization under Lowy's watch heralded a re-alignment towards Asia. Though Australian players still predominantly sought careers in the prestigious European leagues, a growing number were drifting into the lucrative Asian player-markets. In January 2012, 186 Australian players were reported to be playing in professional leagues across Europe, Asia and North America. Of these, 125 players were based in Europe, 55 of whom were scattered through the various levels of the English professional game. But increasingly more players were being attracted to Asian leagues, particularly in South-East and North Asia. Of the 55 Australians playing in Asia, six were in the Chinese league, eight in the K-League and another four in the J-League.[3] Furthermore, several Socceroos now ply their trade in Asia. The Australian captain, Lucas Neill, and Marco Bresciano play in the lucrative United Arab Emirates Pro League, while Josh Kennedy and Jade North are based in the J-League. Come the Asian Football Confederation (AFC) club championships, Australian clubs will inevitably be facing off against Asian teams featuring Australian players.

This shift is only recent. Nevertheless, it provides an opportunity to both observe and dissect how Australia, as a new AFC member country, dealt with the shift from the 'English Book'[4] to a more outward view of itself and of Asia. This paper explores these changes and the accompanying re-branding of 'soccer' to 'football' – hence the official name changes from the Australian Soccer Federation (ASF) to the Football Federation of Australia – and the impact of the re-alignment of confederation membership from Oceania to Asia. Central to these changes were the increased business and marketing opportunities for players, the A-League's franchisees and the FFA in the globe's fastest-growing football market. This shift has enabled the FFA to form links with some of Australia's more internationally focused businesses. As one of the nation's most well-known sporting teams, the Socceroos are much sought-after for corporate sponsorship. The national airline, Qantas, is currently the team's chief sponsor. Hence, the team is packaged as the Qantas Socceroos for an increasingly competitive Asian airline market. No doubt, the airline and the FFA are greatly assisted by utilizing the kangaroo to peddle their products throughout the region.

Signposts to the Asian footballing century

A number of key signposts encapsulate this shift in the recent direction of Australian football. They also signify important aspects of the sport's re-alignment from 'soccer' to 'football'; from local community leagues to a national corporatized league; and from the Oceania to the Asian confederation. The first of these signposts occurred in February 2003 when the Socceroos squad convincingly defeated England in a full international at the West Ham ground in London's East End. The fixture was very much out of the 'English Book' of Australian sport, which traditionally sought acceptance on the cricket fields, tennis courts and rugby pitches of 'the mother country'. With the victory, Australian soccer proved its worth in the game's most lucrative market. Most tellingly, of the 18-man Socceroo squad, every member played for clubs either in England or Western Europe.

The second signpost in the shift towards Asia occurred in June 2005 in London's West End. At the home of the Fulham Football Club, Craven Cottage, the Socceroos played a home match against the New Zealand All Whites. Both teams were playing a 'trans-Tasman' fixture more than 10,000 miles from their Oceanic home. Because the Socceroos were European-based, home was determined by the location of the players' clubs as much as by the nationality on their passports. The fixture was indicative of the game's marginal place on the Australian sporting landscape. With the folding of the National Soccer League (NSL) with its assortment of diverse but mostly non-Anglo ethnic[5] clubs in 2004, there was no elite Australian club competition/league on a national level. But the fixture also marked the end of an era. It would be one of the last that Australia would play as a member of the Oceania Confederation. The following August, Lowy's FFA finally launched the franchise-based A-League, and 'football' replaced 'soccer' as the preferred brand. In November, the Socceroos ended a 30-plus year drought by qualifying for the 2006 World Cup. By the time of the Cup, the Asian Confederation had become the new home of Australian football and the Australian clubs were embarking on their first foray into the Asian Club Championship.

The third signpost occurred in Hanoi's My Dinh Stadium. In mid-2007, Australia took part in their first Asian Cup. After a successful World Cup campaign, the Socceroos expected to breeze through the tournament. With Japan, South Korea and Saudi Arabia, the Australians, with eight EPL players, were justifiably considered pre-tournament favourites. Many of the players approached the tournament with a conspicuous bravado and swagger. The team captain Lucas Neill declared:

> I really think we've got a squad that can handle the conditions. Enough of us have played on the biggest stage now that we won't be intimidated by the teams we're going to play against, and I really see the standard we're expecting to set taking us all the way to the end.[6]

But at My Dinh, the Australians faltered in the quarter-final when the EPL-based Kewell and Neill missed from the spot in a penalty shoot out against the Japanese. The less fancied but very able Japanese had exploited the Australians' over-confidence and poor preparation. An opening draw against Oman was followed by a crushing 3–1 defeat against the tournament's eventual winners, Iraq. The defeat prompted the Australian coach, Graham Arnold, to question the commitment of his highly paid European players. The press immediately speculated on a rift between these players and the coach though the rumours were scotched with a morale-saving 4–0 victory over minnows Thailand. But speculation and questions about Australia's football future in Asia surfaced with the defeat to Japan. Observers thought the Australians had misjudged the strength of Asian football, and if not better prepared, would struggle to qualify for the next World Cup. The apparent motivation for seeking AFC membership – an easier path to the World Cup Finals – had suddenly become more problematic.

Furthermore, around this time another problem was emerging. The failure of A-League clubs to challenge their more cashed-up and highly skilled North Asian opponents in the AFC Club Championship highlighted the weakness of the new corporatized football structure. Franchise indebtedness would increase, evident in the folding of the Auckland and North Queensland ventures, and the A-League would become a supplier of footballing labour to more highly leveraged Asian leagues. By the 2011 Asian Cup, three Australian internationals were playing in Asian leagues, and the relatively unknown Saso Ogenovski had been voted the '2010 Asian footballer of the year' after leaving Adelaide for the K-League. He now captains the Qatari club, Umm-Salal, joining his more illustrious international colleagues, Neill and Bresciano, in the lucrative Gulf States' football market. According to the FFA, more Australian players were choosing to follow Ogenovski's path. By March 2011, there were 44 Australians playing in AFC leagues with eight in Indonesia and South Korea, six in China and five each in India and Japan.[7] Within a year, another 11 had joined them.

The fourth signpost, and arguably the most far-reaching, occurred in October 2012 when the Labour Party Prime Minister, Julia Gillard, launched the Australian Government's White Paper, *Australia in the Asian Century*. Couched as a major policy initiative, the paper was an extension on past governments' attempts to economically enmesh with the booming Asian economies. As the paper outlined, the rise of Asia promised to be 'a defining feature of the twenty-first century', and provided Australia with not only unrivalled economic opportunities, but also the chance to bolster cultural, educational and other 'people-to-people' links within the region. The overwhelming emphasis was on fostering an environment to facilitate trade liberalization and regional economic integration, while hitching Australia's future prosperity to the rapidly expanding Chinese and Indian economies, in particular. But the paper also recognized that this could not be achieved without greater cross-cultural engagement. There was to be a renewed emphasis on the teaching of Asian languages and stress on building links through social and cultural institutions. This will be 'a whole-of-Australia effort', the paper declared, in which 'businesses, unions, communities and governments [would be] partners in a transformation as profound as any that have defined Australia throughout our history'.[8]

Seated alongside Gillard at the event was the FFA Chair, Frank Lowy. His think-tank, the Lowy Institute for International Policy, was hosting the White Paper's launch. Lowy, generally, was not overtly Asian-oriented. As Chair of the retail property developer, Westfield, his business interests were concentrated in Australasia, Britain and North America. But his think-tank was very much involved in monitoring Australia's engagement with its region. Given Lowy's position with the FFA, the Institute also keenly scrutinized Australian football's foray into the AFC. To coincide with the FFA joining the AFC, the Institute's Anthony Bubalo published a policy paper, 'Football Diplomacy', in November 2005. As Bubalo explained, AFC membership constituted Australia's 'first significant sporting relationship with Asia', and his paper explored ways by which the country could exploit this relationship to improve its image and links within the region.[9]

Lowy, the Institute and the FFA were therefore well prepared to exploit government moves to promote greater Asian engagement. In preparation for the Government's White Paper, the FFA prepared a submission in March 2011. Advancing on 'Diplomacy', the submission emphasized the FFA's unique situation as 'one of the few Australian organisations to enjoy full membership of an Asian supranational organization'. Consequently, football provided a 'unique opportunity for all levels of Australian government, business and society to engage with our fellow Asians'. With an estimated 85 million players – 20 million in advance of European numbers – football had become entrenched within the Asian sporting landscape.[10] The submission was particularly pertinent because the 2015 AFC Asian Cup was to be staged in Australia. With a potential television audience in excess of 250 million, according to the submission, the Cup would provide an opportunity to showcase Australia throughout Asia. The submission recommended the involvement of government, business and the education sector in a series of initiatives that would utilize the Cup and football, in general, to bolster Asian engagement. These initiatives included the establishment of a 'Football Asia Council to coordinate commercial, cultural and public diplomacy programs with Australian participation in Asian football competitions'; the appointment of a government-funded 'International Relations Manager' to coordinate Australia's diplomatic efforts with FFA initiatives; and the formation of the Football Business Club, Australia, to meld networking opportunities with AFC-sponsored events. Involved in all these initiatives was the leveraging of business and government financial support in exchange for the FFA's much touted unique access throughout the region.[11]

The White Paper, however, was more concerned with broader business and diplomatic imperatives than sport. This was not surprising, given Asia's marginal place in Australia's largely Eurocentric sporting culture. But the Paper did acknowledge football's potential role in fostering Asian engagement. Unlike cricket whose influence is limited mainly to South Asia and its diasporas, football offered 'a significant, ongoing sporting relationship with ... Asian and Middle Eastern countries, [which] compliment[s] our diplomatic and other links'. In particular, the White Paper noted the opportunities presented by the Asian Cup. Not only would the Cup enable Australia to showcase its expertise in staging major sporting spectacles, but also it would 'promote Australian tourism, trade and other interests in Asia'.[12]

Shortly after the White Paper's release, the Lowy Institute staged an invitation-only seminar entitled 'Football Diplomacy – Australia's Engagement with Asia through Football'. It was the fifth and final in a line of signposts pointing Australia towards Asia's footballing century. According to the blurb, the seminar was a continuation of the Lowy Institute's quest to enhance diplomatic links and business networks through the FFA's membership of the AFC and the staging of the Asian Cup. Among the invited speakers were the Trade Minister, Craig Emerson, and Christopher Fong, the Vice-President of the Indonesian conglomerate, the Bakrie Group. Numbered amongst Bakrie's international investments is its ownership of the A-League franchise, the Brisbane Roar. Fong told the seminar that Bakrie bought the Roar for both 'footballing reasons' and the access it provided to 'Australian technology and expertise'. Ownership of the Roar, he added, had 'opened an amazing amount of doors'.[13] For the likes of Lowy, Fong's presence at the seminar was proof that Australia's footballing engagement with Asia was entering a new phase. Asian conglomerates were not only prepared to associate their name with FFA products – such as Hyundai's sponsorship of the A-League – but also to buy a stake in Lowy's footballing bazaar. For the business-minded Lowy, the FFA's embrace of Asian football was paying-off. The FFA's fortunes were firmly aligned to cash in on the emerging Asian footballing century.

The pre-condition

The signposts only offer half the story behind Lowy's foray into Asia. The journey was by no means seamless and, partially, was in response to forces well beyond Lowy or the FFA's control. At the time, the FFA – and the Australian Government – was a victim of dubious business practices, apparent in the bidding process for the 2022 World Cup. But a mere business analysis of Australian football neglects important cultural aspects.

The oft-portrayed view from sport administrators and supporters is that in order for a sport to become more prominent and financially viable, it needs sufficient levels of media coverage and broadcasting rights. This view was evident in Gallop's hubris over the FFA's recent broadcast rights deal. Sports form a sizeable share of leisure time and media reporting. But the Australian sports landscape currently serves up a series of contradictions. National leagues have been formed in almost every registered sport. However, the most popular spectator sport – Australian rules – has no international component and draws income support which has enabled fulltime professionalism. Yet, the most popular international sport – football – has struggled to draw sufficient spectator numbers and suffered income and media-wise, while the game's most talented players predominantly have sought full-time status in British and European professional leagues.[14]

While the AFL and rugby league command the most sizeable slices of the sponsorship and media pies, football has slowly secured its place in Australia's overcrowded football market. For approximately three decades, Australia unsuccessfully attempted to join the AFC. When it finally did on 1 January 2006, Australia was re-designated from 'Oceanic' to 'Asian'. AFC membership was the culmination of a series of decisions and manoeuvres that combined to have significant and enduring impacts on the sport in Australia, as well as serving to re-position more general commentary regarding the country's geopolitical identity and future. The move must be situated within the general context of Australia's economic and socio-cultural shift from its traditional British links to an increasing enmeshment with Asia. During the 1980s, the Hawke Labour government sought to realign Australia's economic and strategic interests with South-East and North Asia. But this realignment had limits. The subsequent Keating Government's attempts to promote Australia as an Asian country were repulsed by Malaysia and Singapore. Though there was a shift back towards Australia's traditional strategic links under the Howard Government, economic enmeshment with the region intensified. Indicative of this trend was Australian football's decision to join the AFC and Howard's support for Lowy's push to corporatize the sport.

A necessary pre-condition for Australia's move into Asia was a corporatized, franchise-based A-League. This altered the dynamics of identity politics in football and the broader society shifting the game at the elite level from its multicultural or ethnic roots to a corporate assimilationist model. As Howard was a critic of multiculturalism, arguing that it pandered to sectional rather than national interests, his government financially supported the shift. But serious questions remain about the extent to which Australia has embraced Asia. This paper suggests that the complex interplay of football, national identity and regionalism has not facilitated any paradigm shift in attitudes surrounding Australia's place in Asia. It has merely reinforced that all that binds Australia to Asia is economic opportunism and in football's case, the endless quest for a bigger market acquired through a formal realignment from Oceania to the AFC.

With the establishment of a financially secure A-League, qualification for the past two World Cups, and finishing runner-up to Japan in the 2010 Asian Cup, football now seems to be firmly entrenched on the Australian sporting landscape. By scheduling its season during the Australian summer, the FFA has avoided the winter stoush between codes for sponsors and broadcast times and carved out a permanent spot in the Australian sporting calendar. With city and regionally based teams replacing the ethnically-oriented ones, the elite level competition has been radically changed from a small market and fractiously administered organizational structure, into a franchised-based competition with potential mass market appeal. Lowy, with Howard's support, has shifted the organization of the game from clubs representative of non-Anglo ethnic communities. Hence, an expression of Australia's ethnic diversity has been transformed into a corporate assimilationist mould, better suited to the emerging global football structure and the political agendas of conservative politicians keen to see the back of multiculturalism.

A most un-Australian game

Howard and Lowy seemingly forget that football was the most un-Australian of games. While Australia's traditional sporting paths led back to the playing fields of England, football became more socially and ethnically inclusive than Anglo-centric sports. Long before Lowy's foray into Asia, Australian football had developed informal links with the country's near north. In 1923 and 1926, Chinese teams from Hong Kong toured Australia. This was followed by Australian visits to the Dutch East Indies in 1928 and 1931. Australia also toured New Caledonia in 1933 and hosted an Indian team five years later. This tour is significant because it occurred nine years before the first official tour to Australia by an Indian cricket team. While Australia remained a white and fearful outpost of the Empire on the periphery of Asia, football formed part of Australia's formative ties with the region. These ties occurred at a time when Australia's external affairs were determined by Whitehall and the Australian Government was tentatively establishing its first diplomatic missions in London and Washington, and more tellingly, in Tokyo and Chungking. In straying from Australian sport's traditional path, football's engagement with the region played a small part in forging the way for these diplomatic initiatives.

The un-Australianness is also seen in the game's embrace of ethnic diversity. Only recently have migrant groups filtered into the old Anglo-Australian domains of cricket and tennis. In contrast, migrant groups gravitated to football and ethnically-based clubs became expressions of migrants' identities within the broader Australian community. As head of the Jewish club, Sydney Hakoah, Lowy was part of football's ethnic past. Hakoah was one of many ethnic clubs that played in the various major city-based state leagues from the 1950s onwards. These clubs sprouted from the influx of migrants recruited as factory fodder during Australia's post-war industrialization. Clubs such as the Greek-based Hellas, the Maltese George Cross, the Yugoslavian Just and the Italian community's Juventus and Marconi emanated from this influx.

But their establishment created a rift with the traditional Anglo-oriented clubs and administration. Concerned that the latter did not represent their interests, NSW migrant clubs established a rebel administration and competition in 1957 under the banner of the NSW Federation of Soccer Clubs. In 1961, the Federation joined with its Victorian and South Australian counterparts to form the ASF. This development institutionalized football as a migrant sport. While cricket, rugby and Australian rules were considered national games, 'soccer' was derisively dubbed 'wogball'. As well, most of the television coverage ignored the local game and focused on the elite English and European leagues and periodic tours by leading European clubs. The game filtered into public prominence every four years, as Australia battled – usually unsuccessfully – to compete in the World Cup.

In 1974, Australia did qualify for the World Cup finals in West Germany. The team was a product of Australia's post-war migration comprising four local-born players, three Englishmen, three Scots, four Yugoslavs, and a Hungarian and German. Though out-classed, the team's qualification fuelled the impetus for the formation of the NSL in 1977. Football was the first sporting code in Australia to establish a fully-fledged national league competition. The main instigator was Frank Lowy, who won support from the chairman of the ASF, Sir Arthur George. In the inaugural season, 14 teams competed from Adelaide, Melbourne, Sydney, Brisbane and Canberra. The teams were drawn from the existing state leagues, and so were predominantly ethnic based. Lowy pressured the teams to surrender their ethnic names, so as to broaden the League's public appeal. Only Lowy's Hakoah did so, re-branding itself the Sydney City Slickers. The other clubs' reluctance signified that they, in being established when migrants were meant to assimilate into Australian society, used the game to reaffirm their ethnic roots. Given that the NSL's launch coincided with the release of the Galbally Report in support of multiculturalism, there seemed no reason for the clubs to abandon their ethnic identities.

Throughout the 1980s and 1990s, periodic accounts of clashes between rival ethnic groups at state and national league matches appeared in the populist press. The clashes were employed to tarnish the game's image and denigrate multiculturalism. For the likes of Lowy, these clashes and the (over)association of the sport with ethnicity thwarted the former from becoming Australia's global game and recognizing its full potential in local and regional sporting marketplaces. Consequently, the ethnic connotation had to be removed and the sport needed to be legitimized as 'football', not besmirched as 'wogball'.

The new global football order

To fully comprehend the reasons behind these changes, an exploration is required of the new global football order that emerged during the 1970s. Lowy was not alone in seeking to corporatize the game or broaden its appeal to the widest possible market. Indeed, he was merely responding to changes that had altered the game globally.

While the post-war Australian game grew on its migratory roots, a new global football order was emerging fostered by decolonization. The old colonial empires had fragmented resulting in the proliferation of new nation states throughout Africa, Asia, the Pacific and Central America, many of which established national football federations aligned with FIFA. As Goldblatt indicates, in 1945 FIFA had 54 members, half of whom were European. By 1974, FIFA's membership had expanded to

140 with European and South-American members comprising only 33% of the total.[15] The biggest surge in member nations came from Africa where 31 states joined FIFA between 1958 and 1967. This altered the power balance within FIFA. In 1961, the English FA's, Sir Stanley Rous, assumed the presidency. He was of the old school committed to public service, amateurism and keeping politics out of sport. Such attitudes were prevalent among Australia's Anglo-centric sporting administrators, most notably in cricket and tennis. As with Rous, they were incapable of dealing with the global impact of decolonization on sport and its politics. Rous's backing for the whites-only Football Association of South Africa and his reluctance to grant the African Confederation automatic entry into the 1966 World Cup eroded any support he might have secured from the new member constituency. Hence it was no surprise in 1974 when he was unseated by the Brazilian, Joao Havalange.

Havalange was arguably the most important sporting administrator of the post-War era. He had tapped into South and Central American rumblings about the Euro-centric control of World football. More significantly, he had garnered support from Asian and African federations through politicking on a reformist agenda that offered greater inclusiveness to football's developing world. Of particular appeal to these confederations was Havalange's proposal to lift the number of World Cup places from 16 to 24, thus ensuring greater African representation. But Havalange's most significant contribution was the commercialization of the World Cup. With the head of Adidas France, Horst Dassler, Havalange devised a strategy to exploit the emerging synergy between corporate sponsorship, the global television market and sport. In so doing, he created the blueprint for football's new corporatized global order.

This new order extended to the top European leagues. Many of the World's leading players were lured to Italy's Serie and Spain's La Liga during the 1980s. But this changed in the 1990s when the interconnection of multinational corporatism and satellite pay-television transformed the English first-division into the World's richest and most prestigious competition the EPL. The EPL's chief executive, Richard Scudamore, suggested that English football during the 1990s achieved 'the triple play – losing the hooligans, luring big money at home [and] expanding overseas'. But Scudamore failed to note that this was achieved at the expense of the traditional supporters. As in the corporatization of the Australian game, the traditional fan was expendable.

In 1992, the English FA's top clubs split from the four-tier divisional structure and formed the EPL. The split was motivated by the clubs' increasing displeasure at having to surrender valuable broadcasting revenues to lesser clubs which did not have the same drawing-power. The split sparked a bidding war for TV-rights to the new league. The rights were finally secured by Rupert Murdoch's British Sky Broadcasting (BSkyB) for £308 million for over three years. With the global popularity of the EPL, the rights have since escalated markedly. In 2007, BSkyB paid £1.7 billion for a three-year deal. This increased to £1.8 billion in 2010, but jumped dramatically in the most recent deal signed in mid-2012. Under the new arrangement, BSkyB and the British telecom company, BT Group, paid £3 billion for the 2013 – 16 rights, an increase of 69% on the 2009 figure. With the increase in internet streaming fragmenting the media market, BSkyB's determination to secure its hold on the EPL rights undoubtedly inflated the market price.[16] Based on the EPL's global reach, eight of its clubs currently number among the top 20 revenue earners in the global game, while the EPL ranks only behind the US-based National

Basketball Association (NBA), Major League Baseball and the National Football League (NFL) in gross sporting revenues.[17]

This injection of revenue has provided the platform for EPL clubs to purchase the World's best players. The impetus for this global market in football flesh was the 1995 Bosman decision in the European Court of Justice. Before the decision, European leagues had restricted the number of foreign players per club. But the Bosman ruling declared void these restrictions because they violated the free movement of labour within the European Union (EU). Though restrictions remained on players from outside the EU, the ruling broadened the market for footballers and resulted in the Europeanization and, subsequently, the globalization of the EPL. This is evident in large number of Australians currently playing in the English leagues.

As arguably the World's premier football market, the EPL has also attracted the attention of foreign sporting entrepreneurs and well-heeled enthusiasts. Consequently, clubs that were once locally owned, in many cases within their communities, are now partially or solely in foreign hands. Of particular significance is the investment of American sporting entrepreneurs. In May 2005, Malcolm Glazer, a part-owner of the NFL's Tampa Bay Buccaneers, assumed a controlling share of Manchester United amidst much consternation from its diehard supporters. He has since been joined by the Cleveland Braves' proprietor, Randy Lerner, who in 2006 purchased a controlling interest in Aston Villa. In February 2007, Tom Hicks and George Gillett diversified their American ice hockey and baseball interests when they purchased Liverpool. In so doing, they joined Chelsea's Russian oil oligarch, Roman Abramovich, Queen's Park Rangers' (QPR) Malaysian part-owner, Tony Fernandes and Manchester City's Abu Dhabi-based financier, Mansour bin Zayed Al Nahyan as investors in the English game. While Fernandes uses his QPR association to promote his Air-Asia budget airline, Mansour is part of a Gulf States' push to diversify oil revenues into major sporting clubs and events. Since assuming control of the club, Mansour has spent in excess of £480 million on players and bought City, its first league title since 1968.

This influx of foreign capital and the EPL's global reach signifies that it is *the* global brand with greater earning potential than other major leagues and sporting competitions. Indicative of this global push, the League's marketers, Saatchi and Saatchi, dropped 'English' from the EPL brand to present a 'single, unified global identity'. This recognized that the Premier League had moved well beyond Britain's shores.

Australia, Asia and the global order

Australia's entry into the Asian football market replicates Australian foreign policy initiatives of the 1970s and 1980s. With Britain joining the European Common Market, and the USA beating a strategic retreat from Asian military adventurism, Coalition and Labour governments were left with no option but to embrace the region or face isolation. The embrace was founded primarily on economic opportunism, as Australian primary producers and manufacturers sought new markets. Australian football's entry into Asia followed a similar path. Isolated in the Oceania Confederation, Soccer Australia by the 1990s endeavoured to enter the substantially larger Asian market. While Oceania harboured only 500,000 participants in the game, the Asian Confederation boasted approximately 46 million, the largest number of all the confederations.

But the sport's influential non-Anglo ethnic base in Australia was viewed by some, such as Frank Lowy, as a fractious agglomeration of service-oriented organizations that were too unique, relatively small and lacking the necessary financial and media support – an impediment to broadening Australian football's appeal both locally and overseas. Lowy's view was supported by Soccer Australia chairs, David Hill and Neville Wran. They put forth the view that 'ethnic' rivalries were 'un-Australian' and not only stifled the sport's acceptance, but also thwarted its commercial potential. Indeed, in an attempt to broaden the National League's appeal, Hill introduced clubs Perth Glory and Sydney's Northern Spirit in 1996 as well as others that drew upon iconic and popular Australian rules names – Carlton and Collingwood. Carlton and Collingwood quickly floundered but the founder of the Carlton Soccer Club insisted that the demise of his club was the result of Soccer Australia's unwise decision to rush the inclusion of Collingwood Warriors – a 'new' club that was actually a rebranded Heidelberg United (Greek affiliated) club from the Victorian State League.

> [I]t was a mistake for David (Hill) to allow Collingwood Warriors in because they gazumped the Carlton Soccer Club. They hoodwinked a lot of neutrals that we would have naturally have marketed to. I mean we were there at the first game and they had a massive crowd. I think thirteen or fifteen thousand but basically it was downhill from that point on because people realised that it wasn't really going to be a new neutral soccer club. It was a re-badging or a re-establishing of an existing club.

Dabscheck[18] reported that six years after Carlton was declared defunct, the contracted players from 2000 season had only been paid approximately one-third of money owed. Sydney's Northern Spirit club overspent on players, while Perth Glory established a sizeable supporter base built somewhat ironically around the English migrant base. It served as the one-club per city setup which became the 'benchmark' for the new A-League.[19]

But change was not easily achieved, given that Soccer Australia was, like many sports organizations, struggling with competing interests[20] from state governing organizations and club representatives within each state. An opportunity emerged in 1993 when reports began to surface in Britain and Australia alleging that Australian coaches and officials had received illegal 'kick-backs' for acting as player agents in the international transfer market. Amongst those named were the then Australian coach, Eddie Thomson, his predecessor, Les Schenflug and the President of the Marconi Football Club, Tony Labozzetta. Soccer Australia's Chairman, Neville Wran, appointed the former head of the National Crime Authority, Donald Stewart, to investigate the allegations. So apparently damning was Stewart's final report, it was published only under the protection of parliamentary privilege. Stewart not only highlighted the endemic corruption within the game, but also suggested that the game's national development was impeded by its ethnic base. As the report was tabled by the Liberal senator, Michael Baume, it was seen in Labor Party quarters as an attack on the party's migrant constituency. This politicized the issue. Seemingly, it became a means by which the Howard Government could bolster its case against multiculturalism. The Howard government policy put forth an assimilationist-driven form of multiculturalism that required adherence to a singularized cultural grid.[21]

But it was not until 2003 that 'the ethnic game' was laid to rest. The Howard Government had been approached by Soccer Australia chairman, Ian Knop, to investigate the game's administration and its under-achievement on the international stage. The former chair of the accounting firm, KPMG, David Crawford, was appointed to lead the inquiry. Crawford was asked to investigate the efficiency and effectiveness of the game's structure and governance. Of the 230 submissions received by Crawford, all painted a damning portrait of the game's administration. It was riddled with divisiveness and 'inappropriate behaviour', and focused on 'local or factional issues' rather than the broad whole-of-sport development and 'bigger picture' issues. Hence, the report concluded that '[t]he current structure of soccer in Australia is ineffective, does not work and needs changing'. Furthermore, the NSL was bankrupt with debts of $AUD8 million. Crawford recommended an interim committee to be established, chaired by Frank Lowy, to restructure the game's administration. Under Lowy, the NSL and Soccer Australia were scuttled and a new non-ethnic based league implemented. The initiative was substantially bankrolled by the Howard Government. Crawford's report had shown that the game's multicultural roots were at fault which suited the government's agenda. Multiculturalism gave way to corporate assimilation. The new League would be based around one-team regional centres and marketed to appeal to a mass audience, both locally and in Asia.

Lowy's achievement has the potential to alter the Australian sporting landscape. The A-League promptly secured sponsorship from the South Korean conglomerate, Hyundai, and a $AUD120 million television-rights deal with Foxtel. Sponsorships also trickled in from Asian conglomerates and smaller concerns to clubs. Melbourne Victory signed with Samsung, while the provincially based Gosford club, Central Coast Mariners, attracted support from Toshiba. Most interesting of all, the cash-strapped Perth Glory secured a $AUD750,000 sponsorship from the Singaporean-based Delong Holdings. Undoubtedly, these companies viewed the League as a means for promoting their products in Australia and Asia. And the League will depend upon team sponsorship and broadcast rights for funding their operations. So long as the FFA broadcaster needs sports programming to maintain its pay TV subscriptions, the FFA will likely benefit as the national footprint for the major codes of AFL and NRL is more regionalized than the FFA. As Australian clubs' profiles grow in the Asian region, more of this corporate revenue may flow into the League. However, the broadcast rights for Asian Cup, the AFC Champions League, and Asia qualifying rounds for the FIFA World Cup are exclusively owned by World Sport Group for $US 1 billion through 2020. Drawing on Havalange's formula, the amount will be determined on the global or regional reaches of these clubs.

Understanding the change

Much of the published literature has primarily examined and discussed the need for change within the game because of the alleged failures and mismanagement associated with NSL clubs,[22] the mediation of the sport[23] and its Anglo-centric re-centring.[24] These discussions were invaluable in excavating the contested terrains regarding the sport itself, as well as some of the issues bound up in identity and promotion. This contribution furthers this research knowledge base by drawing upon the theories of organizational change to shed light on how the shifts and changes in Australian football were brought about and how this has resulted in the place of Australia within the AFC becoming all but normalized.

Researchers[25] have emphasized the importance of power as the key determinant for understanding the process of change in organizations. The micro politics of interest groups – be they separate clubs, collectives, media outlets and influential figures like Lowy may well adhere to different rationalities, values, outcome preferences when competing with each other. Furthermore, Pettigrew and colleagues[26] maintain that the micro politics are inextricably linked to the broader macro politics and cultural processes at work in the world at large. As well, they insist that understanding organizational change requires the attention to the front stages and back stage use of power, public overt exercises in power and unobtrusive covert actions such as those involving Lowy and the FFA as they seek financial and voting support from the Australian government, the AFC and FIFA.

The ramifications of these developments on Australian football, in general, are far reaching. The capacity of the A-League to expand on its embryonic global base is far greater than those traditional codes which have developed along the crimson line of Empire. But this development may come at a cost. The establishment of a League based on the synergy of corporatism, sport and global media has inevitably undermined the organic roots of the sport. In Britain, some fans have responded to the new corporatism by forming supporter groups and demanding a voice in the administration of their clubs. Though there was some discontent on the A-League's establishment from some supporters loyal to the long established clubs, there has been no substantial backlash. Nonetheless, the League is a product of an evolving neoliberal sporting culture, in which clubs are carefully constructed to maximize spectator membership, media support, merchandise revenue and sponsorship. Players now wear shirts that have sponsor logos as the most visual icon. The shirt no longer signifies a community or place but instead a commercial space for hire. The formation of the A-League confirmed the additional commercial imperative. Frank Lowy has insisted that Fox TV money be channelled to the FFA and that each A-League club must be privately funded. At the elite level, the league has been transformed into a commercial venture, governed by albeit semi-regulated market forces, with designs on expanding into football's Asian and global markets. Time will tell if the community's loss is worth the market's gain. But the boost in funding and media coverage will likely confirm the future of Australia's place in Asia – an outcome perhaps facilitated by the planned or otherwise sequence of organizational change. Notwithstanding the associated issues, without doubt, the transformation of 'soccer' to 'football', the NSL to the A-League, and the Oceania to the Asian Confederation falls under the classification of significant change. Amis and associates contend that such change may well be undermined by its rapidity and emphasized the importance of sequence rather than the taken-for-granted (and often detrimental) need for rapid change.

> What is important is the *sequence* in which organization elements are altered. Our research clearly shows the importance of changing high impact decision-making elements early in a transition process. Thus, even though change may progress at a slower pace after the initial generation of momentum, the early alteration to high-impact elements sends a clear message that the changes being implemented will be substantive and enduring.[27]

Featherstone[28] reminds us that much of the analysis of sport and post colonialism is contained by gender specificity and an over reliance upon issues of national identity. Yet, the very national identity of Australia's participation in the AFC competitions may be the cornerstone of the impetus to join and compete. Televised sport has been the backbone of subscriptions for pay-TV providers. Sage has highlighted both the direct and indirect linkages between mass media organizations and major sports.

> Radio and television segments ... essentially provide advertising for sports. No other privately owned, profit-making industry receives as much free publicity for its product. Of course, the reciprocal business aspect of this is quite clear: The more interest is generated in commercial sports, the greater the profits for the mass media.[29]

In his study of the Olympics, Chalip[30] utilized the concept of polysemy to explain and examine how the world's most-watched event provides multiple pathways meanings directed to audiences. That is, fundraisers and marketers could leverage an array of pliable signifiers to generate support, interest and/or sales. The build-up and announcement of the World Cup bid was widely considered a failure with criticism directed at the FFA for naivety and the Federal government for wasting taxpayers' money. The FIFA balloting count which resulted in one vote only for Australia nevertheless, generated considerable interest and served as a rally point in the preparation for the Asia Cup bid. Unless Lowy and close associates were utterly ill-informed, it might be the case that Lowy and FFA had a good idea that the Australian bid would not win. But for the lead-up to the bid announcement, the FFA and Lowy astutely succeeded in extracting millions of dollars in public subsidy, enthusiastic and sustained media support for the Socceroos (public funded) and the FFA clubs (private ownership) for The Asia Cup bid that was notably uncontested. The 2015 Asia Cup might be a more lucrative opportunity for Australian leveraging into Asia via the contest, elements of festival, pre- and post-contest marketing, football-based tourism and opportunities to coordinate commercial, cultural and public diplomacy. But, although a forthright advocate for Australia's membership of the AFC, one of the Lowy Institute's Research Fellows averred that Australia remains on the cultural and geographical periphery of Asia:

> it should be recognised that membership of the AFC will not make Australia any more Asian than the Persian Gulf countries that are also members of the Confederation. Nor will football help Australia overcome all of the prejudices, misconceptions and historical legacies – both Australian and Asian – that still complicate its ties with the region.[31]

Building upon the 'Asian Century' opportunity

Australia has not changed so much from 'Oceanic' to 'Asian' but has leveraged an opportunity to re-align Confederation membership (and all the nascent commercial opportunities) from OFC to the AFC. The commercial imperative has de-constructed multiculturalism by dismantling foundation clubs and re-constituting the elite level of the sport with a bevy of relatively bland monikers.

Noted commentator and former Socceroo, Craig Foster,[32] looks forward to the moment when Australia wins the FIFA World Cup. Will Australia win the trophy as an Asian country or, as the Lowy Institute is careful to point out, an AFC member? Australian football supporters, in general, may well look forward to the moment when a current second-tier club such as Wollongong/South Coast Wolves (twice NSL Champions & Oceania Club Champion) or Adamstown Rosebud (founded 1889) wins the FFA Cup and thus is the Australian representative for all clubs in the AFC Cup Winners Cup – and re-aligns suburban football to national football to Asian football and a sustainable inclusive future.

The new broadcast rights deal (for the period 1 July 2013 – 30 June 2017) has just been announced to mixed reviews. It is an increase which will enable player payments but the salary cap remains the same and, significantly, it is lower than the better-supported leagues in China, Japan and Korea. As Australian businesses backed by the Federal Government seek more fruitful engagement with Asia, so too does Australian football. Football in Australia has always been at the forefront of new competitive endeavours – both domestically and internationally. With the next hundred years heralded as 'the Asian century', it is not surprising that the touted prosperity of Asia and the AFC also includes ambitious football countries on the geographic fringe such as Australia.

Notes

1. The Melbourne *Age*, 20 November 2012.
2. http://www.transfermarkt.co.uk/en/asien/asien/wettbewerbe.html (accessed 25 November 2012).
3. http://www.ozfootball.net/ark/Abroad/2012-01.html (accessed 25 November 2012).
4. Bhabha, 'Orientalism'. Bhabha used the term 'English Book' to draw attention to the ethnocentrism of 'English' values, literature and knowledge dominance in the colonial world.
5. Within popular Australian discourse 'ethnic' has usually referred to population groups other than English as first language Anglos and Celts and Aborigines and Torres Strait Islanders. Furthermore, immigrant population groups from Asia and Africa have more frequently been connotively referred to as racial groups rather than acknowledged as ethnic groups. But most prominent clubs in football were formed around non Anglo Celtic immigrant groups.
6. Opinion divided but Socceroos need Neill. September 25, 2009. http://wwos.ninemsn.com.au/article.aspx?id=867351 (accessed October 22, 2012)
7. Football Federation of Australia, *FFA Submission to the Australia*, 17–18.
8. Australian Government, *Australia in the Asian Century*, 1–3.
9. Bubalo, 'Football Diplomacy'.
10. Football Federation of Australia, *FFA Submission to the Australia*, 1–2 and 6.
11. Ibid., 24–6.
12. Ibid., 268–9.
13. *Australian Financial Review*, 24–25 November 2012.
14. Wagg and Crabbe, 'Holding their Own'; Hay, 'Our Wicked Foreign Game' and Stoddart, 'Illusion or Reality'.
15. Goldblatt, 'The Ball is Round,' 515–6.
16. *Wall Street Journal*, 14 June 2012.
17. Deloitte Football Money League, 'Real Madrid Stays at the Top'.
18. Dabscheck, 'Moving Beyond Ethnicity'.
19. Hay, 'Soccer in the West'.
20. Four Corners, 2002.
21. Hallinan and Hughson, 'The Beautiful Game', 2.
22. Hay, 'Our Wicked Game'.
23. Baker and Rowe, 'Mediating Mega Events', Rowe and Gilmour, 'Getting a Ticket to the World Game' and Rowe, *Sport, Culture and the Media*.

24. Danforth, 'Is the "World Game"', Hallinan and Hughson, 'The Beautiful Game in Howard's Brutopia', Hughson, 'Football, Folk Dancing and Fascism', James et al., 'Where to Now, Melbourne Croatia?' and Miller, 'The Unmarking of Soccer'.
25. Crozier and Friedburg, *Actors and systems* and Giddens, *Central Problems in Social Theory* and Pettigrew, 'Studying Organizational Change'.
26. Pettigrew et al., 'Studying Organizational Change'.
27. Amis et al., 'The Pace, Sequence and Linearity'.
28. Featherstone, 'Postcolonial Cultures'.
29. Sage, 'Globalizing Sport', 167.
30. Chalip, 'Construction and Use of Polysemic Structures'.
31. Foster, 'Fozz on Football'.
32. Ibid.

References

Amis, J., T. Slack, and C. R. Hinings. 'The Pace, Sequence and Linearity of Radical Change'. *Academy of Management Journal* 47, no. 1 (2004): 15–39.
Baker, S. A. and Rowe, D. (2012) 'Mediating Mega Events and Manufacturing Multiculturalism: The Cultural Politics of the World Game in Australia'. *Journal of Sociology*, doi: 10.1177/1440783312451782.
Bhabha, H. K. *Narration and Nation*. London: Routledge, 1990.
Bubalo, A. 'Football Diplomacy Policy Brief'. Lowy Institute for International Policy, November, 2005. http://lowyinstitute.cachefly.net/files/pubfiles/Bubalo%2C_Football_diplomacy_stripe.pdf
Chalip, L. 'The Construction and Use of Polysemic Structures: Olympic Lessons for Sport Marketing'. *Journal of Sport Management* 6 (1992): 87–98.
Cockerill, M. 'Lowy Names Task Force to Set Ball Rolling on Premier League, *The Sydney Morning Herald*, October 14, 2003. http://www.smh.com.au/articles/2003/10/13/1065917345660.html?from=storyrhs
Cockerill, M. 'Money Talks as Socceroos Make East Asia Debut,' *The Sydney Morning Herald*, August 30, 2012. http://www.smh.com.au/sport/football/money-talks-as-socceroos-make-east-asia-debut-20120829-25149.html
Cockerill, M. 'The Decline of the Wollongong Wolves', *Illawarra Mercury*, August 18, 2012. http://www.illawarramercury.com.au/story/270048/the-decline-of-the-wollongong-wolves
Crozier, M., and E. Friedberg. *Actors and Systems* (A. Goldhammer, Trans.), Chicago: University of Chicago Press. (Original work published in 1977), 1980.
Dabscheck, B. 'Moving Beyond Ethnicity: Soccer's Evolutionary Progress'. In *The Games are Not the Same: The Political Economy of Football in Australia*, ed. B. Stewart, 199–236. Carlton: Melbourne University Press, 2007.
Danforth, L. M. 'Is the "World Game" an "Ethnic Game" or an "Aussie Game"? Narrating the Nation in Australian Soccer'. *American Ethnologist* 28, no. 2 (2001): 363–87.
Featherstone, S. *Postcolonial Cultures*. Edinburgh: Edinburgh University Press, 2005.
Football Federation of Australia, *FFA Submission to the Australia in an Asian Century White Paper*. March 2011.
Foster, C. *Fozz on Football*. Melbourne: Hardie Grant Books, 2010.
Giddens, A. *Central Problems in Social Theory: Action, Structure and Contradiction in Social Analysis*. London: Mamillan, 1979.
Goldblatt, D. *The Ball is Round: A Global History of Football* (515–6). London: Viking, 2006.
Hallinan, C., and J. Hughson. 'The Beautiful Game in Howard's Brutopia'. In *The Containment of Soccer in Australia: Fencing Off the World Game*, ed. Hallinan and Hughson, 1–8. London: Routledge, 2010.
Hallinan, C., J. Hughson, and M. Burke. 'Supporting the "World Game" in Australia: A Case Study of Fandom at National and Club Level'. *Soccer in Society* 8, no. 2 (2007): 283–97.
Hay, R. 'Our Wicked Foreign Game: Why has Association Football (Soccer) not Become the Main Code of Football in Australia?' *Soccer in Society* 7, no. 2/3 (2006): 165–186.

Hughson, J. 'Football, Folk Dancing and Fascism: Diversity and Difference in Multicultural Australia'. *The Australian and New Zealand Journal of Sociology* 33, no. 2 (1997): 40–55.

James, K., C. Tolliday, and R. Walsh. 'Where to now, Melbourne Croatia?: Football Federation Australia's use of Accounting Numbers to Institute Exclusion Upon Ethnic Clubs', *Asian Review of Accounting* 19, no. 2 (2011): 112–24.

Masters, R. 'TV Deal a Great Fillip for Code', *The Sydney Morning Herald*. November 1, 2012. http://www.smh.com.au/sport/a-league/tv-deal-great-fillip-for-code-20121031-28kcm.html

Miller, T. 'The Unmarking of Soccer: Making a Brand New Subject'. In *Celebrating the Nation: A Critical Study of Australia's Bicentenary*, ed. T. Bennett, P. Buckridge, D. Carter, and C. Mercer, 104–120. Sydney: Allen and Unwin, 1992.

Moore, P. 'Soccer in the West: The World game in Australia's Western Periphery'. In *The Containment of Soccer in Australia: Fencing Off the World Game*, ed. Hallinan and Hughson, 84–95. London: Routledge, 2010.

Pettigrew, A. M., R. W. Woodman, and K. S. Cameron. 'Studying Organizational Change and Development: Challenges for Future Research'. *The Academy of Management Journal* 44, no. 4 (2001): 697–713.

Rowe, D. *Sport, Culture and the Media: The Unruly Trinity*. 2nd ed. Maidenhead: Open University Press, 2004.

Rowe, D. *Global Media Sport: Flows, Forms and Futures*. London: Bloomsbury, 2011.

Rowe, D. 'The Bid, the Lead-Up, the Event and the Legacy: The Global Cultural Politics of Awarding and Hosting the Olympics'. *British Journal of Sociology* 63, no. 2 (2012): 285–305.

Rowe, D., and S. A. Baker. 'Truly a Fan Experience? The Cultural Politics of the Live Site' In *We Love to Hate Each Other: Mediated Football Fan Culture*, ed. R. Krøvel and T. Roksvold, 301–17. Nordicom: Gothenburg, 2012.

Rowe, D., and C. Gilmour. 'Getting a Ticket to the World Game'. In *The Containment of Soccer in Australia: Fencing Off the World Game*, ed. Hallinan and Hughson, 9–26. London: Routledge, 2010.

Sage, G. *Globalizing Sport: How Organizations, Corporations, Media, and Politics are Changing Sports*. Boulder, CO: Paradigm Publishers, 2010.

Stoddart, B. 'Illusion or Reality: Aspects of Contemporary Australian Sport'. *Sport in Society: Cultures, Commerce, Media, Politics* 9, no. 5 (2006): 749–61.

Wagg, S., and T. Crabbe. 'Holding Their Own': Australian football, British Culture and Globalization. In *The Containment of Soccer in Australia: Fencing Off the World Game*, ed. Hallinan and Hughson, 57–72. London: Routledge, 2010.

Index

Page references in *italic* indicate Figures.

Abbey, Ebenezer 119
Abdulhamit II, Sultan 45
Abdullah Ahmad Badawi 66
Abhishek, R. 106
Aboagye, Felix 116, 119
Abramovich, Roman 182
Adamstown Rosebud 187
Adanaspor 46
Adorno, T.W. 149
AFC *see* Asian Football Confederation
African Confederation 181
African footballer migration 106–20; and athleticism and experience 115–16; and colonialism 106, 107, 108–11; determining factors 115–18; and the diffusion of football in South and South-East Asia 107–8; and economic disparity 116–17; geographical trends 111; legal challenges 115; and mobility 117–18; and the modern world football system 118–19; number of players per country in South and South-East Asia *112*; players' origin and supply channels 112–14; South and South-East Asian path 111–15; traditional colonial route 108–11
Afro-Brazilians 148, 149
Air Asia 67
Akers-Jones, David 32
AKP (Justice and Development Party, Turkey) 50
A-League 156, 158, 159–68, 173–4, 175–9, 183, 184, 185; market value 174
Alegi, P. 107
Althusser, Louis 149
Amateur Sports Federation and Olympic Committee of Hong Kong (ASF&OC) 25, 27; HKFA feud 25, 30–2, 33
Amis, J. et al (quoted) 185
Anatolian clubs 45, 46
Anderson, B. 94
Aoji coal mine 100
Apparao, Kakinada 82–3

Arcanjo, Miguel 109
Arema FC 38, 44
Argentina 75, 86, 87
Arnold, Graham 175
ASF&OC *see* Amateur Sports Federation and Olympic Committee of Hong Kong
'Asian Century' 157–9, 165, 167, 168, 186–7; Australian signposts to 174–8
Asian Cup 1, 2, 31, 125; and Australia 158, 167, 173, 175, 176, 177, 179, 186–7; broadcasting rights 184
Asian financial crisis (1998) 5
Asian Football Confederation (AFC) 2, 42, 183; Australia's membership 4–5, 157, 158, 173–87; Champions League *see* Champions League, AFC
Asian Games 25, 28, 29, 31, 32
Au Chi-yin 29
Australia 156–68, 173–87; AFC membership 4–5, 157, 158, 173–87; and the Asian Cup 158, 167, 173, 175, 176, 177, 179, 186–7; Asian entry and the global order 182–4; *Bradley Report* 166; broadcasting rights deal 2013–17 187; building upon the 'Asian Century' opportunity 186–7; club sponsorships 184; *Crawford Report* and New Football era 156–7, 163, 165–6, 184; 'cultural xenophobia' 157; and the 'ethnic game' 179–80, 183–4; FFA *see* Football Federation Australia; football as an un-Australian game 179–80; football diplomacy 157; Hawke government 178; Howard government 166, 178, 183–4; Keating government 178; A-League *see* A-League; multiculturalism 157, 158, 166, 178, 179, 183, 184; National Soccer League (NSL) 156, 157, 163, 164, 175, 180, 184, 185; New Australia, New Football, and the 'Asian Century' 157–9, 165, 167, 168; New Football's justification: politics and billions 164–6; and the new global order 180–4;

INDEX

Old Soccer–New Football 156–68, 174–8; 'Project Sydney' Del Piero experiment 159–62; signposts to the Asian footballing century 174–8; Socceroos 161, 174, 175, 186; and the World Cup 167, 175–6, 178, 180, 186
Australia in the Asian Century White Paper 157, 176–7
Australian Soccer Association 156

Baaptu (East Bengal fan) 87, 88
Bahrain 38
Baker, J. 68
Bakrie, Aburizal 40, 42
Bakrie, Nirwan 40, 42
Bakrie Group 177
Bandyopadhyay, K. 78, 80
Banerjee, Mamata 84, 85
Banerjee, Sivaji 76
Bangladesh 111, 117
Bangladesh war 75, 83, 84
Bardasono (PSSI chairman) 39
Barker, C. 97
Basu, Sailesh 80
Battini, Adrien 47, 48–9
Bauman, Z. 167
Baume, Michael 183
Beckham, David 160, 173
Bedlington, S. 64
Beijing Summer Olympics (2008) 4
Bekamenga, Christian 117
Ben Barek, Larbi 108, 118
Bengal 74–88; and the Bangladesh war 75, 83, 84; British colonialism and football 75, 77–9, 80; cinema and football 77–8, 79, *79*, 82, 83; club rivalries 80–1, 84, 88; football/fan cultures 76, 78–81, 82–8; 'Ghoti-Bati' and the ball as (Foucault's) pendulum 77–86; growing up in 75–6; and immigration 82; and Latin American football 75, *85*, 86, 87; Left Front 83; masculinity and football 77–8, 80; media and football 85; myths/myth-making and football 76, 78, 81, 83, 86–7; nationalism/sub-nationalism and football 78–9, 80–1, 82–4, 86–8; Naxalite movements 84; partition 75, 78, 82, 83, 84; politicization of football 82–4; refugees 82, 83; riots 83
Ben-Porat, G. and Ben-Porat, A. 5
Besiktas JK 45, 48, 49
Black Stockings 44–5
Borussia Dortmund 148
Bosman ruling, European Court of Justice 109, 182
Bradley Report 166
Brazil 75, *85*, 86, 87; Afro-Brazilians 148, 149; Brazilian players in Asian leagues 147, 150; Japanese-Brazilians 147–8, 149; and the J-League 147, 150; race and collective identity 149; racial democracy 149
Brazilian Serie A 147
Bresciano, Marco 174, 176
Brisbane Roar 164, 177
British colonialism 44–5, 75, 77–9, 80, 107
British East India Company 11
broadcasting rights 46, 48, 110, 118, 130, 135, 181, 184, 187
Brundage, Avery 30
BSkyB 181
BT Group 181
Bubalo, Anthony 176
Bundesliga 137
Bursa 49
Bursapor 49

Calcutta 75, 76, 78, 81, 82, 84, *85*, 86, 88
Cambodia 106, 111, 114, 117
Cameroonians 112, 113, 119
Carlos, Roberto 49, 149
Carlton FC 183
Carniel, J. 160, 166, 167
Celaya FC 151
Central Coast Mariners 184
Cha, V.D. 3
Chadwick, S. and Clowes, J. 130
Chalip, L. 186
Champions League, AFC 1, 4; broadcasting rights 184
Changsoo (South Korean) 96
Channing, Leslie C. 26–7, 28, 33
Chattopadhyay, Bankim Chandra 77
Chaudhuri, A. 113, 114, 116
Chelsea 85
Cheng, Maximo Antoney 27
Cheonam incident 98–9, 101
China 4, 107; Chinese Civil War 25; Chinese involvement in football in Singapore 14–17, 18; Hong Kong and the ROC 25, 26, 29, 31, 32, 33; and the SCC 12–13; Sino – Japanese relationship 4
Chinaglia, Giorgio 76
Chinese Football Association Super League 4
Chinese Football Club 15, 16
Chinnamul (Ghosh film) 82
Chowdhury, I. 77
City of God (film) 86
Cochrane, L. 115–16, 117
Collingwood FC 183
Collingwood Warriors 183
Colombijn, F. 39, 44, 107
colonialism 2–3, 39, 44–5, 75, 77–9, 80; and African football labour migration 106, 107, 108–11; decolonization 180
Coluna, Mario 108
commercialism 30, 32, 45–6, 48, 158, 163–4, 166–7, 177–8 *see also* broadcasting rights

192

INDEX

Communist Party of India 83, 84
consumerism 1
Copa Libertadores 150
Cosmos, New York 75, 76, 85
Crawford, David 164, 184
Crawford Report 156–7, 163, 165–6, 167, 184
Cross-Causeway competition 58

Darby, P. 116, 118; et al. 108, 109
Darul Adab Association 19
Darul-Adab club 19
Darul Adab Football Cup 19
Darul-Bahar club 19
Dassler, Horst 181
Davis, M. 157, 159, 163, 167, 168
decolonization 180
De Latour, E. 112
Delong Holdings 184
Del Piero, Alessandro 159–62, 173
Dhanraj 82–3
Dhanyi Meye 83
Diagne, Raoul 108
Dimeo, P. 81
Djohar Arifin Husein 40, 42
Dokdo 101
Dolles, H.: and Schweizer, R. 127; and Söderman, S. 127
Douglas, S. 60
Doyun (South Korean woman) 101–2
Drogba, Didier 110
Dutch colonialism 39, 107
Dutch East Indies 108

East Bengal FC 80–1, 82–3, 84, 87
East India Company 11
Economist (US) 125
Egypt 108, 109
Elpis FC 45
Elrick, Major 26
Emerson, Craig 177
Emperor's Cup 124–5
Emrence, Cem 45
Endo, Yasuhito 150
Engels, Friedrich 150–1
English Premier League (EPL) 67–8, 161, 181–2
Enjung (South Korean woman) 100
EPL *see* English Premier League
Erdogan, Recep Tayyip 49–51
Ergenekon affair 50
Erhat, Itir 47–8
Erker, E.K. 111
Eto'o, Samuel 110
European Union (EU) 182; and Turkey 48–9, 51
Eusebio da Silva Ferreira 108, 109, 118

FAM *see* Football Association of Malay
fan cultures 5, 82–8

FAS *see* Football Association of Singapore
FC Barcelona 135, 146
FC Bayern Munich 135
Featherstone, S. 186
Fédération Internationale de Football Association *see* FIFA
Fenerbahce SK 45, 48, 49–50
Fernandes, Tony 182
FFA *see* Football Federation Australia
FIFA (Fédération Internationale de Football Association): agents licensed by 113; and Australia 166; central role in football 3; and Hong Kong 27, 28, 32; and Indonesia 38, 39, 40, 42, 112; power balance changes 180–1; 'say no to racism' mission 146; and Singapore 58, 59; World Cup *see* World Cup
financial crisis, Asian (1998) 5
Fisher, R. and Wakefield, K. 130
Follows, Dennis 32
Fong, Christopher 177
football: African footballers in Asia *see* African footballer migration; Asian countries studied *see* Bengal; Hong Kong; Indonesia; Japan; Malaysia; Singapore; South Korea; Turkey; Australian engagement with Asia *see* Australia; broadcasting rights 46, 48, 110, 118, 130, 135, 181, 184, 187; civilization by soccer 18–19; club sponsorships 184; commercialism 30, 32, 45–6, 48, 158, 163–4, 166–7, 177–8 *see also* broadcasting rights; diplomacy 157, 176–7; Eurocentricity 157, 181; fan cultures 5, 82–8; globalization *see* globalization; hooliganism 40, 44; of Latin America *see* Latin America; and masculinity 77–8, 80; militancy 46–7; modern world football system 118–19; network of value captures 127–37, *128*; as a new Asian regionalism 4–5; new global order 180–2; overview of football in Asian society 1–2, 5–7; player salaries 116–17; politicization of 37–51, 82–4, 145–7; professionalization of *see* professionalization of football; televised 62, 67, 68, 85, 87–8, 125, 137, 173–4, 177, 184 *see also* broadcasting rights; as western coloniality and national aspiration 2–3; World Cup *see* World Cup
Football Association of Indonesia (PSSI) 39–40, 42, 43
Football Association of Malay (FAM) 58–60, 61, 62, 63, 65–6
Football Association of Singapore (FAS) 57, 60 *see also* Singapore (Amateur) Football Association (SFA/SAFA); exclusion from Malaysia Cup 64–6; withdrawal from Malaysia Cup 61–2, 66, 68
Football Association of South Africa 181
Football Business Club, Australia 177
'Football Diplomacy' 176–7

INDEX

Football Federation Australia (FFA) 156, 174, 178, 186; 2012 television deal 173–4; National Competitions Review 163
Football Union for the United States of Indonesia 39
Foster, Craig 186
Fox Sports 173–4, 185
Freyre, Gilberto 149
Fukuda, Kenji 150, 151

Galatasaray SK 45, 48–9
Galeano, Eduardo (epigraph) 144, 152
Gallop, David 173
Garrincha (Manuel Francisco dos Santos) 149
Gawler, Norman 18
George, Sir Arthur 180
George Cross FC 179
Ghanaians 119
Ghatak, Ritwik 82
Ghosh, Robi 83
Gillard, Julia 176
Gillett, George 182
Giulianottti, R. and Robertson, R. 5
Glazer, Malcolm 182
globalization 1, 3–4, 5; and African footballer migration *see* African footballer migration; of football and neoliberal multiculturalism of Latin America 145–52; global diffusion of football and football labour migration 110, *110*; research on globalization of football 126
Goldblatt, D. 180
Golkar 40, 41
Gopal, Shanti 76
Gothia Cup 137
Gramsci, Antonio 149
Gul, Abdullah 50
Gulen, Fethullah 50
Gullick, J.M. 69
Guti 49
Guttman, A. 2

Hakoah Sydney 179, 180
Halid, Nurdin 39, 40–2
Hall, S. 97, 101, 103, 104, 152
Hallinan, C. and Hughson, J. 157, 161, 166
Haobo (journalist) 27
Harada, M. and Matsuoka, H. 126
Havalange, Joao 109, 181
Hellas Verona FC 179
Herzog, Chaim 65
Heskey, Emile 159
Hetherington, K. 94
Hicks, Tom 182
Hill, David 183
Hirose, I. 125, 126
HKFA *see* Hong Kong Football Association
Hobsbawm, E. 96

Hong Kong 25–34; ASF&OC – HKFA feud 30–2, 33; and the Asian Games 25, 28, 29, 31, 32; as Football Kingdom of the Far East 26, 28, 33; match-fixing allegations 27, 28; and the Olympics 25, 27, 28, 29, 30–3 *see also* Amateur Sports Federation and Olympic Committee of Hong Kong (ASF&OC); professionalizing football 26–30, 32–4; and the ROC 25, 26, 29, 31, 32, 33; shamateurism in football 25, 26–7, 28–33
Hong Kong Chinese Footballer's Fraternity 29
Hong Kong Football Association (HKFA) 25; ASF&OC feud 25, 30–2, 33; and the professionalizing of football 26–30, 32–4; Rules Revisions Committee 30; and shamateurism 26–7, 28–33
Hong Kong League 25
Hong Kong Rangers 32
Hong Kong Senior Challenge Shield 25, 27
Hong Kong Times 27, 29, 33
hooliganism 40, 44
Hornby, Francis Villiers 12
Howard, John 166, 178, 179
Husein, Djohar Arifin 40, 42
Hutchison, Tommy 33
Hyundai 184

IFA *see* Indian Football Association
Imogene FC 45
India: and African footballer migration 106, 107; and African players 113; Bengal *see* Bengal; I-League 113; and the World Cup 108
Indian Football Association (IFA) 78, 80; IFA shield 78, 80, 83, 86
Indonesia: African players 112–13, 119; Committee to save the Indonesian Football (KPSI) 40–2; Democratic Party (PD) 40; and Dutch colonialism 39, 107; FIFA ranking 112; Football Association of Indonesia (PSSI) 39–40, 42, 43; football hooliganism 40, 44; football–politics–business nexus 43–4, *43*; football popularity 40; interests of political figures in clubs at regional level *41*, 43; Javanese struggle against Papuans 38, 44; league rivalries undermining performance 37, 40–2; nationalism 39; New Democratic Party 40; player salaries 116; polarization legacy in football 38–40; politics of football 38–44; Turkish soccer comparison with Indonesian 37–51; and the World Cup 108, 111, 112
Indonesian Democratic Party of Struggle (PDIP) 40
Indonesian Premier League (LPI) 40, 42
Indonesian Super League (LSI) 40, 42, 113
International Olympic Committee (IOC) 27, 30, 33

INDEX

Internazionale Milano 148
IOC *see* International Olympic Committee
Iraq 3, 175
Israel: footballers and fans 5; and Singapore 65
Istanbul 45, 49
Istanbulspor 46

Jaelim (South Korean woman) 95
Japan 3, 4, 124–37; creating a new market for football in Asia and 135–7; Emperor's Cup 124–5; football development in 125–6; JFA *see* Japanese Football Association; J-League *see* J-League; Latin American football and the Japanese diaspora 144–52; *Nikkei* (Brazilians of Japanese descent) 147–8, 149; Sino – Japanese relationship 4; and South Korea 3, 93, 101–3, 104; and value captures 131–7; women's national team (Nadeshiko Japan) 132–3; and the World Cup 102, 103, 125, 126, 132
Japanese Football Association (JFA) 124, 127, 137; JFA declaration (2005) 131–2, *132*; Nadeshiko Japan 132–3
Jardine FC 32
Javanese 38, 44
JFA *see* Japanese Football Association
J-League 4, 124, 125–6, 131–7, 174; Brazilian players 147, 150; development of match attendance and revenues *136*; fan attendance *134*, *135*; market value 174; value captures and the development of 131–7
Johor, state 64, 65
Johor Challenge Cup 17
Johor Football Club 17, 58
Jong, Theo de 33
Joori (South Korean woman) 96
Just FC 179
Juventus 146, 161, 162, 179

Kadikoy FRC 45
Kaftan, Eylam 45
Kapadia, N. 107, 108
Kayseri disaster 46
Kayserispor 46
Kedah 67
Keesuk (South Korean) 101
Keita, Salif 109
Kelantan 67
Kennedy, Josh 174
Kewell, Harry 175
Khan, Ahmed 82–3
King's Cup 2
K-League 4, 174
KMB (Kowloon Motor Bus) 32
Knop, Ian 184
Kookannog, T. 107

Kowloon Motor Bus (KMB) 32
KPSI (Committee to save the Indonesian Football) 40–2
Kuala Muda Naza FC 67
Kurds 37–8

Labozzetta, Tony 183
Laclau, E. 152
Lanang (reporter) 44
La Nyalla Mattalitti 40, 42
Laos 38, 117, 119
Latin America: and Bengal football 75, *85*, 86, 87; football and the Japanese diaspora 144–52; nationalizing the foreign 150–1; neoliberal multiculturalism and the globalization of football 145–52; and the political ideology of football 145–7; race and collective identity 149
Lawson, John 11, 12, 17, 18
Lee Hsien Loong 66
Lee, P.P. 62–3
Lee Wai-tong 33
Leifer, M. 64
Lerner, Randy 182
Leung, Raleigh 27, 30
Liga MX 147
Light, R. and Yasaki, W. 125–6
Lions XII 57, 69
Little, C. 3
Liverpool FC 67, 182
Lowy, Frank 163, 166, 173–4, 176, 177–8, 179, 180, 183, 184, 185, 186
Lowy Institute for International Policy 176, 177, 186, 187
LPI (Indonesian Premier League) 40, 42
LSI (Indonesian Super League) 40, 42, 113

Mabaoang, Emmanuel 112
McDonald, M. et al. 125
McKenzie, James 12, 17, 18, 20
MacTavish, I.M. 27, 30
Magee, J. and Sugden, J. 107, 110
Mahathir bin Mohamad 65
Mahony, D. et al. 126
Majumdar, B. and Bandyopadhyay, K. 75, 78, 80
Malang 38, 44
Malaya, HMS 58
Malaya Cup (later Malaysia Cup) 18, 58–60, 61, 63, 68
Malay Policemen 19
Malay Royal Engineers 19
Malaysia 3; African player recruitment 113; and colonialism 107; FAM *see* Football Association of Malay; Merdeka Tournaments 2–3, 61; Singapore and the Malays *see* Singapore–Malaysian football relations; and the World Cup 111

INDEX

Malaysia Cup (previously Malaya Cup) 61–2, 63–6, 68
Malaysian Super League 57, 66, 67, 69
Mallarangeng, Andi 38
Manasi 80
Manchester United 67, 85, 135, 146, 148, 182
Mangan, J.A. 3
Mansour bin Zayed Al Nahyan 182
Manzenreiter, W. 126; and Horne, J. 102
Maradona, Diego 86, 87
Maranhão, T. 149
Marconi FC 179
Marx, Karl 146, 150–1
masculinity 77–8, 80
Matheson, Jardine 32
Matsouka, H. et al. 126
Mattalitti, La Nyalla 40, 42
Mauzy, D. and Milne, R.S. 64
Maxwell, W.E. 16–17
Melbourne Heart 162
Melbourne Victory 184
Merdeka Tournaments 2–3, 61
Mexico: Asian/Japanese footballers in 150–1; First Division, Liga MX 147; Japanese players in Mexican football clubs 147–8; nationalism 149
Mfede, Louis-Paul 115
Milla, Roger 112, 113, 116, 119
Miller, Thomas C.B. 20
Minhee (South Korean woman) 101
Mitra, Nabagopal 77
Miura, Kazuyoshi 'Kazu' 150
Moda FC 45
Mohammedan Sporting Club 80, 84
Mohun Bagan AC 74, 75, 76, 78, 80, 84–5, 86–7
Mohun Bagan (film) 83
Mok Hing 30
Morrow, S. and Hamil, S. 130
multiculturalism 145–52, 157, 158, 166, 178, 179, 183, 184
Mutiara Hitam, Sport & Management 113

Nadeshiko Japan 132–3
Najib Abdul Razak, Mohammad 66
Nakamura, Shunsuke 150
Nakazawa, M. 126
Nandy, Moti 76, 77, 82
Nanninga, Dick 33
nationalism: Bengali (sub-nationalism) 78–9, 80–1, 82–4, 86–8; football, the working classes and 144; football as national aspiration 2–3; Indonesian 39; Mexican 149; pan-Korean 100; role of football club in 149; Turkish 45
Naxalite movements 84
Neill, Lucas 174, 175, 176
neoliberalism 145–52

Netherlands, colonialism 39, 107
Netherlands Indies Football Association 39
Netherlands Indies Football Union 39
Newcastle Jets 159
New York Cosmos 75, 76, 85
Neymar 149
Nigerians 87, 109, 111, 113, 119
Nikkei (Brazilians of Japanese descent) 147–8, 149
Nogawa, H. and Toshio, M. 126
North, Jade 174
Northern Spirit 183
North Korea 3, 92, 97–101, 103, 104
NSL (National Soccer League, Australia) 156, 157, 163, 164, 175, 180, 184, 185
NSW Federation of Soccer Clubs 180
Nurdin, Dodi Reza Alex 43

O'Donnel, Scott 116
Ogenovski, Saso 176
Okorie, Chima 113, 114, 116, 119
Onana, Jules-Denis 112, 114, 116
Ono, Shinji 159
Ono, Yuto 151
Ophüls-Kashima, R. 126
Orlowitz, D. 159
Ōsumi, Y. 126
Othman Wok, Inche 61, 62, 63
Ozal, Turgut 48

Pachuca 147, 150, 151
Pahang 63–4
Palmer, Clive 163
Panigoro, Arifin 40, 42
Papuans 38, 44
Paul, Gostho 80, *81*
Pedra Branca 65
Pelé 75, 76, *77*, 149
Perón, Juan Domingo 145
Persebaya 1927 42
Persebaya (Surabaya) 38, 42, 44
Persib FC 44
Persija FC 44
Perth Glory 183, 184
Peterson, R. 87
Pettigrew, A.M. et al. 185
Pique, HMS 19
Plover, HMS 19
Pohan, Ramadhan 42
Poli, R. 109, 111
political economy 4
Porat, A.B. 75
professionalization of football 3–4, 116; Hong Kong 26–30, 32–4; Indian League 113; Turkey 45–6
'Project Sydney' Del Piero experiment 159–62
PSSI (Football Association of Indonesia) 39–40, 42, 43

INDEX

PT. Djarum 43
PT. Liga Indonesia 43
Puebla FC 151

Queen's Park Rangers (QPR) 182

RA (Royal Artillery) 16
racism 145, 146
Radio France International 109
Raffles Institution 16, 19
Rahman, Abdul 59–60
Rajat Jayanti (Barua film) 77–8
Real Madrid 135, 146
Redhead, S. 87
Renaissance Capital 49
Rodrigo, Lenny 61
Rodrigues, Albert 28
Ronaldinho 149
Ronaldo 149
Rous, Sir Stanley 181
Rowe, D. 130
Roy, B.C. 83
Royal Artillery (RA) 16, 20

SAFA *see* Singapore (Amateur) Football Association
Said, E.W. 98, 100, 103
Saleh, P.B.A. 83
Sales, A. de O. 31, 33
Salvadoran-Honduran Football War 145
Samsung 184
Santos FC 148, 150
São Paulo 148
Saptapadi (Kar film) 79, *79*
Saravanamuutu, J. 68
Sarbadhikari, Nagendra Prasad 78
Sarel, Clement 11
Sarup, M. 99
Sato, Minori 151
Saudi Arabia 3
SBS (Special Broadcasting Service) 162, 173–4
SCC *see* Singapore Cricket Club
Schenflug, Les 183
Scottish influence on football in Singapore 12–13, 16, 17, 18, 20
Scoular, Robert 12, 16, 17, 18, 20
SCRC (Straits Chinese Recreation Club) 14, 15, 16, 17
Selangor Club, Kuala Lumpur 18, 67
Selangor Rugby Union 61
SFA *see* Singapore (Amateur) Football Association
Shimizu, S. 126
Shiraishi, T. 69
Singapore 3, 10–20, 51; Chinese involvement in football 14–17, 18; civilization by soccer 18–19; and the European scene 16; FAS *see* Football Association of Singapore; footballing beginnings for the local communities 14; footballing pioneers 12; introduction of football to 11–13; and Israel 65; and the Malays *see* Singapore–Malaysian football relations; military 12–13, 17; People's Action Party (PAP) 60, 61; post-1894 expansion of football 17–18; SAFA/SFA *see* Singapore (Amateur) Football Association; Scottish influence on football in 12–13, 16, 17, 18, 20; S-League 66–7; Warren Challenge Shield 17, 19
Singapore (Amateur) Football Association (SFA/SAFA) 10, 20, 58–9, 60 *see also* Football Association of Singapore (FAS); SFA Challenge Cup 16–17
Singapore Cricket Club (SCC) 10, 12–13, 16, 17, 18, 58
Singapore Free Press 16
Singapore–Malaysian football relations 57–69; 1950s, start of deteriorating relations 58–60; 1960s 60–2; and the 1963 merger of Singapore and Malaya 60; 1970s 62–4; 1980s 64–5; 1990s 65–6; 1996 withdrawal of Singapore from Malaysian League 66; 2012 return of Singapore to the Malaysian League 66–8; and civilization by soccer 18–19; Cross-Causeway competition 58; and the EPL 67–8; indigenous Malays in Singapore 14; Singapore's exclusion from Malaya Cup 58–60, 63, 68; Singapore's exclusion from Malaysia Cup 64–6; Singapore's withdrawal from Malaysia Cup 61–2, 66, 68
Singapore Recreation Club 13, 15, 16
Singapore Volunteer Artillery (SVA) team 17
Sing Tao FC 32
Sivas 46
Sivasspor 46
S-League 66–7
Slot, Owen 115
Smart, B. 147
Smith, A. 92, 94, 95, 97, 99
SNFA (Straits National Football Association) 15
Socceroos 161, 174, 175, 186
Sócrates 149
Soh Ghee Soon 60
South and South-East Asia, African footballers *see* African footballer migration
South China 27
South China Morning Post 30
South Korea 3, 92–104; *Cheonam* incident 98–9, 101; and Japan 3, 93, 101–3, 104; K-League 4, 174; Lee Myung-bak administration 98; national identity 92–104; and North Koreans 3, 92, 97–101, 103, 104; and pan-Korean nationalism 100; post-colonial consciousness 100–3; and the World Cup 93, 94–7, 98–9, 100, 102–3

INDEX

Special Broadcasting Service (SBS) 162, 173–4
Sriwijaya FC 43
Star 68
'Steelbacks' 12
Stewart, Donald 183
Straits Chinese Recreation Club (SCRC) 14, 15, 16, 17
Straits National Football Association (SNFA) 15
Straits Times 59, 61
Sugden, J. and Tomlinson, A. 102
Sugimoto, A. 125–6
Suharto 39
Sumino, M. and Harada, M. 126
Sungyun (South Korean woman) 95
Surabaya 38, 44
Suzuki Cup 38
Sydney City Slickers 180
Sydney FC 159–62, 164, 173
Sydney Hakoah 179, 180

Tabata, Rodrigo 148, 151
Taemin (South Korean woman) 96, 102
Tai, Y.T. 68
Takahashi, Y. et al. 126
television: football broadcasting rights 46, 48, 110, 118, 130, 135, 181, 184, 187; televised football 62, 67, 68, 85, 87–8, 125, 137, 173–4, 177, 184
TFF (Turkish Football Federation) 48, 50
Thailand 106, 107, 111; King's Cup 2
Thomson, Eddie 183
Tiger Beer 67
Tiger Cup ASEAN championship 38
Timor-Leste 38
Tinkler, Nathan 163
Toisutt, George 42
Toshiba 184
towchang ('pigtail') 15
Trabzon 49
TrabzonSpor 49
Triandafyllidou, A. 97–8, 101
Tung Wah 27
Türk, Hikmet Sami 48
Turkey: AKP 50; Anatolian clubs 45, 46; and British colonialism 44–5; broadcast rights 46, 48; commercializing football 45–6; Committee of Union and Progress 45; corruption 37, 46, 48; Ergenekon affair 50; and the EU 48–9, 51; football militancy 46–7; Genc (Youth) Party 46; Indonesian soccer comparison with Turkish 37–51; Kurds in 37–8; liberalization 48; match fixing 37, 46, 50; nationalism 45; politics of football 44–51; professionalizing football 45–6; sexual innuendo in chants and slogans 47–8; women in 47; Young Turks 45
Turkish Football Federation (TFF) 48, 50
Turkish Super League 46

UltrAslan 47
Uzan, Cem 46

value captures 127–37, *128*
Vanegas, Fernando 151
Van Limbergen, K. et al. 44
Vargas, Getúlio 145
Vasconcelos, José 149
Vedic Village 88
Venkatesh, P. 82–3
Verdy Kawasaki 125
Vidacs, B. 102–3
Vietnam 106, 107, 116
Vivekananda, Swami 77, 78

Wallerstein, I.M. 110, 118, 119, 151–2
Warren Challenge Shield 17, 19
Watt, W. McGregor 58, 68
Weah, George 110
Weeks, J. 94
Western Sydney Wanderers 159
Weston, John Charles 27
Wharton, Arthur 108
Wok, Inche Othman 61, 62, 63
Wollongong/South Coast Wolves 187
World Cup 3, 4–5, 108, 109, 111; 1938 Cup 149; 1966 Cup 181; 1970 Cup 145; 1990 Cup 110; 2002 Cup 3, 4, 5, 110, 148, 162; 2006 Cup 175; 2010 Cup 103, 110; 2022 Cup bidding 178; and African football 108, 109, 110, 111, 118; and Argentina 87; and Australia 167, 175–6, 178, 180, 186; broadcasting rights 184; and Havalange 181; and Indonesia 38, 39, 111, 112; and Japan 102, 103, 125, 126, 132; and South Korea 93, 94–7, 98–9, 100, 102–3; televised 87–8
World Sport Group 184
Wran, Neville 183

Yildirim, Aziz 50
Yiu Cheuk-yin 26, 29
Yokohama Marinos 125
Young Turks 45
Yuen Long FC 32
Yura (South Korean woman) 99